Master Index
and Illustrated Symbols

Master Index and Illustrated Symbols

By the Editors of Time-Life Books

TIME-LIFE BOOKS, ALEXANDRIA, VIRGINIA

Signposts to the Unknown

Through a wealth of symbols, the fifteenth-century painting at left conveys a supernatural understanding of the cosmos and of time. In circles that ring the earth at the center, deities represent days of the week, signs of the zodiac give meaning to the night skies, and depictions of human activity reveal a belief in the heavens' ability to shape life. Outside the circles, puffing cherubs symbolize the four winds while God and a heavenly host oversee it all from above.

"What we call a symbol is a term, a name, or even a picture that may be familiar in daily life, yet that possesses specific connotations in addition to its conventional and obvious meaning," wrote Swiss psychiatrist Carl Jung. "It implies something vague, unknown, or hidden from us." In this way, mystical symbols link the sphere of everyday consciousness with something undeniably outside it, in many cases with what some consider a world of paranormal phenomena and occult experience.

Thus it is appropriate that this index to the preceding thirty-two volumes of Mysteries of the Unknown—a series of books dedicated to exploring and recounting humankind's age-old belief in a supernatural realm that flickers on the periphery of known reality—should include a richly illustrated guide to mystical symbols. These symbols come from all over the world and throughout history. Some mean one thing in one culture and quite another elsewhere. Others are virtually universal.

The index entries—from "Miss A" to "Jacob Zwinger"—are referenced to the various volumes of the series by two-letter codes, which are explained in a key running along the bottom of each page. Italicized page numbers refer to illustrations while those in standard roman type indicate text.

A

A, Miss: and ghosts, HN 84-85, 86, *87*; trance of, HN 85
A, Mr.: PH 105
Abbatabbari: MA 17
Abbot Beere: and Chapel of St. Edgar, PP 121
Abbott, David P.: PS 34
Abbott, Edwin A.: TS *136*
Abduction by aliens: UP 57, *58-63*, 79-86, 129, 141-143, *144. See also* UFOs; *specific headings*; AE *index*
Abduction of Proserpina, The (Dürer): CD *15*
Abelard: CC 56
Aberfan (Wales): avalanches in, DD 132, PP *32-33*, 34
Abiff, Hiram: AW 9, 97-98
Abir: MY *22*
Abishag (biblical figure): SI 38, *40*
Abominable Snowmen: EM 16, MC 18, 100, 102, 103, 104, *105-106, 122-123*, 124, MW 44, 59. *See also* Hominoids *in MC index*
Aborigines, Australian: CD *60*, EE 50, MA 21, MW 34, 38, 93, 95-96, 97, 127; and Ayers Rock, TS 15; and extraterrestrials, ML 29-32; and time, TS 36-37; and *wandjina*, ML 38
Abortions: herbs for, WW *37*
Abracadabra: MA *38*; history of, MA 17
Abraham (biblical figure): CD 58, DD 37, EE 52, MY 91, UV 24
Abraham the Jew (magician): MA 23-25
Abra-melin (sage): MA 23
Abrams, Albert: PH 80
Abraxas: MA 60
Absolute, the: SE 61, 62
Absolutists: defined, CD 127
"Abt Vogler" (Browning): SS 94
Abu Ali al-Husayn ibn Abd Allah

ibn Sina: *See* Avicenna
Abu Bakr Muhammad ibn Zakariya ar Razi (Rhasis of Persia): SA 30
Abū Ma'shar: CC 53, 57
Abu Musa Jabir ibn Hayyan: *See* Geber
Abyssinia: *See* Ethiopia
Acacias: EE 107
Academy of Applied Science: Loch Ness monster research of, MC 77-78, 85, 87, 89
Acevedo, Carlos: AE 60
Acheron River (Greece): MQ 56, SE *74*; site on, MQ *57*
Achille Lauro (ship): DD 137
Achilles: SI 65
Achote plant: MB *111*
Acid Bath Vampire: *See* Haigh, John George
Acropolis: CD 56, MY 60
Actaeon: and Diana, WW 23
Actors: and superstitions, MA 110-111, 116, 118, 121, 128-129, 137
Actual entities: defined, MB 20
Acupressure: PH 49
Acupuncture: EE 38, 136, 137, MA 114, PH 44, 47-50, *48, 49*, 51, 54-57
Adam (biblical figure): MB 42, ML 24, MW 102, SA *51*, TN 110, TS *40*, UV 20, *22*; characteristics of, CD 58; diet of, SI 13; and Eden, UV *7, 12-13*; and Eve, CD *27, 56*, 59; and Gnostics, CD 59; and Golgotha, EE 27; as hermaphrodite, CD 48-49; and Lilith, CD 80, WW 15-16; longevity of, SI 12, 13; and Daniel Colin Munro, SI 13; and tree of knowledge, EE 95; and tree of life, SI 13
Adam, Sigmund: and poltergeists, MM *50, 51-53*
Adam and Eve (Rembrandt): CD *27*
Adamenko, Victor G.: psychotronics research of, MM 76, 79
Adam of Domerham: ML 56-59
Adams (captain): MY 134
Adams, Mrs.: AE 106
Adams, Evangeline: CC 131-132, *133*, 139, PS 120-121
Adams, F. C.: Loch Ness monster

photograph by, MC *75*
Adams, Henry: HN 112
Adams, Hester Ann: gift drawing by, UV *72*
Adams, Janette: AE 106
Adams, John: MY 58, UV 72
Adams, John Couch: CC 46
Adams, John Quincy: AW 86, VP *75*; ghost of, HN 107
Adams, Marian: statue of, HN *112-113*
Adams, Samuel: AW *74*, 77
Adamski, George: and alien encounters, AE 20-21, UP *74*, 76
Adare, Viscount (fourth earl of Dunraven): MM 115, 116
Addams, Charles: CC 89
Addison's disease: MB 54
Adelard of Bath: CC 56
Adeline, Guillaume: WW 58
Adelphi Theatre: HN *31*; and ghosts, HN 31
Adena culture: MP 123
Ader, Robert: PH *130*, 131
Adhémar, Countess d': AW 64, SA 100
Adler, Alfred: DD 127
Adler, Margot: WW 116; and neopaganism, WW 97-98, 119; and Wicca, WW 104, 114-115, 122
Adler, Mortimer: SE 68
Adolescents: and poltergeists, HN *54*, 55, 58, 72
Adonia: MY 67
Adonis: CC 40, MY *67*
Adoptive Masonry: AW *103*
Ado River: EM *56*
Adramelech (demon): MA *98*
Advent: MY 114
Adventist movement: UV 57
Advertisements: MA 113
Aelian: EE 59; and toads, WW 14
Aelianus, Claudius: and Atlantis, MP 20
Aeneas: MW 90
Aeneid (Virgil): UV 23, 33
Aeolus episode in *Odyssey*: MQ 55
Aepyornis maximus: MW 65, 69
Aerial Phenomena Research Organization (APRO): AE 24, 57, UP 53, 69
Aerobics: SI *42*, 94
Aeromancy: defined, VP 35
Aerospace Defense Command:

ANGEL. *Often depicted blowing a trumpet (above) to represent its role as a herald of divine will, the angel is the symbolic embodiment of the invisible link between God and mortals in monotheistic religions.*

AE Alien Encounters; AW Ancient Wisdom and Secret Sects; CC Cosmic Connections; CD Cosmic Duality; DD Dreams and Dreaming; EE Earth Energies; EM Eastern Mysteries; HN Hauntings; MA Magical Arts; MB The Mind and Beyond; MC Mysterious Creatures; ML Mysterious Lands and Peoples; MM Mind over Matter; MP Mystic Places; MQ Mystic Quests; MW The Mysterious World;

ANDROGYNE. *In alchemy, uniting man and woman in a single two-headed being stands for a fusion of opposites that leads to immortality. The androgyne may also signify procreation and the primal force of life.*

and investigation of UFOs, UP 119

Aeschylus: UV 96

Aesculapius: DD 32-33, PH 13, 15, 85

Aeson (father of Jason): MQ *35,* SI *27;* and Medea, WW *23*

Aetherius Society: PS *100;* and cosmic batteries, UP 78, *80-81*

Aetos, isthmus of (Greece): MQ *61*

AFB-14 (U.S. Navy vessel): MW 71

Africa: MW *maps 8-9, 34-35,* 64, 98, 132; Mother Goddess in, EE 27; vampires in, TN 136

African-Americans: *See* Blacks

Afterlife: CD 82, 85, 99, 124, 126-127, PV 59

Agamemnon (king of Greece): DD 32

Agartha: and hollow earth theory, MP 138

Agassiz, Louis: DD *117*

Agastya: SI 11

Agates: MA 101

Age: and biological rhythms, TS 90-95

Aggression: CD 68-69

Agha, Zaro: SI *15-22*

AGLA: MA *38, 55*

Agle, David P.: PH 129

Agnagna, Marcellin: MC *91-92, 96*

Agnes, Hurricane: PS *14-15*

Agnes, Saint: MY 127

Agneya weapon: ML 32-33

Agnosia: defined, MB 50

Agobard (archbishop of Lyons): MW 40-41; and UFOs, UP 14-15

Agogwe: MW 65, 67-69

Agor, Weston: PS 107, 130

Agricultural rituals: MY 37. *See also* Harvest celebrations

Agriculture: CD 49, 55; of Maya, ML 19; and Rudolf Steiner, UV 110, 118

Agri Dagi (as local name for Mount Ararat): MQ 67

Agrippa, Heinrich Cornelius: AW 26, MA 31-32

Agung, Mount: MY 25

Ahimsa: defined, EM 39

Ah Puch (god): TS 34

Ahriman (god): CD *29,* UV *113;* characteristics of, CD 26-28, 28-29, 40, 82

Ahu: ML *84-85,* 87

Ahura Mazda (god): TS 22. *See also* Ohrmazd

Aigla Saga: TN 37

Ainus: EM 20, ML *30*

Aion (Mithraic cult figure): AW *17*

Airaudi, Oberto: UV 141

Air Florida Flight 90 crash: CD *108-109;* and Arland D. Williams, Jr., CD 106-107, 108

Air Force: *See* U.S. Air Force

Air hand: VP *54, 60. See also* Palmistry; Palmists

Airline pilots: and superstitions, MA 102, 129

Air Materiel Command (Ohio): and investigations of UFOs, UP 38. *See also* Project Sign

Airport Mesa: EE 65

Airscrew: VP *28*

Airships: in fiction, UP 19; sightings of, UP 19, 22

Aiwas (guardian angel): AW 120

Ajanta (India): MW 93

Ajútap: defined, MA 80

Aka: MA 90

Akapana: MW *82*

Akashic records: PP 95; defined, PV 123. *See also* Cayce, Edgar

Aken, Myrna Joy: PS *39;* disappearance and murder of, PS 35-36, 39; and Nelson Palmer, PS 35-36, 37, 39; and Clarence Van Buuren, PS 36-37, 39

Akers, David: and Yakima Indian Reservation UFO window site, UP 133-134

Akitu: MY 23

Akkadians: AE 91

Akuakus: symbols of, ML *93, 96*

Akwambo: MY *83*

Alacitas Fair: MY 128

Alalouf, Serge Léon: PH *91*

Alamogordo (New Mexico): TS 58

Alasco, Albertus: SA 59

Alaska: MW 43, PS *10-11*

Albatross (king): UV *141*

Albedo: MW 127

Albert (prince of Britain): CC 113

Albertus, Frater: *See* Riedel, Albert

Albertus Magnus (a.k.a. Universal Doctor): CC 59-62, CD 83, 130, SA 31-33, *32*

Albert Victor (prince of England): SI 26

Albigenses (Christian sect): MQ 118; Cathar stronghold, MQ 118, 124, 127-128, *129. See also* Cathars

Albright, Elizabeth: PS *127*

Alchemists: and elixirs, SI 6, *30,* 32; and gold, SI 32, 34; and immortality, SI 13, 32, 34; religious beliefs of, SA 82. *See also specific headings;* SA index

Alchemy: EM 52-53, MA 31-33, 61, MB *75,* MW 113, *119,* 122, *123,* 125-127, 133-134, MY 39, 64, *127,* UV 60; background of, SA 19, 20; characteristics of, CD 36, 37, 70; decline of, CD 37-38; defined, MA 31, 61, VP 46-47; goals of, SE 54; and gold, CD 36, 37; history of, MA 31, 61; as influence on grail legend, MQ 117; mystical, SE 54; origins of term, SA 19; of Rosicrucians, AW 50, 54, 55-56, 61, 70-72; symbols of, AW 62. *See also* SA *index*

Alcibiades: MY 39

Alcibiades I (Plato): SE 44

Alcock, Harry: MW 19, PE 8

Alcock, Leslie: ML 52

Alcohol: MB 116; and dreams, DD 114; and psychokinesis, MM 61

Alcor Life Extension Foundation: SI *98,* 116, *120-121,* 123, 130

Alcott, Bronson: UV 81, 82-84, *83*

Alcott, Louisa May: CC 88, UV 82, 84

Alcuin of York: CC 53, 54-55

Aldrin, Edwin (Buzz): and first moon landing, UP 120

Alecton (gunboat): MC 22-23

Alectryomancers: defined, VP 34

Alembic: SA *38-39,* SE *54;* defined, SA 29

Alexander, Greta: PS 24-27, *26*

Alexander, James: and Cleopatra's Needle, MP *60-61*

Alexander, Jim: MW 30

7

Alexander, John B.: PS 90-91; psychic research, military applications of, PP 144

Alexander, Rolf: and cloud busting, MM *16-17*

Alexander II (czar of Russia): MM 115, SS 22-23, 40

Alexander III (king of Macedonia): VP 11

Alexander III (pope): ML 64

Alexander VI (pope): PE *84*

Alexander the Great: CC 23-*24*, CD 64, DD 23, 42, MA 25-26, MW 6, 40, 102, 104, 133; water of life sought by, MQ 33

Alexandra (czarina of Russia): PH 86

Alexandra (queen of England): VP 82

Alexandria (Egypt): MW 113, 133, *134*, SA 19, 23; psychic archaeologists' expedition to, MQ 100, *101*. *See also* Egypt

Alexandrian tradition: WW 108, 112

Alexis (prince of Russia): PH 86

Alfassa, Mirra (a.k.a. Mother): and Auroville (India), UV 145, 148; death of, UV 149; and karma-yoga, UV 147; and Paul Richard, UV 145, 146; and Sri Aurobindo, UV 145-146, 147

Algard tradition: WW 112

Algonquin Indians: AE 112

Alibard, Thomas-François D': EE 70

Alice (Indian): MA 78

Aliens: MW 42-43, 79, MY *86-87, 92;* and ancient-astronaut theory, UP 13; and the Bible, UP 12, *14, 15, 17;* encounters with, UP 64-86, *68, 69, 72;* faked accounts of, UP 16; in legend, UP 12-18, *13, 14;* motivation of, UP 28, *29-35. See also* Anunnaki; Extraterrestrials; Space Brothers; UFOs; AE *index*

Alighieri, Jacopo: DD 143

Alioto, John: VP 25

Allagash affair: AE 16, 17, *18-19,* 20, *24-27,* 28

Allah: MY 91

Allahabad (India): MW 93, SI *16-21*

Allan Apples: MY 96

Allegewi tribe: ML 25

Allen, William Frederick (pseud. Alan Leo): CC *116*

Allen, Woody: SE 132

Allgood, Sara: DD 142

All Hallows' Eve: MY 81, *96-97, 98,* WW 43

Alliette (Tarot reader): VP 125-127

Allis, Chris: MB 135

Allison, Dorothy (psychic): PP *132-133,* PS 43-*45*

Allison, Ralph: MB 83, 87

Alloys: SA 17, 18, 21

All Saints' Day: MY 96-97, 98, WW 43

All Souls' Day: MY 97, 98, SE 22-23

Allyn, Edward: CD 84

Almagest (Ptolemy): CC 36

Al Mamun, Abdullah: and Great Pyramid, MP 49-51

Almanacs: CC 75-76, 101-106, *102, 103,* 107, 112, 113, 135; by Bauhaus, UV *121;* Maya, TS *102*

Almas: MC 18, 100, *108,* MW 59-*60;* characteristics of, MC 107, 110, 112; footprints of, MC *108-109;* history of, MC 107; and Neanderthal theory, MC 112; sightings of, MC 107-112; Zana, MC 106, 110-112. *See also* Hominoids in MC *index*

Along Beach (Vietnam): MW 75

Alpert, Richard (a.k.a. Baba Ram Dass, Ram Dass): EM *138-139,* MB 112, 115, 116, 117

Alpert, Shell: and alleged UFO photograph, UP 97

Alpha and Omega: AW 156

Alpha and Omega Lodge of the Stella Matutina: MA 62

Alpha waves: DD 97, 118. *See also* Sleep; MM *index*

Alphitomancy: defined, VP 35

Alphonsus Liguori, Saint: out-of-body experience of, PV 17

Alps: MW 53

Alt (priest): CD 91

Altars: SA 35

Alter, Minerva: SE 93

Altered States Research (ASR): PP 69

Alternate reality: *See* Parallel universe

Alternating-current generator: MB 57

Alternative healing: PH 7-10, 20, 44. *See also specific types of alternative healing*

Althing: EE 32

Altman, Nathaniel (palmist): VP 60-63

Alto Anchicayá Dam: MW 27, 31-32

Alton Barnes (England): crop circles in, EE *14-15*

Altruism: *See* CD *index*

Aluminum: refining of, ML 22

Alvarez, Jose: and Levelland UFO sighting, UP 68

Alvarez, Luis: and Robertson report, UP 55

Alves da Costa, Joaquim: ML 135-136

Ama (god): VP 36

A-Ma (goddess): MY 28

Amala (feral child): TN 62-63, 64

Amalgamated Flying Saucer Clubs of America, Inc.: and Gabriel Green, UP 79

Amalric (king of Jerusalem): MQ 122

Amana Society: UV 75

Amanda (witch): MC 37

Amanita muscaria: EE 102

Amaringo, Pablo: paintings by, MB *108-111*

Amarnath Cave: EM *46-47;* and Shiva, EM 43, 47

Amaterasu (goddess): MY *116*

Amazing Margery: *See* Crandon, Mina

Amazonian headless tribe: MQ *29*

Amazons: CD 63-64, MW 8

Ambrose, Saint: out-of-body experience of, PV 17

Ambrose, Steve: AE 104

Ambrosia: SI *10-11*

Ambrosius, Aurelius: and Stonehenge, MP 82, 84

Amen (god): MW 100-102

America, discovery of: *See* ML *index*

America B.C. (Fell): ML 133

American Association for the Advancement of Science: PP 27, 57, TN 93-94; and UFO symposium, UP 122

American Cryonics Society (ACS): SI 116

American Fertility Society: SI 112

American Indians: *See* Indians, American; *individual tribes*

American Institute of Phrenology: VP 76

American Psychological Association: DD 59

Americans: and time, TS 98-99

American Sign Language (ASL): MB *42-43*

American Society for Psychical Research (ASPR): DD 139-140, MY 54, PE 35, PP 35, 42, 50, SE 19, 139, SS 81, TS 113; and clairvoyance, PP 85; and Mina Crandon, SS 117; founding of, HN 86, MM 19, 57, PP 24, PV 20; and ghosts, HN 19-20; and hauntings, HN 86; and mediums, PP 36, 38-39, 40; and near-death-experience research, PV 62; and obsession, study of, PP 43; and out-of-body-experience research, PV 20, 36; and poltergeists, HN 86; and remote viewing, PP 85; and spirit photography, PP 44-45, 47; and Ingo Swann, PP 83

APPLE. In the Greek myth depicted in this etching, nymphs called the Hesperides cultivate magical apples that grant eternal life. The fruit has come to symbolize immortality, and for this reason, felling an apple tree is considered unlucky.

Amesha Spentas: CD 26
Amethysts: MA 101
Am Fear Liath Mor: MW 17, 19, 20
Amida Buddhists: UV 6. *See also* Buddhists and Buddhism
Amityville (New York): HN 100-101, MW 27
Ammianus Marcellinus: CC 49
Amnesia: MB 78; dissociative, AE 110; doorway, AE 27
Amorites: AE 91
Amos (biblical figure): VP 10
Amoy (China): EM *8-9*
Amphetamines: and dreams, DD 114
Amphitheater: Roman, at Hissarlik site, Turkey, MQ *37*
Amphitrite (goddess): SA *27*
Amphorae: ML 137
Amrita: SI *16*, 17, 18; defined, SI 16
Amulet ring: MA *56*
Amulets: CD *12. See also* Charms; Talismans; MA *index*
Amundson, Ronald: EE 125
Amusia: defined, MB 50
Analog computer: ML 16-17, *18*
Analysis of Mind, The (James): SE 65
Ananta (serpent): TS *24*
Anârqâq (shaman): PP *76-77*
Anasazi: MW 80-81; background of, ML 115-116; buildings by, ML *80-81;* Sun Dagger of, ML *118-119*
Anastasia Beach (Florida): MW 75
Anastasius (pope): PV 99, SE 45
Anat (goddess): WW 13. *See also* Mother Goddess
Anathema: defined, TN 40
Anati, Emmanuel: area studied by, MQ *44-45*
Anatolia: gold in, SA 17
Anaxagoras: CC 20
Anaximander: CC 21, 23, UV 25
Anaximenes: CC 21-23
Ancestor stones: MW 76
Ancestor visions: MQ *12-13*
Ancestor worship: *See* Shinto
Anchor stones, possible: MQ 91, *92, 94*
Ancient and Mystical Order Rosae Crucis: AW 70-72; administration building of, AW *71*

Ancient Arabic Order of the Nobles of the Mystic Shrine: AW *108-109*
Ancient-astronaut theory: UP *13. See also* Extraterrestrials
Ancient Secret, The (Anderson): MQ 124-125
Ancilia: MY 19
Andersen, Hans Christian: PE 93
Anderson, Herbert H.: SA 114
Anderson, Jack: PS 80, VP 23
Anderson, James: AW 89
Anderson, Lady Flavia: MQ 124-125
Anderson, William: PS 71
Andes: writing system of, ML *24-25*
Andes Mountains: MW 116-117
Andrade, Antonio de: EM *28*
André, John: DD *140*
Andreae, Johann Valentin: AW *54-55*, SA 85, UV 42
Andreasson, Betty: AE *23;* and abduction by aliens, AE *12-13, 14-15,* 23, 24, 26, 28, *30,* 36, 37, UP 62, 84-86; drawings and paintings by, AE *24, 28, 30, 31, 37;* dreams of, AE 37; hypnosis and hypnotic regression of, AE 13, 15, 23, 30-32, 36, 37; and Whitley Strieber, AE 120; theophany

of, AE 30-32, *31;* and triads, AE 120; and UFOs, AE *64;* and Fred Youngren, AE 64
Andretti, Mario: MA 129
Andrew, Saint: MY *105*
Andrew Jackson (ship): HN 80, MW 27
Andrews Air Force Base (Maryland): and UFO sightings, UP 53, 55
Androgyny: CD 48, 68, *69,* 70
Anesthetics: ergot as, EE 100; ether as, MB 104; laughing gas as, MB 102; mandrakes as, EE 96; and out-of-body experiences, PV 16, 36; trances as, MB 103-104
Angel, J. Lawrence: PS 40
Angel consciousness: defined, CD 136
Angelica: WW *38*
Angelic Doctor: CD 130
Angel meditation: UV *145*
Angelo, Sam: PH *16*
Angels: AE *43, 45,* 48, *52-53,* DD *50, 51,* MY *90,* SE *68-69. See also* CD *index*
Anger: CD 87
Anghiera, Peter Martyr d': MQ 34
Angkor (Cambodia): MW 93
Angkor Wat: ML *69, 70-71*

Anglo-Saxon churches: dowsing at, MQ *104-105*
Anglo-Saxons: and witches, WW 25
Angra Mainyu (god): TS 22
Angus, Miss (scryer): VP 50
Ani (Egyptian): MA 52
Anima/animus: DD 88-91; defined, CD 70
Animal magnetism: PH 20-27, 87-90, SA 92
Animal mutilations: causes of, AE 41; of cows, AE *40,* 41; of Lady, AE *40*
Animals: as criminals, TN 40; divination with, VP *37, 38-39,* 40, *42;* and earthquakes, EE 59-60, 61; and extrasensory perception, PP 58-59, *110;* and ghosts, HN 24, 133; and meteorology, EE 64; and out-of-body-experience research, PV 40, *41, 42;* and sleep, DD *104-105;* stories of, on Noah's Ark, MQ *82. See also* Forest People; *specific animals*
Animals, endangered: and artificial insemination, SI 110, and cryopreservation, SI 110-111; and in vitro fertilization, SI 110-111
Animal spirits: MB 13
Animism: defined, WW 115; in Indonesia, SE 33; Tylor's views of, SE 21; and Wicca, WW 115
Anir (son of Arthur): ML 47
Ankh: defined, SA 119
Ankrah, Joseph A.: PS 76
Ann, Saint: MY 65
Ann Arbor (Michigan): and UFO sightings, UP 106-110
Anne (nun): CD 115
Ann the Word: *See* Lee, Ann
Annwn: defined, ML 44-45, 56
Anomalistic psychology: PP 74
Anorexia: defined, HN 35
Ansbach: Werewolf of, TN *84-85*
Anschluss: PS 64
Anson, Jay: HN 100
Antaeus: SE *80*
Antelope (Oregon): EM 131
Anthesteria: MY 19
Anthony of Padua, Saint: out-of-body experience of, PV 16-17

9

MY *The Mystical Year;* **PE** *Phantom Encounters;* **PH** *Powers of Healing;* **PP** *Psychic Powers;* **PS** *The Psychics;* **PV** *Psychic Voyages;* **SA** *Secrets of the Alchemists;* **SE** *Search for the Soul;* **SI** *Search for Immortality;* **SS** *Spirit Summonings;* **TN** *Transformations;* **TS** *Time and Space;* **UP** *The UFO Phenomenon;* **UV** *Utopian Visions;* **VP** *Visions and Prophecies;* **WW** *Witches and Witchcraft*

ANKH. *This Egyptian symbol, shown here in an illustration from the* Book of the Dead, *represents the unquenchable life force. Gods were said to hold an ankh before a pharaoh's nose to confer upon him the breath of immortality.*

Anthropomancy: defined, VP 32, 38; by Druids, VP 38
Anthroposophical Society: AW 143, EE 130, SE 103
Anthroposophy: MP 30, MY 136; defined, SE 103; and Rudolf Steiner, UV 102, 110, 115, 118, 119
Antidotes: to magic spells, WW *38, 39*
Antikythera mechanism: ML 16-17, *18*
Antileptoquarks: EM 142
Anti-Masonic Party: AW 84
Antimatter: UP 24
Antinous: CC *35*
Antioch Chalice: discovery of, MQ 106
Antioxidants: SI 69
Antisurvivalists: defined, PE 68
Antlers: MY *84-85*
Antoninus, Marcus Aurelius (Roman emperor): SI 136
Antonio, Fray (Spanish priest): MQ 40
Antony, Saint: CD 82-83, MY 72
Ants: EE 107, EM 27; killer, MC *128-129;* soldier, CD 109
Ant Teacher: EM 90, SI 11-12
Antwerp Cathedral: clock tower of, TS *108*
Anu (god): AE 94, 96, CC 17
Anubis (god): MA 48, *50-51,* MC

56, ML *127*
Anunnaki: AE *94;* defined, AE *90;* robot emissary of, AE *90. See also* Aliens
Anuradhapura (Ceylon): bo trees in, EE 83
Anxiety states: chronic, MB 116
Aoki, John: PS 126
Aomata: defined, ML 97
Aomori Nebuta: MY 66
Aoyama Cemetery: MW 34, *37, 38*
Aoyama Tessan: PE 76
Apache Indians: EE 52-54, MA 74, SI 67
Apantomancy: defined, VP 32
Apep (serpent-devil): MA 51
Aphasia: defined, MB 45
Aphrodisiacs: EE 99, MA 99, SI *67;* types of, SI 67, 74
Aphrodite (goddess): CC *40,* CD 62-63, EE 76, WW 17
Apocalypse: MW 105; and Essenes, UV 33, 35
Apocalypse of Peter (Anonymous): CD 85
Apocalyptic literature: CD 85
Apollo (god): CC *38,* CD 43, EE 29, MW 85, 90, 104, SA *73, 75,* VP 10, 107
Apollo 1 (spacecraft): AE 62, PS 41
Apollo 13 (spacecraft): MA 118-119
Apollo 14 (spacecraft): EE 124, PP

54-55
Apollonia, Saint: MY 132
Apollonius of Tyana (magician and philosopher): MA 45
Apophis (demon): CD *14*
Apostle of Greenland: *See* Egede, Hans
Apostles: MY 50, 105
Apothecary shop: PH *64*
Apothem: and Great Pyramid, MP 55
Apparent: defined, PE 83
Apparitions: *See* Ghosts
Apple blossoms: divination with, VP 40
Apples: MY 96, 97, 126
Appleseed, Johnny: MY 89
Apple trees: EE 92. *See also* Trees
Applied cybernetics: PS 80
Apports: SS 54, *55,* 59, 109
Apricots: SI *52*
April Fool's Day: MY 26
APRO: *See* Aerial Phenomena Research Organization
Apsu (planet-god): AE *93;* background of, AE 92
Apuleius, Lucius: AW 16, MA 52
Aquarius (zodiac sign): CC *90,* 139, MY 104, 127
Aquarius, Age of: CC 145, 153, PP 98, UV 138
Aquila (constellation): CC 35
Aquino, Michael: and Satanism, CD 78-79; and Set, CD 78, 80; and Temple of Set, CD 96
Arab countries: superstitions in, MA *126*
Arabia: and distillation, SA 39; gold in, SA 17
Arabs: EE 96, SI 32; and pyramids, MP 48; vampires of the, TN 111; and zero, TS 29
Arachne: SE *74*
Aradia (witch): WW 102, 104
Arapaho Indians: Ghost Dance of, DD 30
Arapesh people: CD 62
Ararat, Mount (Turkey): MW 99, MY 35; appearance of, MQ 67-68, *68-69;* and Noah, ML 22, 34. *See also* Noah's Ark *in* MQ *index*
Arawak Indians: MA 82-83
Arcana: defined, SA 64, 89
Arc de Triomphe: EE 67

Archaeoastronomy: MP 94, 98; and Great Pyramid, MP 47, 63-65
Archaeology: PP 118-127. *See also* Biblical quests; Psychic archaeology; MQ *index*
Archangels: CD *131-133*
Archery: MB 104; in Japan, MM *121*
Arches: of Maya, ML 19; on Tonga, ML 97, *98*
Archetypes: AE 111, DD 79, 81; anima, DD *88-89;* animus, DD 89, *90-91;* child, DD *86-87;* defined, MB 20, VP 122, 140, WW 115; father, DD *84-85;* hero, DD *92-93;* and Carl Jung, DD 57, 73, 81, 85, 87, 89, 91, WW 115; mother, DD *82-83;* shadow, DD *94-95;* and Montague Ullman, DD 79. *See also* Dreams; Jung, Carl Gustav
Archimedes: ML 18, SE 18
Architectural model: ML *108*
Ardachie Lodge: HN *35,* MW 19; and hauntings, HN 33-34
Arderydd, Battle of: MQ 137; site, MQ *132-133*
Ardhanarishvara: *See* Shiva
Arecibo (Puerto Rico): and radio telescope, UP 124, *127. See also* Search for extraterrestrial intelligence
Ares (god): CC 41, CD 63-64
Argei: MY 37
Argentinum Astrum (AA): AW *116-118,* 147, MY 93; artwork for, AW *147*
Argo (galley): MQ *50, 54, 55;* voyage of, MQ *49-61*
Argo (Jason's ship): EE 80, MW *13*
Argonauts: WW 20
Argüelles, José: CC 146, MY 69
Arias, Oscar: MA 6
Aries (zodiac sign): CC 11, 13, 21, 24, 32, 36, *80,* 138, 139, 143, 154, MY 23, 31
Aristarchus of Samos: CC 25, 29, 93
Aristeas of Proconnesus: SE 28-31
Aristophanes: and torture, WW 82
Aristotle: AW 9, 13, CD 34, 56, DD 34-35, 107, MA 31, MC 45, ML 27, MW 134, SE 42, 46-50, 118;

AE *Alien Encounters;* **AW** *Ancient Wisdom and Secret Sects;* **CC** *Cosmic Connections;* **CD** *Cosmic Duality;* **DD** *Dreams and Dreaming;* **EE** *Earth Energies;* **EM** *Eastern Mysteries;* **HN** *Hauntings;* **MA** *Magical Arts;* **MB** *The Mind and Beyond;* **MC** *Mysterious Creatures;* **ML** *Mysterious Lands and Peoples;* **MM** *Mind over Matter;* **MP** *Mystic Places;* **MQ** *Mystic Quests;* **MW** *The Mysterious World;*

and elements, EE 51, 62, 66, 70, 76; and Geber, SA 29; and graphology, VP 92; and palmistry, VP 81; and physiognomy, VP 66; and Plato's Atlantis, MP 20; and torture, WW 82. *See also* SA *index*

Arjopas: defined, EM 81

Arjuna (disciple): TS *25*

Ark, of Noah: *See* Noah's Ark *in* MQ *index*

Ark of the Covenant: MQ 46-48

Arlacchi, Pino: AW 112

Arlington Street Church: women's spirituality conference and, WW 96-97

Arm (ghost): PE *43*

Armen, Jean-Claude: and gazelle-boy, TN 65-66; and Théodore Monod, TN 66; sketch by, TN *65*

Armenia: ancient kingdom (Urartu), MQ 67, *map* 67; and Noah's Ark, MQ 70

Armenians: archbishop, MQ *77*; ark stories of, MQ 75, 80-81

Armstrong, Neil: UP 120

Arnau de Villanova: SA 33, 34, 49

Arnold, Benedict: AW *83*, 111, DD 140

Arnold, Dorothy: TS 131

Arnold, Kenneth: MW 42, MY 56; and Cascade Mountains UFO sighting, UP 36-37, 38, *39*, 56, 69, 74, 131

Arnold, Matthew: CC 89

Aroma therapy: PH 112-*113*

Arorae Island: ML 97

Arpa: MW 120

Arrival apparitions: PE 99-100. *See also* Doubles

Arrow of time: TS *59*

Arrows, secret: defined, EE 115

Arroyo, Laura: MW 27, 30-*31*

Art (demon): WW 55

Artemidorus Daldianus: DD 35-37, 127

Artemis (goddess): CC 39, MW 104. *See also* Diana

Arthen, Andras Corban: WW 99, 128-129, *130-131*, 135

Arthritis: EE 100, SA 116

Arthur (of Britain): MW 85, 87, PE 130; and Arthurian legends, and Glastonbury, MQ 123; and grail legends, MQ 111, 112, 114, 117, *119, 120-121*; and Merlin, MQ 130. *See also* ML *index*

Arthur, Desmond: MW 19, 20

Arthur's Stone: ML *52-53*; background of, ML 51

Artifacts: American Indian, MP *126-127*

Artifacts, ancient: *See* MQ *index*

Artificial insemination: SI 112, 113. *See also* In vitro fertilization

Artificial intelligence (AI): MB 125-126, SI 88. *See also* Robots

Artificial sunlight: TS *84*

Arts and crafts movement: UV 35, 36, 85

Arturo (ghost): PE 124, *125*

Arunachala: EM 90

Arunta tribe: EE *90*, MW 34, 38, TS 37

Aryans: ML 20, WW 13-15

Asanas: PH *70-71*

Ascension Day: MY 39, 40

Ascension Island: ML 101-102

Asceticism: EM *36, 37*, 50

Asclepius (god): WW 17-18

Aserinsky, Eugene: DD 96, 97

Ashe, Geoffrey: ML 52; and axes, ML 129; and Brendan, ML 123

Ashley House séance: SS 41, 42. *See also* Home, Daniel Dunglas

Ash Manor: HN *116, 117, 119*; and ghosts, HN 114-118

Ashmole, Elias: CC 106, SA 56

Ashqelon calf (figurine): MQ *48*

Ashram: EM *128*

Ash trees: and healing rituals, EE 91-92

Ashurbanipal (king of Assyria): CC 8

Ash Wednesday: MY 136

Asia: MW *maps* 34-35, 58, 92, 126

Asian Development Bank: EE 132

Asians: and sacred places, TS 6

Asiatic Brethren of the Rosy Cross: AW 63

Asimov, Isaac: MM 34

Asket (alien): AE 99

Asking Festival: MY 101

Aslan, Ana: SI 75

Asmat: EM 95; warrior, SE *14*

Aśoka (king): EM 40-41

Aspens: EE 96. *See also* Trees

Aspergillum: CD *97*

ASPR: *See* American Society for Psychical Research

Assam (India): MW 59

Assassins: AW 12, *32, 33*; initiation of, AW 32-33; and Knights Templars, AW 39. *See also* individual assassins

Association for Research and Enlightenment (ARE): PH 31, 32, VP 22; and Edgar Cayce, PP 93, 95

Association for the Scientific Study of Near-Death Phenomena: PV 72

Assyria: haruspicy in, VP 34-35; numerology in, VP 107; white magic in, MA 17-19

Assyrians: AE *91*; flood stories, MQ 64, 80; and Gilgamesh epic, MQ 33, 80

Astarte (goddess): WW 13. *See also* Mother Goddess

Asteroids: MY 57

Asthma: herbs for, WW *36*

Astor, John Jacob: EE 100

Astragali: defined, VP 110

Astral body: MA 22, MB 118, PV 16-19, 21, 25, 34-35, *46-66*. *See also* Out-of-body experiences; Spirit

Astral messages: PP 42

Astral projection: defined, PV 21; and werewolves, TN 89, 91

Astral travel: PP 82-83, 86. *See also* Out-of-body experiences

Astro*Carto*Graphy: CC *149*

Astro-economics: PS 118-119, 121-124

Astrolabe: CC 53, *58, 101*, PS 121

Astrologers: CC 17-21, 26-29, 52-53, *137*. *See also* individual astrologers

"Astrologie und Okkultismus" (radio broadcast): PS 68

Astrology: CD 34, 36-37, MA 26, MW 12, 113, 127, 133, *134*, UV 60; and alchemy, SA *24-25*; branches of, CC 57-59; characteristics of, SA 21; defined, CC 10; humanistic, CC 150; psychological, CC 131; theories of, CC 143-148; use of, PP *94-95*. *See also* PS *index*

Astronauts, ancient: UP *13*. See

ARROW. Thanks to the mythological Eros (above), who fired magical arrows at people to smite them with love, the arrow has come to symbolize amorous desire. Shot through a heart, an arrow signifies the male principle uniting with the female.

also Extraterrestrials

Astronomers: *See individual astronomers*

Astronomical alignments: MP 90, 91-92, 94, 110, 112-113, 119, *120*

Astronomy: EE 54, MW 133, PS 118; defined, CC 10; and Maya, ML 19; and Pythagoreans, TS 47

Asura (demon): TS *26-27*

Asvattha: and bo trees, EE 83; and Hindus, EE 93-95. *See also* World trees

Atamara (Indian chief): MQ 34, 39

Atargatis (goddess): MY 28

Ataxia: defined, MB 78

Athame: WW *120, 127*

Athanor Fellowship: WW *128-131, 134-135*

Atharva-Veda: EM 33

Athelhampton Hall: MW 19

Athena (goddess): CC 41, CD 56, 61, EE 79, MY 60, SE 74, WW 17

Athens (Greece): MW 15

Athletes: and visualization, MB 125, MM 126, *132-133*

Athoeter: defined, SA 101

Athols: MW 59, 62. *See also* Bats

Atkinson, R.J.C.: and Stonehenge, construction of, MP 92, 94

Atlanta child murders: PS 44; and Dorothy Allison, PS 43, 44; and Wayne Williams, PS 44

Atlantic Humped Snake: MC 28. *See also* Sea serpents

Atlantis: ML 26-28, MP *map* 17, MW 14, *map 15,* 85, MY 22; colonies of, MP 15; description of, MP *6-7, 8-9;* destruction of, ML 27, MP *12-13;* legends of, ML 19; MP 14-36; popular interest in, MP *23,* 24; possible location of, ML 26, MP 15, *16,* 20-21, 23; and pyramids, relationship to, MP 67; rulers of, at temple of Poseidon, MP *10-11,* 16-19

Atlantis: The Antediluvian World (Donnelly): ML 27-28, MP 21-26

Atlas: CC 22

Atman: CD 49; defined, EM 37, PV 99. *See also* Spirit

Atmospheric halos: at Stonehenge, MP 102

Atomic bomb: ML 33

Atoms: and John Dalton, SA 115; defined, EE 51; and Democritus of Ionia, SA 20, 23; dissection of, TS 66; and Max Planck, TS 55. *See also* Primordial atom

At-Taum (angel): CD 31, 122

Attis: MY *24*

Attunement: and Findhorn Foundation, UV *142-143,* 144

Atum (god): MQ 78, TS 20

Atwood, Mary Anne: *See* South, Mary Anne

Aubrey, John: PE 85, VP 47; and Stonehenge, construction of, MP 88-89

Audition colorée: MB 52

Auditory hallucinations: MB 44-45. *See also* Hallucinations

Augury: defined, VP 33; Etruscan, VP 33; and haruspicy, VP 35; Roman, VP 33-34

Augustine, Saint: CD 32, 129, DD 107, EE 80, SE 50, 70, TS 38, 41-42; and City of God, UV 30; and Thomas More, UV 39

Augustine of Hippo, Saint: CC 50-52, WW 45

Augustus (Roman emperor): CC 34, MY 49

Augustus the Strong (king of Saxony): letter by, SA 89

Aurameter: EE *136*

Aura Rhanes (alleged alien): and Truman Bethurum, UP 76, 78

Auras: AE 110, AW 144, *145,* PS 113. *See also* MB *index*

Aurora australis: and hollow earth theory, MP 149

Aurora borealis: and hollow earth theory, MP 146, 149, *155;* mistaken for UFOs, UP 14; and twin earth theory, MP 139-140. *See also* Northern lights

Auroville (India): UV 145, *146-147, 148-149,* 150-152

Auspices: defined, VP 33

Ausso (alien): AE *25;* and Carl Higdon, AE 10, 26

Austen, Jane: CC 88

Austin, Stephen F.: EE 99

Australia: MW 75, 127

Australopithecus: MW 65, 69

Austromancy: defined, VP 35

Authority figures: CD 94-95

Autism: MB 62, TN 64, 69

Autogenic training: PH 138

Automatic behavior: TS 87

Automatic writing: SE *106,* 109; and John Alleyne Bartlett, ML *60,* 61, PP 119; and Frederick Bligh Bond, ML 60, PP 119, *120;* description of, PP 42; and Marguerite Du Pont Lee, PP 44-45. *See also* SS *index*

Automobiles: and superstitions, MA 121, 129, *130*

Autophany: PE 95, 97

Autoscopy: PE 95-97

Autosuggestion: MB 123, PH 123; description of, PP 24

Autumnal equinox: *See* Equinoxes

Avalon: CD 126, EE 92, ML 48, 52. *See also* Afterlife

Avarice: CD 87

Avatamsaka Sutra (Buddhist text): MB 10, 22

Avatars: SI 9, UV 115; defined, EM 124

Avebury Stone Circle: MW 85; as site of fertility rituals, MP *86-87*

Aveni, Anthony: and Nazca lines of Peru, MP 119

Averill, Richard L.: MM 61

Ave Roma immortalis case: SS 96. *See also* Cross-correspondences

Averroës (philosopher): SE 50

Aveyron, wild child of: *See* Victor (feral child)

Avicenna (a.k.a. Abu Ali al-Husayn ibn Abd Allah ibn Sina): EE 58, SA 30, *31,* 64, 65

Avis, Jean: CC 76

Avis family: and abduction by aliens, UP 84

Awa: defined, MA 84; and *kahuna ana'anas,* MA 84, 85

Axes: ML 129

Axinomancy: defined, VP 35

Ayahuasca: MB *108-109*

Ayers Rock: MW 93, 95-96, *97,* TS *14-15;* and Pitjantjatjara Aborigines, TS 15

Aymara Indians: SE *22-23*

Ayres, William: ML 101

Ayton, Hugh: MC 60

Ayton, Jim: MC 60

Ayton, William A.: SA 127-128

Ayurveda: PH 63-66, 67-68, 72, PS 98; defined, SI 32; and sweating, SI 114. *See also* Eastern healing; Indian healing

Ayurvedic Institute: PS 98-99

Aztec calendar stone: flood story depicted by, MQ 78

Aztecs: EE 101, ML 28, MW 79, 113, 115, PH 38, SE 20, UV 23-24; cosmogonies of, TS 37; and directions, TS *30;* and Mother Goddess, EE 26; and sacrifices, EE 26, TS *37*

B

BEAR. This 15-foot-high wooden grizzly, symbolizing supernatural power, was used by the Bellacoola in British Columbia, perhaps as a guardian for a home. When the hunters killed a bear, they held rites over its body out of reverence for its soul.

B, Mr.: TS 127
B., Mrs.: HN 33; ghost of, HN 34
Ba: SE 16, *17*, 24
Ba (Egyptian astral body): PV *16-17. See also* Astral body; Spirit
Baal (god): ML 133, WW 16
Baba, Neem Karoli: MB 117
Baba, Sai: EM 24
Baba, Satya Sai (a.k.a. Satyanarayana Ratnakara Raju): EM 24-25, 58
Babaji: EM 118, SI 8-11, 30
Babel, Tower of: ML 34, UV *20-21*
Babies: MB *54-55*
Babies, abduction of: AE 43, *48*-49
Babylon: haruspicy in, VP *34-35*; and seers, VP 9
Babylonia: vampires in, TN 110
Babylonian priest (Berossus): MQ 70
Babylonians: AE 91, CC 14-21, CD 24, 80-82, EE 72, ML 22
Bacchus (god): MA *106*, MY 100
Bacchus, Temple of: MW 125
Bach, Edward: PH 114
Bach, Richard: and SCANATE, PS 81; and *Taurus*, PS 83
Backster, Cleve: EE 107-109; psychokinesis research of, MM *74*
Bacon, Francis: AW *57*, EE 58, ML 27, MM 10, UV 42, VP 27; and alchemy, SA 80, 83-85; and Atlantis, possible location of, MP 20; and Rosicrucianism, SA 83-85; and witches, TN 38
Bacon, Roger: CC 59, 64, SA *33*, 34, SI 32, 39, VP 45
Bacteria: cloning of, SI 85-88; longevity of, SI 72
Baden-Baden (Germany): baths in, SI *131-137*
Badon, Mount: ML 47
Baggally, Wortley: SS 64
Baghdad (Iraq): MW 133-134;

characteristics of, SA 25-29; design of, EE 33
Ba-gua: EE *117*
Bahram I (ruler of Persia): CD 31
Baia: EE *62*
Baigent, Michael: MQ 125, 127
Bailes, Julian: SI 123
Bailey, Richard: MQ *105*
Bailly, Charles: MW 63
Bainbridge, Kenneth T.: SA 114
Bain-marie: SA 24
Baker, Russell: and UFO possibilities, UP 109
Balbillus: CC 34
Balder (god): MA 119
Baldness: SI 89, 93. *See also* Hair
Baldoon Castle: HN *16-17*, MY *71*
Balefire: defined, WW 107
Balfour, Arthur J.: HN 30, PV 19, SS 97, *98*, 99, VP 82; and Arthur Conan Doyle, SS 101; and Mary Catherine Lyttelton, SS 80-81, 92, 96-99; and Henry Sidgwick, SS 74; silver box of, SS 97, *99*
Balfour, Francis Maitland: SE 104, 107, SS *74-75*, 80
Balfour, Gerald: SE 104, 107; and Cross-Correspondences, SS 92; and Henry Sidgwick, SS 74
Bali: EM 60-69, MW 127; death rituals in, EM *64-65*, PE 55, PV *102-103*, SE 33, *34-37*; vampires in, TN *112*
Ball, Joseph A.: PS 82
Ball court: MY *13*
Ballechin House: HN *125*; and hauntings, HN 122-123, 124-128, 137
Ballen, Lloyd: and Levelland UFO sighting, UP 69
Ballinger, Bill: ML 98
Ball lightning: EE 70; as possible explanation for UFOs, UP 26-27, 69, 104, 105. *See also* Lightning
Balomain (demigod): MY 120
Balsamo, Giuseppe: *See* Cagliostro, Alessandro di Conte
Balsamo, Joseph: *See* Cagliostro, Alessandro di Conte
Balthazar (feral child): TN 68, *69*
Bamburg: witch trial in, WW 88-95
Bande Mataram (journal): UV 146
Bandiagara cliffs: ML *76-77*

MY The Mystical Year; PE Phantom Encounters; PH Powers of Healing; PP Psychic Powers; PS The Psychics; PV Psychic Voyages; SA Secrets of the Alchemists; SE Search for the Soul; SI Search for Immortality; SS Spirit Summonings; TN Transformations; TS Time and Space; UP The UFO Phenomenon; UV Utopian Visions; VP Visions and Prophecies; WW Witches and Witchcraft

BLOOD. *In this early-19th-century engraving, Aztec priests tear the heart from a sacrificial victim, offering up his blood—a universal symbol of life—as a gift to the sun god.*

Bandini, Ralph: MC 33-34

Baney, Ralph: MQ 43

Bangladeshis: SI 22

Bank of China: EE 35

Banks, Joseph: SA 78-79

Banshees: MY 100, PE 38, 42

Bantam cocks: MA 101

Bantu society: EE 53

Banya: SI 114

Banyan tree: EE 77, 82, EM 12-13. See also Trees

Baobabs: EE 84-85. See also Trees

Baphomet: AW 36, 37, 38, 115. See also Crowley, Aleister

Baptism: and floods, EE 74-76

Baptists: UV 65

Baquet: MM 92, 93. See also Hypnosis and hypnotic regression

Bara, Theda: as vamp, TN 135

Baradiin, Badzar: MC 107

Baraduc, Hippolyte: and near-death-experience photographs, PV 62, 63

Barbara, Saint: MW 113

Barbari, J. de: painting by, TS 39

Barbary apes: VP 40

Barbault, Alexandre: SA 132, 133, 134, 135

Barbault, Armand: SA 132-135; and elixirs, SA 132-135; and Mutus Liber, SA 132

Barbault, Jacqueline: SA 132

Barber, Theodore: MB 92

Barbers: MA 19-20

Barclay, John: MC 42-43

Bardo Thodol (Buddhist text): MB 114, PV 58. See also Book of the Dead, Tibetan

Barham, Jay: as healer and medium, PV 65

Barinth (abbot): ML 122

Baris dance: EM 68-69. See also Dances

Barker, J. C.: and Aberfan coal-waste avalanche, PP 34

Barker, William: PV 118

Barking Tree (spirit guide): and Taryn Krivé, SS 15, 148

Barkoczy, Countess: AW 103

Barnard, Eugene E.: and out-of-body-experience research, PV 16

Barnes, Harry G.: UFO sighting, UP 53, 55

Barnett, Grady Landon (Barney): AE 82; and Roswell UFO crash, UP 74-75

Barnum, P. T.: MC 62

Barombi Mbo, Lake (Cameroon): EE 53, MW 99

Barometers: EE 63

Barong (spirit): EM 69

Barrett, Lady: and patient's death-bed vision, PV 60

Barrett, William: PE 21, SS 71; and near-death-experience research, PV 60-62

Barron, Frank: MB 107

Barros, João de: ML 67

Barrow Neurological Institute: SE 18-19

Barrows: excavation of, MP 91; and ley theory, MP 95

Barrows, Gordon: PE 99

Barrymore, Lionel: CC 81

Bartholomew, Saint: MW 6-7

Bartlett, John Alleyne: and automatic writing, ML 60, 61, PP 119; and Frederick Bligh Bond, ML 61

Bartlett, Joseph: VP 67

Bartok, Eva: EM 121

Barton, Clara: VP 80

Basant Panchami: MY 130

Basil, Saint: UV 102

Basilisk: MC 12, MW 53; purple, EM 49

Basket Maker peoples: TS 7

Basoga: EE 90

Basques: ML 31

Bass Strait: MW 43

Bastet (goddess): SI 70

Bat: EM 29

Batcheldor, Kenneth J.: psychokinesis research of, MM 25

Bath (England): SI 24

Bathhouse: ancient, site of, MQ 102

Báthory, Elizabeth: TN 123-125, 126, 127

Baths: in Baden-Baden (Germany), SI 131-137

Bathurst, Benjamin: TS 129

Bats: MW 62, 65, 70, TN 128-129; bumblebee size, MC 20; and Great Pyramid, MP 54, 55; vampires as, TN 109, 134. See also Athols

Batteries: ML 23

Battlefields: hauntings of, PE 129-139

Battle of Blythe Road: AW 156

Battle of Britain: MW 20

Battle of Glendale: MW 121

Battle of Little Bighorn: MA 78-80

Battle of Nechtansmere: PE 132-133

Battle of the Spoilt Dyke: MW 121

Baudelaire, Charles-Pierre: CD 93

Bauhaus: UV 121, 128, 129, 130, 131

Bauhütten: UV 129

Baulieu, Étienne: SI 75

Baumgardner, John: MQ 93

Baunscheidt, Carl: PH 118

Bavaria: werewolves in, TN 84-85

Bayless, Raymond: and poltergeists, HN 59

Baynes, Cary F.: VP 121

Bayraktutan, M. Salih: MQ 93

Beacons: PS 85

Bead lightning: EE 70. See also Lightning

Beads: quartz, ML 24

Beahrs, John: SS 152, 153

Beaked whale: MC 41

Beal, James: EE 61

Beamships: See UFOs

Bean, Beverly: AE 83

Beans: MA 99

Bearden, Thomas E.: and psychotronics, MM 80

Bears: MW 65, 66, 119-120; rituals regarding, TN 10; as totems, TN 8

Beastie: See Loch Ness monster

Beast of Gévaudan: MW 53, 55-59, TN 88

Beast of Truro: MW 47, 49-50

Beat Generation: EM 137

Beatles: EM 122

Beatrice Foods: natal charts of, PS 118-119

Beauchamp, Christine: MB 78

AE Alien Encounters; AW Ancient Wisdom and Secret Sects; CC Cosmic Connections; CD Cosmic Duality; DD Dreams and Dreaming; EE Earth Energies; EM Eastern Mysteries; HN Hauntings; MA Magical Arts; MB The Mind and Beyond; MC Mysterious Creatures; ML Mysterious Lands and Peoples; MM Mind over Matter; MP Mystic Places; MQ Mystic Quests; MW The Mysterious World;

BEE. *In the traditional spiritual teachings of several cultures, bees symbolize the souls of mortals, probably because souls are believed to swarm around the divine unity as bees swarm around their queen.*

Beauchamps, Mr. and Mrs.: PE 32
Beauty and the Beast (fairy tale): CD 46, *47*
Beavor Lodge: PE 115-119
Bechtel, Stefan: MB 83-85
Becker, Ernest: CD 107
Becker, Raymond de: DD 37
Becker, Robert D.: PH 54
Becket, Thomas a: MW 19, PE 104
Bedford, James: SI *98*, 118-119
Beecher, Henry Ward: VP 78, *80*
Beelzebub (demon): MA *94*
Beenham, Ethel: SS *124*, 128
Beerbohm, Max: DD 142
Beer Hall Putsch: and Adolf Hitler, PS 58, 62, *63*; and Nazis, PS 58
Bee therapy: PH 21
Beetles: divination with, VP 40; dung, CD *12*
Behaviorist psychology: school of, PP 49
Behavior modification: MM 57; and hypnosis, MM 98
Beheading: SE 15, 21
Behemoth (demon): MA *95*
Beijing (China): design of, EE 33; Inner City of, EM *10-11*; Forbidden City of, EE 33, EM 10, MW *127, 128*
Being and Nothingness (Sartre): SE 69-71
Beissel, Johann Conrad: and Ephrata commune, UV 60, 61
Bekker, Balthasar: and witch hunts, WW 72
Bel (god): ML 133
Belacane (character in *Parzifal*): MQ 111
Belcher, Miss: WW 61
Belgian Society for the Study of Space Phenomena: AE 80
Belgium: UFOs in, AE *80-81*
Bell: SA *61*
Bell, Mrs.: AW 102
Bell, Elizabeth: and poltergeists, HN 93-98
Bell, John: death of, HN *95*; and hauntings, HN 93, 94, 98; and poltergeists, HN 93, 94, 98
Bell, John, Jr.: HN 95
Bell, Luce: and hauntings, HN 93, 95; and poltergeists, HN 93, 95
Bell, Richard: and hauntings, HN 93, 94, 95; and poltergeists, HN 93, 95

Belladonna: MB 55, TN 94, WW 32. *See also* Hallucinogens
Bellamy, Rev. Arthur and Mrs.: PE 58
Bellon (ghost): HN 130
Bell Plantation: MW 27
Bell Rock: EE 65
Bell Witch (ghost): HN 93-98; and exorcism, HN 93
Belmez (Spain): MW 34
Beloff, John: MM 8
Belphegor (demon): MA *95*
Beltane: WW 123, *134-135. See also* May Day
Belt fastener: ML 22
Ben (master gunner on frigate *Aggie*): alleged reincarnation of, PV 114
Benares (India): EM *18-19*
Bender, Hans: and hauntings, HN 32-33; poltergeist research of, MM 38, 42, 43, 44, 51, 52, 53
Bender, Peter: and Koreshanity, MP 151
Benedict, Saint: WW 42
Benedict XIV (pope): CD 116
Benet, Sula: and longevity, SI 41, 43-45
Benevolent and Protective Order of Elks: AW 12
Benford, Gregory: and tachyonic antitelephone, TS 70

Bengala (ghost): PE 62
Benin: SI *102-103*
Benjamin (baby born without brain): PH 82
Benjamin, Alfred: PH 78
Benjamin, Harold H.: PH 132
Ben Macdhui (mountain): MW 16-17, 19, *20-21*
Bennett, Allan (a.k.a. Bhikku Ananda Metteya): AW *121*, 153-155, EM *92*
Bennett, Edward: DD 74
Bennett, John: EM *121*; and Georgei Ivanovitch Gurdjieff, MB 100-101, 104
Benoit, Adolphine: and poltergeists, HN *54*
Benson, Herbert: PH 122, 137, 139; Transcendental Meditation research of, MM 119
Bent, J. Theodore: MQ 41
Bentham, Jeremy: CD 128
Bentreshyt: alleged reincarnation of, PV 104
Bentwaters Royal Air Force Base (England): and Rendlesham Forest UFO sighting, UP 132, 136-141
Benveniste, Jacques: PH 120-121
Beowulf: MC 100
Beradt, Charlotte: DD 41
Béraud, Marthe: *See* C., Eva
Berdaches: CD *64-65. See also*

Gender
Beresford, Arabella: MW 19
Bergier, Jacques: SA 120-123; death of, PS 71; and Gérald Messadié, PS 71; and *Nautilus*, PS 71, 72; and psi-warfare experiments, PS 72
Bergman, Ingmar: DD 38
Bergson, Henri-Louis: MB 20
Beringia: ML 115
Berini, Daisy: and ghosts, HN 102
Berini, Joe and Rose: and exorcism, HN 104; and ghosts, HN 102, 103; and poltergeists, HN 103-104
Berini, John: HN 102; and poltergeists, HN 103
Berkeley, George: SE 56-57
Berkland, James: and earthquakes, EE 59-61
Berlin Wall: PS *22-23*
Berlitz, Charles: MQ 89; and Roswell UFO crash, UP 74-75
Bermuda: MW 75
Bermuda Triangle: EE 65, MW 79, 83, MY 19, 99, 115, TS 132-133; episodes in, MP 37, *42-43, 44 45;* and *Mary Celeste,* MP 38-39
Bernard, Claude: TS 100
Bernard, Raymond: and hollow earth theory, MP 152-153
Bernard of Clairvaux, Saint: AW 33-36, *37*, MQ 118, 120
Bernays, Martha: DD *61*; and Sigmund Freud, DD 60, 61
Bernays, Minna: DD *61*; and Sigmund Freud, DD 61
Bernbaum, Edwin: MQ 22, 30; Khembalung quest of, MQ 30-31
Bernhardt, Sarah: VP 85
Bernheim, Hippolyte: hypnosis research of, MM 94
Bernini, Giovanni Lorenzo: HN 131
Bernstein, Jerome: DD 81, 83, 85, 87, 89, 91, 93, 95
Bernstein, Morey: MY 102; as hypnotist, PV *116-118*
Berossus (Babylonian priest): CC 26, MQ 70
Berries: rowan, WW *38*
Berry, John: CD 65
Berry Pomeroy (castle): PE 40
Berserkers: TN 36-37

15

Bertha: WW 27. *See also* Holda

Bertrand, Eugene: and Exeter UFO sighting, UP 99-*102*, 104

Bertrand, Victor: TN 126; trial of, TN 126; as vampire, TN 126

Besant, Annie Wood: AW *136, 140, 142*, EM *87*, 88, MY 115, UV 115-118; and Helena Petrovna Blavatsky, AW 137-140, EM 87; cremation of, AW *143*; in India, AW 128, 141-142, *143*, EM 86; and Jiddu Krishnamurti, AW *143*, EM 87, 88; and Order of the Star in the East, EM 87; and Comte de Saint-Germain, AW 64-65; and Theosophical Society, EM 86, 87; and William Butler Yeats, AW 150

Besant, Frank: AW 140

Besold, Christoph: AW 54-55, SA 85

Bessent, Malcolm (psychic): DD 148-149, PP 16, PS *111*, TS 117

Beta waves: characteristics of, MM *82-83*, 108; and self-mutilation, MM 112

Bethune, Thomas Greene ("Blind Tom"): PV 118, *123*

Bethurum, Truman: and encounters with aliens, UP 76, 78

Betony: WW *39*

Betoro Bromo (god): MY 126

Bettara-Ichi: MY 94

Bettelheim, Bruno: CD 44; and autism, TN 64; and feral children, TN 57, 64

Betty, L. Stafford: and poltergeists, HN 54, 55

Beutel, Tobias: CC 101

Bey, Rahman: MM 110

Béziers (France): CD 33

Bezoars: MA *106*

Bhagavad-Gita: EM 64, TS 25; and yoga, EM 37

Bhaktisiddhanta: EM 124

Bhakti yoga: defined, EM 37, 116; and Ramakrishna, EM 116. *See also* Yoga

Bhoma (god): SE 34, *36*

Bible: MQ 41, PS 118, SI 12; and alleged alien visitations, ML 29, UP *15*, 17; alleged UFO sightings in, UP 12-*14*; and cosmogonies, TS 19; flood stories in, ML 33-

34; giants in, ML 24; illustration from, MQ *46-47*; and *Mutus Liber*, SA 70, *77*; numerology in, VP 106, 107; psi-warfare experiments in, PS 73; psychic detection in, PS 27; seers in, VP 10, 14

Biblical quests: MQ 41-48. *See also* Noah's Ark *in* MQ *index*

Bicameral: defined, MB 44

Bicyclist: and virtual reality, MB *134-135*

Bien Boa (spirit guide): PP *40*, SS *66-67*

Big bang theory: TS 61-62, 67

Big Bear City (California): MW 27

Bigfoot: MC 18, 98-99, *114, 118, 119*, MW 44, 47, MY 95; characteristics of, MC 99; defined, MC 98; footprints of, MC 99, 116, *117, 119, 120, 121, 124, 125*; history of, MC 99-100; sightings of, MC 98, 99, *114*, 117, *118, 119*, 120. *See also* Hominoids *in* MC *index*

Big Foot (Indian): MW 111

Big Gray Man: MW 17, 19, 20

Bighorn Medicine Wheel: MW 79

Big Muddy Ranch: EM 131

Bihari, Bernard: PH 44

Billboard: MW 27, 30-*31*

Billington, James H.: AW 92

Bilocation: CD 116-118

Bimini (island): in fountain of youth stories, MQ 34, 39

Bimini Road: and Atlantis, possible location of, MP 33

Bin (oracle): VP 119

Bindele: defined, MA 14

Bindu: defined, CD 11

Binet, Alfred: VP 92

Bingham, Hiram: ML 73

Binns, Ronald: MC 81-82

Binski, Sigurd R.: psychokinesis research of, MM 62-63, 64

Biodynamic farming: EE 128-131, UV 118. *See also* Agriculture; Farming

Bioenergetics: PH 101

Bioenergy: PH 98, 99-100

Biofeedback: MB 126, MM *122*, PH 9, 135-*137*, and Thomas Budzynski, DD 118; characteristics of, MM 124, SI 104; defined,

PE 128; Elmer Green's research on, MM 124-125; and hypothermia, SI 104, 109; and longevity, SI 109; and theta waves, DD 118; and Roy L. Walford, SI 104, 109

Biological-clock theory: SI 66

Biological rhythms: *See* TS *index*

Biophysics Laboratory: PS 84

Biowork: PS 94

Bird (ghost): PE *44*

Bird, Christopher: EE 108, PS 77

Bird, Eric: MC 37-38

Bird, J. Malcolm: and Mina Crandon, SS *110, 111*-112, 114, 115, 117; and *Scientific American's* tests of mediums, PP 38-39

Bird, Junius: ML 131

Bird, Sheila: MC 37-38

Birdmen: ML *88-89*

Bird of paradise, greater: EM *94*

Birds: EE 131, ML *24-25*, TS 82, *83*; blackbirds and witches, WW 12; divination with, VP *38-39*, 40, *42*; as image of soul, SE *16-17*; on Noah's Ark, MQ *72*, 82; spirit, in vision quest, MQ *14-15*, 17. *See also* Animals

Birth: and superstitions, MA 130

Birth chart: CC *118-127, 142*

Birth control: UV 78

Birthmarks: and reincarnation, PV 108-109

Birthstones: MY *17, 49, 81, 113*

Bisclaravet: *See* Werewolves *in* TN *index*

Bisham Abbey: HN *12-13*; and ghosts, HN 12

Bishop, Bridget: MY 52; as witch, WW 76

Bishop, Eleanor: PP *105*

Bishop, Washington Irving (mentalist): PP *103*, 104, *105*, 106-107

Bishop-fish: MC *54. See also* Human-beasts

Bisi, Giannetto: photograph by, UV *123*

Bisket: MY 29

Bismarck, Otto von: DD 37

Bison: and Indians, TN *31*

Bisson, Juliette: SS *68*; and Eva C., SS 67-68, 70

Bjora, Steve: MC 16

Bjorksten, Johan: SI 66-69

Bjornsson, Hafsteinn (medium): SE 99, 100

Black, Dora: SE *64*

Blackburn, Douglas: telepathic tests of, PP *28-29*; thought transference of, PP 26-27

Black Canon (ghost): HN 90

Black Death: MY 40

Black Elk (medicine man): visions of, PP *78-79*

Blackfeet Indians: MA *79*

Black Forest: SI *132-133*

Black Friar (ghost): PE *39*

Black Hat Dance: MY *106-107*

Black Hills: MW 79-80

Black holes: AE 116, TS 63-64, *65, 73*, 117, UP 24, *146-147. See also* Rotating black holes

Black Madonna: CD 58. *See also* Virgin Mary

Black magic: MA 15, 17, 48, SI 30; and Catholicism, MA 90-92; and hand of glory, MA 92; and love, MA 92-93, 99, 100; and potions,

BOAT. *An ancient emblem of the passage between this world and the next, a boat is seen in the Egyptian tomb painting below transporting the dead into the nether regions.*

MA 92, 99; and sex, MA 92, 93-99; and sorcerers, MA 25; and spells, MA 92, 93, 100; and white magic, WW 23-25. *See also* Magic

Blackmore, Susan: out-of-body experience of, PV *37;* and out-of-body-experience research, PV 44

Blacks: and Shakers, UV 68; and superstitions, MA 135; and voodoo, MA 82

Black sabbaths: MA 48

Blacksmiths: MA 19-20

Black Spot I (Kandinsky): AW *163*

Black stage: SA 48, 49

Black Stone: MY 91

Black Tuesday: PS 112. *See also* Stock market crash (1929)

Blackwood, Algernon: MA 64

Bladder Festival, Inuit: MY 117, TN *32 33*

Blair, Lawrence: EM 95, MA 33-34

Blair, Lorne: EM 95, MA 33-34

Blair, Robert: SE 49

Blaise, Saint: MY 130

Blajini (spirits): MY 27

Blake, William· CC 88, CD 136, EM 137, MB 102, MY 104, SE 49, VP 66; and Atlantis, MP 20; death as viewed by, PV *74-76;* engraving by, SE *48,* 49; near-death experience of, PV 75

Blance, R. S.: MW 38

Blanchard, William: AE 81

Blasphemy: punishment for, WW *83*

Blavatsky, Helena Petrovna (a.k.a. HPB): AW *126,* 128, 130-132, 135-137, CC 116, 130, EM 84, *86-87,* MY *65, 84,* 115, PV 21; and alien visitors, UP 16; and Atlantis, ML 28; background of, EM 84, ML 28; and Annie Wood Besant, AW 137-140, EM 87; and British Society for Psychical Research, EM 86; and Christianity, AW 131; and Alexis and Emma Coulomb, AW 134; death of, AW 137, EM 84, 86; and Ignatius L. Donnelly, ML 28; and drugs, AW 128, 129; experiments of, PV 20-21; and Richard Hodgson, AW 134-135; and

Daniel Dunglas Home, AW 129, 132; in India, AW 132-134, PV 21-22; and Lemuria, ML 12, 28; and magic, EM 84; and mahatmas, AW *132-133,* 134, 140, EM 85-86; as medium, AW 129; and Henry Steel Olcott, AW 124-125, 129-130, EM 84; out-of-body-experience beliefs of, PV 21; plagiarism of, AW 131; and Ramaswamier, AW 133, 135; and reincarnation, PV 22, SE 45; and Comte de Saint-Germain, AW 64; and Alfred Percy Sinnett, AW 133-134; sketch by, AW *127;* and Society for Psychical Research, AW 134-135, 141, PV 22; and Rudolf Steiner, UV 115; and Theosophical Society, EM 84, 85, MQ 19, 27, PV 20, 22, 103; and Theosophists, UV 87, 115; in Tibet, AW 129; travels of, AW 128-129, 135, EM 84; and untouchables, EM 85

Blavatsky, Nikifor: AW 128

Blavatsky, Yuri: AW 129

"Blessed Damozel, The" (Rossetti): SS *97,* 99

Blessing of the Throats: MY 130

Blimp: MY *22*

Blindfold Carriage Test: PP 103, *107,* 108, 114

Blind persons: and occipital lobe, MB 51; and "sonar," MB 54. See *also* Sight

"Blind" target: defined, MM 63

Blind Tom: PV 118, *123*

Bliss-consciousness: TS *28*

Block, Gladys: SI 75

Block Island: MW 27

Blofeld, John: and *I Ching* diviner, VP 115, 116-117, 119

Blok, Alexander: UV 121

Blood: TN *125;* and Aeson, SI *27;* and Elizabeth Báthory, TN 123-125; circulation of, SI 14-15; and Innocent VIII, SI 27-30, *32,* 60; and Medea, SI *27;* transfusions of, SI 6, 27-30, 60

Blood circulation: SA 64, 92

Blood Countess: *See* Báthory, Elizabeth

Bloodletting: PH *42*

Blood Spring (Chalice Well, Glastonbury, England): MQ *116,* 123-124

Bloodwort: SI *59;* and folk medicine, SI 59, 60

Bloom, Claire: MA 137

Blossom House: UV *127*

Bloxham, Arnall: TS 126; as hypnotist, PV 114

Blue Book: *See* Project Blue Book

Blue bottles: PS *30-31*

Blue God (a.k.a. Krishna): UV *9*

Blue Lake: EE *46-47*

Blumberg, Jeffrey: SI 75

Blumenschein, Adam: MW 36

Blumrich, Josef F.: and alleged biblical UFO sightings, UP 14, *15*

Bly, Robert: CD *61*

Blymyer, John: WW 98

Blythe, Henry: as hypnotist, PV 113-114

Blythe Giant (California): MP 119-121, *135*

Board of Rites: EE 35

Boats, paper: MW 34

Bob (dog): MY 60

Boban, Claudine: and brooms, WW 19

Bobo (sea serpent): MC 33. *See also* Sea serpents

Boccaccio, Giovanni: DD 141-143

Boccioni, Umberto: UV *123*

Bocock, Kemper: spirit photographs of, PP 44, *45*

Bodenham, Anne: WW *60;* and the occult, WW 60

Bodhanath stupa: CD *98,* MY *112*

Bodhidharma: EM 53, 55, 57, 147

Bodhisattva: CD 122, EM 77

Bodhisattva Avalokitesvara: PV *120*

Bodin, Jean· TN 83

Bodkins· WW *80;* defined, CD 83

Body double: PV 17, 20, 31-32, 40-41

Body temperature: TS 81, 95

Bodywork: PH *106,* PS 94

Boece, Hector: ML 25

Boeche, Raymond: and Rendlesham Forest UFO sighting, UP 136, 141

Boehme, Jakob: AW *53,* CC *109*

Boer War: MA 121

Boethius: VP 109

Bogen, Joseph: SE 119

Boggs, Wade: MA 128

Bogomil (priest): CD 32

Bogomils: CD 32

Bohemia: vampires in, TN 116

Bohm, David: MB 26-28, SE 130-131, *135,* 139

Bohr, Niels: MB 25, TS *68;* and Albert Einstein, TS 68; and quantum mechanics, TS 65, 68

Bokors: MA 88, 89

Boleyn, Anne: MW 19, PE 106

Bolton, Frances T.: and Parapsy-

17

BULL. *This massive beast has long signified strength and fertility and was sacred in ancient Egypt, Greece, India, and the Middle East. The head below, carved from stone with gilded wooden horns, was used in bull-cult rituals on Crete.*

chology Foundation, PP 86; and psychic research, PP 56

Bolton Priory: and ghosts, HN 90

Bombast von Hohenheim, Philippus Aureolus Theophrastus: *See* Paracelsus

Bombers: MY *115*

Bon (religion): HN 127, PV 127; festival, MY *60-61*, SE *30-31*; masks of, TN *42*; sacred land of, MQ 25

Bona Dea (goddess): MW 124, MY 115

Bonaparte, Marie: DD *67*

Bonaparte, Napoleon: CC 84, DD 42-43, PS *75*; armies of, MQ 122

Bonatti, Guido: CC 48-49, 64

Bonaventure, Saint: CD 116

Bond, Frederick Bligh: ML *60*, PP 126; and automatic writing, ML 60, PP 119, *120*; and John Alleyne Bartlett, ML 61; and Glastonbury Abbey, ML 59-63, PP 118-120, *120-122*

Bonfim Church: PH *28-29*

Bonhomme Richard (ship): AW *80-81*

Boniface of Montferrat, Marquis: MQ 122

Bonpo sect: and Kailas, TS 11

Booker, John: CC 102

Book of Changes: See I Ching

Book of Constitutions (Anderson): AW 89

Book of Dyzan: See Stanzas of Dyzan

Book of Mormon: UV 59

Book of Shadows: WW 104, 105, 107, *118*

Book of the Dead, Egyptian: AW 16, CD *14*, 85, MA *50-51*, 51-52, MQ 78, SE 24, 25, 26

Book of the Dead, Tibetan: CD 85, MB 114, PV *58*, 134-135; near-death experiences in, PV 59

Books of hours: and calendars, TS *104*

Book tests: SS 90-91

Boone, Daniel: EE 100, ML 125

Booth, David: PS *17*

Booth, John Wilkes: MW 28

Bordeaux Academy of Sciences: TN 121

Borden, Lizzie: physiognomy of,

VP 79-81

Boreas (wind): CD 23

Boredom: effect on test results, MM 62

Borfimah: defined, TN 44; of leopard-men, TN 44

Borgia, Cesare: VP 67

Borgia, Roderigo: PE *84*

Borley Rectory: HN *67, 68-69,* MW 19, PE 126-127; and ghosts, HN 66, 68; and poltergeists, HN *65-69*

Borobudur: MW 93

Borron, Robert de: MQ 118-120, 123

Bors (character in Arthurian legend): MQ 120, *121*

Borysenko, Joan: PH *138*

Bosch, Hieronymus: death as viewed by, PV *68*; painting by, TS *41*; triptych by, SA *69*

Bosco, Father Giovanni: DD *36*

Boston Phrenological Society: VP 75

Boston Society for Psychic Research (BSPR): PP 38, SS 117

Boston Strangler case: TN 130; and Peter Hurkos, PP 130-132

Boston Tea Party: AW *74-75*, 76, 78

Boswell, James: SE 57, 58

Boswell, Urania: MA 101

Botanicas: MW 115

Botanomancy: defined, VP 35

Botany: EE 102-103, 105

Bo trees: EE 77, *83. See also* Trees

Böttger, Johann Friedrich: SA *88*; letters by, SA *89*

Botticelli, Sandro: VP *106*; painting by, UV *12*

Boullan, Abbé: MA 64

Boullée, Étienne-Louis: cenotaph by, UV *32*

Boundary stone: CC 10

Bounteous Immortals: CD 26

Bounty (ship): ML 95

Bourne, Ansel: MB 77-78

Bourne, Samuel: photographs by, EM *16-19, 30*

Bourstev, Igor: MC *106*

Bouyer, Frédéric Marie: MC 23

Bovis, Antoine: EE 25; and pyramid power, MP 65-66

Bowers, Barbara: MB *30;* and au-

18

BRIDGE. In this painting, souls of the deceased contend with a narrow bridge, symbol of the journey between life and the eternal. Good souls cross successfully into heaven, while sinners tumble into the river that flows to the underworld.

ras, MB 29-37
Bowers, William: PS 71
Bowes Lyons (earls of Strathmore): PE 37
Bowles, Joyce: and UFO sighting, MP *108-109*
Bowls: bronze, MQ *124;* Gundestrup cauldron, images from, MQ *130, 133, 135, 136-137;* Sacro Catino, MQ 121-122, *125*
Bowness, Charles: MA 102
Bowthorp, Ben: ark sighting of, MQ 90
Bowyer-Bower, Eldred: PE 27-30
Boxing Day: MY 46
Boyle, Robert: PH 87. *See also SA index*
Boynton Canyon: EE *65*
Bozzano, Ernesto: and ghosts, HN *22*, 30
Bradley, Marion Zimmer: WW 122
Bragdon, Claude: AW 168
Brahan Seer: *See* Odhar, Coinneach
Brahe, Tycho: CC 92, 94-97
Brahma (divine principle): PV 99
Brahma (god): CD 25, DD *28, 71,* EM 119, TS 23, 24, VP 106; the Creator, EE 93; and Carl Jung, DD 71
Brahman: MB 22-25; defined, EM 37
Brahminism: *See* Hindus and Hinduism
Brahms, Johannes: DD 117, SI 133
Braid, James: hypnosis research of, MM 94, *95*
Brain: DD 100-101, 105, MB *16;*

CAT scan images of, SE *130;* contents of, MB 39-40; defined, MB 39; maps of, MB *81;* model of, SE *125;* organization of, CD 66-68; and time dilation, TS 89. *See also specific headings*
Brain death: SE 138
Brainstem: DD 100, 103
Brainwashing: characteristics of, MB 99; and Patricia Hearst, MB 98. *See also* Trances
Brain waves: alpha waves, MM *82-83,* 86, 108, 112, 119; beta waves, MM *82-83,* 108, 112; delta waves, MM *82-83,* 108; theta waves, MM *82-83,* 105, 108, 109
Bramasuganandah: and Ant Teacher, EM 90; and yoga, EM 89, 90
Brandano, Bartolomeo: VP 14
Brandenburg (Germany): penal code of, WW *82*
Brandler-Pracht, Karl: CC 130
Brangwyn, Frank: SE 112
Brant, Joseph: AW *101*
Bran the Blessed (Celtic hero): MQ 109, 110; castle of, MQ *112*
Brasseur de Bourbourg, Charles-Étienne: and Atlantis, ML 27, 28; and Maya, ML 27; and Mu, MP 26
Bratton, Ernest (a.k.a. Dr. Buzzard): MA 9
Braun, Dr.: WW 92
Brazel, Mac: and Roswell UFO sighting, UP 39
Brazil: MW 42, 75, 113; deaths caused by aliens in, AE 41-42;

UFOs in, AE 42
Brazilians: and time, TS 97-99
Bread: MY *59*
Breast ornament: of Mixtecs, TS *37*
Breath control: SA 106
Breathing: and yoga, EM 40
Breeding program: AE *37;* and Betty Andreasson, AE 36, 37. *See also* Genetic experimentation
Brejack, George: PS 44
Brendan, Saint: and America, discovery of, ML 120, 121-122; and Geoffrey Ashe, ML 123; background of, ML 121-122; and Christopher Columbus, ML 123
Brennan, Barbara Ann: PH 96-99
Breton: werewolves in, TN 79
Breton, André: DD 7
Brewer, Robert: PS *127*
Brezhnev, Leonid: MA 8, PH 100
Brice, Fannie (comedic actress): and mind reading, PP 107
Bricout, B. (medium): SE 100, 102
Bride (goddess): MY 130
Bride's Beds: MY *130*
Bridger, Jim: PS *77*
Bridges, Marilyn: and earth drawings, photography of, MP *128-137*
Bridget, Saint: MY 130
Briggs, Mr. and Mrs.: and hauntings, HN 89
Briggs, Benjamin Spooner, Sarah, and Sophia: MY 99
Briggs, Denis: MQ *104;* dowsing sites, MQ *104-105*
Briggs, Lori: AE 123
Briggs, Rachel: and hauntings, HN 88-89
Brigham, William Tufts: fire walking of, MM 103-105
Brighton trunk crime: and Eugenie Dennis, PS 34, *36*
Brigit (goddess): MY 130
Brigue, Jehanne de: WW 57
Brinkley, John Romulus: SI *63-64*
Bristlecone pines: SI *72;* longevity of, SI 23, 72
Britain: MW *maps* 18, *34-35;* Battle of, MW 20; crop circles in, AE 75; and psi-warfare experiments, PS *68-69*

British: and time, TS 99
British Overseas Airways: MW 42
British Premonitions Bureau: PP 34
British Society for Psychical Research: EM 86
British UFO Research Association (BUFORA): AE 105-106
Britten, Emma Hardinge: SS *30-31*
Broad, C. D.: SE 65, *66-68,* 107, 108
Broadside: MC *27*
Broca, Pierre-Paul: MB *50,* VP 81; and left brain/right brain, MB 45, 49; and limbic system, MB 50
Brocken: MY 32
Brockwood Park: EM 120
Brodie-Innes, J. W.: MA 62
Broman, Francis: EE *110*
Bromhall, J. Derek: SI *57*
Bromo, Mount: EE *68-69,* MY 126
Bron (character in grail legends): MQ 110-111, 119, 123
Brontë, Emily: out-of-body experiences of, PV 15
Bronze Age galley: voyage of Ulysses retraced in, MQ *19, 61*
Bronze bowl: MQ *124*
Brook Farm: UV 81, *82*
Brooklyn Enigma: MB 87
Brooks, Ronald: SI 107
Brooms: WW *19, 54, 112, 120-121*
Brossy, Jacques: SE 100, 102
Brotherhood of Luxor: AW 129
Brotherhood of the New Life: UV 79
Brotherhood of the Rosy Cross: MY 71. *See also* Rosicrucians and Rosicrucianism
Brougham, Lord Henry: PE 32-33
Broughton, Richard: PS 94
Brown, Agnes: and pigs, WW *61*
Brown, A. J.: MB 78
Brown, Bernard: ML 25
Brown, Harold: and investigations of UFOs, UP 110-111
Brown, Jerry: PH 57
Brown, John: VP 78
Brown, J. Randall (mentalist): and Washington Irving Bishop, PP 105
Brown, Melvin E.: AE 83
Brown, Paul Clement: PS 128-130

19

Brown, Rosemary: SS 138

Brown, Sister Barbara: MM 124

Brown, Mrs. Sybil: and Aberfan coal-waste avalanche, PP 33

Brown, T. Townsend: and National Investigations Committee on Aerial Phenomena, UP 69

Browne, Thomas: MB 45, MQ 41

Browning, Elizabeth Barrett: MY 63, 134; and Daniel Dunglas Home, SS 39, 43, *44-45, 46-47, 48-49, 50-51;* and spiritualism, SS 39

Browning, Robert: MY 63, SI 130; and Daniel Dunglas Home, SS 39, 43, *44-45, 46-47, 48-49, 50-51*

Brown Lady: MW 19, 21-22, *23*

Brown-Séquard, Charles-Édouard: SI *58,* 60-62

Brslanast: MY *44-45*

Bruan: MW 62

Brueghel, Jan (the Elder): paintings by, SA *26-27,* UV *12-13*

Brueghel, Pieter (the Elder): paintings by, MP *140-141,* UV *20-21*

Brulé Sioux Indians: EE 101

Brummer, Carrie: PH *133*

Brunhilda: SI 97-99

Bruno, Giordano: CC 93; and mind, MB 7, 58

Brunton, Paul (a.k.a. Raphael Hurst): EM 88, 89-*91,* 92

Bruyere, Rosalyn: PH 103-104

Bryant, Ray: alleged previous incarnation of, PV *115*

Bryant, Steven: EM 130

Bryant, William Cullen: EE 104

Bryce, James: MQ 76, *81*

Bubonic plague: SA 96-97

Buchanan, James: UV 58

Buchanan, Joseph Rodes: PS 30

Buckingham (English duke): HN 116-117

Buckland, Raymond (a.k.a. Robat): WW 109-110, 112

Buckland, Rosemary (a.k.a. Lady Rowen): WW 109, 110

Buckstone, John: ghost of, HN 31

Budapest, Z: WW 108, *112,* 116

Buddha (a.k.a. Siddhartha Gautama): EE 77, MY 115, SS 136, 137; background of, EM 40, MY 115; and Alexandra David-Néel,

EM *72,* 73; and dharma, EM 53-55; and enlightenment, EM 40, 101; and hippie, EM *96;* and Kashyapa, EM 55; and meditation, EM 40, PV *133;* and "middle way," EM 40; and nirvana, EM 40, 101; and Peter D. Ouspensky, EM 85; paintings of, PV 133, UV *29;* sculpture of, MB *27;* search for burial site of, MQ 40-41; statues of, EM *22-23, 72,* 85, *96,* ML *107,* MY *29, 41,* SA *11,* UV *104;* and yoga, EM 40

Buddha Amida: EM 22-23

Buddhist New Year: celebration of, EM 51, *52*

Buddhists, Mikkyō: CC 56; hearth, CC *56*

Buddhists and Buddhism: AW 35, 133, MA 64, MW 93, MY 115, SA 10, UV 11; and afterlife, CD 85; and angels, CD 122; and Aśoka, EM 41; and bodhisattvas, CD 122; and bo trees, EE 83; in China, EM 51, 53; and *chöd,* EM 76; and Confucianism, EM 53; and consciousness, MB 25; decline of, EM 41; and dharmakaya, MB 22; and directions, TS 30, *31;* and dreams, DD 23, 37-39; and dualities, CD 35-36; and Eightfold Path, CD 99; and enlightenment, CD 99, *104,* TS 29, 37; and floods, EE 76; and Fuji, EM 20; growth of, EM 41, 53; and Himalayas, EM 43; Aldous Huxley as, MB 106; and Kailas, TS 11; and karma, CD 111; in Korea, EM *100,* 101, *104-105;* and magic, EM 40; and meditation, EM *104-105,* MB 102; and mind, MB 26; and mysticism, CD 111-114; and nirvana, CD 99, EM 101, PV 127; and Padmasambhava, EM 41; and Pure Land, CD 126; and reality, MB 22; and reincarnation, CD 99, 111, PV 102; and Chogyam Trungpa Rinpoche, EM 133, 134; rites of, CD *102-103, 104;* and sacrifices, TS 37; and samadhi, CD 36; and Taoism, EM 53, 55; in Thailand, EM *108-109;* in Tibet, EM 41; and transmigration, EM 37; and

zero, TS 29. *See also* Amida Buddhists; Pure Land Buddhism; Shambhala; Tantric Buddhism; Tibetan Buddhism; Zen Buddhism; Zen Buddhists

Budhi: defined, EM 121

Budker, Paul: MC 37

Budzynski, Thomas: DD 118

Buer (demon): MA 97

Buffalo: MW 110

BUFORA: AE 105-106

Bulgaria: vampires in, TN 113

Bulgarians: CD 25; heresies of, WW 49-50

Bull: CD *9,* MY *31,* 120, *121, 125,* SA *72, 74, 76*

Bull, Harry: HN 66

Bull, Henry Dawson Ellis: and poltergeists, HN 66, PE 126

Bull, Samuel (ghost): PE 119

Bullard, Thomas E.: and abduction by aliens, AE 26-27, 28, 29, 30, 32, 34; and UFOs, AE 64

Bullet train: TS 98-99

Bullheads: as totems, TN *9. See also* Fish

Bulloch, Karen: PH 131

Bulwer-Lytton, Edward (Lord Lytton): and hollow earth theory, MP 146

Bundy, Ted: TN 130

Bunyan, John: SE 60

Bunyip: MW 59, *63-65*

"Bunyip aristocracy": MW 65

Buoyancy motor: SA *95*

Buraq: MY 33

Burch House: MB *76, 77*

Burckhardt, Johann Ludwig: ML 75

Burden, Jane: UV 36, *37, 38*

Burdick, Clifford: and giants, ML *25, 26*

Burgot, Pierre: TN 82, 83

Burgoyne, Cuthbert: MW 68

Burials: EE 26, PE *53-57, 92-93. See also* Live burials

Burial suit: SA *111*

Buried-alive trick: EM 92

Burma: and reincarnation beliefs, PV 108

Burned-over District, spiritualism in: SS 19-22

Burnham, Sophy: CD 124

Burning brand: *See* Cone of power

Burning Time: *See* Witch hunts *in* WW *index*

Burns, Barbara: and Silva Mind Control, MM 120

Burns, Ed: AE *57*

Burroughs, Catharine (a.k.a. Ahkön Norbu Lhamo): EM 135

Burry Man: EE *103,* MY 68-69

Burtis, C. Edward: SI 13

Burton, Julian: PE 65, 72; and Mrs. Burton, PE 65

Burton, Maurice: Loch Ness monster research of, MC 80, 81, 82

Burton, Robert: and werewolves, TN 87-88

Burus (swamp creatures): MC 70, MW 59

Bush, George: MA 6

Bushmen: CD 109

Bush schools: MA 13

Bush spirits: MW 133

Business: and extrasensory perception, uses of, PP 134-140

Bute, third marquis of: HN *124;* and ghosts, HN 123-124

Buterbaugh, Coleen: HN 39; and retrocognition, HN 39; and time slips, TS 112-114, 126

Butler, Edward: DD 130-131

Butler, E. M.: MA 45

Butterflies: migration of, TS 82, *83*

Butter Lamp Festival: MY *20*

Bux, Kuda (mentalist): eyeless sight act of, PP 108-*109*

Buzzard, Dr. (a.k.a. Ernest Bratton): MA 9

Buzzum: SI *54-55*

Byg, William: VP 45

Byland Abbey (England): and alien visitors, UP 16

Byrd, Eldon: EE 108; metalbending research of, MM 30-31

Byrd, Richard: AW *111;* pole explorations of, MP 152-153, *154*

Byron, George Gordon: MY 30, PE 39; and John Polidori, TN 132-133

Bystander apparitions: PE 26-27. *See also* Crisis apparitions

Bystander effect: CD 110-111

Byzantine structures in Egypt: building, Marea, MQ *102-103;* cistern, Alexandria, MQ *101*

AE Alien Encounters; AW Ancient Wisdom and Secret Sects; CC Cosmic Connections; CD Cosmic Duality; DD Dreams and Dreaming; EE Earth Energies; EM Eastern Mysteries; HN Hauntings; MA Magical Arts; MB The Mind and Beyond; MC Mysterious Creatures; ML Mysterious Lands and Peoples; MM Mind over Matter; MP Mystic Places; MQ Mystic Quests; MW The Mysterious World;

C

C., Eva (née Marthe Béraud, a.k.a. Eva Carrière): PP 40, SS 64-70, 67, 69

Caacrinolas (demon): MA 97

Cabal (dog): ML 47

Cabala and Cabalists: AW 22-29, CD 25, MA 26-31, 35, 54-59, MW 133; characteristics of, SA 23; defined, VP 105; and Nicholas Flamel, SA 46; and high magic, MA 31; history of, MA 54; and magic circles, MA 59; and numerology, VP 105; and Paracelsus, SA 65; and talismans, MA 35, 39; and Tarot, VP 127, 137; texts of, MA 54, 59. See also individual Cabalists

Cabalistic Square: MW 133

Cabinet of Dr. Caligari, The (film): MM 97

Cabot, Laurie: WW 124-125

Cabral, João: MQ 26-27

Cabreras, Count de: TN 120

Cacella, Estevão: MQ 26-27

Cadbury Castle: PE 130-131

Cadbury Hill: ML 51-52

Caddy (sea serpent): MC 38. See also Sea serpents

Caddy, Eileen: EE 133; and Findhorn Foundation, UV 142, 143, 144

Caddy, Peter: and devas, EE 134-135; and Findhorn Foundation, EE 133-134, UV 142, 143, 144; and Landscape Angel, EE 135

Caduceus: MB 14

Caedmon: CD 135

Caesalpino, Andrea: and botany, EE 102-103

Caesar, Julius: AW 17, 18-19, CC 34, DD 42, MP 88, MY 22, 115, 137, SI 89, VP 35; and calendars, TS 104

Caesar Forman Healing Center:

MW 108

Caffeine: and psychokinesis, MM 61

Caffeine of Europe (a.k.a. Filippo Marinetti): UV 122

Cage, John: EM 137

Cagliostro, Alessandro di Conte (a.k.a. Giuseppe Balsamo, Marquis di Pellegrini): AW 64, 100-101, 105, MA 44, SA 100-102, VP 84; and Colombe, MA 42-43; and high magic, MA 44; as magus, MA 42-44, 45; and Masons, MA 42-43, 44, SA 102; names of, MA 50

Cagliostro, Lorenza Feliciani: AW 100

Cairo (Egypt): fig trees in, EE 77

Calcination: defined, SA 55

Calculus: MB 20

Caldwell, Jonathan E.: and pseudo UFOs, UP 45

Caledonia Mills (Canada): MW 25, 27

Calef, Robert: and witch hunts, WW 72

Calendars: background of, ML 17; and books of hours, TS 104; and Julius Caesar, TS 104; and Egyptians, TS 103; and French revolutionary government, TS 104, 105; and Gregory XIII, TS 104, 105; and Maya, ML 19, TS 34, VP 12. See also Gregorian calendar; Julian calendar; Roman calendar; Sacred calendars; Solar calendars

Calendar stone: Aztec, flood story depicted by, MQ 78

Caleuche (ship): MW 32, 33

Calf idol: MQ 48

Caliburn: ML 48

California: earthquakes in, EE 59-60

Caligula (Roman emperor): CC 47, VP 109

Callanish Stone Circle (Outer Hebrides): MW 85; and summer solstice, MP 76-77

Calloway, Hugh G. (pseud. Oliver Fox): DD 113; out-of-body experiences of, PV 22-25, 27, 33; Theosophical beliefs of, PV 25

Calmet, Augustin: and vampires,

CAT. Embodying both good and evil, this animal was held sacred by ancient Egyptians, who buried pet cats with bronzes such as this one. But cats later became associated with powers of darkness and are still often regarded as omens of bad luck.

TN 120-121

Calpurnia: DD 42, MY 22

Calvados Castle: and exorcism, HN 93; and hauntings, HN 92-93

Calvary: EE 27

Calvert, James F.: and North Pole, MP 153

Calves: SI *85*

Calvin, John: CC 69, VP 20; and witches, WW 66

Calvinists: UV 65

Cambodians: and disappearances, TS *137*

Camelot: ML 51-52, 63, MQ *119*, 120, MW 87

Cameron, Teresa: and ghosts, HN 36, 37

Cameroon: MW 65, 70

Camillo, Giulio: MB 56-58

Camlan, battle of: and Arthur, ML 47, 51, 56; and Mordred, ML 47

Campanella, Tommaso: UV 40

Campbell, Alex: MC 67, *72*

Campbell, Duncan: VP 40

Campbell, Joseph: CD 55, DD *29*, EE 26, ML 103, MQ 111, 114; and Mother Goddess, WW 13; and Venus figurines, WW 11

Campbell, Mrs. Patrick (a.k.a. Mrs. Pat): DD 142

Campbell, Steuart: MC 83, 84

Campbell, Virginia: and polter-geists, MM 46-48

Camp Cassadaga: MW *105-109*, 113

Camp David (Maryland): MQ 30

Camus, Albert: CC 87

Canada: MW 47; biodynamic farming in, EE 130; Iroquois Indian site in, MQ 98, *99*

Canadian Archaeological Foundation: PP 123, 125

Canaries Current: ML 120

Canary: divination by, VP *39*

Canary, John: PH 68

Cancer (disease): and visualization, MB 96, 125, MM *136-137*

Cancer (zodiac sign): CC 36, *83*, 94, 139, MY 55

Canches, Master: SA 46

Candelabra of the Andes: MP 113, *115*

Candle clocks: TS 106, 109

Candlemas: MY 130

Candles: and magic, MA *131-133*

Candles, Feast of: WW 123

Candomblé: PH 23

Cannibalism: CD 82, ML 95

Cannon, Joseph G.: ghost of, HN *106-107*

Canoes: outrigger, ML *99*

Canon Episcopi (Anonymous): WW 46, 47, 62

Canseliet, Eugene: CD 70; and Fulcanelli, SA 120, 123-124

Canterbury Tales, The (Chaucer): CC 66, SA 56

Cantharides: SI 67

Canyon de Chelly: MW 79, TS 7

Cao Guojiu: SA *113*

Cape Cod Ark: SA 136

Cape of Good Hope: MW 75

Capillary dynamolysis: SA *130-131*

Capital punishment: UV 92

Capitol, U.S.: HN *106-107*

Capnomancy: defined, VP 32

Capone, Al: CC 89

Cappadocia (Turkey): MW 99, UV *102-103*

Capra, Fritjof: MB 25

Capricorn (zodiac sign): CC 74, *89*, 139, MY 119, 127

Caracalla (Roman emperor): SI 136

Caracalla Therme: SI 133, *136*

Caravels: ML 119

Carbon dating: in ark study, MQ 88-89; of Shroud of Turin, MQ 108

Carbon dioxide: SA 93

Cardan, Jerome: CC 72

Cardiac, Jean: PV 118

Cargo cults: MW 127, 130-133

Carib Indians: MA 82-83

Caribou: effigy of, TN *32*

Carini Castle: MW 34, 36-37

Carlson, Dan: EE 131-133

Carl Theodore (duke of Bavaria): AW 104

Carlyle, Thomas: AW 100

Carmelites: MY 25

Carnac (France): MW 85, *87-88*; ruins at, EE 57, 58

Carne Rasch, Frederick: PE 83-85, *86-87*

Carnival: MY *136-137*

Carolus Linnaeus: VP 67

Carp: MY *128-129*

Carpathian Mountains: MW 53

Carpenter, Dorothy: MW 27-28

Carpenters: MY 62

Carpio, Miguel: SI 43

Carpzov, Benedict: and witch hunts, WW 42

Carrière, Eva: *See* C., Eva

Carrington, Hereward: PS 34; and Mina Crandon, SS 110-112; and out-of-body-experience research, PV 25, 27; and Eusapia Palladino, SS 64; and polter-geists, HN 72-73; MM 41, 46

Carritte, Dr.: and poltergeists, HN 99, 101

"Carrying death away": MY 26

Carson, Johnny: DD 127, MM 34

Carson, Lord Edward: PP *10-11*

Carter, Charles: CC 132, 143-145

Carter, Howard: MY *27;* and Tut-ankhamen's tomb, MP *64*

Carter, Jimmy: AE 108, MM 36; and UFO sighting, UP *128*

Cartesian dualism: MB 10, 13. *See also* Dualism

Carthaginians: ML 117

Cartomancy: defined, VP 123. *See also* Tarot; Tarot readers

Cartwright, Rosalind: DD 114

Carus, Paul: EM 136

Caruso, Enrico: CC 132

Carvalho de Oliveira, Wellaide Cecim: AE 41-42

Carver, George Washington: EE *104*, 105

Carvings: used by shamans, TN *10*

Cary, Winifred: MC *73*

Casanova, Giovanni: SA 101

Cascade Mountains (Washington): and UFO sighting, UP 36-37. *See also* Arnold, Kenneth

Casey, Caroline: CC 126, 142, 143, 148, 155

Casey, Harry: and geoglyphics of North America, MP 121

Cash, Betty: and UFO sighting, UP 8-9, *10-11*

Cash-Landrum incident: UP 8-9, *10-11*, 132

Cassadaga: MW *105-109*, 113

Cassini, Samuel de: and witch hunts, WW 72

Cassiodorus: CC 52

Castagno, Andrea del: fresco by,

VP *109*

Castaneda, Carlos: MA 115

Castello de la Rotta: PE *124-125*

Castillo: MY *8-9*

Casting of magic circle: WW 128

Castle, Henry N.: MA 85

Castle, Katherine (Kit): MB 83-85, *86*

Castle Dinas Brän (Wales): MQ *112*

Castlerigg (England): legend of, MP *69*

Castration: CD 68-69

Castration complex: defined, CD 60

Castro, Fidel: CC 84

CAT: *See* Computerized axial to-mography

Cataclysmos: MY 51

Catacomb, Roman: Christian painting from, MQ *72*

Catalepsy: and Washington Irving Bishop, PP 104; defined, TN 111; and Wolf Messing, PP 111-113

Catal Hüyük (Turkey): CD 54

Catchings, John (psychic): PP 133, PS *49, 52-55,* 56-57

Categorical imperative: CD 127-128

Caterpillars: arctic woolly bear, SI 107

Catfish: EE *60*

Cathars (Christian sect): AW 26-32, CD 32-33, MQ 118, 124, 127-128, PV *100-101*, SE 45, WW 12, 50, 51; alleged reincarnation of, PV 99, 101; ruined temple of, MQ *129. See also* Albigenses; Manicheans; *specific Cathars*

Cathedral of the Future (Feininger): UV *128*

Cathedral Rock: EE *65*

Catherine de Médicis (queen of France): CC 69, *72,* MA 55, VP 18, *47*

Catherine of Aragon: PE 39

Catherine of Siena, Saint: MB *95*

Catherine the Great (empress of Russia): SA 102

Catholics and Catholicism: CD 31; and alchemy, SA 45; and big bang theory, TS 62; and black magic, MA 90-92; and Cathars, AW 26-32, CD 33; and exorcism,

COW. Like the god Krishna, seen herding cows at twilight in this painting, Hindus try to ensure the well-being of the cow. They consider it a symbol of life and fertility, associated with a divine beast whose milk spawned the first life on earth.

CD 33-34, 88, 90, HN 137; and Freemasons, AW 92, 96, 97, 111-112; and Manicheans, AW 26, CD 32; missionaries, MQ 26-27; and possession, CD 90; and Rosicrucians, AW 46-48; and Montague Summers, TN 122, *124;* and voodoo, MA 82. *See also* Christians and Christianity

Catlin, George: painting by, ML *125*

Cat Parade: MY *36*

Cats: MA 118, 135, MW *106-107,* MY *121,* SI *70,* WW 12; devil in form of, WW 49; and elderly persons, SI *70;* in England, MA 118; as ghosts, HN 107, PE *41, 121;* mummy of, WW *12;* and out-of-body experiment, SE 88-89; Schrödinger's, TS 68; sleep studies with, DD *101;* superstitions about, WW 12

Caucasus Mountains: MW 59, SI 39-43

Caude: Werewolf of, TN 86

Cauldron: WW *121*

Cauldrons, magical: Celtic, MQ 109, 112; Greek, rejuvenating, MQ *35*

Causality: defined, TS 120; and precognition, TS 120; violation of, TS 71, 77

Cautio Criminalis (Spee): WW 72

Caveat for Alchymists, A (Plattes): SA 98

Cave Dwellers: ML 14

Cavendish-Bentinck, William: DD *145*

Caves: France, MQ *128;* Greece, chapel in, MQ *59;* and oracles, EE 54; in Superstition Mountains, EE 52-54

Cayce, Edgar: CC 91, MB 29, MY 22, 97, 123, PH 9, 30-33, *31,* PP 84, *90-91,* 123, SS *133,* 149; abilities of, PP 91-96; alleged previous incarnations of, PV 123; and Atlantis legend, MP 14, 30-33, *31,* 36; and channeling, SS 132; healing by, SS 27, 132; karma beliefs of, PV 124; and New Age movement, PP 101; as seer, PV 122-124, VP 22-23, *24;* trances, VP 22

Cayce, Hugh Lynn: SS 132

Cayce, Leslie B.: PP *90-91*

Cazeau, Charles: and pyramid power, MP 66

Cazotte, Jacques: as seer, VP 6-7, *8,* 20

Cebes: SE 43, 44

Cecco d'Ascoli: CC 64

Cecilia, Saint: SI *26-27;* incorruption of, SI 26, 30

Cefn Bryn (Wales): ML 51

Celery, wild: WW *37*

Celestial Abyss course: MB *118-119*

Celestial Burial: PV *136-137*

Celestial computer: ML 16-17, *18*

Celestial Hierarchy, The (Dionysius): CD 130

Celibacy: UV 64, 65, 70-74, 75

Célie, Maman: MA 81

Celle, Clara Germana: CD 71, *72-73,* MY 59; and possession, CD 71-77

Cells: and gerontologists, SI 66; and Leonard Hayflick, SI 71; types of, SI 82-83

Cellular Cosmogony, The, or, the Earth a Concave Sphere (Teed): MP 147-148, 149

Cellular error theory: SI 66

Cellular therapy (CT): SI 64-*65,* 66

Celsus (physician): SA 63, SI 32

Celtic Revival: AW 128

Celts: AW 11, 17-19, CD 126, SI 24, ML 132-135, VP 35-38; Gundestrup cauldron, images from, MQ *130, 133, 135, 136-137;* and goddesses, WW 29; and grail legends, MQ 109, 110, 112; king (Gwenddolau), Merlin as bard of, MQ 133; Irish torque, MQ *136;* sacrifices of, AW 19; shrine of, ML *50;* temple of, AW *18;* and witches, WW 25, 29-30. *See also* Druids

Cementation and Propitiation Festival: MY 90

Census of Hallucinations (SPR): HN 72, PE 25

Centaur: MC *57,* MY *103. See also* Human-beasts

Center for Applied Intuition (CAI): and William Kautz, PS 108, 109, 130

Center for the Treatment of Ritualistic Deviance: CD 96

Center for UFO Studies (CUFOS): UP 121; background of, AE 24, 25; and J. Allen Hynek, AE 25; and Philip J. Imbrogno, AE 57; and Edward Walters, AE 70

Central America: giants in, ML 25

Central Hindu College: AW 141-142

Central Intelligence Agency (CIA): MB 104, PS 76-77, 80, 81-82, 83, 85, 91

Central Phrenological Society: VP 72

Central Premonitions Registry: PP 34

Centuries (Nostradamus): CC 70, VP 18-*19*

Cephalomancy: defined, VP 35

Cephalopods: *See* MC *index*

Cephalus: SE *16*

Ceques: and Nazca lines of Peru, MP 98, 119

Cerberus (demon): CC 47, MA *96-97*

Cerebellum: MB 6-7, 41

Cerebral cortex: MB 39, 40, 41-44, 59, 106; and John Carew Eccles, SE 123; model of neuron in, SE *116. See also* Left brain/right brain

Cerebrum: SE 138

Cerei: MY 119

Cereologists: AE 75

Ceres (goddess): MY 129. *See also* Isis

Cerne Giant (England): MP 126, 127, *137*

Cernunnos (god): MQ 136, WW 28-29; and Horned God, WW 107

Ceromancy: defined, VP 35

Cervé, Wishar: and Lemuria, ML

23

10, 83
Cewa tribe: MA 11
Chac (god): CC 60-61
Chachapoyan Indians: MQ 43
Chaco Canyon: ML 80, MW 81-83, MY 16
Chacruna: MB 108
Chaffee, Roger: AE 62
Chagall, Marc: paintings by, DD 10-11, 12, 13
Chair, interrogation: WW 84
Chakra-puja: defined, CD 69
Chakras: AW 138-139, 144, MA 64, PH 72, 74, 105, 108; defined, CD 69, DD 148; symbols of, MB 15
Chalcomancy: defined, VP 35
Chaldea: numerology in, VP 107
Chaldeans: CC 20
Chalice: SA 10, WW 120; Holy Grail as, MQ 106, 119, 123, 126
Chalice Well (Glastonbury, England): MQ 116, 123-124
Chalicotheria: MW 67
Challacombe, Mr. and Mrs. J. P.: PE 89
Challenger (space shuttle): PS 20-21, TS 86
Chalybeate spring: MQ 135
Chambered nautilus: TS 48
Chamberlain, Richard: and poltergeists, HN 58
Champ (lake monster): MC 62, 63, 77, MW 47, 49-50. See also Lake monsters
Champagne, Jean-Julien: SA 120
Champlain, Lake: MW 47, 48
Champlain, Samuel de: MC 62, MW 49
Chanctonbury Ring (England): and ley theory, MP 106-107
Chandler, Helen: TN 137
Chandley, Margo: SS 133, 150-152
Chandra: See Harto, James S.
Chang: MY 110-111
Changing Woman: MY 83
Chango (orisha): MW 113, 114-115
Channelers: SS 7-17, 131-132. See also UFO channelers; individual channelers
Channeling: PP 84, 96, 97; defined, PV 43, SS 131-133, 150-153

Channon, Jim: PS 94
Ch'an school: EM 53, 55. See also Zen Buddhism
Chanting: EM 125
Chaomos: MY 120
Chaos: CD 23, 24
Chaos (god): EE 22
Chapel: cave, in Greece, MQ 59; on Isle of Man, WW 110-111
Chapel of St. Edgar: vision at, PP 121
Chaplin, Charlie: SI 65
Chapman, George: PH 34-36, 35
Chapman, John: DD 135, MY 89
"Chapter on Dreams" (Stevenson): DD 46
Charaka: PH 65, 66
Charcot, Jean-Martin: MB 75; hypnosis research of, MM 94, 95
Charge: defined, WW 107
Charge of the Goddess: and Gerald Brosseau Gardner, WW 104; purposes of, WW 102, 116, 126
Chari, C. T. K.: reincarnation research of, PV 110
Charing Cross underground station: and ghosts, HN 31
Chariots of the Gods? (von Däniken): ML 32, MP 113-116, UP 13, 14
Charlemagne (king of the Franks): CC 53-55, EE 33, MW 88-89, PH 21; and paganism, WW 43-44
Charles (prince of Hesse): AW 65, SA 101
Charles (savant): MB 60; and savant syndrome, MB 38-39, 62
Charles I (king of England): CC 102, 107-109, MW 22, PE 50, 134; and William Harvey, SI 14, 15; and Thomas (earl of Arundel and Surrey), SI 14
Charles II (king of England): CC 106, HN 56, MW 19, PE 106, PH 87
Charles VI (king of France): MA 48-49
Charles IX (king of France): VP 18
Charles Haskell (ship): HN 80-81
Charleton, Walter: and Stonehenge, MP 85-86
Charm necklaces: MW 127
Charms: MA 126, WW 107. See also Amulets; Talismans

Charny, Geoffrey de: MQ 108, 122-123
Charon (boatman): SE 74
Charon (satellite of Pluto): CC 47
Charroux, Robert: ML 29
Chartres (France): MW 119, 125
Chartres Cathedral: MY 10
Charybdis (whirlpool): EE 72, MQ 59
Chase, Stanley N.: MM 101
Chase, Truddi: MB 81, 82, 83, 87
Chase family burial vault: MM 38-39
Chastel, Jean: MW 57-59
Chaucer, Geoffrey: CC 66, SA 56
Chavez, M. S.: and Socorro encounter with aliens, UP 73
Cheh'pi wanunyanpi (flesh offering): MQ 12
Cheiro: See Hamon, Count Louis le Warner de
Chelmsford trial: WW 60
Chema (Chemes): SA 19
Chemical philosophy: SA 80
Chemical Wedding of Christian Rosenkreutz, The (Andreae): AW 54-55, 57, 58, SA 83, 85
Chemistry: SA 35; and alchemy, SA 43; and Paracelsus, SA 63
Chemosit: MW 65, 66-67
Cheng, George: VP 26
Chenoweth, Mrs. (medium): SE 92
Cheops: MW 99, MY 11. See also Great Pyramid of Cheops in MP index
Chephren: MP 56; pyramid of, MY 11
Chernenkov, Mikhail: ML 33
Chernobyl: TS 86
Cherokee Indians: EE 100
Cherry, Donald: drawings by, PS 40-41
Cherubim: CD 131
Chess: MB 49
Chessie (sea serpent): MC 39-40, MY 38. See also Sea serpents
Chesterton, G. K.: MA 64; and ghosts, HN 118
Cheval, Ferdinand: architecture by, UV 44-45
Chevreul pendulum: MM 101
Cheyenne Indians: CD 65, MA 74, MW 79, UV 18
Ch'i: See Qi

Chicago warehouse fire: and spirit photography, PP 46
Chichén Itzá: MW 79; ruins, MY 8-9
Chicomecoatl-Xilonen (goddess): SE 21
Ch'i kung: EE 106
Chilam Balam of Chumayel (Anonymous): TS 32
Child archetype: DD 86-87
Childbirth: herbs for, WW 37
Child blessing: WW 136
Child of the Water: MY 83
Children: MA 122, 136-137; and reincarnation, PV 96-98, 103, 105-106, 106-110, 111, 118. See also Prodigies
Children of the Sun: TS 13
"Child's Gaze, A" (postcard): CD 92
Chiles, C. S.: and Montgomery UFO sighting, UP 42
Chilled bloodless perfusion: SI 122-123
Chiloé Island: MW 27, 32, 33
Chilseong-je: MY 123
Chimney: EE 62
Chimpanzees: EE 69, MB 42-43. See also Animals
China: CD 50, 56, MW 34, 38; alchemy in, SA 103-113; Buddhism in, EM 51, 53; dominoes in, VP 112; earthquakes in, EE 61; effigies in, MA 23; ginseng in, EE 99; and immortality, SA 103; lamas in, EM 78, 79; palmistry in, VP 81; physiognomy in, VP 70-71; transformations in, TN 42; vampires in, TN 110
China Illustrata (Kircher): EM 29
Chindi: MA 78
Chinese: and aluminum, refining of, ML 22; and America, discovery of, ML 114-115, 117; and cellular therapy, SI 65; cosmogonies of, TS 19, 27-29; exploration by, ML 120; and flood stories, ML 34; and giants, ML 25; and magical foods, SI 6, 36-37; and sacrifices, TS 37; and snakes, SI 35; and space, TS 27-32; and tigers, SI 67; and time, TS 27-32, 35
Chinese Academy of Sciences: MC

24

CANOPY. *In this 16th-century Persian miniature, a Mogul potentate takes his repose beneath a canopy, which, as a small-scale representation of heaven, magically protects the divinely chosen ruler from earthly harm.*

113

Chinese healing: PH 46-47, 57-58. *See also* Eastern healing

Ching: SI 39

Chinnery, Mabel: ghost photograph by, HN *26*

Chiothetists: PH 87

Chiou Chu (general): ML 22

Chipko: EE *92*

Chippewa Indians: EE 100

Chiromancy: *See* Palmistry; Palmists

Chiron (centaur): MC *57. See also* Human-beasts

Chiropractic: MA 114

Chithurst Forest Monastery: EM *140-141*

Chlorpromazine: MB 74, TN 91

Chöd: EM 76-80, *79*

Choisnard, Paul: CC 131, 140

Cholera victim: and premature burial of, TN *114-115*

Chomo-Lungma: EE 27

Chorea Gigantum (Charleton): MP 85-86

Chovahonni: defined, MA 100

Choyo-no-Sekku: MY 84

Chresmomancy: defined, VP 35

Chrétien de Troyes: MQ 111

Christ: crucifixion of, EE 95; and Gethsemane, EE 79; and Golgotha, EE 27. *See also* MQ *index*

Christ Church Graveyard: MW 27

Christian IV (king of Denmark): CC 95

Christianopolis (Andreae): UV 42

Christians and Christianity: AW 17, 20, MW 99, WW 10, 12, 42-45, 49; in Alexandria (Egypt), SA 23; and Helena Petrovna Blavatsky, AW 131; and dreams, DD 37; and dualism, MB 10; and reincarnation as viewed by, PV 98, 101; and resurrection, SE 51; and transformations, TN 37-41; and vampires, TN 111; and werewolves, TN 88. *See also* Catholics and Catholicism; CD *index*

Christian Science: MB 124, PH 124-125, SE 32

Christie, Agatha: PS *32;* disappearance of, PS 29, 32; and Arthur Conan Doyle, PS 29, 32

Christmas and Christmas tree: MY *120,* 121

Christmas Eve: WW 43

Christmas rose: WW *34*

Christopher, Milbourne (magician): and Lady Wonder, PP 110

Christopher, Saint: MY 49, 64

Chromotherapy: PS *101*

Chronic anxiety states: MB 116

Chronobiology: TS 79, 80

Chuang Chou (a.k.a. Chuang-tzu, Master Chuang): CD 12, DD 22, 23

Chu Hua: VP 119

Chukchi: MW 127; burial rituals of, PE 53; tools of, PH *9*

Chula Vista (California): MW 27, 30

Chung-Ch'iu: MY 89

Chung K'ang (emperor of China): CC 20

Chung Yeung: MY *92*

Church, George W.: PS 81

Church archaeology: dowsing use in, MQ *104-105*

Churches: eighteenth-century, flares lighting, MQ *57;* and ghosts, HN 90-91. *See also specific churches and ghosts*

Churchill, Winston: CC 135, MA 118, MB 88, PE 112, SI 65; psychic experience of, PP 20

Church of Carmel: MA 64

Church of Jesus Christ of Latter-day Saints: UV 58-59

Church of Saint Catherine (Fierbois, France): and Joan of Arc's sword, PP *18-19*

Church of Saint Katherine Cree: MY 94

Church of Saint Michael: ruins of, ML *54-55,* 56

Church of Satan: CD *97;* decline of, CD 96; and Anton Szandor La Vey, CD 78, 80, 96

Church of Scientology: PS 84

Churchward, James: and Lemuria, ML 6, 8, 83; and Mu, MP 27, 28

Churingas: defined, EE 50

CIA: *See* Central Intelligence Agency

Ciaran, Saint: MY 19

Cicero, Marcus Tullius: AW 9, CC 32-34, EE 29

Cinderella (fairy tale): CD 44-45

Cinnabar: EM 53, SA *110,* SI 34, TS 32

Cinquefoil: WW *33*

Circadian rhythms: TS 80

Circe (goddess): MQ *56,* 58, 59

Circe (witch): WW *22;* and henbane, WW 35; and Odysseus, WW 19-20

Circle dance: ML *110, 111*

Circle Limit IV (Escher): CD 20

Circles: AE 111, MA *38*

Circle Sanctuary: and Selena Fox, WW 112, 125-126

Circus Maximus: MY 72

Cistercians: and witches, WW 54

Cistern: Byzantine, in Alexandria, Egypt, MQ 101

Cities of the Plain: MQ 43

City of Dawn: *See* Auroville

City of God: UV 30, 39

City of Man: UV 30, 39

City of Peace: EM 27

City of Pease, The (Wicker): UV 73

City of the Sun (Campanella): UV 40-42

Civilian Saucer Investigation (CSI): and UFOs, UP 69

Civil War, English: MY 128

Clairaudience: PP 17, 18, 133-134

Clairvoyance: EM 118, PS 7, 111; and apparitions, PE 35; and CIA, PS 80, 81; and Gerard Croiset, TS 115; defined, DD 147, MM 57, PS 7, 25, 80; and Eileen Garrett, TS 114, 115; and Uri Geller, MM 29, PS 124; and Heinrich Himmler, PS 65; and Peter Hurkos, TS 115; and Harold Puthoff, MM 29-30, PS 80; and Russell Targ, MM 29-30, PS 80, 81; and witches, WW 35. *See also* Extrasensory perception; Intuition; PP *index*

Clairvoyant dreams: DD 139-141. *See also* Dreams *in* DD *index*

Clans: defined, TN 6; purposes of, TN 8; and totems, TN 8, 30

25

CIRCLE. *An emblem of eternity, a circle has neither beginning nor end and embodies all directions: up, down, left, and right. Given spokes, as in this rose window from the Cathedral of St. Denis, it is a wheel, symbolic of the cycle of death and rebirth.*

Clarion (alleged planet): UP 76, 78

Clark, Mrs. B.: MC 62, 63; lake monster sketch by, MC *62*

Clark, Champ: ghost of, HN *106-107*

Clark, David: MC 37

Clark, Jerome: and investigations of UFOs, UP 23

Clarke, Arthur C.: SI 46

Claros oracle: MW 99, 104, VP 11-14

Clatford (England): crop circles in, EE *12-13*

Claudius (Roman emperor): CC 34, MY 133

Clavie: MY 125

Clay: EE 58; animal made of, ML *20;* bottle made of, ML *110*

Clay, Henry: AW 86

Cleckley, Hervey: MB 79

Clem, Weir: and Levelland UFO sighting, UP 68-69

Clemens, Alonzo: MB 62

Clemens, Harry: PP 14-15, *16*

Clemens, Samuel (a.k.a. Mark Twain): CC 88, DD 131, EE 63, SI 133; hand print of, VP *67;* and palmistry, VP 64-65, *66,* 81, 82; psychic experience of, PP 14-15, *16*

Clement, Saint: MY 103

Clement of Rome, Saint: out-of-body experience of, PV 17

Clement V (pope): AW 38, 39, *97,* MY 21

Clement X (pope): MY 90

Clement XII (pope): AW 96, 97

Clement XIV (pope): PV 17

Cleopatra's Needle: MP 57, 60-61

Clepsydras: *See* Water clocks

Clergy: as witches, WW 41, 56

Clerke, May: PE 32

Cleveland, Grover: VP 82

Cliff Palace: ML *81*

Climate: and continental drift, EE 64-66; and ice ages, EE 64

Clinique La Prairie: SI *64, 65;* and Paul Niehans, SI 64

Clinton, DeWitt: AW 85

Clocks: TS *108, 109,* 110; haunted, PE 30, 31; and monasteries, TS 109; and Sylvester, TS 109

Clodius, Publius: MY 115

Cloning: *See* SI *index*

Clooties: MA *113*

Close encounters: of the first kind, AE 25; of the fourth kind, AE 25; of the second kind, AE 25; of the third kind, AE 25, UP 65, *68-69, 70-73;* three kinds of, UP 121-122

Close Encounters of the Third Kind (film): AE 120; and alien visitors, UP 28, *32-33*

Closure: defined, TS 100

Clothing: and superstitions, MA 134

Cloud busting: MM *16-17*

Cloud Nines: UV *151*

Clouds: mistaken for UFOs, UP *20*

Cloud spirits: MA 46, *47*

Club of Rome: VP 28

Clutterbuck, "Old Dorothy": and Gerald Brosseau Gardner, WW 103

Clymer, R. Swinburne: AW 68

Coal waste: MY *94-95*

Cobb, John: MC 66

Cobra: EM *38-39*

Cocaine: MB *113. See also* Hallucinogens

Cochran, Jack: Bigfoot drawing by, MC *114*

Cockatrice: MC *12*

Cock Lane: HN *62;* and poltergeists, HN 61-70, *63*

Cockrell, H. L.: Loch Ness monster photograph by, MC 74

Coconsciousness: SS 152, 153

Cocytus, Lake: SE *80*

Code of Hammurabi: WW 62

Codex Magliabechiano: SE *20;* illustration from, SE *20*

Codices: and Maya, ML 27, VP *12-13*

Coelacanths: MC *23,* MW 47; discovery of, MC 18-19, 44, 84

Coevolution: defined, CD 62

Coffee grounds: reading, VP *40*

Cogito: SE 50, 52, 69

Cohausen (physician): SI 38-39

Cohen, Mary: PV 113-114

Cohen, Nicholas: PH 130, *131*

Cohoon, Hannah: gift drawings by, UV *71, 72*

Coincidences: TS 120-121, 122, 125, 137

Coins: Phoenician, ML *66;* third-century, Noah's Ark on, MQ *72*

Coitus reservatus: SI 39; defined, UV 78

Colby, George P.: MW 106, 113

Colby, Kenneth: MB 128

Colby, Lake: MW 108

Colby Memorial Temple: MW *107*

Cold reading: PP 98, 102

Cole, Nat King: CC 91

Cole, T. C., Jr.: and hypnosis, MM 96

Coleman, William Emmette: AW 131

Coleridge, Samuel Taylor: DD 46

Coley, Eileen: and Eileen Garrett, PP 84

Collagen: SI 94

Collective percipience: defined, HN 88

Collective phenomena: defined, PE 31

Collective unconscious: DD 70, 73, 81, 153, EE 51, MY 64, TS 121; and archetypes, AE 111, MB 20; defined, AE 111, SA 130, SE 117, TN 31; and dreams, DD 41; and Budd Hopkins, AE 127; and Carl Jung, AE 101, 111, 120, MB 20, 23, PP 21, SA 130, 132; and lycanthropy, TN 31; theory of, defined, VP 122; and UFOs, AE 101; and Jacques Vallee, AE 120. *See also* Jung, Carl Gustav; Unconscious

Collie, Norman: MW 16-17

Collier, Constance: MA *112*

Collindridge, Michael: MM 48, *49-50*

Collins, Norman: MC 76

Collins, Polly: gift drawing by, UV *73*

Collyer, Anne: PE 25, 26, 30

Colombe (medium): MA 42-43

Colombia: artifact from, MQ *28-29;* in El Dorado legend, MQ 29

Colorado Bureau of Investigation: AE 41

Colors: MA 36, 37, 118-119, 126, 129, 130-134

Color therapy: PH *108-109*

Colt, Oliver (crisis apparition): PE 23, 30

Columba, Saint: MC 60-61, MW 85

Columbia (space shuttle): PS 20

Columbus, Christopher: CC 20, MW 83, UV 58, *73;* and America, discovery of, ML 17, 114, 117, 120; and Brendan, ML 123; and Ponce de León, MQ 34

Column: ancient, excavation of, MQ *103*

Comanche Indians: EE 101; and hunting, MA 74; and rituals, MA 68

Combe, George (phrenologist): VP 72, 75

Combermere, Lord: and poltergeists, MM 39

Combermere, Viscount: ghost of, HN *26*

Combustion: defined, EE 66

Comets: CC *28,* MY 57, VP *34;* mistaken for UFOs, UP *20*

Coming of age ritual: EM 65

AE *Alien Encounters;* **AW** *Ancient Wisdom and Secret Sects;* **CC** *Cosmic Connections;* **CD** *Cosmic Duality;* **DD** *Dreams and Dreaming;* **EE** *Earth Energies;* **EM** *Eastern Mysteries;* **HN** *Hauntings;* **MA** *Magical Arts;* **MB** *The Mind and Beyond;* **MC** *Mysterious Creatures;* **ML** *Mysterious Lands and Peoples;* **MM** *Mind over Matter;* **MP** *Mystic Places;* **MQ** *Mystic Quests;* **MW** *The Mysterious World;*

CRANE. *A Chinese emblem of longevity, the crane is also a mystical intermediary between the mortal world and the realm of the Eight Immortals. The crane on this embroidery sample holds peaches, another symbol of long life, in its bill.*

Coming Out Ceremony: MY *82-83*

Committee for the Scientific Investigation of Claims of the Paranormal (CSICOP): CC 129, 141-142, 150, MM 31-32, 34

Commodus (Roman emperor): SI 24

Communes: *See* Intentional communities

Communion (Strieber): AE 24, 120, UP 62, 143

Community of Jerusalem: UV 74, 75

Companion ghosts: defined, PE 71

Companion planting: EE 131

Company 164: SA 117

Company of Avalon: ML 61

Comparative Miracles (Smith): CD 115

Compass: EE *113;* of geomancers, TS *35*

Compendium Maleficarum (Guazzo): woodcuts from, WW *44-46*

Complexion: SI *90-91*

Computer clothing: MB 130

Computerized axial tomography (CAT): MB 132, PH 76, *77,* SE 129, *130*

Computers: TS *88-89;* analog, ML 16-17, *18;* and artificial intelligence, MB 125-126; and biological rhythms, TS 89; brain compared to, DD 100-101; and mind, MB 125-128; and mind prints, PS 132; and psi powers, PS 131; and time, TS 89; and transmigration, MB 126

Concave earth theory: MP 147-148

Concentration camps: CD 80

Conception Bay: MC *46-51*

Concerning the Spiritual in Art (Kandinsky): AW 162

Conclave (Tuieta): AE 124-126

Concurrent dreams: DD 149-150. *See also* Dreams *in DD index*

Condon, Edward U.: AE 78, UP 115-*116*

Condon committee: UP 48, 115-121, 126, 138

Condorcet, Marquis de: AW 80

Condor I: MP 117-119

Condwiramurs (character in *Parzifal*): MQ 112, 114, 117

Cone of power: WW 103, 104, *132-133*

Confabulation: AE 40

Confessio Fraternitatis Rosae Crucis (Anonymous): AW 53-54, 57, SA 83

Confessions (Saint Augustine): CC 50-52

Confessions (Crowley): AW 122

Confessors: defined, CD 110

Confrontations (Vallee): AE 41, 121

Confucians and Confucianism: MW 93, UV 6; and Buddhism, EM 53; characteristics of, EM 51; and Taoism, EM 53

Confucius: CC 27, CD 56, EM 51, MY *89,* VP 117

Confucius, Temple of: MW *93*

Congo: MC 77, *map 93*

Conjure balls: MA 81-82

Connolly, Brian: HN 73-74

Connor, Patrick: PS 77

Connors, Jimmy: MA 128

Conquistadors, quests of: El Dorado, MQ 29; Fountain of Youth, MQ 34, 39-40

Conrad, Joseph: CC 88, SI 46

Conrad of Marburg: WW 51

Consciousness: PS 109; characteristics of, MB 103; defined, MB 14, 39. *See also specific headings*

Constable, John: EE 104

Constant, Abbé: *See* Lévi, Éliphas

Constant, Alphonse-Louis: AW *65,* 66, 68

Constantine the Great (Roman emperor): CC 49, MY 84, 86

Constantino, Tony: AE *27*

Constantinople: sack of, MQ 122

Constellations: CC *14-15, 29, 35;* circumpolar, CC *32-33*

Constructivists: and El Lissitzky, UV 125; and technology, UV 124

Consus (god): MY 72

Contagious magic: MA 15, MW 133. *See also* Magic

Conte du Graal, Le (The Story of the Grail; Chrétien de Troyes): MQ 111

Contemplation: EM 137

Contiguity law: MA 15

Continental drift: and Atlantis, MP 33-34; and Francis Bacon, EE 58; and climate, EE 64-66; and Alfred Wegener, EE 58-59

Contributions to the Theory of Natural Selection (Wallace): MB 14

Control Data: PS 116-117

Controlled dreaming: MM 126

Controls: *See* Spirit guides

Conversion hysteria: PH 105

"Conveyor belts": ML 120

Conwell, Rev. Russell H. and Sarah: PE 63-64, *67*

Cook, Carolyn: MB 90

Cook, Connie: MB 90

Cook, Duane: AE 68-70

Cook, Elizabeth: MW 80

Cook, Florence: MY 68, SS 52-*58,* 60

Cook, James: and Easter Island, ML 86, 87

Cooke, Hope: CC 7

Coolidge, Calvin: EM 119

Coombe-Tennant, Winifred (a.k.a. Mrs. Willett; medium): SE 97, 104-107, SS *96,* 99; automatic

writing of, SS 92, 97

Cooper, Blanche (medium): SE 98-99

Coover, John E.: and psychic research, PP 48

Copeland, Miles: PS 76

Copernicus, Nicolaus: CC 25, 91, 93, *95, 96,* CD 37-38, SA 79, SE 50; and solar system, TS 51, 53

Copper: symbol for, SA *24*

Copperhead: MB *94*

Corbet, Sybell: ghost photograph by, HN *26*

Corbould, Henry: astral body as viewed by, PV *18*

Corder, William: DD *136*

Cordière, la (Jehanne de Brigue): WW 57

Corhampton Downs farm: crop circles at, EE *8-9*

Corkell, Bridie: PV *119*

Corn: MY 42, 65

Cornaro, Luigi: SI 76

Corn dances: MY *51,* 58

Corn dollies: MY *73*

Cornell, A. D.: and ghosts, HN 128-129; and suggestibility, HN 128-129

Cornel trees: EE 91. *See also* Trees

Cornély, Saint: MW 88, MY 86

Cornerstones: MA 120

Corn god: ML *106*

Corn Jester: MY *45*

Corn Spirit: MY 73, 81

Cornwall: MW 45, 85, *86-87*

Corona discharge imaging: *See* Psychic auras

Coronado, Francisco Vasquez de: MW 80

Corporations: and use of graphology, VP 86, 92

"Corpse": defined, SA 24

"Corpse Who Dances": EM 75

Corpus callosum: MB 45-47

Corpus Christi: MY 54

Corpus Hermeticum: AW 24, MQ 109

Corregidor (Philippines): hauntings on, PE 138

Correspondences theory: SA 79-80. *See also* Microcosm/macrocosm

Cortés, Hernán: MW 115, UV 24, VP 34

27

CHIMERA. Here cast in bronze, this hybrid creature from Greek mythology—a mix of lion, goat, and serpent—embodies evil in complex form. In particular, as common use of the term implies, a chimera is symbolic of an illusion or false rumor.

Cortezar, Gerardo: MW 31
Cortisol: and biological rhythms, TS 81
Cory, Charles Edward: SS 85
Cory, Giles: execution of, WW 75
Cory, Martha: witch trial of, WW 75
Corydon, Benjamin: HN 76
Cosmetic surgery: and Henri de Mondeville, SI 89; types of, SI 95
Cosmic breath: MW 127, 128
Cosmic consciousness: EM 119, PP 21
Cosmic Dance: UV 9
Cosmic fishing: See Intuition
Cosmic Loom (Elwell): CC 145
Cosmic mirror: SA 110
Cosmic Tree: UV 6
Cosmic trees: See World trees
Cosmobiological experience: defined, EE 24; and Mircea Eliade, EE 24-26
Cosmogonies: See TS index
Cosmological constant: defined, TS 60
Cosmology: in Bali, EM 63; defined, TS 19
Cosmos: CC 51, 94
Costa, Teresa: and poltergeists, MM 44
Coué, Émile: PH 123; and Silva Mind Control, MM 120-122
Coulomb, Alexis and Emma: AW 134
Council of American Witches: and

Wicca, WW 113
Council of Constantinople: PV 99
Council of Nicea: MY 30
Council of Three Hundred: UV 26
Counseling: astrological, CC 150-152
Counselor ghosts: defined, PE 71
Count Dracula Fan Club: TN 136
Count Dracula Society: TN 136
Countercomposition V (Doesburg): UV 133
Courtaut (wolf): TN 81
Court de Gébelin, Antoine: VP 125
Courtenay-Latimer, Marjory: MC 18
Courtship: and superstitions, MA 130
Courtship in Loch Ness (Scott): MC 80, 82-83
Cousett, Mary: PS 24-27
Cousins, Norman: MB 124, PH 6-7, 117, 118
Cousteau, Jacques: MC 78
Cousteau, Philippe: ML 95
Coven: defined, WW 107
Covenant of the Goddess: WW 126; and Wicca, WW 113
Covindassamy: levitation of, MM 117
Cowan, Thaddeus M.: MP 123
Cow horns: and biodynamic farming, EE 128, 129, 130
Cowley, Luke: HN 52, 53
Cowpox: MA 136
Cowrie shells: VP 36-37

Cows: EM 38-39; mutilation of, AE 40, 41
Cox, Esther: house of, HN 98; and poltergeists, HN 98, 99-101
Cox, Jennie: and poltergeists, HN 98
Cox, Julian: transformations of, TN 41
Cox, Robert: and Kline disappearance case, PP 132-133
Cox, William E.: metal-bending research of, MM 32-33; psychokinesis research of, MM 64, 66, 70
Coxe, Daniel: AW 73
Coxie, Michiel van: painting by, UV 22
Coyne, Lawrence J.: and encounter with UFO, UP 126-127
Coyote (trickster): and Nez Percé Indians, TN 52-53
Crab: MY 55
Crabtree, Adam: and multiple-personality disorder, SS 152-153
Crack in the Cosmic Egg, The (Pearce): MB 85
Craft, the: See Wicca
Craft Laws: WW 104
Craig, Mary: PP 20-21, 24-25
Crandon, Le Roi Goddard: PP 38-39; and Mina Crandon, SS 104-109, 108, 110; death of, SS 117; and Harry Houdini, SS 114-115
Crandon, Mina (pseud. Margery): mediumship of, PP 38-39, 40,

50. See also SS index
Cranes: SA 108-109
Cranshaw, Stella: MM 19; and levitation of table, MM 20
Crash retrievals: See UFOs; specific headings; AE index
Crater, Judge Joseph Force: PP 131
Crawford, Arch: CC 7, PS 121-123, 124
"Crawford Perspectives" (telephone hotline): PS 121
Creation myths: of Navajo, EE 24; of Pimas, EE 76. See also CD index; Cosmogonies in TS index
Creation of Eve, The (Bartolo di Fredi): CD 56
Creative visualization: defined, MM 126. See also Visualization
Creech Hill: haunting of, PE 12-13
Creek Indians: EE 100
Cremations: MY 116; in Bali, EM 64-65, PV 102-103; of Chogyam Trungpa Rinpoche, EM 132, 134
Cremlach: MW 85
Creosote bushes: SI 72
Cretans: CD 54
Crete (island): MQ 52-53; and Atlantis legend, MP 36; and Minoan civilization, MP 34
Crew, Jerry: MC 119
Crichton-Stuart, John: HN 124; and ghosts, HN 123-124
Crick, Francis: DD 100, 107
Crick Stone: EE 57-58
Criminal investigations: and hypnosis, MM 98
Criminals: animals as, TN 40; insects as, TN 40
Crios Bride: MY 130
Crisis apparitions: defined, HN 21, PE 24-25, 47, 86, 111, PV 19; of family members, PE 18-19, 20-21, 23, 25-26, 27-30, 30-31, 32, 33-35, 36; hauntings compared with, PE 111, 119. See also Ghosts; Out-of-body experiences; individual crisis apparitions
Crispin and Crispinian, Saints: MY 96
Critias (Plato): MP 15, 16, 19
Critique of Pure Reason (Kant): SE 58-59, UV 111
Croesus (king of Lydia): PS 74; and Delphic oracle, PP 17

AE Alien Encounters; AW Ancient Wisdom and Secret Sects; CC Cosmic Connections; CD Cosmic Duality; DD Dreams and Dreaming; EE Earth Energies; EM Eastern Mysteries; HN Hauntings; MA Magical Arts; MB The Mind and Beyond; MC Mysterious Creatures; ML Mysterious Lands and Peoples; MM Mind over Matter; MP Mystic Places; MQ Mystic Quests; MW The Mysterious World;

CROW. *Said to enjoy the frequent company of all-knowing divinities, the crow has long represented mysterious powers of divination. On this ancient Greek cup, the bird is depicted with Apollo, founder of the famous oracle at Delphi.*

Crofts, James (duke of Monmouth): PE 106

Croiset, Gerard (psychic): TS *115;* clairvoyance of, PP *126,* 127, 129-130, *131;* and psychometry, PP 127; and Yorkshire Ripper case, PP 134

Cro-Magnons: ML 17, MW 60; afterlife beliefs of, PV 59; and sympathetic hunting magic, TN 26-27; and transformations, TN *25-27, 26, 29*

Cromniomancy: defined, VP 35

Cronus (god): CC 43, 44, CD 24, TN 34, TS *21,* UV 22, *23*

Crookall, Robert: and out-of-body-experience research, PV 33-34, 35

Crookes, William: SS 52-53, 56-*57, 58*

Crop circles: AE *77,* MY *61;* in Britain, AE 75, EE *6-15,* broadsheet about, EE *20;* and cereologists, AE 75; characteristics of, AE 75-76, EE 7; effects of, AE 77, *78-79;* growth of, EE 7; patterns of, EE *20-21;* and Stonehenge, EE 6; theories about, EE 7, 20; and UFOs, EE 20

Cross, James Jasper: PS 41-43

Cross-correspondences: SE 97, 98, SS 91-99; defined, SE 97

Crosses: EE 95, MA *39, 40;* of Christ, MQ 115; from wood of Noah's Ark, alleged, MQ 70, 71, *77*

Cross-linkage theory: SI 66-69

Crotser, Tom: claims of, MQ 47-48

Crow Indians: MW 79; vision quest of, DD 31

Crowley, Aleister (a.k.a. Mahatma Guru Sri Paramahansa Shivaji): EM *93,* MA 45, 48, *65,* MC 84, MY *93,* SA 128; and Gerald Brosseau Gardner, WW 104, 105; and Great Pyramid, mystery of, MP *51;* and Hermetic Order of the Golden Dawn, MA 64, 65; and magic, MA 65; magic wand of, MA *57;* and Order of the Silver Star, MA 65; and sex, MA 65; and Tantrism, MA 65; Tarot cards by, VP *144-145;* as Tarot reader, VP *126,* 129. *See also*

AW *index*

Crown: SA *12*

Crows: and witches, WW 12

Crucible: SA *40-41, 73*

Crucifixion: MY 28

Crucifixion complex: CD 118-119

Cruikshank, George: PE 34

Crusades and Crusaders: AW 26, 31, 33-36, MQ 111, 121, 122, 123

Cryobiology: SE 132, 133, SI 109, 115, 122; defined, SE 132

Cryocapsules: SI *117, 120-121, 127,* defined, SI *124;* purposes of, SI *116*

Cryonics: SE 132, *133;* defined, SE 132. *See also* Cryonic suspension *in* SI *index*

Cryonics Institute: and Robert C. W. Ettinger, SI 116, 117

Cryonics Interment: SI 119-122

Cryonics Society of New York: SI 12

Cryonic suspension: SE 132, *133. See also* SI *index*

Cryopreservation: SI 109-*113*

Cryoprotectants: SI 109, 110, 116, 122, 123, 128

Cryosurgery: SI 109

Cryptomnesia: defined, PV *112;* and hypnotic regression, PV 112-113, 115, 124, 125; and Countess Maud, PV 113, 124. *See also* Past-life therapy

Cryptozoology: MW 45-47; defined, MC 18, 20

Crystal balls: MA *56,* MW *108,* VP *48,* 50; and John Dee, MA 22, PS 74; and Jeane Dixon, PS *9;* and psychic detection, PS 27; pur-

poses of, PS 74; use of, PP *98-99*

Crystal Chain: UV 121; and Paul Scheerbart, UV 126; and Bruno Taut, UV 126

Crystal gazing: MY *39*

Crystal Gazing and Clairvoyance (Melville): VP 50

Crystal healing: PH *105, 110-111*

Crystal House: UV *127*

Crystallomancy: VP 49-50. *See also* Scryers; Scrying

CSI: *See* Civilian Saucer Investigation

CT: *See* Cellular therapy

Cuba: MW 113

Cubit: and Great Pyramid, MP 54, 55, 58, 63

Cudhodana (king): DD 39

Cudi, Mount (Cudi Dag; Turkey): MQ 67; stone structure on, MQ *74*

Cuffe, Henry: MY 21, VP 123

CUFOS: *See* Center for UFO Studies

Cullen, Paul Stedman: EE 99

Cult & Occult (Smith): MA 126

Cult of the Dead: MA 44

Cult of the Head: ML *50*

Cults: *See individual cults*

Cultural archetypes: AE 111

Cultural Revolution: EE 35

Culver, Roger B.: CC 140

Cumae: MW 85, *90*

Cumberland, Stuart (mentalist): PP 107

Cummings, Eryl: MQ 84

Cummings, Robert: PS 41-43

Cummins, Geraldine (medium): SE 102-106, 107; psychic messages of, MP 25

Cuneiform: on clay tablets, MQ *80*

Cunningham, Mr.: DD 140

Cunning men: *See* Psychics

Cup: WW *120*

Cups (Tarot suit): VP 130, *140-141. See also* Tarot; Tarot readers

Curaçao (ship): HN 83

Curie, Marie: CC 87

Currach: defined, ML 122

Curran, Pearl: SS 85; mental linkage of, PP 42

Currer-Briggs, Noel: MQ 122

Curry, Roland: MC 16-17

Curse of Macbeth: MA 115, 116, 137; and Harold Norman, MA 110-111; and Laurence Olivier, MA 116; and Herbert Beerbohm Tree, MA 112

Curses: MW 127

Curtis, Mark: photograph by, AE *74-75;* and Edward Walters, AE 73, 74

Custer, Elizabeth: MY 56

Custer, George Armstrong: MA 80, MW 80, MY 56

Custer State Park: MW 80

Custodio di Faria, José: MM 91

Cutolo, Nicola: PS *96-97, 101*

Cutten, John: HN *122*

Cybele (goddess): CC 40, MY *24, 27, 42;* and Phrygians, WW 23

Cybele, Lady: as witch, WW 108

Cybernetics: applied, PS 80

Cyberspace: *See* Virtual reality

Cyclic time: defined, TS 42

Cyclopes: CD 24

Cyclops (Navy vessel): MY 19

Cyclops myth: artifact depicting, MQ *53;* basis for, possible, MQ 53; re-creating, MQ 52

Cygnus X-1: TS 63, *65*

Cylicomancy: defined, VP 45. *See also* Scryers; Scrying

Cyr, Donald: and atmospheric halos at Stonehenge, MP 102

''Cyrurgie'' (Mondeville): SI 89

Cyrus the Great (king of Persia): CD 80-82

Cytowic, Richard: MB 52

Czartoryski, Count: and Wolf Messing, PP 113

Czeisler, Charles A.: TS 86

Czetli, Nancy: PS *45-47*

29

Daedalus (frigate): MC *31*, MY 67

Dagda (god): MQ 109

Dagobert II (Merovingian king): MQ 125

Daguerreotypes: PS 30

Dahinden, René: MC *116, 117;* Sasquatch research of, MC 118-119, 124

Dahlfeld, Edith: and ghosts, HN 18

Daily Mail (London newspaper): Abominable Snowman expedition, sponsorship of, MC 105; buru expedition, sponsorship of, MC 70; and search for Loch Ness monster, MC 68

Daim, Wilfrid: DD 144-145

Daisetsu: *See* Suzuki, Teitaro

Daisyworld: EE *122-123*

Dakini: defined, HN 127

DAL (parallel universe): AE 99

Dalai Lamas: EM *130,* MQ 26, MW 93, 127, MY 110, PV 120, *121,* VP *45;* background of, EM 133; and Alexandra David-Néel, EM 70-71, 74, 80; in exile, EM 70, 133; and Thomas Merton, EM 142; and Nobel Peace Prize, EM 130; as political leader, EM 133; and Potala, EM 15. *See also* Buddhists and Buddhism; Tibet

Dalang: defined, EM 60

Dali, Salvador: DD 21; and double images, DD *20-21;* and Sigmund Freud, DD 19; paintings by, DD *18, 19, 20-21*

Dalkey, Norman: and Delphi method, PP 135

Dalrymple, James: HN 16

Dalrymple, Janet: MY 71; ghost of, HN 16

Dalton, John: SA 115

Damanhur: UV *140-141*

Damascius: VP 45

Damballah (god): MA 83

Dames, Edward: PS 90

Damian, John (a.k.a. Maister John the French Leich): attempted flight of, SA 56-58; and James IV, SA 56; as physician, SA 56

Damiani (psychic investigator): MM 12

Dance of Life, The (Hall): TS 100

"Dance of the sun": CD 121

Dances: of Aborigines, MA *21,* around maypole, CD *55;* in Bali, EM *66-69;* circle, ML *110, 111;* of Death, DD *38;* and Georgei Ivanovitch Gurdjieff, UV *105,* 108-109; and Point Loma Universal Brotherhood and Theosophical Society, UV *94-95;* and Shakers, UV *64-65,* 69-70; of Sufis, CD *112-113,* 114; and Tantric Buddhism, EM *103;* whirling, of Shakers, SS 24-25

Dancing in the Light (MacLaine): PV 44, SS 140

Danes, as constructors of Stonehenge, MP 85-86

Daniel (biblical figure): DD 29, MY 94

Daniels, Laura Jean: TS 16, 17

Dante Alighieri: AE 43, CC 64, *67,* CD 130, DD 141-143, SE 49, 72-87, VP 16

Danziger Goldwasser: SA 116

Da Passano, Andrew: SI *71*

Daphnomancy: defined, VP 35

Dariex, Dr.: and hauntings, HN 93

Dark Ages: CD 58, SA 31

Dark day: MY 38

Darkness Girl: TS *31*

Darley, John: CD 111

Daruma: EM 49; doll, EM *49*

Darvulia, Anna: and Elizabeth Báthory, TN 123

Darwin, Charles: CC 90, CD 93, 107-109, EE 105, MB *21,* MP 62, MQ 74, SS 23, VP 81; and Atlantis, MP 24; and mind, MB 21; and Henry Sidgwick, SS 73; and Stonehenge, MP 91; theory of evolution, MB 13, 14, 21, ML 28, 29, MP 26, PP 49

Darwin, Mike: and cryonic sus-

30

DEMON. Endowed with supernatural powers, including the ability to change form at will, and ever ready to do the bidding of witches and sorcerers, demons such as this Japanese oni are said to personify evil and Satanic influence.

pension, SI 118, 119
Darwin's Bulldog: ML 29
Dasaratha (king of India): MY 30
Dashwood, Francis: MW 119, 121-125
Dass, Baba Ram: *See* Alpert, Richard
D'Assier, Adolphe: TN 121; and body-double research, PV 20; and vampires, TN 121
DataGlove: MB *130-131*
Datta, Narendranath: *See* Vivekenanda, Swami
Datura: MW 113
Davenport, Ira: SS *36-37;* and Harry Houdini, SS 36; and John King, SS 60
Davenport, William: SS *36-37,* 60
David (biblical figure): ML 24; and Abishag, SI 38, *40;* and gerocomy, SI 34-38, *40*
David (grandson of Prester John): ML 66
David (postmortem apparition): PE 46-47, 52
David, Louis: EM 72
David-Néel, Alexandra (a.k.a. Mademoiselle Myrial): MQ 27, PE 98; background of, EM 72-73; and Buddha, EM *72,* 73; and *chöd,* EM 76-80; and Dalai Lama, EM 70-71, 74, 80; death of, EM 84; and enlightenment, EM 80-81; fame of, EM 83-84; and *gomchen,* EM 81; and Legion of Honor, EM 84; and Lumbini Gardens, EM *72-73;* and *lunggom,* EM 75-76; and magic, EM 84; and Philippe Néel, EM 73-74; and nirvana, EM 81; as opera singer, EM *72,* 73; photographs by, EM *76-79;* and *phurba,* EM 76; as pilgrim, EM *75,* 81; and sex, EM 73-74; and Emanuel Swedenborg, EM 72-73; and Theosophical Society, EM 84; and *thumo reskiang,* EM 81-83; travels of, EM *72-75,* 81-83; and Sidkeong Tulku, EM 76; and Aphur Yongden, EM 77, 81, 83, 84
Davidovits, Joseph: and pyramids, construction of, MP 67
Davidson, David: and Great Pyramid, measurements of, MP 63

Davidson, Gordon: UV 153
Davies, Fredrick: VP 147, 148; as Tarot reader, VP 146-149
Davis, Adelle: SI 75
Davis, Andrew Jackson: PH 20, 27-*30,* 90-91, SS 26, 27-*28,* 29, 132; as seer, VP 20-22; and trances, VP 22
Davis, Arthur: MA 6
Davis, Edward: ML 83-84
Davis, Gordon: SE 98-99
Davis, James: and psychic research test data, PP 60
Davis, Kathie: and abduction by aliens, AE 24, 34, 36; child of, AE *37;* drawings by, AE *24, 37;* hypnosis of, AE 36; pregnancy of, AE 36; scar of, AE *34;* and visitation by aliens, UP 142, *144*
Davis, Neil: AE 104
Davis, Wade: and zombies, MA 88, 89
Davis Land: *See* Easter Island
Davitashvili, Dzhuna (psychic healer): PH 99-100, 103, PS *103;* and remote viewing, PP 63
Dawe, Leonard: TS 122
Dawes, William: AW 77
Dawn Man: TS *31*
Dawn of Astronomy, The (Lockyer): MP 65, 91-92, 110
Day, Albert: PH 104
Daydreaming: and ego, MB 104; and trances, MB 103
Day-force: CD 36-37
Daykeepers: defined, DD 26
Day of the Dead: MY *98,* SE 22-23
Day of the Dolphin, The (film): MB 117
D-Day: MY 34, TS 122
De, Abhay Charan: *See* Prabhupada, A. C. Bhaktivedanta Swami
Deacon, Richard: CC 152
Dead Sea (Israel-Jordan): search for Sodom and Gomorrah in, MQ 43
Dead Sea Scrolls: CD 132, UV 34
Dean, Douglas: PS *106;* and extrasensory perception, study of, PP 135, PS 107; and precognition, PS 107; and telepathy, PS 106
Dean, James: MY *90*
De Anima (Aristotle): SE 49

Deasil: defined, WW 107
Death: CD 12, 13, DD *38;* attempts to overcome, MQ 22-23, 31-34, 39-40, 109; certificate, MA *88;* compacts, PE 32-33, 52-58; defined, SI 113-114; festivals, MY 102; god of, ML *113;* hormone, SI 71; mask, SA *9;* moment of, SE 138; penalty, UV 92; and superstitions, MA 130-134; Tibetan Buddhist beliefs about, PV 58, 135, 136-137. *See also* Near-death experiences; Postmortem apparitions
Deathbed experiences: *See* Near-death experiences
Death-Bed Visions (Barrett): PV 60-62
Deathwatch beetles: divination with, VP 40
Debaraz, Louis: witch trial of, WW 80
De Beverley, Constance (ghost): PE 16
Décadas da Asia (Barros): ML 67
Decatur, Stephen: ghost of, HN *110-111;* house of, HN *110-111*
Decline effect: of psychic ability, PP 53, 63
De-coo-dah: and earthen mounds of North America, MP 122, 123
Decreasing Oxygen Consumption (DECO): SI 71
Dee, John: AW 153, CC 72-75, MA 21-22, ML 45, MY *39,* SA *58;* and Albertus Alasco, SA 59; and alchemy, SA 59; and astrology, PS 74; background of, SA 58; code name of, PS *76;* and crystal balls, PS 74, VP *48;* death of, SA 59; and Elizabeth I, PS 74, SA 58, 59; and Edward Kelley, MA 45, 57, SA 58-59; and Mary Tudor, SA 58; and mirrors, MA *57;* and psi-warfare experiments, PS 74; and Walter Raleigh, SA 58; and Rosenberg, SA 59; and Rosicrucianism, SA 83; and Rudolf II, SA 59, 60; as scryer, VP 45-*49;* and séances, SA 59; talisman of, VP *48;* and "the nine," PS 74; and transmutation, SA 58-59; and visions, SA 59

Deep Quest: and psychic archaeology, PP 124
Deer headdresses: MY *123*
DeFeo, Ronald, Jr.: HN 100
De Florinville, Seigneur: VP 17
De Forest, Lee: VP 27
De Gandavo, Pedro de Magalhães: CD 64
De Gasparin, Agénor: séance research of, MM 11, 13, *24,* 25
De Gaulle, Charles: SI 65, TS 117
De Gomara, Francesca Lopez: and Atlantis, possible location of, MP 20
De Guaita, Stanislas: AW 68
Dei Gratia (ship): and *Mary Celeste,* MP 38-39
Deilde: MW 32, 34
Deildegasts: MW 32, 34
Deimos (satellite of Mars): CC 41
Deities: Christian, PV 16, 69, 73; communication with, PP 75, *76-77, 78,* 80-81; Egyptian, PV 98; gender of, CD 11; Hindu, PV 98-99; Tibetan Buddhist, PV 135. *See also* Gods; *individual deities*
Déjà vu: defined, TS 116
De Kerlor, W.: psychic predictions of, PP 28
De Koros, Alexander Csoma: Shambhala investigation of, MQ 27
De Landa, Diego: and Atlantis, ML 27, 28; and Maya, ML 27
Delaney, Gayle: and dreams, DD 80, 127; and incubation, DD 80; and nightmares, DD 115; and psychic dreams, DD 135
Delaney and Flowers Center for the Study of Dreams: DD 80
Delaware Indians: ML 25
De Leau, Mr.: and hauntings, HN 38
De Leau, Ernie: and hauntings, HN 38
De Leau, Esther: and hauntings, HN 37, 38
Delilah (biblical figure): SI 93
Delirium tremens (DTs): DD 114
Delmer, Denis Sefton: PS 68
De Loys, François: MC 101
Delphi: MW 85; valley of, TS *8-9*
Delphi Associates: disbanding of,

31

DRAGON. Known in the Christian world as vile embodiments of the devil Lucifer, dragons such as this one are regarded in Asian cultures as benevolent creatures associated with the Chinese yang, the mystical, creative force in the universe.

PS 117; and extrasensory perception, business applications of, PP 136-140; and Keith Harary, PS 113, 116; purposes of, PS 113; and stock market, PS 113, 115, 116 117; and Russell Targ, PS 83, 113, 116; and Anthony White, PS 113, 116

Delphic oracle: PS *74,* TS 9, VP 10-11, 14; and Apollo, EE 29; and Cicero, EE 29; clairvoyance of, PP 17; enclosing of, EE 29-30; and James Frazer, EE 29; and Mother Goddess, EE 29; and Plutarch, EE 29; and Diodorus Siculus, EE 29. *See also* Oracles

Delphi method: applications of, PP 135-136; development of, PP 135

Delta Force team: PS 93-94

Delta waves: DD 97; characteristics of, MM *82-83,* 108. *See also* Sleep

Delvaux, Paul: paintings by, DD *14, 15*

Demaison, André: and gazelle-boy, TN 64-65

De Markoff, E.: MQ 79

Dement, William C.: DD *101,* PV 36; and sleep, DD 99-100

Demeter (goddess): CC 47, 85, EE 54, MY *86,* 94, 130, SA *26-27,* WW 23

Demigods: UV 22-23

DeMille, Cecil B.: CC 84

De Mille, Richard: MA 115

Demiurge: SE 118; defined, CD 29

Democritus of Alexandria: SA 23

Democritus of Ionia: SA *23,* SE 49; and atoms, SA 20, 23; and physics, SA 23

Demon Detector: defined, HN 136

Demoniac: defined, CD 90

Demonic possession: MY 59

Demonifuge medicine: MY 122

Demonolatreiae (Remy): WW 78

Demonologist: defined, WW 68

Demonology: CD 83

Demonology (James I): WW 7, 8

Demons: AE *46-47, 48-49,* 51, CD *9, 14, 79-80, 83-84,* 86, 89, 90, *93-94, 96,* MA *94-98,* MY 20, 32, 56, 59, 89, 107, SI *16;* and Chris-

tians, CD 82; defined, HN 137; and Origen, CD 82; and Zoroaster, CD 122. *See also* Ghosts

De Morgan, Augustus: SS 22

Denckla, W. Donner: SI 71

Dennis, Christy: AE 38

Dennis, Eugenie: and David P. Abbott, PS 34; and Brighton trunk crime, PS 34, 36; death of, PS 34

Dennis, Glenn: and crash retrievals, AE 83; drawings by, AE *84;* and Kevin D. Randle, AE 83; and Donald R. Schmitt, AE 83

Deno meter: HN *73;* defined, HN 73

Dentistry: ML *22;* psychic, PH *96-97*

Denton, William: PS 30-33

Deoxyribonucleic acid: *See* DNA

Depersonalization theory: PV 63-64, 78. *See also* Near-death experiences

Deprenyl: SI 74

Depression: MB 88. *See also* Mental illnesses

De Puységur, Marquis: PH 90;

hypnosis research of, MM 94, *95*

DeQuincey, Thomas: AW 61

Deren, Maya: CD 86

De Revolutionibus Orbium Coelestium (Copernicus): CC 93

Dermo-optical perception: PP *143*

Dermo-optic vision: defined, MM 23. *See also* Extrasensory perception

Dervishes: MY *114-115;* and Paul Lucas, SA 42-43, 47; whirling, CC *55. See also* Sufis

DeSalvo, Albert: and Boston Strangler case, PP 132

Descartes, René: AW 56-57, CD 38-40, DD 23, 44, MB *11,* MY 100, SA 85, SE 50-51, *52-56,* 123, 124; and animal spirits, MB 13; criticism of, MB 10; diagram by, SE *53;* and dualism, MB 13; and mind, MB 11-13; and pineal gland, MB 11-13, 19; and "simple natures," MB 11; and space, TS 42; theories of, MB 10-11

Descent from the Cross, The (Beckmann): DD *152*

Descent of Man into the Vale of

Death, The (Blake): PV *74*

Deschamps, M.: TS 120-121

Description of Greenland (Egede): MC 26

Desert Center (California): and encounters with aliens, UP 76, 78

Desert men: ML *63*

Desideri, Father (Roman Catholic missionary): MQ 27

De Silva, Colonel: PE 62

De Solla Price, Derek: ML 16-17

Desmond, Countess of: SI 14

Despards: haunted house of, PE 110-111, 112, 123

De Stijl group: AW 158

Detective work: *See* Psychic detection *in* PS *index*

Determinism: defined, SE 70

Deukalion (god): EE 74

Dev, Guru: EM 121

Devas: and Peter Caddy, EE 134-135; defined, EE 134; and Dorothy Maclean, EE 134, 135, UV 143, 144

Devereux, Paul: AE 106; and dowsing rods, MP *96-97,* 98; and Dragon Project, MP *96-97*

Devereux, Robert (second earl of Essex): VP 123

Devereux, Robert (third earl of Essex): PE 134

Devil Dance: MY 134

Devilfish: ML 32

Devil post: MA *10*

Devils: MA 13, SE *82-83;* and Gypsies, MA 100, 101; in Liberia, MA 13. *See also* Demons; Satan

Devil's Boulder: MY *99*

Devil's marks: WW 79; and bodkins, WW 80; defined, WW 63

Devil's Trill (Tartini): DD 45

Devotion (Mondrian): AW *158*

Dew: characteristics of, SA *72;* collecting of, SA *72,* 132-133; distilling of, SA *72;* heating of, SA *73;* origins of, SA 70

Dewi Danu (goddess): EE 132

De Wohl, Louis: CC 136, *138*

DeYoung, Kaye: MB 85

Dhami: defined, EM 50

Dharma: PH 63; and Buddha, EM 53-55; defined, EM 121; and Kashyapa, EM 55

Dharma Bums (Kerouac): EM 138

32

DRUM. *Symbolic of sacrificial altars in diverse cultures, drums like the one being played by this Siberian shaman serve as vehicles of powerful magic, mediators between the dread world of the spirits and the earthly world of humans.*

Dharmakaya: defined, MB 10, 22

Diabology: defined, CD 82

Dialectic: TS 41

Dialectical materialism: CD 40

Diamond, Louis: PH 129

Diamond Composition with Grey Lines (Mondrian): AW *160*

Diana (goddess): CC *39*, MY 28, *69*, WW 12, 23, 27. *See also* Dianic cult

Dianic cult: and Margaret A. Murray, WW 100, 102, 112. *See also* Diana

Diaphragmatic breathing: defined, MM 118. *See also* Levitation

Diary of a Drug Fiend, The (Crowley): AW 122

Diaz del Castillo, Bernal: MW 115

Dice: VP *110-111*; psychokinesis experiments and, MM 58-66, *58, 59, 60, 63, 67*

Dice throwing: computer version of, MM *63. See also* Micro-PK; Psychokinesis

Dickens, Charles: CC 90, DD *42-43*, 131, HN 22, PE 60; hypnosis by, MM 96

Dickinson, Emily: CC 88

Dictionnaire Infernal (Plancy): MA *94-98*; engraving from, WW *14*

Die astrologische Rundschau (Brandler-Pracht): CC 130

Diefenbach, Karl: AW 164

Diego, Juan: CD 119, MY 117

Die Kunst Chiromantie (Hortlich): VP 81, 82

Diencephalon: MB *12*

Dienheim, Wolfgang: MA 33

Dies Natalis Invicti Solis: MY 120-121

Diet: of Adam, SI 13; and gerontologists, SI 6; of Hunzakuts, SI 43, 47, *52, 53,* 54, 55; and Daniel Colin Munro, SI 13; in Vilcabamba (Ecuador), SI 43

Diet supplements: of Durk Pearson, SI 75-76, *80;* of Sandy Shaw, SI 75-76, *80*

Diev: MY 119

Diffraction spectral analysis: AE 74

Diffusionists: characteristics of, ML 116-117; defined, ML 116; examples of theories of, ML *103-113;* and Barry Fell, ML 131; and Joseph Mahan, ML 135; and Mystery Hill, ML 131

Digges, Leonard: CC 72

Digitalis: WW 36

Dill: WW *39*

Dilmun: UV 18-20

Dimensions: number of, TS 17-19, 70, 136

Dimensions (Vallee): AE 120, 121

Diminishing spell: MA *38*

Dimond, E. Gray: PH 51

Dinas Brän (castle; Wales): MQ *112*

Dine: MW 79, 81

Dinetah: MW 81-83

Dingwall, Eric J.: MM 20; and Mina Crandon, SS 115-116; and Eileen Garrett, PP 86; and Carlos Mirabelli, SS 120; and Eusapia Palladino, SS 59

Dinsdale, Tim: MC 72, *78,* 84; Loch Ness monster film by, MC 73, *74-75,* 77, 81, 82; Loch Ness monster research of, MC 72-73, 80

Diocletian (Roman emperor): MA 31, MW 133, SA 19

Diodorus Siculus: AW 19, EE 29

Diogenes: SE 49, TS 40

Dionisopoulos-Mass, Regina: MA 11, 12

Dionysian cult: AW 13, *14,* 16

Dionysian rites: WW 23, *24*

Dionysius (monk): CD 130-131

Dionysus (god): CD 61, MY 121, SE 31-32; and rites of followers, TN 34; transformations of, TN 34

Dior, Christian: PS 128

Directions: TS 19, *30-31;* cultural conceptions of, TS 30-31

Dirigible: MY *22*

Disabled persons: and virtual reality, MB *135*

Disappearances: and Dorothy Arnold, TS 131; and Benjamin Bathurst, TS 129; and Bermuda Triangle, TS 132-133; and Cambodians, TS *137;* and First Fourth Norfolk, TS 131; and Flight 19, TS 132-133; and David Lang, TS 131-132; and UFOs, TS 137. *See also individual cases*

Discourse on Method (Descartes): SE 51, 52

Discover (magazine): AE 57, *58-59*

Discovery of Witches (Scot): WW 78

Diseases: *See* Sickness

Disinformation: AE 88

Disney, Walt: PS 111

Displacement: PS 115; and Sigmund Freud, DD 66

Dissection: of witches, WW *55*

Dissociative amnesia: AE 110

Dissociative personality: *See* Multiple-personality disorder

Dissolution: HN 90, 91; defined, HN 90

Distillation: SA 39

Divination: defined, MA 26, VP 7, WW 107; various types of, VP 35. *See also* Seers; *specific types of divination*

Divine Comedy (Dante): AE 43, CC 64, CD 130, DD 141-143, SE *72-87. See also* Inferno

Divine power: defined, WW 107

Divine Powers Metaphysical Center: MA 7 8

Diving-duck trick: EM 92

Diving reflex: SI 101

Divining Hand, The (Bird): PS 77

Divining rods: coat hangers used as, MQ *104-105*

Diwali: MY *101*

Dixon, Jeane: PS *9,* 10; as seer, VP *23-25*

Dixon, John Peters: and extrasensory perception, business applications of, PP 136

Djajapura (New Guinea): MW 34

DNA: SI *68;* defined, SI 66; and Human Genome Project, SI 73; mitochondrial, CD 60; and proteins, SI 66; and RNA, SI 66

Doctor Faustus: See The Tragicall History of Doctor Faustus

Doctors: CC 65, 76-78; in Egypt, MA 19; and magic, MA 17-19, 19-20. *See also* Sickness

Doctrine of signatures: EE 96

Dodd, E. R.: SE 108

Dodge, Jamie Kellam: witch trial of, WW 125

Dodona, forest of: EE 80

MY The Mystical Year; PE Phantom Encounters; PH Powers of Healing; PP Psychic Powers; PS The Psychics; PV Psychic Voyages; SA Secrets of the Alchemists; SE Search for the Soul; SI Search for Immortality; SS Spirit Summonings; TN Transformations; TS Time and Space; UP The UFO Phenomenon; UV Utopian Visions; VP Visions and Prophecies; WW Witches and Witchcraft

Dodson, Lucy: and mother's apparition, PE 59

Dodson, Richard Lee: and Kline disappearance case, PP 133

Doesburg, Theo van: UV *133;* painting by, UV *133;* and de Stijl, UV 132

"Dog days": MY 67

Dog-headed men: MC *57. See also* Human-beasts

Dogon (West African tribe): buildings of, ML *76-77;* burial rituals of, PE *53, 56-57;* divination among, VP *36-37*

Dogs: divination with, VP 40; and Isis, MA 22; and psi-warfare experiments, PS 74, 76

Doğubayazit (Turkey): Phantom Ark's proximity to, MQ 90, 92

Dohada: EE 110

Dojos: MW 130

Doll festival: MY *19*

Dolls: CD *30,* MY *19, 24, 73, 114, 130;* and voodoo, MA *87-88. See also Tihus*

Dolma (goddess): EM 42

Dolma Stone: EM *42*

Dolmen: MA *16,* MW 125; characteristics of, EE 54-57; definition of, MP 81

Dolphin, David: and porphyria, TN 93-94

Dolphins: and John Lilly, MB 117, 122. *See also* Rowe, Neville

Dome of the Rock: UV *24*

Dominic, Saint: AW *31*

Dominions: CD *131*

Dominoes: VP *112-113*

Domitian (Roman emperor): CC 34

Dommeyer, Frederick C.: SE 94-95

Donaldson, Thomas: SI *98;* and Alcor Life Extension Foundation, SI 116; brain tumor of, SI 96; and cryonic suspension, SI 96, 98, 116

Doña Paz (ferry): CC 152

Donar (god): EE 92

Donghua, Master: SA 113

Dönitz, Karl: SI 26

Don Juan (Byron): PE 39

Donnelly, Ignatius Loyola: ML 27-

28; and Atlantis legend, MP 21-26

Dool, Claas Arientz van den: certificate awarded to, WW *71*

Doors of Perception, The (A. Huxley): MB 104

Doorway amnesia: AE 27

Dopamine: MB 74; and Deprenyl, SI 74; and Parkinson's disease, SI 83

Doppelgänger: *See* Doubles

Doppler effect: characteristics of, TS 60; and UFOs, TS 137

Doré, Gustave: drawing by, MW *72;* illustrations by, SE *72-87*

Doris (childbirth patient): near-death experience of, PV 60, 62

Dorjieff (Siberian lama): MQ 26

Dormion, Gilles: and Great Pyramid, construction of, MP 46

Dorr, George B.: SE 95, 97

Dorsett, Sybil: background of, MB 79-80; and multiple personality disorder, MB 79-80; painting by, MB *83;* and Cornelia Wilbur, MB 79-80

Dory: MC *46-51;* defined, MC 47

Doshas: PH 65-66, 67, PS 98

Dostoyevsky, Fyodor: CC 87, SI 133

Doubles: history of, PE 85; out-of-body experiences compared with, PE 94-95; and telepathy, PE 88, 89; and vardøgrs in Norway, 100. *See also individual doubles*

Dove: on Noah's Ark, MQ *72, 82;* as symbol, SE 16

Downer, Craig: MW 31-32

Downing, Barry H.: and alleged biblical UFO sightings, UP 12, 14

Dowsing: EE *91, 136,* MA 135; and Elizabeth Albright, PS *127;* and Robert Brewer, PS *127;* and Paul Clement Brown, PS 128-130; in church archaeology, MQ *104-105;* defined, TS 128; equipment used in, PS *126, 127,* 128, 130; and Ian Fleming, PS 68, 69; of Uri Geller, MM *35,* 36; and Harry Grattan, PS *126;* and Heinrich

Himmler, PS 65; how to, PP *139;* and Thomas Lethbridge, TS 128, 129; and ley theory, MP *96-97,* 98; and Clayton McDowell, PS *126;* map dowsing, MQ *100,* PP 138, PS *122,* 124-126; and Louis Matacia, PS 77; and mining, PS *122-123, 125,* 128-130; and Nazis, PS 59, 68; and psi-warfare experiments, PS 74, *77-78;* and psychic detection, PS 27; and psychic emissions, PP 138; and Vietcong tunnels, PS *77-78;* for water, PP *138;* and Colin Wilson, TS *133;* and J. W. Young, PS 128

Doyle, Arthur Conan: MM 57, 115, PS 29, *32-33;* and Arthur Balfour, SS 101; and Mina Crandon, SS 110, 115; and Kingsley Doyle, SS 100, 101; and Arthur Ford, SS 121; and Harry Houdini, SS 102-104, *105,* 115; and Oliver Lodge, SS 100; and J. B. Rhine, PP 50, SS 116; and Society for Psychical Research, SS 100, 101; and spiritualism, PP 50, 87, SS 100, 101, 102; and Zancigs' thought-transference act, PP 108

Doyle, Lady: automatic writing of, SS 103-104, *105*

Dozier, James: PS *92-93;* and Gary, PS 91-92; and Red Brigades, PS 91-92

Drackenburg, Christian Jacob: SI 14

Dracul: defined, TN 104

Dracula (a.k.a. Vlad III, Vlad Tepes, Vlad the Impaler): MC 9, TN *104, 105,* 106-107

Dracula (film): TN 137; Bela Lugosi in, TN *137*

Dracula (Stoker): TN 104, 109, 111, 133-134, VP 127

Dragon Boat Festival: MY 54

Dragon bone medicine: MA 107

Dragon Hill (England): MP 126-127

Dragon Play: MY 128

Dragon Project: MP *96-97*

Dragons: CD *8-9, 36-37,* MC 7, *8-9,* ML *105,* MW 53, 94, MY *31, 54, 65, 128,* SA *51, 53, 109;* and earthquakes, EE *60-61;* Komodo, MC *20-21;* Merlin's prophecy of, MQ *130-131;* as sacred animals, EE *113,* 114, 115; sea, MC *18, 19. See also* Animals

Dragon's Triangle: MW 93, 94-95

Dragon Throne: MW 127, 128

Drake, Frank: MY 28; radio message of, AE *108;* and search for extraterrestrial intelligence, UP 124

Drawing Down the Moon: and Andras Corban Arthen, WW *130-131;* and Athanor Fellowship, WW *130-131;* characteristics of, WW 105, 116; and Wicca, WW 116

Drawing Down the Moon (Adler): WW 97, 104, 114-115

Drbal, Karl: EE 25; and pyramid power, MP 66

Dream, The (Kupka): AW *165*

Dream, The (Rousseau): DD *8-9*

Dream body: and Frederik Willem van Eeden, DD 110

Dream City (Klee): UV *130*

Dreaming spot: MQ *10-11*

Dream machine: DD 113

Dream research: and psychic abilities, PP 69-74; and REM activity, PP *66;* and sensory deprivation, PP 67; and telepathy, PP 66

Dreams: CD 38, MB 20, MY 22, 35, 57, 60, 100; as alternate explanation for near-death experiences, PV 77; and Malcolm Bessent, TS 117; and John William Dunne, TS 123; and John Godley, TS 128; and John Gribbin, TS 117; interpretation of, MA 19; out-of-body experiences compared with, PV 16, 42, 44; of Chuck Rak, AE 17; of Susan Ramstead, AE 36; and H. E. Saltmarsh, TS 128; and the unconscious, TN 31; of Jack Weiner, AE 16, 17; of Jim

34

DANCE. Because ancient Goddess worshipers believed she spawned the universe by dancing over the Waters of Chaos, dance came to symbolize creation. By dancing, these celestial nymphs hope to persuade the deities to reshape the world.

DOVE. Their white feathers emblematic of purity and grace, capable of flight to the highest reach of heaven, the doves below represent the souls of the dead. Perched on the branches of the tree of life, they partake of divine fruit and fear no evil.

Weiner, AE 16, 17; and John H. Williams, TS 128. *See also* Archetypes; Incubation; Nightmares; Night terrors; Psychic dreams; REM sleep; Vision quest; DD *index*
Dreams, Feast of: MY 124-125
Dreams and How to Guide Them (Saint-Denis): DD 107
Dreams of knowledge: defined, PV 24, 42. *See also* Calloway, Hugh G.
Dream state: PP 68
Dream symbols: bones, DD 57; clocks, DD 12; fire, DD *34;* horses, DD 12; houses, DD 16, 57, 59; purposes of, DD 33, 59; sexual connotations of, DD 35; skeletons, DD 15; skulls, DD 57;

snakes, DD *32-33;* water, DD 35
Dream-telepathy research: PS 111. *See also* Telepathy
Dream Telepathy (Ullman and Krippner): DD 146
Dreamtime: MW 95, 96; characteristics of, TS 15, 36-37
Dreamwork: DD 23, 64; and Sigmund Freud, DD 64
Drepung Monastery: PV *132-133*
Drescher, Thomas: EM 130
Drexler, K. Eric: SI 128-130
Driesch, Hans Adolf Eduard: SE 118, *119*
Driesen, Basil von: PE 61
Drive bands: MB *32-33*
Driving simulator: MB *135*
Drona Parva: and UFO sighting, UP 12

Drop-in contacts: SE 99-107
Drown, Ruth: PH 80
Druffel, Ann: and abduction by aliens, AE 124; and aliens, AE 123-124; and Lori Briggs, AE 123; and Emily, AE 123; and D. Scott Rogo, AE 121; and Sara Shaw, AE 123; and Tujunga Canyon incidents, AE 121; and UFOs, AE 124; and Jacques Vallee, AE 123-124; and Jan Whitley, AE 121
Drugs: MB 93; and dreams, DD 114; and near-death experiences, PV 77, 78. *See also* Anesthetics; Hallucinogens
Druids: AW 11, 12, 17-18, ML 50, MP 20, *88-89,* MW 17, 125, MY *55, 97,* VP 35; abolition of, AW 19; anthropomancy by, VP 38; and Christianity, AW 20; Merlin as, MQ 136; and mistletoe, EE 95-96; and oaks, EE 80, 92; pyromancy by, VP 38; revival of, AW 19-20; sacred object of, MQ *124;* and sacrifices, AW 18-*19, 20,* VP 38, and Stonehenge, EE 54, MP 86, 88, 89 90, 91, 100-*101*
Druids' Altar (Ireland): MP *72*
Drums: MW *120,* WW *121*
Drury, Edward: and ghosts, HN 29
Drury, William: HN 56; and poltergeists, HN 57-58
Druse: reincarnation beliefs of, PV 108
Dry cupping: PH *42-43*
Dryden, John: MB 87
Dry-sand trick: EM 92
Dualism: SE 51-52, 89, 124, 130; Broad's brand of, SE 68; characteristics of, MB 9; and Christianity, MB 10; defined, CD 26; and René Descartes, MB 13, SE 43-44; and John Eccles, MB 18, 19; and mind, MB 9; and Plato, MB 10
Dualities: defined, CD 18
Duba-duba: SE 39
Dubček, Alexander: PS 13
Duchenne, Guillaume: PH *88, 89*
Dudak, Rita: DD 130-131
Dudley, E. E.: SS 116, 117
Dudley, Guilford and John: PE 106

Dudley, Marshall: AE 75
Dughdov (mother of Zoroaster): CD 26
Du Maurier, George: MM 96
Dumu-zi (god): WW 16
Dunbar, David: HN 16
Dunbar, Helen Flanders: PH 129
Duncan (king of Scotland): MW 86
Duncan, Gilly: execution of, WW 7; as witch, WW 6-8
Duncan, Kelly: CD 106-107
Duncan Forest Museum: AE 33
Dundes, Alan: MA 9, 124
Dung beetle: CD 12
Dunikowski, Zbigniew: and alchemy, SA 119, *122, 123;* and z-rays, SA 119, *122*
Dunne, Brenda J.: PS 88, SE 135, *136,* 139
Dunne, John William: DD 134, MY 35, TS 123, *127;* and J. B. Priestley, TS 124; as seer, VP 8, 9, *11;* and serialism, TS 123-124, 127
Dunninger, Joseph (mentalist): and hoaxes of mediums, SS 123, *127, 128;* and Bess Houdini, SS *120, 122;* mind-reading act of, PP 113-*114*
Dunvegan Castle: MW 120-121, *124*
Durante, Jimmy: MA 134
Duration: defined, TS 100
Dürer, Albrecht: engraving by, CD *15*
Durga (goddess): MY 88
Durga Puja: MY 88
Durupinar, Ilhan: MQ 90-91
Dusares (god): ML 75
Dutch West India Company: ML 84
Dwarfs: ML 102
Dying: emotional stages of, PV 64
Dying Chrysanthemum (Mondrian): AW *158*
Dymaxion house: UV *150*
Dynamism of an Automobile (Russolo): UV *122*
Dynamo Jack: MA *32,* 34
Dynamometers: SI 61
Dyson, Frank: and relativity theory, TS 50-51
Dzonokwa: MY *78-79*
Dzu-teh: defined, MC 104

35

EAGLE. *Though long associated with destructive gods of storm and war, eagles—such as this Sun Bird carrying an American Indian to the gates of immortality—sometimes represent the sun and other deities known for benevolence and justice.*

Ea (god): CC 17

Eady, Dorothy (a.k.a. Omm Sety): PV *107;* alleged previous incarnation of, PV 104-105

Eagle: MY 95, SA *52,* SE 16

Eames, Wilberforce: ML 136-137

Early, Loretta F.: and stigmata research of, MM 113

Early British Trackways (Watkins): MP 94, 98

Earrings: MA 118

Earth: AE *90-93;* satellite photograph of, AE *89*

Earth drawings: MP 126-127, 128, *129-137. See also* Geoglyphics; Nazca lines of Peru

Earthen mounds (North America): MP *124-125;* builders of, MP 122

Earth hand: VP *54, 61. See also* Palmistry; Palmists

Earthlights: AE *107;* defined, AE 106, *107*

Earth Mother: MW 85, MY 20, 42, 51, 130

Earth power: defined, WW 107

Earthquakes: EE 59-61, MW 15, MY 131; in Alaska, PS *10-11;* prediction of, VP 25-27, *41-43;* in San Francisco, PS 105

Earth Resources Technical Satellite: photograph by, MQ 64, *66*

EarthSpirit Community: WW *134-135. See also* Athanor Fellowship; Wicca

East Africa: gold in, SA 17

Easter: MY 23, 30, 136

Easter Bunny: MY 30

Easter Island: MW 93. *See also* ML *index*

Eastern Europe: trees in, EE 91

Eastern healing: PH 45, 46, 54, 55, 57, 58-60. *See also* Ayurveda; Chinese healing; Indian healing; Japanese healing; Tibetan healing

Eastern mountain lion: MW 50. *See also* Beast of Truro

Eastern Star: AW 103, 109

East Indian rope trick: EM 92

Eastwood, Clint: SI 76

EAT: AE 34

Eaton, Henry: and ghosts, HN 37

Eavesdropping: MB *24*

Eberbach Valley: MW *34,* 35-36

Eberhardt (captain): MW 51

Ebertin, Elsbeth: CC 130-131, *134,* PS 58-59

EBEs: *See* Aliens

Ebisu (god): MY 94

Eccles, John Carew: DD 152, MB 18, 19, 20, SE 123-*124,* 139

Ecgfrith (king of Northumbria): PE 132

Echeverria, Loreto: CD 121

Echmiadzin monastery: alleged Noah's Ark relics in, MQ 70, 71, 77

Ecker und Eckhoffen, Hans Carl von: AW 63

Eclectic school: MW 105

Eclipses: CC *20,* MY 6-7, PS 123

Ecliptic: CC *11, 12, 13,* 39

Ecstasy: defined, PV 45; passive state of, PH 10

Ecstatic trances: *See* Trances

Ectoplasm: and Eva C., SS 64, 66, *67,* 68-69; and Mina Crandon, SS *114,* 115; defined, SS 61; description of, PP *38-39,* 40; hoaxes, SS *128;* and Eusapia Palladino, SS 61; and Stanislava P., SS *65;* production of, PP 40-41

Eddington, Arthur: EM 142, SE 130; and arrow of time, TS 59; and relativity theory, TS 50-51, 58

Eddy, Mary Baker: MA 62, MB *124,* PH 91, 124-*125*

Eddy, William: MA 124

Eden: CD 126, EE 95, MW *6-7,* UV *7, 12-13;* and paradise myths, UV 18, 20

Edgar Chapel: ML 61

Edgehill: battlefield of, PE 129, *134-135*

Edgerton, Harold (Doc): as inventor, MC 78; Loch Ness monster research of, MC 85, 89

Edict of Milan: CC 49

Edimmu: See Vampires

Edison, Thomas A.: CC 90, EE 105, PE *116;* and hypnagogic state, DD 117; reincarnation beliefs of, PV 103, *105;* Theosophical beliefs of, PV 103

Edric the Wild (knight): WW 49

Education: and Rudolf Steiner, UV 111, 112, 113, 118-119. *See also* Raja-yoga school

Edward I (king of England): AW 98, ML 56-59, PE 103

Edward II (king of England): SA 33

Edward IV (king of England): PE 104, 105

Edward V (king of England): PE 104

Edward VI (king of England): PE 106

Edward VII (king of England): AW 91, VP 82; coronation procession of, DD *144-145*

Edward VIII (king of England): VP 82

Edward Augustus (prince of England): VP 69

Edwards, Frank: and National Investigations Committee on Aerial Phenomena, UP 69

Edwards, Harry: PH 33-*34*

Edwards, Michael: MM *78*

Edward the Confessor (king of England): PH 87

Eeden, Frederik Willem van: DD 107-110, 113

Eel, giant: MW 75

Eels: MA *129,* MC 44, 85, ML 98

Effigies: in China, MA *23;* in Portugal, MA *12*

Egede, Hans: MC 26; sea serpent research of, MC 26, 42

36

Egg, cosmic: CD 10, 23, TS *24*

Eggebrecht, Arne: ML 23

Eggs: MY 17, 23, 25, *30*, SA *75*; and cosmogonies, TS 19-20, 23, *24, 25, 27*

Egg-stone: ML *54*

Egidi (Mongol prince): MC 107

Ego: MB 41, 71, 92, 104; defined, CD 36, DD 73, MB 41, 104; and enlightenment, MB 101; and Sigmund Freud, DD 73

Egungun: MY *51*

Egypt: and alchemy, SA 19; and astral body beliefs, PV *16-17*; and Atlantis legend, MP 34, 36; *Book of the Dead*, MQ 78; doctors in, MA 19; and Dorothy Eady, PV 104-105; geomancy in, EE 33; gods in, MA 51-54, PV 98, *107*; gold in, SA 17, *18*; kings of, PV 104, *107*; magic in, MA 19, 51-52, 54; and Minoan civilization, MP 35; Mobius Society expedition to, MQ *100-103*; and Mu, MP 26; popular interest in, MP 57; and reincarnation beliefs, PV 98, seers in, VP 10; use of dice in, VP 110; use of numerology in, VP 105. *See also* Alexandria; Egyptians; Giza; Pyramids

Egyptian Rite: AW 100-101

Egyptians: ML 22-23, 83, 117, TS 20, 103, 107; and afterlife, CD 85; and angels, CD 122; and cats, SI 70, WW 12; and cellular therapy, SI 65; complexion of, SI 90; and evil, CD 80; and immortality, SI 23; and ka, CD 122; and Mother Goddess, CD 50, 56; mummies of, SI 23, 99, *100*; pyramids of, SI 23-24; and snakes, CD 14; wigs of, SI *93*

Ehrenberg, Philipp Adolf von: and witch hunts, WW 69-70

Eidetic imagery: defined, VP 52

Eidetic memory: MB 53-58, 62. *See also* Memory

Eiffel Tower: PS *89*

Eight: in dice, VP 111; in numerology, VP 103, 108

Eighteen: in dice, VP 111

Eightfold Path: CD 99

Eight Immortals: AE *53*, SA 112, *113*

Eight principal patterns: PH 58

Eiheiji monastery: EM *106-107*

Eileen (double): PE 94, 95

Einstein, Albert: CC 91, *142*, 148, EM 119, MB 25, MM 72, SE 130, 134, 135, 139, TS *57*, 70, 137, VP 8-9; and Niels Bohr, TS 68; and coincidences, TS 137; and ether, TS 55; and fourth dimension, AE 121; and gravity, TS 58; and Institute for Advanced Study, TS 54; and Carl Jung, TS 121; and light, TS 55-57; and Joost Meerloo, TS 137; and Wolf Messing, PP 113; as musician, TS 55; and Isaac Newton, AE 115; and photoelectric effect, TS 65; and Max Planck, TS 65; and quantum mechanics, TS 65, 68; and relativity theory, AE 115, 118, TS 50, 51, 54, 55-57, 58, 59, 60, 75; and space-time, TS 58, 60; and telepathy, opinion of, PP *26*; and time, AE 121; and time dilation, TS *56*, 57; and time travel, TS 120

Eisenberg, David: PH 58-60

Eisenhower, Dwight D.: PE 112

Eisenstein, Sergei: CC 90

Eitel, Ernest: EE 36

Ejecatl (spirits): MW 115-116

Eka Dasa Rudra: MY *25*

Ekeko (god): MY 128

Elamites: AE 91

Elbe (ocean liner): MA 85

Eldepryl: SI 74

Elder Edda (Anonymous): EE 93

Elder Futhark: MA 27, *28-29*

Elders, Brit: AE 105

Elders of Mu: ML 14

Elder trees: EE 92. *See also* Trees

El Dorado legend: MQ 29

Eldridge, Tom: PS 47-48

Electric girl: HN *54*, 55

Electricity: ML 23

Electro-acupuncture: PH 49

Electrode caps: EM *124*

Electroencephalograph (EEG): defined, MM 108

Electromagnetic energy: and James Beal, EE 61; and Francis Hitching, EE 61-62; and Dolores LaChapelle, EE 62

Electromagnetic radiation: MM 79-80; and telepathy, PP 140

Electromagnetism: and psychic phenomena, PP *70-71*

Electroplating: ML 22-23

Electroshock therapy: MB *75*

Electrotherapy: PH 88-89

Elements: CC *21*, 23, *122-123*, SA *26-27, 51*; and alchemy, SA 26; and Aristotle, EE 51, 62, 66, 70, 76, SA 21, 26, 44; and Robert Boyle, SA 96, 97; characteristics of, EE 51; defined, WW 107; and Empedocles, SA 20, 26; and Paracelsus, SA 64; periodic table of, SA 116; and Plato, SA 21

Elephant bird: MW *59*, 65, 69

Eleusinian mysteries: AW 9, 13-14, EE 54, WW 23

Eleusis (Greece): MW 119

Eleutherococcus: EE 100

Eleven: in dice, VP 111

ELF (extremely low frequency) waves: PS 86

Elfrida (ghost): HN 90

Elgee, Mrs. E. H.: PE 88-89

El Gran: MW 102

El-Hemel: EE 29

Eliade, Mircea: and cosmobiological experience, EE 24-26; and creation myths, CD 18; and fall from grace, CD 18, 23; and gestures of approach, EE 30; and Mother Goddess, EE 24-26; and sacred places, EE 27-29, 30; and shamans, CD 111

Elijah (biblical figure): AE 112, ML 29, MY 24

Eliot, George: MB 89, PS 30

Elisha (biblical figure): PS 73; out-of-body experiences of, PV 16

Elixirs: EM 52-53; and alchemists, SI 6, *30*, 32; and Avicenna, SA 31; and William A. Ayton, SA 127-128; and Armand Barbault, SA 132-135; characteristics of, SA 44-45; effects of, SA 110, SI 34; and Jan Baptista van Helmont, SA 93; and immortality, SA 83, *103*, 110; and Albertus Magnus, SA 32; and Paracelsus, SI 32; purposes of, SA 30, SI 6, 95; recipes for, SI 30-32, 34; selling of, SI *95*; and Taoism, SI 34; and Wei Poyang, SI 34. *See also* Patent medicines; Philoso-

EGG. *Fragile protectors of life growing within, eggs are symbols of fertility and creation. Colored bands on this Tantric cosmic egg represent divine currents of male and female energy, from which all the universe was supposedly created.*

phers' stone

Elizabeth (queen of Bohemia): AW *54*

Elizabeth (queen of Spain): VP 18

Elizabeth I (queen of England): AW 102, CC 72-75, *76-77,* HN 12, ML 45, MW 22, MY 21, 39, PE 85, *88,* 106, PS 74, SA 86, VP 46, 47, 123, WW 7; and John Dee, SA 58, 59

Elizabeth II (queen of England): SI 111

Ella (dreamer): DD 138

Ellen (crisis apparition): PE 18-19,

20

Ellington, Duke: CC 81

Ellis, Havelock: DD 60, 107

Ellora (India): MW 93

Elusive Monster, The (Burton): MC 80-81

Elva (familiar): and Agnes Sampson, WW 7

Elwell, Dennis: CC 143, 145, 148, 152, 153-154

Elysian Fields: CD 126, UV 23. *See also* Afterlife

Embalming: SI *100*

Emblem of the Heavenly Sphere, An

(Collins): UV *73*

Embriaco, Guglielmo: MQ 121; Sacro Catino of, MQ 121-122, *125*

Emelyanov, Valery Nikolaevich: AW 86

Emerald: as Holy Grail, MQ 117

Emerald Table (Hermes Trismegistus): MA 61

Emerald tablet: SA 20

Emergence Ladder: TS *31*

Emergent evolutionists: MB 17. *See also* Evolution

Emerson, J. Norman: MQ *98;* and

psychometry, tests of, PP 123-127

Emerson, Ralph Waldo: PS 108, SE 58, 61-62, SS 27, 136, UV *81,* VP 75, 92; disciples of, SE 61

Emerson, Steven: PS 91

Emerson, Willis George: and hollow earth theory, MP 150

Emery, Douglas: MA 110-111

Emily (abductee): AE 121-123

Emlen, Stephen T.: and extrasensory perception in birds, PP 58

Emmerich, Sister Anne Catherine: and levitation, MM 117

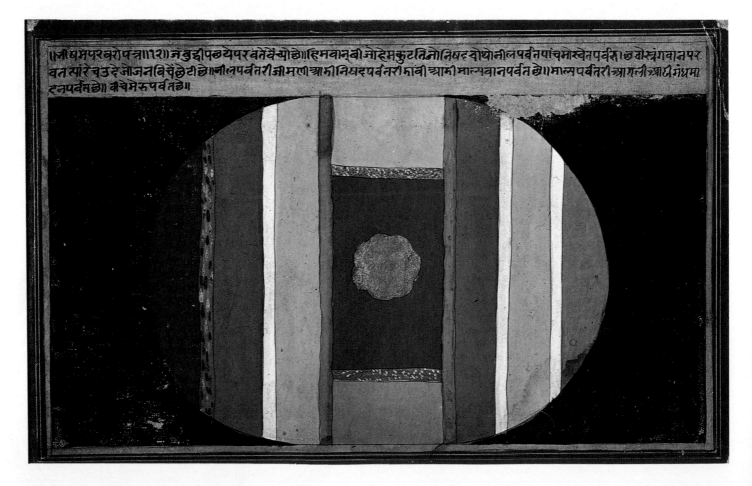

Emotions: and poltergeists, MM 41, 42, 48, 50, 51, 53; and psychokinesis, MM 61, 72

Empedocles: CC 23; and elements, SA 20, 26

Empiricism: SE 56, 57-58

Empusa: TN 110-111. *See also* Vampires

Encausse, Gerard: *See* Papus

Encounter (Escher): CD *22*

Endara, Guillermo: MA 6

Endive: WW *35*

Endocrinology: and Charles-Édouard Brown-Séquard, SI 58, 61

Endorphins: defined, MB 55; possible role in near-death experiences, PV 78

Endura: defined, WW 50

Energy circle: EE 65

Engels, Friedrich: CD 40

England: amulets in, MA *104;* cats in, MA 118; church archaeology, use of dowsing in, MQ *104-105;* crop circles in, EE *6-15;* dominoes in, VP 112; geomancy in, EE 32; Glastonbury sites, MQ *112-113, 116,* 123-124, 128; Merlin in, MQ 130; Rosicrucianism in, SA 86; sand paintings in, MA *14;* Scottish border, area of, MQ *132-133;* superstitions in, MA 118, 134, 135; wells in, EE 76; werewolves in, TN 78-79; and witches, WW *60-61,* 78-79, 80

English Chirological Society: VP 81

Enki (god): AE 94, 96, 97, UV 18-20

Enkidu (character in Gilgamesh epic): MQ 31

Enkidu (hominoid): MC 99-100

Enlightenment: MB 101, MY 41, 115, SI 18, 23, 99; and Buddhists, CD 99, *104,* TS 29, 37; and Hindus, TS 25, 29, 93; and Tantra, CD 69, 70; and women, CD 56. *See also* EM *index*

Enlightenment, Age of: EE 77, SE 56, WW 79

Enlil (god): AE 94-97, CC 17-21

Enmenduranna (Sumerian king): VP 9

Enneagram: UV *106*

Enoch (biblical figure): CC 113

Enquiry concerning Human Understanding, An (Hume): SE 57

Ensoulment: SE 138

Entelechy: SE 118

Entombment, The (Delvaux): DD *15*

Entropy: defined, TS 59

Enuma Anu Enlil (Anonymous): CC 8-9

Envy: CD *87*

Enzymes: SI 69

Eochu Muigmedon (king of Ireland): WW 29

EOM, St.: *See* Martin, Eddie Owens

Eos (goddess): SI 26

Eostre (goddess): MY 23, 30

Epcot Center: survey by, HN 128

Ephrata commune: MW 105, UV 60-61

Epic of Creation (Anonymous): AE 92-97

Epidaurus: DD 80

Epilepsy: EE 96, MB *46,* SA 64-65, SE 119; and abductions by aliens, AE 38, 110; causes of, AE 110; and corpus callosum, MB 45-47; and Wilder Penfield, MB 8, 59; and split-brain operations, MB 45-47; symptoms of, AE 38, 110; and Synchro-Energizer, MB 48; types of, AE 38

Epimenides: SI 97

Epinar Lafuente, Francisco: AW 112

Epiphany: MY 123

Epworth Rectory: HN *60;* and poltergeists, HN 60-61

Equatorium: CC 66

Equinox (journal): AW 147, 154

Equinoxes: ML 118; fall, ML *118,* MY 8, 9, *12-13,* 88, 123, WW 123; and Nazca lines of Peru, MP 112; spring, ML *118,* MY 8, 9, 23, 25, 87

Er: SE 45

Erasmus: PH 119, 122, SA 63

Eratosthenes: CC 29

Erech (Iraq): MW 133

Ere ibeji: MY *38*

Ereshkigal (goddess): WW 13. *See*

also Mother Goddess

Ergot: TN 94, WW *37;* as anesthetic, EE 100; and LSD, EE 100; and witches, EE 101. *See also* Hallucinogens

Er Grah: MW 88

Erickson, Milton H.: hypnosis research of, MM *98,* 123-124

Eric's Saga (Anonymous): ML *122,* 123

Eridu (city): AE 94

Eriksson, Thorvald: ML 124

Erik the Red: ML 123

Eris (goddess): VP 108

Ermacora, G. B.: DD 141, 143-144

Eros (god): TS 19-20

Eroticism: of vampires, TN 109, 134-136

Er Rif (Morocco): MW 65

Error-catastrophe theory: SI 66

Erskine, Thomas: PE 61-63

Ertel, Suitbert: CC 142

Erto, Pasquale: MY *135*

Erwin, William: DD 147

Erzulie (loa, voodoo spirit): CD 86

Erzulie Freda (voodoo spirit): MY 61

Esalen Institute: and Frederick Perls, DD 74. *See also* UV *index*

Esbats: defined, WW 107, 123, 131

Escape artists: PP 103

Eschenbach, Wolfram von: MQ 111-112, 114, 117-118, 124, 125, 127

Escher, Maurits Cornelis: artwork by, CD *19-22*

Eskimos: *See* Inuit

Esoteric Christianity: and Gorgei Ivanovitch Gurdjieff, UV 102; and Rudolph Steiner, UV 102, 114-115

Esoteric Section: AW 137, 140

ESP: *See* Extrasensory perception

Espionage: *See* Psi-warfare experiments *in* PS *index*

E.S.P. Laboratory: EE 25

Essay concerning Human Understanding (Locke): SE 56

Essays on Physiognomy (Lavater): VP 67, 69

Essence: defined, VP 98. *See also* Numerologists; Numerology

Essenes: UV 33-35

Estabrooks, George H.: and psy-

chic research, PP 49

Estebany, Oskar: PH *102-103,* 107

Estero (Florida): MW 105

Estonia: trees in, EE 77

E.T. (film): and alien visitors, UP *34-35*

Etak: ML *99*

E-temen-an-ki (ziggurat): UV 21

Eternal life: *See* Immortality

Eternal recurrence: TS 38

Ethelbert (king of Kent): EE 80

Ether: TS 54; as anesthetic, MB 104; and Albert Einstein, TS 55; and hallucinations, MB *105*

Ether drift: defined, TS 54

Ethical objectivism: defined, CD 127

Ethiopia: ML *map 62,* MW *6-7;* and Prester John, ML 62, 66

Ethiopians: SI 22

Ethnobotany: PH 19

Etruscans: astral body beliefs of, PV *18;* augury of, VP 33; and haruspicy, VP 34-35; and hepatoscopy, VP 32

Etteilla: VP 125-127

Ettinger, Rhea: SI *117*

Ettinger, Robert C. W.: and cryocapsule, SI *117;* and cryonic suspension, SI 113, 114-115, 115-116, 128; and death, SI 113-114; and Arthur Quaife, SI 116

Eucharist: SA 10

Euclid: CC 29

Eudemus (Aristotle): SE 46-49

Eugene III (pope): PH 20

Eugénie (empress of France): and Daniel Dunglas Home, SS 39, 40-*41;* and spiritualism, SS 22

Eugenius III (pope): ML 63

Euler, Leonhard: and hollow earth theory, MP 142

Eunuchs: SI 62

Euphrates River: CD 55

Eurhythmics: CD 69

Eurhythmy: UV 118

Euripides: UV 96

Europe: MW *maps 34-35, 52, 85,* 118

Eurylochus: and Circe, WW 20

Eurynome (demon): MA *94*

Eurynome (goddess): CD 23-24

Euryphamus: UV 28-30

Euskal-Herria: ML 31

39

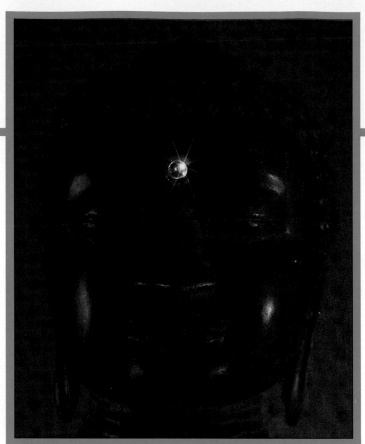

EYE. A gleaming, reflective gemstone marks the location of this Thai Buddha's third eye. In many cultures an eye, especially a third eye, is a symbol of enlightenment, reason, and all-seeing moral authority.

Eva C.: *See* C., Eva

Evans, Mr.: CC 107

Evans, Arthur: and Minoan civilization, MP 34

Evans, Christopher: DD 101-102

Evans, Colin: levitation of, MM *10*

Evans, Hilary: PE 112; and abductions by aliens, AE 102, 111; and Mrs. Adams, AE 106; and UFOs, AE 102, 105-106

Evans, Joan: and retrocognition, HN 50

Evans, Mary Ann: MB 89, PS 30

Eve (biblical figure): CD *57*, EE 95, MB 42, SA *51*, SI 13, TS *40*, UV *22;* and Adam, CD *27, 56, 59;* characteristics of, CD *56-58;* as common female ancestor, CD 60; and Eden, UV *7, 12-13;* and Gnostics, CD 59; and Mother Goddess, CD 59; and Muhammad, CD 58; and paradise myths, UV 20; and snakes, CD 14, 26, 56; and Tertullian, CD 58

Evening Girl: TS *31*

Evening Star (goddess): MA 68

Event at the Observatory (van Allsburg): AE *127*

Event horizon: defined, TS 73

Everest, Mount: EE 27

Everest Reconnaissance Expedition: MC 104

Everglades: MW 44-45, 47

Everglades mink: MW 44

Evergreens: EE 106. *See also* Trees

Evert, Chris: MA 128

"Evidence of Primary Perception in Plant Life" (Backster): EE 108

Evil: CD 79-82, 93, 94. *See also* Sins

Evil Age: MY 134

Evil eye: MW 119, MY 28; and amulets, MA *108;* and children, MA 122; defined, MA 11, 19; and Regina Dionisopoulos-Mass, MA 11, 12; and Georgia, MA 12; in Greece, MA 124-126; and Gypsies, MA 101; history of, MA 17, 121; in India, MA 127; in Italy, MA 122, 124, *136-137;* in Malta, MA 124; in Middle East, MA 127; in Morocco, MA 127; on Nisi, MA 11-13; and Angelina Perella, MA 122-124; protection against, MA 124, *127;* and superstitions, MA 121-126, 127; and the Tuareg, MA *8*

Evolution: EE 105; and Charles Darwin, MB 13, 14, ML 28, 29; and longevity, SI 22, 23; and mind, MB 13-14; and Alfred Russel Wallace, MB 14, 17

Evolution (Mondrian): AW *159*

Ewaipanoma (legendary headless tribe): MQ *29*

Ewen of the Little Head (ghost): PE *45*

Ewes: SI *65*

Exaltation: SA 55

Examination of a Witch (Matteson): WW *76-77*

Excalibur: ML 48

Excavations: *See* Archaeology

Exceptional Cancer Patients (ECaP): PH 127

Excommunications: of animals, TN 40; of Alice Kyteler, WW 55; of Petronilla de Meath, WW 55

Executions: *See* WW *index*

Executive ESP: PS 104-105, 107-108, 115, 130. *See also* Extrasensory perception; Intuition

Exeter (New Hampshire): and UFO sighting, UP 99-106, *100-101*

Existentialism: SE 69, 70

Exodus, Book of: Ark of the Covenant described in, MQ 46; golden calf in, MQ 48

Exon, Arthur E.: AE 84-85

Exon, J. James: and investigation of Rendlesham Forest UFO sighting, UP 136

Exorcism: CD 88, 89-*90*, 91, 92-93, HN *126-127*, MW 133, MY 59, 129, 131, PE 138, UV *140-141;* and Catholics, CD 33-34, 88, 90; and Clara Germana Celle, CD 77; decline of, CD 96; history of, HN 24

Exorcist, The (film): CD 16-17, 17-18

Exotic matter: AE 116

Expectation images: defined, PE 100

Experienced anomalous trauma (EAT): AE 34

Experience vs. logic: SA 34

Experimental physiology: SI 24

Experiment with Time, An (Dunne): DD 134, TS 123, VP 8

Explosion: MY *57*

Expressionists: UV 129

Externalization: defined, PV 39. *See also* Out-of-body experiences

Externsteine: MW 85, 88-90

Extrasensory perception (ESP): PP 24, SE 115; and animals, PP 57, *58-59;* Cleve Backster's research on, MM *74;* and Joseph A. Ball, PS 82; and boredom, MM 62; business applications of, PP 134-140; and decline effect, PP 53, 63; defined, MM 8, PV 108; description of, PP 16, 54, 58; and ganzfeld research, PP *68;* and hypnosis, PP *64-65;* near-death experiences compared with, PV 63; out-of-body experiences compared with, PV 36, 39, 40; and psychokinesis, MM 8; reincarnation compared with, PV 108; reproducing experiments of, PP 56; and J. B. Rhine, MM 56, 57-58, 61-62; and Bernard Rimland, MB 62; and savant syndrome, MB 7, 62; tests of, PP *51-52,* 53, 61-62, 63; types of, PP 16. *See also* Dermooptic vision; Executive ESP; Intuition; Psi phenomena; Psychokinesis; Telepathic dreams; PS *index*

Extra-Sensory Perception (Rhine): PP 54-56

Extraterrestrial Biological Entities (EBEs): *See* Aliens

Extraterrestrial Civilizations (Asimov): AE 115

Extraterrestrials: MW 42-43, 79; artwork about, ML *35-43;* and Australian Aborigines, ML 29-32; and Kiribati Islands, ML 97; and Sasquatch sightings, MC 120-123. *See also* Aliens

Extremely low frequency (ELF) waves: PS 86

Eyeless sight act: and Kuda Bux, PP 108-*109*

Eyelifts: SI *95. See also* Cosmetic surgery

Eye of Horus: MA 9

EyePhone: MB *130-131*

Eyes: MY *55,* 56

Eyos: MY 73

Eyrbyggia (Anonymous): WW 30

Eysenck, H. J.: CC 142, DD 135

Ezekiel (biblical figure): VP 10; visions of, AE 111-112, 123, MW 40, UP 12-*14, 15*

AE Alien Encounters; AW Ancient Wisdom and Secret Sects; CC Cosmic Connections; CD Cosmic Duality; DD Dreams and Dreaming; EE Earth Energies; EM Eastern Mysteries; HN Hauntings; MA Magical Arts; MB The Mind and Beyond; MC Mysterious Creatures; ML Mysterious Lands and Peoples; MM Mind over Matter; MP Mystic Places; MQ Mystic Quests; MW The Mysterious World;

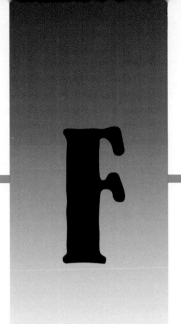

FOOT. *Because the foot keeps the body upright, it has been equated with the soul. Thus ancient Greeks apparently saw lameness as a sign of spiritual shortcoming. This footprint is thought especially holy; it is said to belong to Buddha.*

F, Lieutenant: and transformations, TN 23-24

Fabergé, Carl: amulets by, MA *108*

Fabian Society: AW 128, 140

Facelifts: SI *95. See also* Cosmetic surgery

Fadlallah (terrorist): PS 93

Faery Washing-Woman (ghost): PE 45

Fahrney, Delmer S.: and National Investigations Committee on Aerial Phenomena, UP 69

Fairies: AE *45,* MY 34, *100;* abduction of babies by, AE 43, *48-49;* characteristics of, AE 49; dances of, AE *50;* summoning of, MA 20

Fairlie, Henry: CD 96

Fairy Flag: MW 119, 120-121, *124*

Fairy Stone: MW 88

Fairy tales: CD 41, *43-47*

Faith healing: PH 16-17, 20, PS 95. *See also individual faith healers*

Fakirs: SI 99; on bed of nails, EM *32-33;* and Paul Brunton, EM 90; and Ormond McGill, EM 92; and self-mutilation, MM 108-112

Fall equinox: *See* Equinoxes

Fall from grace: CD 18-23

Falling: dreams of, DD *120-121*

"Fall of the House of Usher, The" (Poe): PE 93

Fall of the Rebel Angels, The (Breughel): MP *140-141*

Falmouth Bay: MC *36,* MW 75

False Faces: MY *124-125*

Famadihana: MY *52*

Fama Fraternitatis (Anonymous): AW 48, 49-50, 51, 53, SA 82-83, *85,* 86

Familiars: defined, MA 118, WW 107; and witches, WW 12, 14

Family (Schöpke): MB *66*

Family ghosts: *See* Crisis apparitions; Ghosts; Postmortem apparitions; *individual ghosts*

Fancher, Mollie: MB 87

Fanes (god): CC *21*

Fang-chung shu: EM 52. *See also* Sex

Fanjeaux, Roger-Isarn de: alleged reincarnation of, PV 101

Fanshawe, Lady Ann: PE 38

Fantastic Horse Cart (Chagall): DD *12*

Fantasy-prone personalities: AE 38, MB 90-92

Faraday, Ann: DD 121

Faraday, Michael: PE 113-114, SS *33;* levitation research of, MM 10-11; and table turning, SS 33

Farewell to Arms, A (Hemingway): PV 11, 58

Fargo (North Dakota): and UFO sighting, UP 44

Farming: EE 132-137. *See also* Biodynamic farming; Organic farming; Psychic farming; Rice farming

Farquhar, Walter: PE 40

Farr, Florence: AW 151, 153, 154, *155,* 156, SA 126

Farrow, Mia: EM *122*

Faruk, Erol A.: AE 76-78

Fasold, David: MQ 90, *91,* 92; Phantom Ark evidence interpreted by, MQ 92-93, *94*

Fate: SE 70

Fate (magazine): and Kenneth Arnold's UFO sighting, UP 39

Fate line: VP *58-59,* 85. *See also* Palmistry; Palmists

Father: as archetype, DD *84-85*

Father-of-all-the-turtles: MW 72

Father Sky: CD *11*

Fátima (Portugal): CD 120-121, MY 36, *93*

Fat Tuesday: MY *136-137*

Faust: CD 84, *85*

Faust (Goethe): CD 93, SA *68*

Faust, Johann: as magician, MA 45, 62

Faustus, Doctor: SI 30

Faustus of Byzantium: MQ 70

Fawcett, Lawrence: and investigations of UFOs, UP 128-129

Fawcett, Percy Harrison: MY 41; and Atlantis, search for, MP *25*

Fawkes, Guy: MY 98

Fay, Anna Eva (mentalist): fakery of, PP 106-107; mind-reading act of, PP 106-107

Faÿ, Bernard: AW *99*

Feast of Candles: WW 123

Feasts: of Shakers, UV 69, *70*

Februalia: MY 130

Feda (spirit guide): and Gladys Osborne Leonard, SS 88-90, *91*

Federation of American Scientists: CC 128, 129

Feichin, Saint: MY 127

Feifei: MC 100

Feilding, F. H. Everard: MM 15, SS 64; marriage of, MM 15, 18

Feinberg, Gerald: MM 29; and precognition, TS 120

Feininger, Lyonel: woodcut by, UV *128*

Feirefiz (character in *Parzifal*): MQ 111, 117

Feldstein, Sol: DD 147-148, 153

Feliciani, Lorenza: SA 102

Felidomancy: defined, VP 35

Fell, Barry: ML 131-134

Fellini, Federico: DD 38

Fellowship: UV 104

Feminism: and Wicca, WW 116-118

Feng bird: SA *108-109*

Feng Meng Leng: DD 23-24

Feng shui: MW 127-128, TS 35. *See also* Geomancy; EE *index*

Feral children: TN *56-69. See also* Gazelle-boys; Monkey-boys; Wolf-children

Feralia: MY 135

Ferdinand II (Holy Roman emperor): WW 92

Ferdinand III (Holy Roman emperor): MA 33, MY 126

Ferdinand of Tyrol (archduke): mirror of, MA *56-57*

Fergus (medieval romance): MQ 135

41

FISH. *Emblem of fertility and formative power, a fish is shown inside the womb of a creator-goddess on the seventh-century-BC Greek amphora below. In the ancient world, the seas were thought to give birth to fish in a supernatural process. To Christians, the fish is a symbol of Christ, who made his disciples "fishers of men." For early Christians, the outline of a fish scratched on a doorpost was a secret sign of refuge.*

Feriae Sementiva: MY 129

Fermi, Enrico: VP 28

Fernandez Gil de Terradillos, Jaime: AW 112

Fernando, Sammy: alleged previous incarnation of, PV 96-98. *See also* Sujith

Ferns: MY 56

Ferrets: black-footed, SI *113;* and witches, WW 12

Fertility: CD 49-50

Fertility cults: AW 13, ML *36-37*

Fertility festivals and rites: MY 32, *33,* 34, 37, 42, 43, 49, *50,* 51, *68-69,* 85, 123, 126, 129, 133

Fertility symbols: EE *22-23;* in India, EE 58; and mandrakes, EE 96; and mistletoe, EE 96; and Newgrange, EE 17-19; and Pimas, EE 76; and Sumerians, EE 76. *See also* Venus of Willendorf

Fesel, Heinrich: CC 134-135, 136

Festival of the Pottery Jar: *See* Kumbha Mela

Festus: and *strigae,* WW 23

Fetches: *See* Doubles

Fête de Gayant: MY *60*

Fête du Roi Potiron, La: MY 85

Fetishes: MA 82

Fetogia (alien): AE 124-126

Fetuses: DD *99,* SE *138,* SI *84;* brain cells of, SI 82-83

F.G. (percipient of postmortem apparition): PE 52

"Field of Being": defined, EM 122

Fifteen: in dice, VP 111

Fight-or-flight reaction: PH 126

Fig trees: in Cairo (Egypt), EE 77; and Christians, EE 77; and Muslims, EE 77; and Romans, EE 91; and Virgin Mary, EE 77. *See also* Trees

Fiji: burial rituals in, PE 53

Filipepi, Alessandro: *See* Botticelli, Sandro

Films: by Ingmar Bergman, DD *38;* and dreams, DD *38;* by Federico Fellini, DD 38; monsters in, MC 127-*137; Prophecy,* MC 136-137; *The Beast from 20,000 Fathoms,* MC 130-131; *The Fly,* MC 127, *132-133; Them!,* MC 128-129; *The Mutations,* MC 134-135; vampires in, TN 109, 136, *137*

Finch, Caleb E.: SI 22-23

Findhorn Foundation: and angel meditation, UV *145;* and attunement, UV *142-143,* 144; and Peter and Eileen Caddy, EE 133-135, UV 142, 143, 144; and farming, EE 133-134, *135-137;* herb garden of, EE *134;* and holism, UV 142; and Dorothy Maclean, EE 133, UV 142, 143, 144; and Lida Sims, UV 143; and David Spangler, EE 135-137, UV 143-144; theories of, EE *134-135;* and Ralph White, UV 144

Fingen: AW 18

Finger, Irene: *See* Hughes, Irene

Fingertips: VP *55. See also* Palmistry; Palmists

Finke, Allen: PS 47

Finland: vampires in, TN 113

Finnegans Wake (Joyce): TS 66

Finns: cosmogonies of, TS 19, 23

Finster, Howard: art by, UV *48-49*

Fire: MA 131; as dream symbol, DD *34;* and myths, DD 34

Fire, Johnny (John Lame Deer): MQ 10, 12, 15, 17

Fireballs: UP 46; mistaken for UFOs, UP *26*

Fire hand: VP *54, 63. See also* Palmistry; Palmists

Fire on the match: and Satya Sai Baba, EM 25, 58

Fires, alchemical: SA *57, 71, 72, 75, 76, 84, 106;* in laboratories, SA 35, *36-37, 38-39;* and Paracelsus, SA 79-80

Firestone: and Atlantis legend, MP 31-32

Fire walking: MM 102-105, *106, 107*

Firmicus Maternus, Julius: CC 49, 50

First Earth Battalion: PS 94

First-footers: MY 123, 128

First Fourth Norfolk: and disappearances, TS 131

First-fruits ceremonies: MY 65, 73, 94

First-husband rites: UV 80

First matter: *See* Prima materia

First Table of the Grail (ritual): MQ 119-120

First time: TS 36

Firth, Mary Violet (a.k.a. Dion Fortune): MA *62*

Fischer, Heinz: and hollow earth theory, MP 151

Fischer, Roland: MB 89

Fish: MY *128-129,* 132, *134;* divination with, VP *42;* rituals regarding, TN *11. See also* Bullheads; Salmon; Sea People

Fish, Leah Fox: SS *22, 34;* apartment of, SS *34;* and James Fenimore Cooper, SS 35; Corinthian Hall, demonstration of, SS 32-33; and Horace Greeley, SS 33, 35; hoaxes of, SS 21, 28, 32; and Washington Irving, SS 35; and Henry Wadsworth Longfellow, SS 35; materializations of, SS 53; and spiritualism, SS 21; table turning of, SS 32; and Daniel Underhill, SS 35; and John Greenleaf Whittier, SS 35

Fish, Marjorie: AE 29; and Hill abduction story, UP 84

Fishbough, William: PH 27, VP 22

Fisher, Martha: MA 126

Fisher King: as Grail King, MQ 114, 117; in grail legends, MQ *110,* 127

Fish falls: TS *135;* and Charles Hoy Fort, TS 134

Fish pig: MC *18, 19. See also* Sea serpents

Fisk, Jim: MY 40

Fitter, Richard: MC 76

Fitzgerald, Ella: CC 81

Fitzgerald, William: and Greta Alexander, PS 24, 25, 27; and Mary Cousett, PS 24, 25

Five: in dice, VP 110-111; in dominoes, VP 112; in numerology, VP 101, 108

Fix, William: and Great Pyramid, MP 67

Flade, Dietrich: and witch hunts, WW 69

Flags, prayer: CD *98*

Flamel, Nicholas: SI 12; and alchemy, SA 42, 46-47; background of, SA 45-46; and Cabala, SA 46; and Canches, SA 46; death of, SA 47; and Pernelle Flamel, SA 46, 47; longevity of, SA 42-43, 45, 47; and Marcel, SA 47; and philosophers' stone, SA 42, 45; religious beliefs of, SA 47; tombstone of, SA *44;* and transmutation, SA 47; and visions, SA 46

Flamel, Pernelle: and Nicholas Flamel, SA 46, 47

Flammarion, Camille: TS 120

Flanagan, G. Patrick: and pyramid power, MP 66

Flandrin, Jean: MA 49

Flashbacks: defined, MB 116

Flat Earth Society, map by: MW *14*

Flatland (Abbott): TS 136

Flaubert, Gustave: CC 88

FLEUR-DE-LIS. *Symbols of life in ancient Egypt, the fleurs-de-lis—"lily flowers"—seen here on the robe and canopy of France's Charles VII also represent the lily an angel supposedly presented to Clovis, first king of the Franks, at his baptism.*

Flauros (demon): MA *97*

Flaying: WW *83*

Flegenheimer, Arthur: *See* Schultz, Dutch

Flegetanis (Jewish astronomer): Wolfram's citation of, MQ 117

Fleming, Abraham: PE 123

Fleming, Alice Kipling: SS 95; automatic writing of, SS 92, 97; and Frederic W. H. Myers, SS 93, 94, 95, 96

Fleming, Ian: CC 136, PS *69;* and dowsing, PS 68, 69; and Nazis, PS 68; and submarines, PS 68, 69

Flesh offering: MQ 12

Flies, The (Sartre): SE 71

Flight 19: TS 132-133; and Bermuda Triangle, MP *42-43*

Flight simulator: MB 126-*127*

Flinders Petrie, William Matthew: and Great Pyramid, measurements of, MP 62-63

Float: MY 136-137

Flood stories: ML 33-34, MQ 64, 67, 72, *78,* MW 15; and American Indians, EE 74; and baptism, EE 74-76; in Gilgamesh epic, MQ 32, 78, 80, 92; and

Greeks, EE 74; and ice ages, EE 74; and Minoans, EE 74; Nineveh, tablet from, MQ *80;* and Noah, EE 74; and Sumerians, EE 74; and Ur excavation, MQ 64, *75*

Flora (goddess): MY 33, 35

Floralia: MY 33

Floral Oracle: VP 40

Florence (Italy): MW 119, *122-123*

Florence, William: AW 108

Florida panther: MW 44

Floromancy: defined, VP 35

Flournoy, Theodore: SS 85

Flower, Joan: as witch, WW 61

Flower, Margaret: and cats, WW 12; as witch, WW 61

Flower, Philippa: and cats, WW 12

Flower Remedies: PH *114*-115

Flowers: divination with, VP 40

Flowers, Jay C.: MB 70

F.L.Q. (Front de Liberation du Quebec): hideout of, PS *42;* and James Jasper Cross, PS 41, 43; and Pierre LaPorte, PS 41, 43

Fludd, Robert (a.k.a. Robertus de Fluctibus): AW 58-*60,* CC 109, MA 50, SA *90-92;* and alchemy, SA 66, 86, 87, 90; background

of, SA 86-87; and blood circulation, SA 92; creation theory of, AW *60-61;* death of, SA 92; engraving by, SA *67;* and William Harvey, SA 92; and Paracelsus, SA 86, 87, 90; and perpetual-motion machines, SA 94; as physician, SA 87-90, 92; and prima materia, SA 90; Rosicrucianism, SA 86, 90, *91*

Fly, The (film): MC 127, *132-133*

Fly agaric: EE 102, TN 36. *See also* Hallucinogens

Flying: dreams of, DD *126-127;* of witches, WW 43, 54

Flying Dutchman (ghost ship): HN 75, MP *40-41,* MY 53, SI 26

Flying ointments: and hallucinations, WW 31, 32, 33; herbs in, WW *32-33*

Flying Saucer (Highstein): AE *128-129*

Flying saucers: *See* UFOs

Flying Saucers (Jung): AE 111, 114

Flying Saucers (Menzel): UP 56

Flying Saucers from Outer Space (Keyhoe): UP 56

Flying Saucer Vision, The (Michell): MP 98-99

Fodor, Jerry: SE 128

Fodor, Nandor: SS 117; and ghosts, HN 95-98, 115-116, 117, 118; and International Institute for Psychical Research, HN 115

Fogarty, Robert S.: UV 137-138

Fogel, Henry: MW *108*

Foggin, Cyril: MW 20

Folk magic: *See* Low magic

Folk medicine: MW 127, 128-129, PH 38-43, *39, 40-41, 42-43;* and bloodwort, SI 59, 60; and garlic, SI 78; in Hawaii, MA 87-90; in Soviet Union, MA 8. *See also specific types of folk medicine*

Folk tales: Dracula in, TN 105; vampires in, TN 111, 112, 134

Follini, Stefania: and biological rhythms, TS 78, 79, 88; isolation chamber of, TS 78, *80*

Foltz, Charlie: AE *18;* and abduction by aliens, AE 17-20; drawing by, AE *19*

Fonda, Claudia: and Lady Wonder, PP 110

Fonda, Jane: SI *94*

Fontanne, Lynn: MA 128-129

Fontes, Olavo T.: and Villas Boas abduction story, UP *85*

Fontinalia: MY 40

Foods, magical: SI 6, 36

Foo fighters: MW 40. *See also* Fireballs; UFOs

Fool card: VP *124, 131. See also* Tarot; Tarot readers

Foote, James: PS 82

Footprints: of Abominable Snowman, MC 100, *102,* 103, 104, 105-106; of Almas, MC *108-109;* of Bigfoot, MC 99, *117,* 119, *120, 124, 125;* of Mokele-mbembe, MC *93;* plantigrade, MC 103-104; of Sasquatch, MC 116

Forbes, J. C.: MC 72

Forbes Air Force Base (Kansas): and UFO sighting, UP 66

Forbidden City, of Beijing (China): EE 33, EM 10, MW 127, *128*

Force feedback steering wheel: MB 135

Forces Occultes (film): AW 99

Ford, Arthur: SS *121*

Ford, Gerald: and UFO possibilities, UP 109, 110

Ford, Henry: CC 84, EE 105, UV 85; reincarnation beliefs of, PV *105*

Forensic graphology: VP 93. *See also* Graphologists and graphology; Psychographology

Forest Dwellers: ML 14

Forest People: TN 51. *See also* Animals

Forgione, Father Pio: stigmata of, MM *115*

Forlì (Italy): MW 53, 59

Formalization: defined, MB 67

Forman, Joan: MW 22

Forman, Simon: MY 122

Fornario, Netta: AW 155

Forster, George: ML 86

Fort, Charles Hoy: TS *134;* and fish falls, TS 134; and paranormal events, TS 133-134; and "rains," TS 134; and teleportation, TS 134; and UFOs, TS 134

Fortenberry, William: and Norfolk UFO sighting, UP *52*

Fortgibu: TS 120-121

43

FOX. Known in most of the world as a living symbol of sly behavior, the fox in Japanese lore is a cunning thief who assumes human form to seduce human beings such as this samurai and steal their life essence.

Fort Knox (Kentucky): and UFO sighting, UP 41

Fort Lesley J. McNair: MW 27, 28-29

Fort Mojave Twins (Arizona): MP 134

Fortuna (goddess): CD 35, TS 20

Fortune, Dion (a.k.a. Mary Violet Firth): AW 152, 155, MA 62

Fortune, Reo: CD 61, 62

Fortune, wheel of: CD 35

Fortune cookies: VP 26-27

Fortunetellers: MA 9, PP 97, TS 95; Gypsies, VP 128; Lucerito, VP 38-39; Macanese as, TS 94-95; the Dogon, VP 36. See also Fortunetelling; specific types of fortunetellers and fortunetelling

Fortunetelling: and J. P. Morgan, PS 111; and Nazis, PS 59; tools of, CC 27; and Cornelius Vanderbilt, PS 111. See also Precognition

Forwald, Haakon: criticism of, MM 67-70; psychokinesis research of, MM 66-70, 67, 71

Foulkes, David: DD 149

Foundation for Research on the Nature of Man: PE 128

Foundry: ML 22

Fountain Grove: UV 78-79

Fountain of youth: EE 76, SI 6-7, 24; German woodcut satirizing, MQ 34; and Herodotus, SI 24; and Ponce de León and, MQ 34, 39-40, SI 24-25

Four: in dice, VP 110, 111; in dominoes, VP 112; in numerology, VP 101, 108

Four Brothers Ziemassvētki (gods): MY 119

Four Corners: MW 79, 80

"Four examinations": PH 57-58

"Four Ghost Stories" (Dickens): PE 60

Fourier, Charles: UV 82

4'33" (musical composition; Cage): EM 137

Fourteen: in dice, VP 111

Fourth dimension: AE 121

Fourth world: defined, EE 43

Fowl: divination with, VP 42

Fowler, A. J.: and Levelland UFO sighting, UP 68

Fowler, Jessie: VP 76

Fowler, Lorenzo: as phrenologist, VP 76, 78, 80, 81

Fowler, Lydia Folger: as phrenologist, VP 78, 81

Fowler, Orson: house designed by, VP 79; as phrenologist, VP 76, 78, 80, 81

Fowler, Raymond E.: AE 27; and Exeter UFO sighting, UP 103; and Charlie Foltz, AE 17; and Chuck Rak, AE 17; scar of, AE 34; and Jack Weiner, AE 17, 27; and Jim Weiner, AE 16, 17

Fowler & Wells: VP 79; employees of, VP 78

Fox, Mrs.: and hauntings, HN 87

Fox, Kate and Maggie: MY 26; Corinthian Hall, demonstration of, SS 32-33; death of, SS 37; decline of, SS 35; and Horace Greeley, SS 33, 35; hoaxes of, SS 21, 28, 32; and Daniel Dunglas Home, SS 42; home of, SS 20; and H. D. Jencken, SS 35; and Elisha Kent Kane, SS 35; and "spirit" rappings, SS 20-21; and Spiritualism, HN 130

Fox, Oliver: See Calloway, Hugh G.

Fox, Selena: MA 131, WW 100-101; and Circle Sanctuary, WW 112, 125-126; and U.S. Army Handbook for Chaplains, WW 99; and World Council of Churches, WW 126

Fox Broadcasting Company: and werewolves, TN 72, 91

Foxe, John: CC 74

Foxes: divination with, VP 37; transformations of, TN 45

Foxglove: MA 99, WW 31, 36

Foxhollow School: MW 27

Fox squirrel, mangrove: MW 44

Fox tribe: SI 114

Foyster, Adelaide: HN 66

Foyster, Lionel: HN 66; and poltergeists, HN 66

Foyster, Marianne: HN 66; messages addressed to, HN 65, 66

Fra, The (magazine): UV 85

France: dominoes in, VP 112; Inquisition in, WW 58-62; Montségur sites in, MQ 118, 124, 127, 128, 129; superstitions in, MA 134; trees in, EE 77; vampires in, TN 126-127; werewolves in, TN 82-87, 88; witch hunts in, WW 58-62, 66-69, 79, 80; witch trials in, WW 55-56, 57-58, 80; wolves in, TN 76, 80, 81

France, Anatole: UV 39

France, Marie de: TN 79

Francé, Raoul: EE 107

Francis, Elizabeth: and Sathan, WW 12; witch trial of, WW 12

Francis, Jerome: PH 88

Francis II (Holy Roman emperor): AW 93

Francis II (king of France): VP 18; tomb of, CD 68-69

Franciscan monk: PS 97

Franciscans of Medmenham: MW 121-125

Francis Ferdinand (archduke of Austria): DD 141, MY 57

Francis of Assisi, Saint: CD 116, 118, MY 86, PS 97; stigmata of, MM 114

Franco, Francisco: AW 112

Frank, Jerome: PH 122

Frankenstein, Victor: MB 88

Frankenstein (M. Shelley): DD 117, MY 30, TN 133

Franklin, Benjamin: AW 73, 80, 89, 90, EE 70, MY 30, PH 90, SI 97; hypnosis research of, MM 92; purported reincarnation beliefs of, PV 104

Fraser, James: MC 71

Frater Albertus: See Riedel, Albert

Fraternitatis Rosae Crucis: AW 68-70

Fraternity of the Inner Light: AW 152, MA 62

Fraunces, Samuel: AW 82

Frazer, James: MA 9; and Delphic oracle, EE 29; and trees, EE 91

Frederick (duke of Württemberg): SA 58

Frederick II (emperor of Germany): and Conrad of Marburg, WW 51; and heresies, WW 51

Frederick II (king of Denmark): CC 94, SA 82

Frederick II (king of Prussia): AW 92

Frederick III (Holy Roman emperor): SI 133

AE Alien Encounters; AW Ancient Wisdom and Secret Sects; CC Cosmic Connections; CD Cosmic Duality; DD Dreams and Dreaming; EE Earth Energies; EM Eastern Mysteries; HN Hauntings; MA Magical Arts; MB The Mind and Beyond; MC Mysterious Creatures; ML Mysterious Lands and Peoples; MM Mind over Matter; MP Mystic Places; MQ Mystic Quests; MW The Mysterious World;

FEATHER. *For the ancient Egyptians, the feather was an attribute of Maat (below), goddess of law and righteousness, and a symbol of truth. It served as the standard against which people's hearts would be measured on Judgment Day.*

Frederick V (king of Bohemia): AW *54*

Frederick Barbarossa, (Holy Roman emperor and king of Germany): ML 64

Frederickson, Oscar: MW 49

Free association: DD 72-73; and Sigmund Freud, DD 60-61, 65

Freeborn, Frances: and poltergeists, HN 52-54, 55

Freeman, Paul: MC 126

Freemasons: CC 101, EE 25, MY 55. *See also* Masons; *specific Freemasons and lodges; AW index*

Freer, Ada Goodrich: HN *129;* and ghosts, HN 122-124, 125-128

Free radicals: defined, SI 69, 78; effects of, SI 69; and garlic, SI 78; and Denham Harman, SI 69, 75; and quinones, SI 75

Free Soul movement: beliefs of, PP 96

Free will: CD 26, 35, SE 70, 71

Fréminville, Chevalier de: MW 87, 88

French Revolution: AW 104-105

French revolutionary government: and calendars, TS 104, *105*

Freud, Amalie: DD *60*

Freud, Anna: CD 60, DD *61, 67*

Freud, Hermann: DD 64

Freud, Jacob: DD *60*

Freud, Sigmund: CC 81, *126-127,* CD 60-61, EE 50, MA 62, MB *22,* MY 64, PE 85, SE 115-117, 119, VP 81; and alchemy, SA 129; and creativity, MB 89; and Herbert Silberer, SA 129; hypnosis research of, MM 94; and Carl Jung, SA 129-130; and Wolf Messing, PP 113; and mind, MB 22; mystical beliefs of, PP *26;* and parapsychology, PP 21; and telepathy, MB 22; theory of the unconscious, and near-death experiences, PV 63; and the unconscious, MB 20, TN 31. *See also* DD *index*

Frew, Karen: MC 39-40

Frew, Robert: MC 39-40

Frey (god): CD *54*

Freya (goddess): MA 28, MY *121,* VP 108; and cats, WW 12; char-

acteristics of, WW 28; and Holda, WW 27; transformations of, WW 28

Friedman, Stanton: AE 81

Friedrich I (king of Prussia): SA 88

Friedrichsbad: SI 133, *134-135*

Froben, Johann: PH 119-122, SA 63

Frogs: and cryoprotectants, SI 109; frozen-hibernator phenomenon of, SI 107; mask of, TN *18;* and regeneration, SI 82; and witches, WW 12

Fromm, Erich: and Teitaro Suzuki, EM 137; and Zen Buddhism, EM 142

From the Earth to the Moon (Verne): VP 27, *28*

Frontal cortex: MB 51

Front de Liberation du Quebec: *See* F.L.Q.

Frost: MY 28

Frost, K. T.: and Minoan civilization, MP 34-35

Frost Giants, Norse: ML 25

Frozen-hibernator phenomenon: SI 107-109. *See also* Hibernation

Fruitlands: UV 82-84

Frum, John: MW 131

Fry, Daniel W.: and encounter with aliens, UP *73*

Fuchi (goddess): EM 20

Fuchs von Dornheim, Johann Georg: *See* Johann Georg II

Fudo Myo-o (god): EM 57

Fu Hsi: VP 117, *118*

Fuji, Mount (Japan): EM 20-21, MW 93

Fulcanelli (alchemist): CD 70, MW 127; and alchemy, SA 119-123; and Jacques Bergier, SA 120-123; and Eugene Canseliet, SA 120, 123-124

Fuld, William: SS 107

''Full Court Dress'' incident (crisis apparition): PE 30-31

Fuller, John G.: and Exeter UFO sighting, UP 102-104

Fuller, John Frederick Charles: AW *147;* artwork by, AW *147*

Fuller, Margaret: PH *97,* UV 80

Fuller, R. Buckminster: CC 83, PS 108-109, UV *150;* architecture by, UV *150-151*

Fuller, Willard: PH *96-97*

Fumigants: MA 22-23

Functionalism: defined, SE 125

Fundamentalists: UV 60

Fundamentalist views: as motive for biblical quests, MQ 41, 63

Fund for UFO Research (FUFOR): UP 131; background of, AE 24; and Bruce Maccabee, AE 71; and Elizabeth Slater, AE 38; and Edward Walters, AE 70

Funeral mask: SI *100*

Funerals: SE 33, *34-41*

Funk, Michelle: SI *106*

Furfur (demon): MA *97*

Furies: CD 24

Furnaces: *See* Fires, alchemical

Furness, Thomas: MB 129, 137; and virtual reality, MB 129, 137

Furry Dance: MY *35*

Furstenberg, Diane von: PS 128

Fuseli, Henry: painting by, CD *84*

Futch, Max: and Project Blue Book, UP 56

Futility (Robertson): PP 28, 30

Futterer, Antonia: MQ 46

Futurists: UV 121, 122, 124; art by, UV *122, 123. See also* Seers; *specific types of divination and seers*

Fu Xi: PH 47

Fyes: *See* Doubles

45

G

G. (crisis apparition): PE 32-33

G., Tessa: TS 127-128

Gabalis, Count de: CC 98

Gabbard, Glen: and out-of-body-
experience theory, PV 44

Gabriel (archangel): CD *132*, DD
39, *47*, 48, 50, 53, 55, EE 32, MY
60

Gackenbach, Jayne: DD 113

Gacy, John: TN 130

Gaea (goddess): WW 15

Gaffney, Matthew: MC 28

Gage, Phineas: head injury of, MB
51

Gahmuret (character in *Parzifal*):
MQ 111

Gaia (goddess): CD 24, EE 22, 120.
See also Mother Goddess

Gaia (theory): characteristics of,
EE 19; and James Lovelock, EE
118-119, 119-124, *122-123*, 137

Gairy, Eric: AE *82*

Galahad (character in Arthurian
legend): MQ *119*, 120, *121*, 123

Galanopoulos, A. G.: MP 35-36

Galaxy 4C41.17: TS *61*

Galaxy M-87: TS 63

Galaxy NGC-1097: TS *65*

Galen: CD 63, PH 16, 85, SI 24;
and Andrew Jackson Davis, VP
22; and Robert Fludd, SA 87; as
palmist, VP 81; and Paracelsus,
SA 64, 65; and George Starkey,
SA 96, 97

Galilei, Galileo: CC 91, 93-94, *100,*
101, SE 50, TS 51-53

Gall, Franz Joseph: VP 69-72, *75*

Galle, Johann Gottfried: CC 46

Gallic Wars (Caesar): MP 88

Gallipoli (Turkey): MW 34; battlefield of, PE *136-137*

Galvanometers: EE 107

Gama, Vasco da: ML 66

Gamblers: MA 129-130

*AE Alien Encounters; AW Ancient Wisdom and Secret Sects; CC Cosmic Connections; CD Cosmic Duality; DD Dreams and Dreaming; EE Earth
Energies; EM Eastern Mysteries; HN Hauntings; MA Magical Arts; MB The Mind and Beyond; MC Mysterious Creatures; ML Mysterious Lands and
Peoples; MM Mind over Matter; MP Mystic Places; MQ Mystic Quests; MW The Mysterious World;*

GOAT. *Associated in Classical times with the lust and potency of satyrs and the god Pan, the goat later became a diabolical symbol—filthy, foul smelling, and black, as depicted in this Goya painting of witches worshiping Satan in the guise of a goat.*

Gamelan: EM 67
Game of Life: UV *141*
Gamow, George: TS *60*
Gander (Newfoundland): and UFO sighting, UP 48-49
Gandhi, Mahatma: AW 142, CC 86, EM 87
Gandillon, George: TN 85-86
Gandillon, Pierre: TN 85-86
Ganesh (god): MY *83*
Ganesha Chaturihi: MY 83
Ganges River: EM *18-19,* MY 125, TS 11, *92-93;* and Hindus, SI 16, *17*-18, *21;* and Shiva, TS 11
Gann, W. D.: PS 118-119
Ganzfeld research: PP 68-69
Garber, Johann: art by, MB *66*
Garcia Gonzalez, Aaron: MW 32
Garden of Eden: CD 126, EE 95, MW *6-7,* UV *7, 12-13;* and paradise myths, UV 18, 20
Gardens: EM *110-111;* and paradise myths, UV *6-15*
Gardner, Frank: PH 129
Gardner, Gerald Brosseau: MW 119, MY *53,* WW 102, 103-107, *109,* 110 112, *113*
Gardner, Joshua: HN 94-95
Gardner, Marshall B.: MP 148-151
Gardner, Martin: MM 31-32, MP 63, 72, PH 36
Gardner, Mary Ann: AE 82
Gardner, Norma: AE 83
Garfield, James: ghost of, HN 107
Garfield, Patricia: DD 110
Gargas Cave: MW 91
Gargoyle Photograph: MC 78, *80,* 90. *See also* Loch Ness monster
Gargoyles: MA *92, 93*
Garinet, Jules: MA 48
Garland King: MY *46*
Garlic: MY 81, 105, SI *78-79*
Garnier, Apolline: TN 84-85
Garnier, Gilles: TN 84-85
Garrett, Eileen: MW 27, MY *22,* PE *71,* PP *88-89,* SS 84-85, TS *114,* VP 42-43, 45, 52; abilities of, PP 84-91; and clairvoyance, TS 114, 115; as medium, HN 116-118, *119,* 130-133, PP 87-88; and New Age movement, PP 101
Garuda (god): AE *44,* EM 144
Garwell, Barbara: DD 137-138, 139

Gary (psychic): PS 91-92
Gary, Romain: VP 25
Garzoni, Tommaso: TN 73
Gasparetto, Luiz Antonio: automatic painting of, SS 138-*139*
Gas sylvestre: SA 93
Gastromancy: defined, VP 45. *See also* Scryers; Scrying
Gate of Remembrance, The (Bond): ML 61, PP 119
Gate of the Moon: UV *55*
Gateway of the Sun: MW *82*
Gathas: CD 26
Gattefossé, René-Maurice: PH 112
Gaudi, Antonio: UV *116;* architecture by, UV *116-117*
Gaudry, Albert: MW 51-53
Gauld, Alan: PV 112, SE 92-93, 94, 98, 100; and poltergeists, HN 55
Gaulos: defined, ML 119
Gauquelin, Françoise and Michel: CC 140-142
Gauric (seer): VP 18
Gautama, Siddhartha: *See* Buddha
Gawai Dayak: MY 50
Gawain (character in Arthurian legend): ML 49, MQ 114, 117, 120
Gawain, Shakti: MB *124,* MM 126; and visualization, MB 123
Gayer, John: MY 94
Gayer, Stan: AE 63-65
Gazelle-boys: TN *64-65,* 66
Gazi, Ahmed ibn Ibrahim al-: MW 102
Gazzaniga, Michael: MB 47-49, 97, SE 120
Gde, Jero: EE 132
Ge (goddess): VP 10
Geb (god): TS 20
Geber (a.k.a. Abu Musa Jabir ibn Hayyan): MW 133, 134, SA 29, *30,* 34
Geckos: SI 35
Gehauds, Jean: WW 83
Gehenna: *See* Hell
Geiges, Leif: poltergeist photographs by, MM *42-43,* 44
Gein, Eddie: TN 130
Geissler, Clara: torture of, WW 72
Gelede: MY 72
Geller, Margaret: MM *26*
Geller, Uri (mentalist): PP 142; and John Aoki, PS 126; and clairvoy-

ance, PS 124; and ESP, business applications of, PP 140; and map dowsing, PS *122,* 124-126; and mining, PP 140, PS *122-123;* powers of, PP 103, *116,* 117; and psychokinesis, PS 124; and Soviet psychic abilities, PP 140; and John Tishman, PS 126. *See also* MM *index*
Gelli, Licio: AW 112
Gelomancy: defined, VP 35
Gematria: MA 54-55, VP 105. *See also* Numerologists; Numerology
Gemini (zodiac sign): CC 36, *82,* 139, MY 38
Gemology: defined, VP 52
Genaba, Edgi: MC 110
Gender: CD 49, 60-62
General Electric High Voltage Laboratory: ML 23
Generator: PH 88
Genesis, Book of: CD 6, SI 12, 13; Noah's Ark in, MQ 63, 64, 72
Genesis West: SI 65
Genetic experimentation: and aliens, AE 35-36, 41, 96-97, 118. *See also* Breeding program
Genetics: CD 109, 128
Genghis Khan: ML 66
Genie: MC *59*
Gennadius: DD 107
Gennaro, Joseph F., Jr.: MC 25
Genoa (Italy): Sacro Catino in, MQ 122
Genovese, Kitty: CD 110-111
Gensheng, Pang: MC 113-114
Gentleman, Wally: AE 104
Geodesic dome: UV *150-151*
Geoffrey de Charny: MQ 102, 122-123
Geoffrey of Monmouth (British historian): MQ 133, 135, 136; and Arthur, ML 48, 49; and Merlin, ML 48; and Stonehenge, MP 82, 84
Geoffrey the Elder: SA 100
Geoglyphics: MP 111, 121-122. *See also specific geoglyphics*
Geomancers: compass of, TS 35
Geomancy: EE 30-32, 33, VP 42. *See also* Feng shui
Geometry: and Pythagoras, TS 43
Geophysical theory of UFOs: UP 134

George (savant): MB *60;* and savant syndrome, MB 38-39, 62
George, Saint: MC 8-9, MY *31*
George I (king of England): and Peter of Hamelin, TN 59
George III (king of England): MW 22
George V (king of England): MC 71, MY 53, SI 26
Georges Bank: MW 27
Georgia (evil-eye practitioner): MA 12
Georgia Mental Health Institute: DD 102
Georgian Wicca: WW 112
Gerald of Wales: TN 79
Geraniums: divination with, VP 40
Gerard (archbishop): CC 62-64
Gerbert of Aurillac: CC 55
German Astrological Society: CC 130
Germanic peoples: WW 25
Germanicus (Roman emperor): MW 104
Germanium: SI 75
Germans: and directions, TS *30*
Germany: amulets in, MA *105, 106, 109;* Inquisition in, WW 62-64; Rosicrucianism in, SA 83, 85-86; trees in, EE 90; vampires in, TN 127; werewolves in, TN 70-73, *72;* witch hunts in, WW 64, 65, 69-78, 79, 80; witch trials in, WW 64, 66, 80, 90-92; wolves in, TN *81*
Gerocomy: SI 38-39, *40,* 60
Gerontologists: SI 6, 22, 41, 46, 66
Gervase of Tilbury: TN 78-79
Gesell, Arnold: TN 63-64
Geshi: MY 55
Gessner (peasant): MA 62, 63
Gestalt therapy: DD 74
Gestapo: PS 66. *See also* Nazis
Gestures of approach: EE 30
Geteit: MW 65, 66-67
Gethsemane: EE 79
Geulincx, Arnold: CD 40
Gévaudan, Beast of: MW 53, 56-59, TN *88*
Ggantija: CD *52,* 54
Ghadiali, Dinshah: PH 108
Ghanta Karna: MY *67*
Ghats: EM *18-19,* HN *127*
Ghose, Aurobindo: *See* Sri Auro-

47

bindo

Ghosh, Mukunda Lal: *See* Yogananda, Paramahansa

Ghost Dance: DD 30, MW 110-111, 113, *114-115*

Ghost dress: MW *114-115*

Ghost Mountain: ML 67

Ghost of the Outback: MW 34, 38

Ghost rockets: UP *27*

Ghosts: MY *70*, 96, 97, 120, 121, 124, 133, PE 24, *34*; arm, PE *43*; bird, PE *44*; cats, PE *41*, 121; dogs, PE 32, 121-123; in Japan, PE *34*, 73-*81*; tiger, PE *62. See also* Hauntings; Poltergeists; *individual ghosts and types of ghosts; HN index*

Ghost ships: HN 75-*83, 76-83*

Giannini, F. Amadeo: and hollow earth theory, MP 152

Giant eel: MW 75

Giant ground sloth: MW 50-*51. See also* Su monster

Giant octopus: MW 75

Giant Rock Space Conventions: UP 78

Giants: ML 24-*26*, 96, 97, 102

Giant squid: MW 71, *73*

Gibbon: MW 62

Gibraltar: MW *map* 15, VP 40; Strait of, MP 16, 20, 36

Gibson, Edmond: PE 49-50

Giddings, T. D.: MW 106

Gideon (biblical figure): DD 37

Gifford, Robert Swain: SE 91, 92; and obsession, PP *43*

"Gift drawings": SS *25*, UV *71-73*

Gigantopithecus: MC 114

Gilbert, Humphrey: MY 39

Gilby, Mrs.: and hauntings, HN 28

Gilgamesh (epic): CD 84, MC 99-100, ML 34, MQ 31-32, VP 9; Assyrian copy, MQ *80;* Assyrian depiction, MQ *33;* flood story, ML 34, MQ 32, 78, 80, 92; and

hollow earth theory, MP 138-139

Gill, Rev. William Booth: and encounter with aliens, UP 70-73

Gilles clan: MC 90

Gill Hall: MW 19, 24-25

Gilson, Étienne-Henry: SE 51

Gimlin, Bob: MC 98-99

Ginsberg, Allen: EM 137-138

Ginseng: EE 99-100, MA 99, PH *59*, SI 67, 75

Gion: MY *62*

Giorgio (ghost): HN 103, 104

Giorgione: painting by, AW *87*

Giotto: painting by, MM *114*

Girden, Edward: MM 62

Girdle: MY 130, SI *95;* of werewolves, TN 95, *98-99*

Giza (Egypt): MP *map* 58-59, 62, MW *99;* construction on, MP 66-67; and Great Pyramid, MP 47; and Great Sphinx, MP *56;* pyramids of, MP *52-53*

"Glacial milk": SI *53*

Glaciers: EE 64. *See also* Ice ages

Gladden, Rose: and werewolves, TN 91

Gladstone, William: AW 141

Glamis Castle: PE 37

Gland grafting: SI *61*, 62

Gland injections: SI 58, 61

Glanvill, Rev. Joseph: PE 22; book frontispiece by, HN *57;* and poltergeists, HN 56-57, 58

Glass, Philip: AE 112

Glasses: microlaser scanner, MB *132-133*

Glass Island: ML 52-56

Glass Pavilion: UV *126*

Glastonbury (England): ML 52-56, MQ 123, 128, MW 85; bowl found near, MQ *124;* Chalice Well, MQ *116*, 123-124

Glastonbury Abbey: ML *60;* and Arthur, ML 44; and Frederick

Bligh Bond, ML 59-63, PP 118-120; excavations at, ML 56-63; and Henry VIII, ML 59, 61; spirits of, PP 119-120, *120-122*

Glastonbury Thorn: EE 88-89, MY 83. *See also* Trees

Glastonbury Tor: ML *54-55*, 56; and Arthur, ML 56, MQ *112-113*, 123

Glastonbury zodiac: ML 44-45, *46*

Glauber's salt: MA 61

Glen Canyon Dam: EE 48

Glendale, Battle of: MW 121

Glider: ML 32, *33*

Global warming: EE 19

Globe: gilded, MW *124-125;* water-filled, as Holy Grail, MQ 124-125

Globe Theater: PE *48*

Globus: defined, CD 31

Gloucester Harbor: MW 75

"Glove anesthesia": PH 139

Gluttony: CD *87*

Glycerol: SI 124

Glymour, Clark: PH 118

Glynn, Carr: MW 22

Glyph: CC 38, 125, MA *41*, MY *63*

Gnomon: defined, TS 44

Gnomonic expansion: TS 44, *48*, *49*

Gnosis: defined, CD 59

Gnostic Gospels: SA 23

Gnostics and Gnosticism: AW 20, 23, 24, 28, EM 72, MA 54, 60-61, VP 124, SA 23, 25. *See also CD index*

Goat: MY *119*

Goat gland treatment: SI 63-64

Gobi Desert: MW 59

Goby, John: as exorcist, HN 137

God: SA *91;* as architect, TS *38;* as chemist, SA 80; names of, MA *38, 39, 40*

God, City of: UV *30, 39*

Goddess worship: *See* Mother

Goddess

Godfrey, Edmundbury: TS 122

Godfrey, William, Jr.: ML 131

Godiva, Lady: MY *66*

God-kings: Khmer, ML 70

Godley, John: and dreams, TS 128

Godman Air Force Base (Kentucky): UP 41

Gods: in Egypt, MA 51-54; gender of, CD 11; Hindu, SI *16. See also* Deities

Gods from Outer Space (von Däniken): MP 113-116

Goebbels, Joseph: CC 135, PS 62

Goethe, Johann Wolfgang von: CD 93, MY 71, *131*, PE *90*, 117, SA 68; out-of-body experiences of, PV 15; and plants, EE 104-105; and Rudolf Steiner, UV 113, 114, 115

Goetheanum: UV *114-115*

Gog (giant): MW *6-7*

Gogh, Vincent van: CC 80

Gogol, Nikolai: PE 93

Goibniu (god): MQ 109

Goidin, Jean-Patrice: MP 46

Golconda (India): MW 127

Gold: CD 36, 37, EM 53; and alchemists, SI 32, 34; Colombian artifact, MQ *28-29;* disk, MA *57;* Irish torque, MQ *136;* King Solomon's, search for, MQ 41-43, *42;* Treasure of Priam, MQ 36. *See also SA index*

Gold, Palace of: *See* Palace of Gold

Goldblatt, David: MB *77*

Golden Age: MY 134, UV 23-25, 28

Golden Bough, The (Frazer): MA 9

Golden calf: MQ *48*

Golden Dawn: *See* Hermetic Order of the Golden Dawn

Golden Dawn Tarot: VP *136-137. See also* Tarot; Tarot readers

AE Alien Encounters; AW Ancient Wisdom and Secret Sects; CC Cosmic Connections; CD Cosmic Duality; DD Dreams and Dreaming; EE Earth Energies; EM Eastern Mysteries; HN Hauntings; MA Magical Arts; MB The Mind and Beyond; MC Mysterious Creatures; ML Mysterious Lands and Peoples; MM Mind over Matter; MP Mystic Places; MQ Mystic Quests; MW The Mysterious World;

GRAIL. Sir Galahad kneels outside a chapel containing the Holy Grail (left). Synonymous with sacred quests since Christ's time, the grail was said to be made by angels from a magical emerald that came off Satan's crown during his fall.

GARDEN. Lovers hand in hand approach the beautiful, idyllic, and peaceful place represented by the garden in this Renaissance work. In alchemy, the garden could be attained only by great efforts and the surmounting of severe difficulties.

Golden Lane: MW 119, SA 60, *62*

Golden mean: TS 47

Golden section: TS *47,* 49

Golden spiral: TS *49*

Golding, Mrs.: and poltergeists, HN 70

Golding, William: EE 120

Gold King (El Dorado): MQ *29*

''Goldmaking'' (Kleopatra): SA *28*

Goldman, Emma: CC 83

Goldsmith, Oliver: and séances, HN 64

Goldwater, Barry: AE 85-88, UP *69*

Goldwyn, Sam: CC 84

Golgotha: EE 27

Goliath (biblical figure): ML 24

Goligher, Kathleen: SS 104

Golok nomads: EM *80-81*

Gomchen: defined, EM 75, 81

Gomorrah and Sodom (biblical sites): ML 33; search for, MQ 43

Gonsalvus, Petrus: TN *82;* children of, TN *83*

Gooch, Stan: MB 41

Good, Sarah: WW 74, 75

Goodall, Jane: EE 69

Good Friday: MY 28

Good ladies of the night: WW 27

Goodly Company, A (Riley): SE 112; artworks from, SE *110-113*

Goodrich-Freer, Ada: VP 52

Gopa (wife of Buddha): DD 39

Gopi: UV *8*

Gorbachev, Mikhail: CC 6

Gordon, Cyrus: ML 128, 135, 136-137

Gordon, Richard: SI 78-80

Gordon, Stan: AE 86

Gorgets: MY *76-77*

Gorilla, mountain: MC *21*

Gorman, George: and Fargo UFO sighting, UP 44

Goshalas: defined, EM 39

Gospel of Thomas (Gnostic text): CD 70

''Gossip about Ghosts'' (Tweedie): PE 28; illustrations from, PE *28-29*

Gothic literature: TN 132; vampires in, TN 132-134, 136

Gotland: MW 85

Gottlieb, Michael: PH 135

Goudsmit, Samuel: UP 55-56

Gould, Rupert: MC 71

Gould, Stephen Jay: CD 62

Gould, Sylvester C.: AW 70

Goulert, Simon: TN 73

Goya, Francisco de: etching by, MB *73;* paintings by, TN *39,* TS *21,* WW *52-53, 56-57*

Grabousa (island; Greece): MQ *54-55*

Graceland: MY 124

Grad, Bernard: PH *102,* 103

Graham, Mrs.: and hauntings, HN 34-35

Graham, Sylvester: UV 77

Graham, Thelma: HN 34, 35

Graham Potentializer: MB 48

Grail: *See* Holy Grail

Grail King (character in *Parzifal*): MQ 114, 117

Grail Messenger (character in *Parzifal*): MQ 114, 117

Gramatica: MB *59*

Grandfather paradox: TS 71

Grandfather Spirit: MQ *14-15*

Grandier, Urbain: MY *105,* WW *48*

Grand Menhir Brise, Le: MW 88

Grand unified theory: TS 63

Granny March's Day: MY 18

Grans, Hans: TN 130

Grant, Allan: photographs by, HN *21*

Grant, Arthur: MC 69

Grant, Ulysses S.: PP 18-20

Graphologists and graphology: Aristotle, VP 92; Alfred Binet, VP 92; defined, VP 66, 86; forensic, VP 93; Jean-Hippolyte Michon, VP 92; techniques, VP 93-*97;* Gloria Weiss, VP 96-97. *See also* Psychography

Grasshof, Carl van (a.k.a. Max Heindel): AW 68

Grateful Dead: EM 125

Grattan, Harry: PS 126

Gratuitous grace: defined, MB 106

''Grave, The'' (Blair): SE 49

Gravediggers: MA 20, TN *117*

Graves: MY *120*

Graves, Robert: CC 84, WW 105, and Doreen Valiente, WW 107; and Wicca, WW 102-104

Gravity: and Albert Einstein, TS 58

Gray, Alonzo: VP 75-78

Gray, Glen: and aliens, UP 129

Gray, Hugh: MC 67; Loch Ness monster photograph by, MC 69

Gray Goose Corporation: and pseudo-UFOs, UP *45*

Gray Ladies: MW 19, 22-24

Great Awakening: UV 60

Great Britain: MW *maps 18,* 34-35; crop circles in, AE 75. *See also* Britain; MQ *index*

Great Buddha of Kamakura: EM *22-23*

Great Cypress Swamp: MW *48*

Great Depression: MY 97

Great Disappointment: UV 57

Great Eastern (ship): HN *78-79*

Great Enclosure: ML *64-65, 66*

Greater bird of paradise: EM *94*

Greater magic: *See* High magic

Great God with Praying Women (rock painting): ML *36-37*

Great Hippostyle Hall: MW 100

Great house (Norse): ML 125-126

Great Houses (Anasazi): MW 80

Great Martian God (rock painting): ML *36*

Great Mother: *See* Mother Goddess

Great Mystery Power: MQ *14-15*

Great Pyramid of Cheops: MW 99. *See also* MP *index*

Greatrakes, Valentine: PH 87

Great Rift Valley: MW 65, *66*

Great Rite: WW 104

Great Serpent Mound (Ohio): MP 122, 123, MW 79; legend of, MP *124-125;* psychic episode at, MP 123-126

Great Soul Trial: SE 15-20, 71

Great Sphinx: MP 56, 66, *67*

Great Spirit: EE 87

Great Temple of Amen: MW 100-*101*

Great Triangle (Peru): MP *129*

Great Wall of China: EE *34,* 35

''Great work'': defined, SA 45

Great Zimbabwe: ML *64, 65, 68,* MW 99, MY 83

Greaves, John: MP 51, *54*

Greece: dice in, VP 110; evil eye in, MA 124-126; fire in, MA 131; fire walking in, MM 105; haruspicy in, VP 34, 35; mythology in, VP 108; palmistry in, VP 81; seers in, VP 10-14; vampires in, TN *110-111, 112-113, 134*

Greeks, ancient: DD 22, 29-37, 80, MB 93, ML 17, SA 19, UV 22-23; and afterlife, CD 126; and beliefs about doubles, PE 85; and cellular therapy, SI 65; cosmogonies of, TS 19-20, 23; and eternal recurrence, TS 38; and floods, EE 74, 76; and hell, CD 84; and Hyperboreans, SI 39; and mandrakes, EE 96, MA 99; and Mother Goddess, EE 29, WW 17; and Noah's Ark, MQ 70; and numbers, TS 45; and oceans, EE 72-74; and oracles, EE 54; and philosophy, TS 38; rejuvenation story, MQ *35;* and sacred places, TS 6; and sacrifices, TS 37; and snakes, CD 14; and space, TS 38; and sundials, TS 107; and time, TS 38; Troy, description of, MQ 36; Ulysses, voyage of, MQ *49-61;* vessels, divine, MQ 109; and water, SI 131; and water clocks, TS 107; and wells, EE 76; and zero, TS 29

49

GRIFFIN. A composite creature, the griffin symbolizes guardianship—its eagle half over the heavens, its lion half over the earth. In this emblem of a medieval Italian bankers' guild, it is shown in a common role as a sentinel over gold or treasure.

Greeley, Horace: SS 33, 35

Green, Alyce: MM 112, PH 138

Green, Celia: PE 95-97; and out-of-body-experience research, PV 33-35

Green, Clay: PP 104

Green, Elmer: PH *136*, 138; biofeedback research of, MM 124-125; self-mutilation research of, MM *109*, 112

Green, Gabriel: and aliens, UP *79*

Green, John: Sasquatch research of, MC 116, 117, 118-119

Green corn dance: MY 58

Green Dragon Tavern: AW 74, *75*, 76

Greene, George Jefferson: MQ 85-86

Greene, Graham: DD 132

Greene, Liz: Tarot cards by, VP *140-141*

Greenhouse effect: defined, EE 66

Green Lady (ghost): HN 8

Greenland: ML 123

Greenlander: TS *85*

Greenlanders' Saga (Anonymous): ML 123-125

Green River Killer: TN 130

Greenstein, Joseph L.: MB 96

Greenwell, Richard: MC *91-92*, 95

Greenwood, Barry: UP 128-129

Greenwood, Jane: MW 55-56

Gregorian calendar: MY 83

Gregory IX (pope): WW 50, 51

Gregory XIII (pope): TS 104, *105*

Gregory the Great (saint and pope): CD 130, MY 21

Gregson, W. H.: HN 68

Grendel: MC 99-100

Grenier, Jean: TN 87; as werewolf, TN 86

Grey, Lady Jane: PE 106, 109

Gribbin, John: TS 117; and precognition, TS 117-118

Grief (Saint-Gaudens): HN *112-113*

Grieve, Donald W.: MC 124

Griffins: MC 7, *14-15*

Griffith, D. W.: CC 90

Griffiths (crisis apparition percipient): PE 33

Griffiths, Gwyn: ML 127

Griggs, Dr.: and witches, WW 73

Grillone (Italy): MW 75

Grimes, J. Stanley: PH 20, 27

Grimoire: See Book of Shadows

Grimoire of Honorius, The (Pope Honorius III): MA 45, 49

Grimorium Verum (Anonymous): MA 93, 99

Grim Reaper: SE *50*

Gris-gris: and voodoo, MA *80-81*, 82

Grissom, Gus: AE 62

Gropius, Walter: UV *129*

Grosseteste, Robert: CC 59

Grosso, Michael: SE 139

Groundhog Day: MY 130

Ground ivy: WW *36*

Ground Saucer Watch, Inc.: AE 105, UP 138-139, 140

Ground sloth, giant: MW *50-51*. *See also* Su monster

Group PK: MM 25

Groveland Fountain Stone: UV *69*

Grover, Margaret: as witch, WW 80

Growth factors: SI 82

Gruber, Elmar: PS 87

Gruhn, Ruth: CD 50

Grünewald, Matthias: art by, MB *91*

Grünwedel, Albert: MQ 27

Gryla the Ogre: MY 118

Guaita, Stanislas de: VP 127

Guanabara Bay: MW 75

Guarayo Indians: SE 60

Guardian angel: AE *48*. *See also* Angels

Guardian Angels Day: MY 90

Guardian of the Threshold (Steiner): UV *119*

Guardian of the Waste Land (Crowley): AW *123*

Guardian spirits: MW 127

Guarico, Luca: CC 69

Guatavita, Lake (Colombia): MQ 29; artifact found near, MQ 28-29

Guazzo, Francesco-Maria: WW 44, 45, 46; woodcuts by, WW *44-46*

Gudmundsson, Ludvik: SE 99

Guell, Eusebio: UV 116

Guell Park: UV *116-117*

Guglielmo Embriaco: MQ 121; Sacro Catino, MQ 121-122, 125

Guild of Physicians: PH 87

Guild of Saint George: UV 35

Guillotin, Joseph Ignace: PH 90

Guillot of Tudela: MQ 117

Guinevere (character in Arthurian legend): MQ 111, 120, ML 48, 56-59

Guiot (Kyot) der Provenzal: MQ 117

Guirdham, Arthur: PV 101

Guising: MY 97

Gujeswari (goddess): MY 104

Gujeswari Jatra: MY 104

Gulf Breeze (Florida): UFOs in, AE 65-75, *69*, *74*, *75*

Gulf Stream: ML 120

Gulielmus Monachus: ML 61

Gulika: defined, SA 127

Gulliver's Travels (Swift): CC 109, SI 26

Gundella (witch): MA 117

Gundestrup cauldron: images from, MQ *130*, *133*, *135*, *136-137*

Gunnbjorn (explorer): ML 123

Gunpowder: SA 34

Gunpowder Plot: PE 109

Gunung Kawi: EM 63

Guoxing, Zhou: MC 113, 114

Guppy, Mrs. Samuel: SS 53-54

Gurdjieff, Georgei Ivanovitch: EM 85, MB 100-101, 104, 112. *See also* UV *index*

Gurdjieff, Ivan: UV 105

Gurdon, J. C.: MP 83

Gur Khan: ML 63

Gurls, Karl: ML 21

Gurnemanz (character in *Parzifal*): MQ 111-112

Gurney, Edmund: PE 21, 24, *25*, SS 71, *78*; ghost research of, PE 23, 31, 47; and hauntings, HN 28; out-of-body-experience research of, PV 19; and Henry Sidgwick, SS 73, 78; and sisters, death of, SS *78-79*; as spirit guide, SS 81, 92

Gurus: defined, EM 118; and Kumbha Mela, SI 19, *20*

Gustavus II (king of Sweden): CC 92

Gustenhover (alchemist): SA 60-61

Guth, Alan: TS 70; and big bang theory, TS 61, 67

Gutheil, Emil: DD 121, 127, 129

Gutowski, Ace: PS 128

Guth, Emil: DD 121, 127, 129

Gwenddolau (Celtic king): MQ 133

Gwrach-y-rhibyn: PE *42*

Gwydion (god): ML 49

Gwynn ap Nudd (king of fairies): ML 56

Gyatso, Tendzin: *See* Dalai Lamas

Gymnastics: and alchemy, SA 106, *107*

Gyoja: defined, EM 58

Gypsies: MA 100-102, ML *31*, MW 119, VP 87-91, *128*

Gyromancy: defined, VP 35

AE *Alien Encounters*; AW *Ancient Wisdom and Secret Sects*; CC *Cosmic Connections*; CD *Cosmic Duality*; DD *Dreams and Dreaming*; EE *Earth Energies*; EM *Eastern Mysteries*; HN *Hauntings*; MA *Magical Arts*; MB *The Mind and Beyond*; MC *Mysterious Creatures*; ML *Mysterious Lands and Peoples*; MM *Mind over Matter*; MP *Mystic Places*; MQ *Mystic Quests*; MW *The Mysterious World*;

HEAD. The head of a Celtic goddess forms the handle of this old Irish bowl; to the Celts the head was the seat of the soul, and it represented the essence of their religion, as the cross does in Christianity.

H

H, Mr.: as werewolf, TN 91

Ha'amonga of Maui: ML 97

Haarmann, Fritz: TN 127, 129-130

Habakkuk (biblical figure): VP 10

Hablik, Wenzel: architecture by, UV *127*; painting by, UV *120*

Hades: *See* Hell

Hades (god): CC 46, *47*, MY 86

Hades, Halls of: site associated with, MQ *57*

Hadrian (Roman emperor): CC 35

Haeckel, Ernst Heinrich: ML 29; and Lemuria, MP 26, *28*

Hagemayer, Curt: MM 50

Haggard, H. Rider: DD 131, *143*, ML 68, MQ 41, MY 60, PE 32

Hagopian, George: MQ 80-81, 90

Hag's taper: defined, WW 38

Hag stones: EE 57

Hahnemann, Samuel: PH 120, *121*

Haida: culture of, TN 6; mask of, CD *32-33*; totem poles of, TN *6-7*

Haigh, John George: TN *131*; as vampire, TN 130

Haines, Richard F.: AE 66

Hair: SI *92-93*. *See also* Baldness

Hair (musical): CC *144-145*, MY 104

Hair-growth stimulators: SI *89, 93*

Haiti: MW 113; transformations in, TN 24-25; voodoo in, CD 86, MA 80, 81, 82-83, 84

Hajj: MY 90-91; defined, EE 52

Halberds: ML 129

Halcyon days: MY 119

Halcyon House: HN *111*

Haldeman, Philip: SS 148

Hale, Virginia: and UFO sighting, UP *103*

Halici, Mehmed Ali: MB 53

Hall, Edward T.: TS 97

Hall, Fergus: Tarot cards by, VP *134-135*

Hall, G. Stanley: and psychic research, PP 48

Hall, Manly P.: Atlantis and pyramids, relationship of, MP 67

Hall, Richard: AE 85, 116; and abductions by aliens, AE 85

Hall, Robert L.: and hysterical contagion theory, UP 123

Hall, Trevor H.: MM 116, SS 37, 42

Halley, Edmond: and magnetic fields, MP 139; and twin earth theory, MP 139, *142;* and UFO sighting, UP 15

Hall-Heroult process: ML 22

Hall of Supreme Harmony: MW 128

Halloween: MY 81, 96-97, 98, WW 43

Hallucinations: PE 31-32, SE *126-127;* and ether, MB *105;* and Roland Fischer, MB 89; and flying ointments, WW 31, 32, 33; ghosts as, HN 30; and hallucinogens, MB 104, 106; near-death experiences compared to, PV 58, 62, 72, 77, 78; and psi experiences, PE 35; and psychiatry, PE 101; and Sasquatch, MC 120-123; and UFOs, MC 120-123; as visions, MB 71. *See also* Auditory hallucinations; Hypnagogic hallucinations

Hallucinogens: EM 138; and Richard Alpert, MB 112, 115, 116; and CIA, MB 104; effects of, MB 115-117; and hallucinations, MB 104, 106; and Timothy Leary, MB 107-115, 116; and near-death experiences, PV 78; and out-of-body experiences, PV 16; and psychic powers, PP 75, 80; and psychoses, MB 104; and shamans, MB 108; and transformations, TN 46-47; types of, MB 104. *See also specific hallucinogens*

Hallvard: and berserkers, TN 37

Halomancy: defined, VP 35

Halos: MB 29, ML *40-43*

Halsydrus pontoppidani: sightings of, MC 40-43. *See also* Sea serpents

Halt, Charles I.: and Rendlesham Forest UFO sighting, UP 132,

51

MY The Mystical Year; PE Phantom Encounters; PH Powers of Healing; PP Psychic Powers; PS The Psychics; PV Psychic Voyages; SA Secrets of the Alchemists; SE Search for the Soul; SI Search for Immortality; SS Spirit Summonings; TN Transformations; TS Time and Space; UP The UFO Phenomenon; UV Utopian Visions; VP Visions and Prophecies; WW Witches and Witchcraft

HAND. A symbol of protection in many cultures, hands such as this version of a talisman known as the Hand of Fatima are believed to ward off the evil eye. The stone in its center strengthens the effect, reflecting the evil back to its source.

136

Ham, Keith: *See* Kirtananda

Hambling, Horace S. (medium): SE *98*

Hameau: and retrocognition, HN *48-49. See also* Petit Trianon; Versailles

Hamilton, Alexander: and UFO sighting, UP 23

Hamlet (Shakespeare): PE 48, SE 68

Hamman: SI 114

Hammerhead bat: MW 70. *See also* Bats

Hammer of Witches, The (Kramer and Sprenger): *See Malleus Maleficarum*

Hammid, Hella: MQ *100,* PS 81, 83; and remote viewing, PP *62, 67;* sketch by, MQ *101;* structures psychically detected by, MQ 100, *101, 102, 103*

Hammurabi, Code of: WW 62

Hamon, Count Louis le Warner de (a.k.a. Cheiro): as palmist, VP 64-65, 66, 81-85, *84;* psychic predictions of, PP 28; salon of, VP *84*

Hanau Eepe: *See* Long Ears

Hanau Momoko: *See* Short Ears

Hancock, John: AW 73, *74,* 77

Hand, Robert: PS *121*

Hand, Wayland: MA 8

Handbook for Chaplains (U.S. Army): WW 99, 113-114

Handfasting: WW *136, 137;* and brooms, WW 19; defined, WW 123, 127

"Hand healing": *See* Laying on of hands

Handicapped persons: and virtual reality, MB *135*

Hand of glory: MA 92, *104*

Handparting: defined, WW 136

Handwriting analysis: *See* Graphologists and graphology; Psychographology

Han dynasty: EE 36

Hannibal: DD 40, MY 27

Hanno: ML 119

Hannover Vampire: *See* Haarmann, Fritz

Hansel, C. E. M.: MM 70

Hansen, Edwin: AE 55

Hansen, Frank: MC 111

Hanukkah: MY 121

Hanuman (god): EM 144

Hanuman Dhoka: MY *130*

Hanussen, Erik Jan: PS *60-61*

Han Xiangzi: SA *113*

Haoles: *See* Whites

Haoma: EE *97*

Hapgood, Charles: ML 135

Happerfield, C.: PE 59

Haraldsson, Eriendur: and near-death-experience research, PV 62-63

Harappa: ML 20

Harary, Keith: PS 113, 115, 116-117, SE 88-89; and Delphi Associates, PS 113, 116; and ESP, PP 136-140, PS 113-115, 116; experiments on, PV 41-42, 44; and Iran hostage crisis, PS 91; out-of-body experiences of, PV *40,* 41-42; and precognition, PS 116-117; and remote viewing, PP *62;* and stock market, PS 113, 115, 116-117; and Russell Targ, PS 113-115

Harder, James A.: and investigation of UFOs, UP 117-118

Hardrada, Harald: MW 121

Hardwar (India): SI 16

Hardy, Ralph: ghost photograph by, HN 27

"Hare Krishna Mantra" (song): EM 125

Hare Krishna movement: EM 122-130, *127;* characteristics of, EM 125, 127; and A. C. Bhaktivedanta Swami Prabhupada, EM 124, 127

Harford, John (postmortem apparition): PE 59

Hargreaves, Gerald: and opera about Atlantis, MP *32-33*

Haribodhini Ekadasi: MY 91

Haridas: EM 40; live burial of, SI 99-100, 101

Haring, Andrea: MW 28

Haring, Keith: art by: AE *134*

Har Karkom (mesa; Israel): MQ *44-45*

Harlow, Alison: WW 122-124

Harman, Denham: and free radicals, SI 69, 75

Harmonic Convergence: CC *146-147,* EE 65, MY 69

Harmonic-periodics: SA 117

Harmony: and Pythagoreans, TS 47, 49

Harmony Society: UV 57, 61, 62; and millennialists, UV 63

Harner, Michael: MW 115

Harner, Robert W.: and Great Serpent, MP 123-126

Harpies: MC 58. *See also* Human-beasts

Harpist: TS *22*

Harris, Lady Frieda: Tarot cards by, VP *144-145*

Harris, Melvin: PV 115

Harris, Steve: AE 63-65

Harris, Susan: PS 86

Harris, Thomas Lake: and Fountain Grove, UV *78-79*

Harrison, George: EM 125

Harrison, Jane Ellen: WW 17; and Mother Goddess, WW 17

Harrowing of Hell (Faust): MA 62, 63

Hart, Carl, Jr.: and Lubbock UFO sighting, UP *50-51*

Hart, Hornell: PE 35

Hart Fell (mountain; Scotland): MQ *134-135*

Hartfell Spa (Scotland): MQ *134*

Hartmann, Ernest: DD 102-106

Hartmann, Franz: PE 93

Hartnoll, Mrs.: PE 41

Harto, James S. (pseud. Chandra): and thought reading, PP *106*

Hartsoeker, Niklaas: engraving by, SA 69

Harun ar-Rashid: SA 29

Haruspices: Soudinos, VP 35; Spurinna Vestricius, VP 35. *See also* Haruspicy

Haruspicy: Assyrian, VP 34-35; and augury, VP 35; Babylonian, VP 34-35; defined, VP 34; Etruscan, VP 34-35; Greek, VP 34, 35; Nepalese, VP *33;* Roman, VP 34, 35

Harvard University: EM 138; Richard Alpert at, MB 115; Timothy Leary at, MB 107, 112-115

Harvest celebrations: ML 116, 134-135, MY 23, 39, 50, 65, 66, 67, 72, 73, 81, 88, 89, 91, 102, 119, 122, 129, *132-133. See also* Agricultural rituals; First-fruits ceremonies

Harvester kachina: MA *46-47*

Harvests: CD 11

AE Alien Encounters; AW Ancient Wisdom and Secret Sects; CC Cosmic Connections; CD Cosmic Duality; DD Dreams and Dreaming; EE Earth Energies; EM Eastern Mysteries; HN Hauntings; MA Magical Arts; MB The Mind and Beyond; MC Mysterious Creatures; ML Mysterious Lands and Peoples; MM Mind over Matter; MP Mystic Places; MQ Mystic Quests; MW The Mysterious World;

Harvey, Andrew: EM 97-98

Harvey, Moses: MC 23

Harvey, William: MA 63, SE 118, *119,* SI 14-15; and circulation, SA 64; and Robert Fludd, SA 92; and Great Pyramid, MP 54

Harz Mountains: MY 32

Hasan-i Sabbah: AW *32, 33*

Hasdai ibn-Shaprut: CC 55

Hasler, H. G.: MC 76

Hasted, John: metal bending research of, MM 33, 86

Hatchet: WW *82-83*

Hatha-yoga: EM 121. *See also* Yoga

Hatshepsut (queen of Egypt): MW 100, SA 17

Hatzic Rock: MW 76-77, 79, *81*

Hauffe, Friederike: HN 130; and poltergeists, HN 129-130

Haught, Warren: and Roswell UFO sighting, UP 39

Haunting apparitions: *See* Ghosts

Hauntings: MW *maps* 18, 26, 34-35; characteristics of, HN 21, 24, 55, 86, PE 111-113, 114, 115, 119; crisis apparitions compared with, PE 111, 119; defined, PE 19; history of, HN 24-25; percentage of persons experiencing, HN 25; postmortem apparitions compared with, PE 111, 119; theories about, HN 30-32. *See also* Demons; Ghosts; Poltergeists; *individual hauntings*

Haupt, Albertine: levitation of, MM 118

Haus der Künstler: MB *64-65;* and Leo Navratil, MB 65; and outsider art, MB 63; symbol of, MB 69

Hauser, Johann: art by, MB *68-69*

Haussay, Chevalier de: PH 90

Haussibut (demon): and la Cordière, WW 57

Havasu Canyon: EE *44-45*

Havasupai Indians: EE 44

Hawaii: MW 93, 96-99, 127; annexation of, MA 85; folk medicine in, MA 87-90; *kahuna ana'anas* in, MA 84-86; spirits in, MA 86-87; volcanoes in, EE 67

Hawes, A. G. S.: MA 86

Hawk-headed man: MC *59. See also* Human-beasts

Hawking, Stephen: CC 148, TS *62, 63;* and big bang theory, TS 62; and black holes, TS 63, 64; and grand unified theory, TS 63; and Roger Penrose, TS 63; and wormholes, TS 70

Hawkins, Gerald S.: and Nazca lines of Peru, MP 119; and Stonehenge, MP 92, 94

Hawk Maiden: MY 118

Hawley, Robert: MB 82

Hawthorn: MY 57

Hawthorne, Nathaniel: UV 81-82, VP 86

Hawtrey, Charles: MA 129

Hay, Louise L.: PH *134, 135*

Hayden, Father: HN 123, 125; as exorcist, HN 137

Hayes, Rutherford B.: UV 77

Hayflick, Leonard: SI 22; and cells, SI 71

Haymarket Theatre: and ghosts, HN 31

''Hayrides'': PH *134,135*

Haywood, James: and witches, WW 80

Head: in Celtic myth, MQ 110

Head crusher: WW *85*

Headdresses: MY *123*

Headhunting: SE 21

Headless horseman: PE *45*

Headless tribe: legendary, MQ *29*

Head line: VP *58-59,* 85. *See also* Palmistry; Palmists

Headpiece: WW *121*

Heads, shrinking of: MW 113, 117-119

Headwork: PS 94

Healers: *See* Shamans

Healing: SS 27, 132; herbs for, WW *36-37;* rituals, and trees, EE 91-92; and touch, PS *95-103*

Healing sanctuary: PH 33

Health line: VP 58-59, 85. *See also* Palmistry; Palmists

Hearers: defined, CD 31

Hearing: sense of, MB 55

Hearn, Mrs. Joe: ML 135

Hearne, Keith: DD 113; and lucid dreams, PP 66

Hearst, Patricia: MB *98-99;* and Dorothy Allison, PS 43, 44; disappearance of, and clairvoyance, PP 132; kidnapping of, PS 43, 44

Hearst, Randolph: PS 44

Heart disease: herbs for, WW *36*

Heart line: VP *58-59,* 85. *See also* Palmistry; Palmists

Heart transplants: SI *83*

Heartwork: PS 94

Heaven: AE *52-53,* CD 18. *See also* Afterlife; Nirvana; Paradise

Hebard, Arthur: psychokinesis research of, MM 75

Hebb, Donald: MB 19

Hebrew, words written in: MW *133*

Hebrew alphabet: MA *39;* and talismans, MA 39, 41

Hebrews: and America, discovery of, ML 117; and cosmos, workings of, ML 24; harvest celebration of, ML 116, 134-135

Hecate (goddess): CC 39. *See also* Isis

Hecate (witch): WW 17-19, *21, 23,* 32

Heceta House: MW *27,* 30

Heckler, Richard: PH *106*

Hédervári, Peter: and Minoan civilization, MP 36

Hedgehogs: and witches, WW 12

Hedin, Sven: EM *82, 83*

Heel Stone: MY *11*

Heflin, Rex: and alleged UFO photograph, UP *88*

Hegel, Georg Wilhelm Friedrich: CD 40, SE 59-61

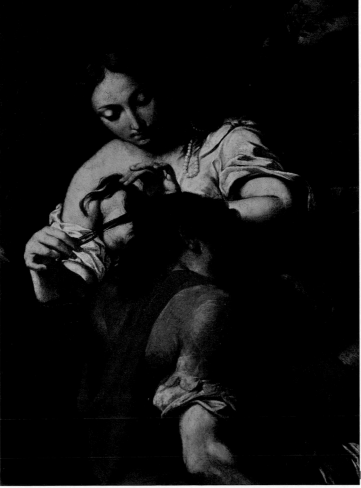

53

Heiaus: MW 96

Heilige Linien: MW 90

Heim, Albert von St. Gallen: near-death experience of, PV 60; and near-death-experience research, PV 60, 63; and time dilation, TS 88

Heindel, Max: AW 68

Heinecken, Christian Heinrich ("the Infant of Lübeck"): PV *122*

Heisenberg, Werner: MB 25, SE 131-134, TS 66

Hejbalik, Karel: PS 74

Helena (empress of Rome): MY 84

Helen of Troy: TN 34

Heliacal rising: defined, TS 103

Helios (god): WW 19

Hell: AE 50-*51*, CD 84-85. *See also* Afterlife

"Hell bank notes": MY *70*

Hellenic invaders: WW 13-15

Hellenism: CC 24

Hell-Fire Club: MW 119, 121-124, 125

Helmer, Olaf: and Delphi method, PP 135

Helmet plate: of Vikings, TN *36-37*

Helmont, Jan Baptista van: EE 70, SA 92, *93-95*

Helms, Jesse: MA 6; and Wicca, WW 126

"Helpless spectator" theory: MB 14

Helvetius (a.k.a. John Frederick Schweitzer): MA 32, MY *127*, SA 14-*16*, 17

Hemicyclium: TS *107*

Hemingway, Ernest: PV 7; near-death experience of, PV 10-11, 58

Hemis kachina: MY *64*

Hemlock: WW *33*

Henbane: TN 73-74, WW *35*; and Circe, WW 35

Henderson, Garry C.: AE 85

Hengist: and Stonehenge legend, MP 82

Henham (England): MW 53, 55

Henley (ghost): HN 116, 117

Henley, Dorothy: HN 117

Henning, A. C.: HN *69*

Henninger, Ronald: and Kline disappearance case, PP 133

Henri (duke of Bouillon): AW 55-56

Henricus (bishop of Greenland): ML 128

Henry (crisis apparition): PE 25

Henry, Naomi: and hypnotic regression, PV 113-114

Henry, Wellington: ghost of, HN *26*

Henry I (king of England): PE 109

Henry II (king of England): PE 104; and Arthur, ML 56, 59

Henry III (king of England): PE 103, 104

Henry VI (king of England): PE 105

Henry VIII (king of England): CC 83, EE 88, HN 90-91, MW 19, 22, PE 39, 106, PH 87, VP 14; and Glastonbury Abbey, ML 59, 61

Henry II (Holy Roman emperor): CC 55

Henry II (king of France): CC 69, 70, VP 18-19

Henry III (king of France): VP 18

Henry IV (king of France): PS 97

Henry II (king of Navarre): VP 18

Henry of Huntington: and Stonehenge, MP 82

Henry of Sayn: and Conrad of Marburg, WW 51

Henry the Navigator (prince of Portugal): ML 66

Henson, Matthew: AW *111*

Heparin: SI 105

Hepatoscopy: CC 15; defined, VP 32

Hephaestus (god): SA *26*

Hera (goddess): CC 43

Heraclitus of Ephesus: SA 20

Herald of Astrology, The (Morrison): CC 113

Herald of Free Enterprise (ferry): CC 152

Herbal healing: PH 58-60, *59*

Herbal remedies: UV *66-67*

Herbert, Benson: MM 26

Herbert, George Edward: MY 27

Herbert, Stella: PE 114

Herb garden: EE *134*

Herbs: MA 63. *See also* WW index

Hercules (mythological figure): DD 87, MC 13, MY 70, SA *77*

Heresies: WW 49, 50, 51; defined, WW 49; trials for, WW 50

Heretics: CD 83

Hering, Constantine: PH 118-119, *120*

Herjolfsson, Bjarni: ML 123-124

Hermaphrodites: CD 48-49, 62-63

Hermaphroditos (god): CD 62-63

Hermes (god): CC 42, CD 62-63, DD 29, MA 61, MQ 56, MY 39, SA 20

Hermes Trismegistus: AW 50, 58, MQ 109; and alchemy, SA 19, 23; background of, SA 19-20; and Emerald Table, MA 61, SA 20; as god, MA 61, SA 83; and Isaac Newton, SA 98; and Thoth, SA 19-20, 23. *See also* Thoth

Hermetic Order of the Golden Dawn: MA 62, 64, 65, MY 53, SA 126-128, VP 127, 129, 137, WW 102. *See also individual members; AW index*

Hermetics: AW 24, 28-*29*, 35

Hermippus, L. Clodius: SI 38

Hermitage Castle: HN *10-11*; and ghosts, HN 11

Hermit of Dole: *See* Garnier, Gilles

Hermotimus of Clazomene: out-of-body experiences of, PV 16, SE 28

Herne (god): characteristics of, WW 28; rites honoring, WW 43

Herne, Frank: SS 54

Hernias: MA 125

Hero: as archetype, DD *92-93*; in myths, DD 93

Herodotus: CC 87, DD 40, EM 27, PS 74, SE 21, 28, 31, SI 24; and Great Pyramid, MP 48-49, 55; reincarnation as viewed by, PV 98; and Tarshish, ML 119, 136

Herrman, James, Jr.: HN *72*; and psychokinesis, HN 72, 73

Herrmann family: and poltergeists, MM 44-46, *45*

Herschel, William: CC 45, 112

Hersh, Seymour: MA 6

Hertzler, Joyce Oramel: UV 33, 39

Herzeloyde (character in *Parzifal*): MQ 111

Hesiod: CD 24, EE 22, UV 22-23

Hess, Harry: EE 59

Hess, Rudolf: AW 99, CC 134, 136, PS 64-65

Hessdalen Valley (Norway): and UFO window site investigation, UP *133-134*

Hesse, wolf-child of: TN 57

Hetepheres (queen of Egypt): SE 28

Heuvelmans, Bernard: MC 38, 44, MW 49, 65-66, 71-72; iceman research of, MC 111; sea serpent research of, MC 37, 38, 43, 44

Hevesy, Guillaume de: and Easter Island, ML 95; and Mohenjo-Daro, ML 20-21; and rongo-rongo boards, ML 95

Hexagrams: MA *38, 40*, TS *33*, VP 121, 122; defined, TS 32, VP 116. *See also* I Ching

He Xiangu: SA *113*

Hexodotus: VP 10

Hex signs: MA *114*, MW 113

Heyerdahl, Thor: MC 32-33, ML *91, 92*; and America, discovery of, ML 120; drawing by, ML *91*; and Easter Island, ML 89-90, 93, 95; and *Kon-Tiki*, ML *93, 95*, 120; and *Ra II*, ML 117-119

hGH: SI 73

Hibernation: DD 105, SI 105-107. *See also* Frozen-hibernator phenomenon

Hibernation-induction trigger (HIT): SI 106

Hibner, Ramona: MW 45

Hichens, William: MW 67, 68

Hickok, James Butler (Wild Bill): PS 77

Hicks, Edward: painting by, UV *40-41*

Hicks, Robert: TS 90

Hickson, Charles E.: MY 92; and abduction by aliens, UP 60, 62

Hidatsa Indians: EE 90

Hidden Channels of the Mind (L. Rhine): CD 68

Hidden Symbolism of Alchemy and the Occult Arts (Silberer): SA 129

Hiei, Mount: monastery on, EM 57, 58

Hieroglyphics: Peruvian find of, MQ 42, 43

Higan: MY 88

Higdon, Carl: and abduction by aliens, AE *10-11*, 25, 26; and

54

HOURGLASS. *Measuring the time relationship between the upper and lower worlds, the hourglass symbolizes the passage of finite time. Here a Mogul, his sands of time running out, ignores kings at his feet and casts his eyes heavenward.*

Ausso, AE 10, *25,* 26; physical examination of, AE 9, 10

High Flight Foundation: MQ 62; Ararat expeditions sponsored by, MQ 62-63, *65,* 94

High History of the Holy Graal, The (Anonymous): ML 44

Highland Fling: UV *94-95*

High magic: and Cabala, MA 31; and Alessandro Cagliostro, MA 44; characteristics of, MA 44, 48, 49; and Aleister Crowley, MA 45; decline of, MA 63; defined, MA 15, 44; in Egypt, MA 51-52; and low magic, MA 44; and pharaohs, MA 51. *See also* Magic; Voodoo

High Sense Perception (HSP): PH 98, 99

Hilda, Saint: PE 16

Hildebrandt, F. W.: DD 60

Hildegard of Bingen, Saint: CD 130, MY *118,* PH 17-20; visions of, SE *127*

Hilgard, Ernest: SS 152

Hilgard, Josephine: MB 90-92

Hill, Barney and Betty: MW 43, MY *86-87;* and abduction by aliens, AE 21, 27, 34, MY 87, UP *58-59,* 60, 62, 79, *82-84;* hypnosis of, AE 29; physical examination of, AE 21, 27, 35; and Carl Sagan, AE 29

Hill, Karen: CD 124

Hill, Napoleon: MB 123

Hill, William C. Osman: MC 106

Hillary, Edmund: MC *105;* Abominable Snowman research of, MC 105-106, 123

Hillenkoetter, R. H.: and National Investigations Committee on Aerial Phenomena, UP 69

Hilliard, Jean: SI *104;* hypothermia of, SI 101, 104

Hillsdale College (Michigan): and UFO sightings, UP *106-107*

Hillside Strangler: TN 130

Hilton, Conrad: and executive ESP, PS 105; and intuition, PS 109; and Stevens Corporation, PS 105

Hilton, James: MQ 27, SI 39, 47

Himalayan Scientific and Mountaineering Expedition: MC 105

Himalayas: EM *16-17,* MC 102-103, MW 44, 59; and Abominable Snowmen, EM 16; and Buddhism, EM 43; and Hinduism, EM 43; and Indra, EM 16; and Kubera, EM 16; and Shiva, EM 16

Hi Matsuri: MY 95

Himilco: ML 119

Himmler, Heinrich: CD 94, 95, MQ 127, 128, MW 89, PS *64-65*

Hinckley, John W., Jr.: DD 137

Hindley, Charles: VP 16. *See also* Shipton, Mother

Hindus and Hinduism: MA 64, MW 93, PH 45, 63, SA 16, SE 124, 131; and afterlife, CD 85; at Allahabad (India), SI 16; and Asvattha, EE 93-95; in Bali, EM 64; and banyans, EE 82, EM 13; and bo trees, EE 83; and Brahman, MB 22-25; and burning embers, MB *97;* and cellular therapy, SI 65; and chakras, MB 15; and consciousness, MB 25; cosmogonies of, TS 23; and cows, EM 39; and creation myths, CD 24-25; and death, CD 12, 13; demons of, SI *16;* and dreams, DD 24, 28; and dualities, CD 35-36; and enlightenment, TS 25, 29, 93; and evil, CD 80; and Ganges River, SI 16, *17-18, 21;* and ghats, EM 19; gods of, SI *16;* and Golden Age, UV 25; and Himalayas, EM 43; and immortality, SI 16; and Kailas, TS 11; and karma, CD 111; and Kumbha Mela, SI *16-21;* and linga, CD 7; and mysticism, CD 114; and nir-

vana, SI 16, 18; and paradise myths, UV 6; and Ramakrishna, EM 117; and reincarnation, CD 111, PV 102, 120, SI 16; and sacrifices, TS 37; and sex, CD 114; and Shiva, CD 80; and snakes, CD 14; and soma, MB 102, 104; and space, TS 23-25; and sweating, SI 114; and time, TS 25, 93; and trances, MB 96, *97;* and transmigration, EM 37; and Veda, EM 29; and Vedanta Societies, EM 117-118; and Vishnu, CD 80, PV *98-99;* and Swami Vivekenanda, EM 114-115, 117-118; and women, CD 56; and Yamuna River, SI 16; and Paramahansa Yogananda, EM 119; and zero, TS 29

Hipparchus of Nicaea: CC 29-32

Hippie: EM *96*

Hippocampus: SE 114; characteristics of, MB 60; and memory, MB 60; and schizophrenia, MB 74

Hippocrates: CC 23, CD 63, DD 33, MB 45, PH 15, 21; and moleoscopy, VP 66; and palmistry, VP 81; and physiognomy, VP 66

Hippolytus: CC 40

Hippomancy: defined, VP 35

Hippopotamus: ML *127*

Hippopotamus, pygmy: MW 47

Hiram (king of Tyre): AW 97

Hiroshige: woodcut by, TN *45*

Hirschborgen: SA 61

Hirsig, Leah: AW 118, *119*

Hissarlik (ruin; Turkey): finds at, MQ *36-37;* and Troy legend, MP 18-19

Historical Library (Faustus of Byzantium): MQ 70

History of Animals (Aristotle): VP 66

History of the World (Raleigh): SI 14

History of Utopian Thought, The (Hertzler): UV 33, 39

Hitchcock, Alfred: CC 84

Hitchcock, Ethan Allen: and alchemy, SA 124-126, 129, 131; background of, SA 124

Hitching, Francis: and electromagnetic energy, EE 61-62

MY The Mystical Year; PE Phantom Encounters; PH Powers of Healing; PP Psychic Powers; PS The Psychics; PV Psychic Voyages; SA Secrets of the Alchemists; SE Search for the Soul; SI Search for Immortality; SS Spirit Summonings; TN Transformations; TS Time and Space; UP The UFO Phenomenon; UV Utopian Visions; VP Visions and Prophecies; WW Witches and Witchcraft

Hitler, Adolf: CC 47, 130-131, 134, 135, CD *92, 95,* DD *41,* 43-44, MY *31,* 99, PE 117, PS *58-59, 64, 65, 66,* SA *120;* as authority figure, CD 95; and Beer Hall Putsch, PS 58, 62, *63;* and hollow earth theory, MP 151-*152;* and Holy Grail, MQ 127; and Wolf Messing, PP 113, PS 66; and Nazis, CD 94; predictions about, PS 58, 62, 66, VP 19, 20, 21, 109; and Wicca, WW 103-104

Hitogata: MY 131

Hittites: CD 122

Hiva: and Easter Island, ML 82, 95

Hiving off: defined, WW 107

H. M. (epileptic): MB 60-62

Ho (astronomer): CC 20

Hoagland, Hudson: TS 95

Hoare, Richard Colt: and barrows, excavation of, MP 91; and Stonehenge, MP *90*

Hoaxes: alleged against Rudi Schneider, MM 21, *22;* of Eva C., SS 66-67, 68, 70; of Mina Cran-

don, SS 114, 116; in ectoplasm, SS *128;* of Fox sisters, SS 21, 28, 32; of Uri Geller, MM 28; in levitation, SS *125;* Loch Ness monster, MC 69, 80, 83; in materializations, SS *129;* of mediums, SS 101-102, 123-*129;* and metal bending, MM 78, *79;* of Stanislava P., SS 65; of Eusapia Palladino, MM 12, 15, SS 58, 60, 61, 62-63, 64; and poltergeists, MM 54; sea serpents, MC 28, 30, 34, *35,* 37, 44; in slate writing, SS *126, 127;* in table turning, SS *125*

Hobbes, Thomas: MB 13, MP 85

Hobbyhorse: MY *34*

Hobgoblins: MY 96

Hobson, J. Allan: DD *106;* and dreams, DD 100, 105; and REM sleep, DD 108

Hoby, Elizabeth: ghost of, HN 12

Hoby, William: HN 12

Hochberg, Marie von: MW 35, *39*

Hodgskin, R. H.: TS 127-128

Hodgson, Richard: AW 134-135,

PV 22, SS 62, 82, 86, 87; bogus spirit photograph of, PP *44*

Hodgson, Shadworth: MB 14

Hodson, Geoffrey: TS *118-119*

Hoerig, Diana: SS *12-13*

Hoerner, Erasmus: MY 59; and Clara Germana Celle, CD 71, 73, *74-75;* and exorcism, CD 77

Hoerner, Sebastian von: AE 115

Hofer, Johann (postmortem apparition): PE 36

Hoff, Frau: WW 27. *See also* Holda

Hofmann, Albert: and Timothy Leary, MB 107; and LSD, MB 104

Hofstadter, Douglas: SE 125-128

Hog, giant forest: MC *21*

Hogan, Ben: MB 125

Hogarth, William: etching by, MW *125*

Hohenheim, Theophrastus Bombast von: *See* Paracelsus

Hohenlohe-Waldenburg-Schillingsfürst, Alexander Leopold Franz Emmerich von: PH 93-95

Hokuei, Shunkôsai: print by, PE *77*

Holand, Hjalmar R.: ML 126-128

Holda (goddess): WW *26-27;* and Diana, WW 27; and Freya, WW 27; names of, WW 27; rites honoring, WW 43

Hole through the Sky: TN *8. See also* Totem poles

Holi: MY *22*

Holiday, F. W.: MC 85

Holika (demon): MY 22

Holism: defined, UV 142; and Findhorn Foundation, UV 142; and Dorothy Maclean, UV 144

Hollandia (New Guinea): hauntings on, PE *138-139*

Holle: WW 27. *See also* Holda

Holliday, Stanley, Jr.: and Mary Cousett, PS 24, 26-27; murder conviction of, PS 27

Hollister, Alonzo: UV *66*

Holloman Air Force Base (New Mexico): and fireball sightings, UP 46

Hollow earth theory: MP 138-155; of UFOs, UP 131

AE Alien Encounters; AW Ancient Wisdom and Secret Sects; CC Cosmic Connections; CD Cosmic Duality; DD Dreams and Dreaming; EE Earth Energies; EM Eastern Mysteries; HN Hauntings; MA Magical Arts; MB The Mind and Beyond; MC Mysterious Creatures; ML Mysterious Lands and Peoples; MM Mind over Matter; MP Mystic Places; MQ Mystic Quests; MW The Mysterious World;

Holly: MY 121

Holmes, Oliver Wendell: VP 75

Holms, Archibald Campbell: PE 95, PV 44

Holocaust, nuclear: ML 32-33

Hologram: SE 129-130, *131*

Holographic model: defined, DD 152-153

Holography: and David Bohm, MB 26, 28; defined, MB 26; and Karl Pribram, MB 26, 28

"Holomovement": MB 28

Holtsman, Ruth: AE 56

Holtz, Michael: EE 133

Holy Blood, Holy Grail (Lincoln, Baigent, and Leigh): MQ 125, 127

Holy Bowl (Sacro Catino): MQ 121-122, *125*

Holy Cross, Feast of the: MY 86

Holy Ghost: MY 43, 50, 55

Holy Grail: MW 85, 99, PS 64; and Joseph of Arimathea, ML 52, 56; search for, ML 49. *See also* MQ *index*

Holy House of Nazareth: MY *84-85*

Holy lines: MW 90

Holyoake, George: UV 60-69

Holy People: EE 19, MW 81-83

Holy places: *See* Sacred places

Holy Spirit: MY 43, 50, 55

Holy Trinity Church: MW 19; and ghosts, HN 91

Holy Week: MY *28*, 30

Holy Wells: MY 40

Home, Daniel Dunglas: AW 129, 132, MM 12, MY 63; alleged levitation of, MM 115-116, *117*; psychokinesis of, MM 11-12. *See also* SS *index*

Home, Everard: MC 42-43

Homeo-acupuncture: PH 49

Homeopathy: MA 114, PH 118-119, 120-121

Homeostatic state: characteristics of, EE 124; defined, EE 120

Homer: DD 32, MB 44, MC 19, 22, SE 26, 27, SI 65, UV 23; and Charybdis, EE 72; and Eleusinian mysteries, EE 54; and Gaia (goddess), EE 22; and hollow earth theory, MP 139; *Iliad*, search for Troy inspired by, MQ

36, 40; *Odyssey*, retracing voyage in, MQ *49-61;* and Troy legend, MP 18-19

Home Rule League: AW 142

Homestead: UV 90, 91, *94*

Homeward: Songs by the Way (Russell): SE 104

Homing pigeons: PS 74

Hominoids: *See* MC *index*

Homo erectus: ML 18

Homo sapiens neanderthalensis: EE 26

Homosexuality: MB 87

Homunculus: MA 48, SA 68, 69

Honan Shaolin Temple: *See* Shaolin monastery

Hong Kong: MW 127; magician in, MA *11*

Hong Kong and Shanghai Bank Building: MW *128*

Honorius, Julius: and pyramids, MP 48

Honorius III (pope): MA 93, 99

Honorton, Charles: DD *151;* and ganzfeld research, PP 68-69

Hood, devil's: CD *95*

Hookala, Daniel: MA *91*

Hooper, Judith: MB 77

Hoover, J. Edgar: CC 89

Hope, Charles: MM 21-22

Hope, Henry T.: MW 129

Hope, Star: and Browning Case, SS 93-95. *See also* Cross-Correspondences

Hope, William: MY 20

Hope diamond: MW 127, *129*

Hopewell culture: earthen mounds of, MP 123

Hopi Indians: MW 79, 81, 83, TN 43, TS 7, UV 20-22; and fourth world, EE 43; and kachinas, MA 46; and Mother Goddess, EE 26; and naming ceremony, EE 26; and Palongawhoya, EE 39; and rituals, MA 68; and San Francisco Peaks, EE 39; and shamans, MA 68; snake dance of, TN *28-29;* and Spider Rock, EE 43; and Spider Woman, EE 43; and superstitions, MA 114

Hopkins, Budd: and investigations of abduction by aliens, UP 141-*143. See also* AE *index*

Hopkins, Harry: MQ 18, 22

Hopkins, Herbert: and alien visitor, UP 77

Hopkins, Matthew: WW *79;* and "swimming," WW 78-79; and witch hunts, WW 78

Hopkinsville (Kentucky): and alien visitors, UP 64-65

"Horla, The" (Maupassant): PE 97

Horn: MA 101

Horn, Siegfried: Crotser's photographs examined by, MQ 47-48

Horn Dance: MY *84-85*

Horned God: and Cernunnos, WW 107; and Margaret A. Murray, WW 100; and Pan, WW 107; and Tammuz, WW 16; and Wicca, WW 10

Horney, Karen: EM 137

Horniman, Annie: AW 151-152, 154, 156

Horns: SI *67*, WW 121

Horoscopes: CC *26*, 74, 118-125; of Albert Einstein, CC 142; of Sigmund Freud, CC *126-127;* by Hans Gerhard Lenz, PS 124; by Grace Morris, PS *118-119,* 123-124. *See also* Astrology

Horses: DD *13*, MA 100; divination with, VP *42;* as dream symbols, DD 12

Horseshoes: MA 118

Hortlich, Johann: VP 81

Horus (god): CD 80, VP 106; eye of, MA 9

Hospital: SA 66

Hospitall of Incurable Fooles (Garzoni): TN 73

Hostage to the Devil (Martin): CD 91-93

Hot-air ballooning: and Nazca lines of Peru, MP 117, *118-119*

Hot cross buns: MY 28

Hot spot: defined, EE 68

Hot springs: in Baden-Baden (Germany), SI *131-137;* in Bath (England), SI 24; and Johannes Brahms, SI 133; and Celts, SI 24; and Fyodor Dostoyevsky, SI 133; and Romans, SI 24, 131; and Mark Twain, SI 133

Hotta Kōzuke: PE *74 75*

Hottentots: CD 109

Hotu Matua (king of Maori): and Easter Island, ML 82, 90, 95; and rongorongo boards, ML 90

Houdin, Jean Eugène Robert: MM 110

Houdini, Bess: MY 97; and Joseph Dunninger, SS *120*, 122; and Arthur Ford, SS 122; and Harry Houdini, SS 120-122

Houdini, Harry: MY 23, *97*, SI 101; escapes of, MM *110-111;* mind-reading act of, PP *106;* and *Scientific American's* tests of mediums, PP 38-39; and slate writing, PP *43;* and Zancigs' thought-transference act, PP 108. *See also* SS *index*

Houdon, Jean-Antoine: sculptures by, AW 80

Houngans: MA 82, 84, *86*

Houris: DD 53

House of Faces: HN *96-97*

House of the Ruler: MW 79

House of the Sun: TS 36

Houses: DD 16; astrological, CC 36, *120-121*, 122, *123;* as dream symbols, DD 16, 57, 59

Houston, Jean: TN 46

Howard, Albert: EE 129

Howard-Bury, Charles Kenneth: Abominable Snowman research of, MC 100, 103

57

HEXAGRAM. Widely identified as the Shield of Solomon or the Star of David, the hexagram also has an older symbolism—the union of male and female. The example on this page contains magical alchemical characters.

Howe, Elias: DD 23, 45-46
Howe, Ellic: AW 146
Howe, R. P.: MW 108
Howitt, William: DD 135-137
How to Live to be 100 (Benet): SI 43
Hoy, David: PH 36
Hoyle, Fred: and big bang theory, TS 61; and Stonehenge, MP 92
HPB: *See* Blavatsky, Helena Petrovna
Hsi (astronomer): CC 20
Hsiao-fu (Feng Meng Leng): DD 23-24
Huacas (gods): MW 116
Huan Ching: MY 92
Hubbard, Bertha: UV 84
Hubbard, Elbert Green: UV *84*, 85; and arts and crafts movement, UV 85
Hubbell, Walter: and poltergeists, HN 98, 99
Hubble, Edwin: and redshift, TS 58-60
Huc, Abbé (French missionary): MQ 27
Hudson, T.: and ghosts, HN 29
Hudson Valley (New York), UFOs in: AE 54-55, 55-59
Hugh (bishop of Jabala): ML 63
Hughes, Howard: CC 89
Hughes, Irene (psychic): PS 41-43; and precognition, PP 98-99
Hughes, Pennethorne: and witches, WW 98
Huichol Indians: EE 100, PP 75, SE 126; rain-making ceremony of, PP *80-81*; shamans and spirits of, PP 80-81
Huitzilopochtli (god): MW 115
Human-beasts: MC *52-59*; Anubis, MC *56*; bishop-fish, MC *54*; Chiron (centaur), MC *57*; dog-headed men, MC *57*; genie, MC *59*; harpies, MC *58*; hawk-headed man, MC *59*; lamia, MC *57*; Maat, MC *58*; mermaids, MC *54*, *55*; merman, MC *54*; Minotaur, MC *56*; monk-fish, MC *54*; satyr, MC *57*, 100; sphinx, MC 53, *58-59*
Human beings, creation of: AE *96-97*
Human Genome Project: SI 73

Human growth hormone (hGH): SI 73, TS 79
Humanist, The (journal): MM 32
Humanization: defined, MB 67
Humanoids: *See* Aliens
Human Personality and Its Survival of Bodily Death (Myers): PE 91, PV 20, SS 96
Human-potential movement: and Georgei Ivanovitch Gurdjieff, UV 107-108; and Aldous Huxley, UV 142; and New Age movement, UV 142
Human sacrifice: Merlin's avoidance of fate as, MQ *130-131*; stone yokes possibly used in, MQ *96-97*
Hume, David: AW 90-91, SE 56, 57, 58
Hume, Hamilton: MW 63
Humors: CC *23*, *71*, *76*
Humphrey, Elizabeth: MM *58*, 62
Hunches: *See* Executive ESP
Hundredth-monkey effect: EE 125
Hungary: superstitions in, MA 134; vampires in, TN 113, 120-121
Hungry ghosts: MW 38; defined, HN 127
Hungry Ghosts Festival: MY 70
Hunt, David: and Exeter UFO sighting, UP 102, 104
Hunt, H. L.: PS 111
Hunt, Valerie: PH 103
Hunter, Dard: designs by, UV 85
Hunters: CD 49-50, 55
Hunting: and Indians, MA 74; and Mandans, MA *74-75*; rituals, MY 85; and shamans, MA *74-75*
Hunting Wild Beasts (Stoneham): MW 66
Hunzakuts: SI *47-55*; characteristics of, SI 39-41; diet of, SI 43, 47, *52*, *53*, 54, 55; family life of, SI 47, *54*; health of, SI 47, 48, 51, 52, 54; longevity of, SI 39, 41, 43, 47, 49, 51, 52, 55
Hunza Valley: SI *47-55*
Huppa Indians: MC 116, 120
Huri moai: defined, ML 95
Hurkos, Peter (psychic): TS *115*; and Boston Strangler case, PP 130-132; clairvoyance of, PP *127*, 130-132
Hurle, Henry: and Druids' influ-

ence on Stonehenge, MP 91
Hurricane Agnes: PS *14-15*
Hurst, Raphael: *See* Brunton, Paul
Hurth, Mrs. Joicey: telepathic experience of, PP *12-13*
Huse, Bertha: DD 140-141
Husk Faces (gods): MY *80*
Huss, Magnus: stigmata research of, MM 113
Hussain (grandson of Muhammad): MY 137
Hussein (king of Jordan): Dead Sea research sponsored by, MQ 43
Hussein, Ahmed: MC 19
Huston, Wayne: and Ravenna UFO sighting, UP 111, 113
Hut (Plains Dweller): ML 14
Hutcheson, Francis: SE 57
Hutchinson, Young: MC 17
Hutton, J. Bernard: PH 34, 36
Huwana (character in Gilgamesh epic): MQ 31
Huxley, Aldous: CC 84, EM 117, MM 62, UV 142; and brain, MB 106; as Buddhist, MB 106; and meditation, MB 117; and mescaline, MB 104-106; and Mind at Large, MB 106; out-of-body experiences of, PV 15
Huxley, Anthony: and plant consciousness, EE 109-110
Huxley, Thomas Henry: ML 29, 118; and consciousness, MB 14, 17
Huxtable, Graham: and hypnotic regression, PV 114
Hyams, Joe: HN *20*, *21*; and ghosts, HN 18-21, 24
Hydesville Rappings: SS 19-21, 22. *See also* Fox, Kate and Maggie
Hydra: MC *13*
Hydrocephalus: SE 129
Hydrologic cycle: characteristics of, EE 70-72
Hydromancy: defined, VP 45. *See also* Scryers; Scrying
Hydropathy: PH 119
Hydrophobicity: AE 76
Hygelo-therapy: PH 119
Hylé: CD 31
Hyman, Ray: MA 135
Hymche: MW 47, 51-53
Hynek, J. Allen: and Ed Burns, AE

57; and Center for UFO Studies, AE 25; and Philip J. Imbrogno, AE *57*; and UFOs, AE 25, 57, 59. *See also* UP index
Hyperboreans: SI 39
Hypermnesia: of Eva C., SS 68-70; defined, SS 70
Hyperspace theory of UFOs: UP 131
Hypertrichosis: MW 56, TN *82*, *83*; defined, TN 94. *See also* Porphyria
Hypnagogic hallucinations: defined, MB 41. *See also* Hallucinations
Hypnagogic images: defined, PV 44. *See also* Out-of-body experiences
Hypnagogic startle: DD 116; defined, DD 97
Hypnagogic state: AE 110-111. *See also* Sleep; DD index
Hypnopedia: DD 117, 118; and Thomas Budzynski, DD 118; and hypnagogic state, DD 117; and J. N. Phiney, DD 117; and Abram Moiseyevich Svyadoshch, DD 117-118
Hypnos (god): DD *24-25*, 29
Hypnosis and hypnotic regression: MB *102-103*, PH 92; cryptomnesia's effect on, PV 112-113; of Monica, PV 88, *89-94*; and multiple personality disorder, MB 80; suggestion's effect on, PV 112; technique of, PV 112. *See also* Past-life therapy; Reincarnation; AE *index*; MM *index*
Hypnotism: PP 35, 69, UV 107, VP 22; tests of, PP *64-65*
Hypogeum: MW 91
Hypothalamus: SE 119; and hypothermia, SI 104, 105; purposes of, SI 104
Hypothermia: *See* SI *index*
Hypothermia Laboratory: SI *110*
Hyslop, James H.: SE 90-92; psychic investigations of, PP 44
Hysteria: CD 118, DD 60-61, 63-64; and Sigmund Freud, DD 60-61, 63-64
Hysterical contagion theory: UP 123
Hyzer, William G.: AE 73-74

58

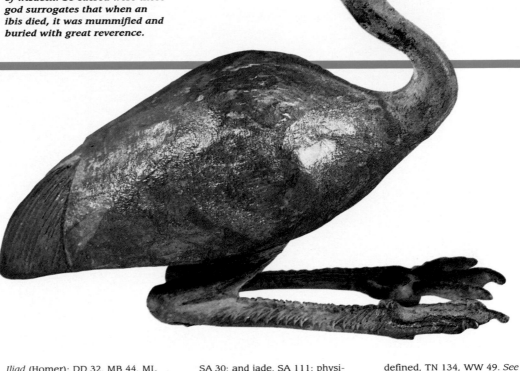

IBIS. Ancient Egyptians considered this large wading bird—depicted here in bronze and wood—a symbol of Thoth, god of wisdom. So sacred were these god surrogates that when an ibis died, it was mummified and buried with great reverence.

Iamblichus: UV 28; and Pythagoras, UV 25, 26, 30
Ianna, Philip A.: CC 140
Ibadan (Nigeria): MW 133
Ibeji: MY 38
Ice ages: CD 50, EE 64, 74, ML 115; history of, EE 64
Iceland: MW *map* 10, 75; geomancy in, EE 32; volcanoes in, EE 69
Icelandic legends: MQ 78, SI 26
Iceman: MC *111*
I Ching (Anonymous): CD 35, MW 127, VP 117; and John Blofeld, VP 115, 116-117, 119; characteristics of, VP 104, 119-122; hexagrams in, VP 116, 121, 122; and Carl Jung, TS 122, VP 119, 122; learning to use, VP 7, 70, 110; and Tao, TS 32; techniques, VP *116, 117,* 119; translations of, VP 117-119, 121, 122; trigrams, VP *118, 120-121;* and Richard Wilhelm, TS 32; yin/yang in, VP 119, *120-121*
Ichthyomancy: defined, VP 35
Id: defined, DD 73
Ida: PH 74
Ideal Palace: UV *44-45*
Idea Medicinae Philosophicae (Severinus): SA 82
Idehd (islet): ML 97-98
Ideogram: MW *127*
Ideoplasts: of Eva C., SS 68, *69,* 70
Ides of March: MY 22
Idol: calf, MQ *48*
Iemisch: MW 47, 51-53
Iemon (samurai): MW *36, 38*
Ifa: MW 114
Igano Kanemitsu: PE *78-79*
Iglulik Eskimos: PP *76-77;* shamans and spirits of, PP 75-77
Igraine (duchess of Cornwall): ML 48
Ik: CD 109-110

Iliad (Homer): DD 32, MB 44, ML 19, SE 26, SI 65; search for Troy inspired by, MQ 36, 40
Ille, Georges: PH 103
Illnesses: causes of, PH 10; and gold, SA 116; and out-of-body experiences, PV 16. *See also* Sickness
Illuminati: *See* Order of the Illuminati
Illusionists: powers of, PP 103
Il Pomarancio: painting by, PV 61
Ilsa (god): EM 50
Imaging: *See* Visualization
Imaging methods: defined, MM 100. *See also* Hypnosis and hypnotic regression
Imaizumi, Yoshinori: MC 43
Imbolc: MY 130, WW 123
Imbrogno, Philip J.: AE *57-59*
Imitative magic: MA 17; and Aborigines, MA *21;* and similarities law, MA 15. *See also* Magic
Imitative noise: defined, HN 24
Immigration and Naturalization Service: EM 131
"Immortalists": SI 116
Immortality: EM 52-53; and alchemy, SA 103, 106, *107;* causes of, SA 103; and cinnabar, SA 110; and dragons, SA 109; and elixirs, SA 83, *103,* 110; in Gilgamesh epic, MQ 31-32; and gold,

SA 30; and jade, SA 111; physical, quest for, MQ 22-23, 31; and tortoises, SA 108; water as source, MQ 32-*34,* 39-40
Immortals: SA 112, *113*
Immortals, Realm of the: SA *112*
Immune system: SI 66
Imo (monkey): EE 125
Imperial City, of Beijing (China): EM 10
Imum Coeli (IC): CC 118
Inanna (goddess): MY 122, WW 13. *See also* Mother Goddess
Incantations: and Isis, MA 52-53; and magic, MA 17-19; about werewolves, TN 95, 96, 100, 102. *See also* Spells
Incas: MW 79, 82, 83, 113, 116-117, SA 16; dentistry of, ML *22;* and Morris Jessup, ML 29; mummified skull of, ML *22;* and Titicaca, TS 13. *See also* Ceques
Incense burner: ML 137
Incident at Exeter (Fuller): UP 102-104
Inconstant (ship): and the *Flying Dutchman*: MP 40-41
Incorruption: of Cecilia, SI 26, 30; defined, SI 30
Incubation: DD 31, *32;* and Gayle Delaney, DD 80; and Indians, DD 31. *See also* Dreams
Incubus: AE *47,* CD 83, *84;*

defined, TN 134, WW 49. *See also* Demons
India: CD 56, MW 14; Buddha's burial site, search for, MQ 40-41; dominoes in, VP 112; evil eye in, MA 127; fertility symbols in, EE 58; fire walking in, MM 105, *106;* flood story, MQ 78; gold in, SA 17; levitation in, MM 117; Mother Goddess in, EE 26; palmistry in, VP 81; sacrifices in, EE 26; trees in, EE 77, *92, 94, 95;* and yoni, EE 57
Indian bride and groom: CC *140*
Indian healing: PH 46, 47, 60. *See also* Ayurveda; Eastern healing
Indian National Congress: EM 86
Indian Point nuclear power plant: AE 56-57
Indians (in India): and aphrodisiacs, SI 67; live burials of, SI 99, *102;* and sweating, SI 114
Indians, American: and America, discovery of, ML 117; and angels, CD 136; artifacts of, MP *126-127;* and berdaches, CD 64-65; and bison, TN *31;* Chachapoyan, MQ 43; and *chindi,* MA 78; Colombian artifact by, MQ *28-29;* and directions, TS *31;* and dreams, DD 30, 114; and earth, spherical nature of, ML 17; El Dorado legend and, MQ

59

29; and evil, CD 80; exploration of, ML 120; and floods, EE 74; fountain of youth, tales of, MQ 34, 39; and ginseng, MA 99; and Golden Age, UV 23; and incubation, DD 31; Iroquois structures, MQ 98, 99; and low magic, MA 76-77, 77-80; and May apple, MA 99; and William Penn, UV 40-41; and redwoods, EE 87; and ritual magic, MA 66, 68, 70, 72, 74; and sacred places, EE 39, TS 6; and Shakers, UV 66, 70; and shamans, MA 77-78; and Sun Dance, MA 78; and time, TS 37, 95; and vision quests, DD 30-31; and Woman in the Wilderness, UV 60. See also individual tribes

Individuation: DD 75

Indonesia: death rites in, SE 33-34; magic in, MA 33-34; farming, EE 132; time in, TS 99

Indra (god): EM 16, SI 13

Industrial Revolution: CD 59, PP 35

Indus Valley civilization: and Mohenjo-Daro, ML 20, 79

Ineffability: defined, MB 114

Infantile unconscious: DD 29

Inferno (Dante): CD 88, VP 16-17

Inferno, The (Koch): CD 88-89

Infirmary: SA 66

Inglis, Brian: SS 70

Ingstad, Anne Stine: ML 125-126

Ingstad, Helge: ML 124-126

Inherka: SE 17

In His Image: The Cloning of a Man (Rorvik): SI 56-57

Initiation: and Andras Corban Arthen, WW 128-129; into Athanor Fellowship, WW 128-129; ceremonies, AW 6, 9; into Wicca, WW 124, 128-129; of witches, WW 44-46. See also Vision quest; specific sects

Inner City, of Beijing (China): EM 10-11

Inner Sanctum: UV 52-53

Inner Self Helper: and Ralph Allison, MB 83; and Katherine Castle, MB 83-85, 86; defined, MB 83; and Kaye DeYoung, MB 85; and Joseph Pearce, MB 85; and tulpa, MB 85

Innocent III (pope): AW 31, CD 33; and Cathars, WW 50

Innocent VIII (pope): SI 32; and blood transfusions, SI 27-30, 60; and Heinrich Kramer, WW 62-64; and longevity, SI 27-30; and Jakob Sprenger, WW 62-64; and witches, WW 62-64

Inquisition: SA 34; and Guillaume Adeline, WW 58; and Cathars, WW 51; characteristics of, WW 51, 58; in France, WW 58-62; in Germany, WW 62-64; history of, WW 50-51; in Spain, WW 79; and Waldensians, WW 58; and witches, WW 51, 52-53, 54

Insects: as criminals, TN 40; divi-

AE Alien Encounters; AW Ancient Wisdom and Secret Sects; CC Cosmic Connections; CD Cosmic Duality; DD Dreams and Dreaming; EE Earth Energies; EM Eastern Mysteries; HN Hauntings; MA Magical Arts; MB The Mind and Beyond; MC Mysterious Creatures; ML Mysterious Lands and Peoples; MM Mind over Matter; MP Mystic Places; MQ Mystic Quests; MW The Mysterious World;

INCENSE. *In this Egyptian tableau, a prince (center) burns the "divine perfume" before the mummified body of a pharaoh (right) to smite that god-king's enemies. Many cultures use incense in burial rites to represent the soul's ascent to heaven.*

10. Epheu.
(Hedera Helix)

IVY. *Symbolic of eternal life and of the soul's triumph over death, evergreen ivy also represents fertility. Ancient nature worshipers may have used it in winter solstice rites to ensure the success of spring crops.*

nation and, VP 40; queens, SI 23

Insomnia: and hypnosis, MM 123

Inspirationists: UV 57, 75

Institute for Advanced Study: and Albert Einstein, TS 54

Institute for Deaf-Mutes (Paris): TN 59

Institute for the Harmonious Development of Man: MB 100; and Georgei Gurdjieff, UV 107, 108, 109; program for, UV *106*

Institute for the Study of American Cultures: ML 135

Institute for the Study of American Religion: and J. Gordon Melton, WW 107

Institute of Psychophysical Research: founded, PV 34

Integratron: and George Van Tassel, UP 78

Intelligence: defined, MA 36; and planets, MA *36, 37, 40*

Intelligence of the Heart: defined, TS 22

Intentional communities: UV 138-139, 142, 153; characteristics of, UV 138, 152-153, defined, UV 17, 137

Intermission: defined, PV 108, 117. *See also* Reincarnation

International Association for Near Death Studies (IANDS): PV 77, 78

International Congress on Quantum Physics and Parapsychology: TS 120

International Fortean Organization: ML 22

International Institute for Psychical Research: and Nandor Fodor, HN 115

International Society for Krishna Consciousness (ISKCON): *See* Hare Krishna movement

International Society of Cryptozoology: MC 40, 90

Interplanetary Confederation Day: MY 93

Interpretation of Dreams, The (Freud): DD 19, 57, 60, 67, 107

Interpretation of Nature and the Psyche, The (Jung and Pauli): MM 72, TS 121

Interrogation chair: WW *84*

Interrupted Journey, The (Barney and Betty Hill): AE 21, 24, 35

In the Wake of the Sea-Serpents (Heuvelmans): MC 38

Inti (god): ML 73

Intihuatana: ML *73*

Inti Raymi: MY *56*

Intruders (Hopkins): AE 36, UP 141-143

Intuition: CD 66-68, PS 107-109, 110, 130. *See also* Clairvoyance; Extrasensory perception; PS *index*

Intuition line: VP 85. *See also* Palmistry, Palmists

Intuitive archaeology: *See* Psychic archaeology

Intuitives: *See* Psychics

Inuit: CD 65, EE 70, SE 13, 21; Bladder Festival of, MY 117, TN *32-33;* burial rituals of, PE 53; masks of, SE *13,* TN *33*

Invisibility: herbs for, WW *34*

Invisible Cap and Cord: MA 7

Invisible College: SA 95, 96

In vitro fertilization: SI 110-111. *See also* Artificial insemination

Invocation: defined, WW 107

Iona: MW 85-86

Ionospheric storms: PS 122

Ipet-isut: MW 100

Iran: ruins in, MQ *114*

Iran hostage crisis: PS 91

Ireland: well in, EE *74;* werewolves in, TN 78, 79; witch trials in, WW 54-55

Irish: ML 120-121

Irish torque: MQ *136*

Irma (patient of Freud): DD 63, 64, 66

Irminsul: EE 33

Iron: MA 101; characteristics of,

SA 21; symbol for, SA *24*

Iron Age: CD 54-55

Ironworkers: MY 103

Iroquois Indians: EE 100, MQ 98, MW 49, PH 15, SE 108; structures, MQ *99;* and time, TS 97

Irving, Washington: AE 114, SI 99

Irwin, Miss: and hauntings, HN 86, 87-88

Irwin, James Benson: and Ararat expeditions, MQ 62-63, *65,* 94

Isaac (biblical figure): CD 58

Isabella (countess of Seaforth): VP 31

Isaiah (spirit): PS 26

Isangoma: MW 136

Isawiyya brotherhood: and transformations, TN 43-44

Isbell, William: and Nazca lines of Peru, MP 119

Ishbel (spirit guide): HN 124, 125

Isherwood, Christopher: EM 117

Ishida, Yasuo: PH 54

Ishmael (biblical figure): MY 91

Ishtar (goddess): AE *90,* CC *10,* 14, *16,* 40, WW 13

Isidore, Raymond (a.k.a. Le Pique assiette): art by, UV *50-51*

Isis (goddess): EM 84, MY *23,* 62, SA 19, SE 26, *27,* VP 106; and dogs, MA 22; and incantations, MA 52-53; and Mother Goddess, WW 13; myth of, MA 52

Isis and Osiris cult: AW *12, 13;* initiation into, AW 16, 58

Isis League of Music and Drama: UV 96

Isis Unveiled (Blavatsky): AW 130-132, EM 84, 85, PV 21

Isis-Urania Temple of the Golden Dawn: AW 151, 156

Islam: MW 99, 102; and dreams,

DD 39; and resurrection, SE 51. *See also* Muslims

"Island beast": MC 22. *See also* Kraken

Island of Magicians, The (Crowley): AW *123*

Islands of the Blest: UV 23

Isle of Avalon: ML 48, 52

Isle of Lewis: MW 85

Isle of Man: MW 119, WW 109, *110-111*

Ismarus (city in *Odyssey*): MQ 50

Isokelekel (warrior chief): ML 102

Isolation: as risk factor, PH 133-135

Isolation chamber: TS 78, *80*

Isolationists: ML 116, 117

Isolde: ML 49, MW 87

Isra: DD 47, *48-49,* 55

Israel: Ashqelon calf, MQ *48;* Har Karkom site, MQ *44-45;* Noah's Ark myths in, MQ 82; seers in, VP 10

Israelites: *See* Hebrews

Italians: and time, TS 99

Italy: amulets in, MA *108;* dominoes in, VP 112, evil eye in, MA 122, 124, *136 137;* and Sacro Catino, MQ 121-122, *125;* and Shroud of Turin, MQ *108-109,* 122; superstitions in, MA 134

Itard, Jean-Marc Gaspard: TN *59;* and Victor, TN 59-60

It Came from Outer Space (film): and alien visitors, UP 28, *29, 30*

Ithaca (island; Greece): MQ *61;* Ulysses' voyage to, retraced, MQ 49-61

Itten, Johannes: UV *130;* and Bauhaus, UV 129, 130; and expressionists, UV 129; and Mazdaznan, UV 130; painting by, UV *130*

Ivan the Terrible (czar of Russia): and Dracula, TN 105

Ivlov, Ivan: MC 107-110

Ivory: MY *116*

Ivory Coast: MW 65, 68-69

Ivy: MY 121; ground, WW *36*

Ixchel (goddess): CD *51*

Iyengar, Bhanu: PE 26

Izana-gi (god): TS 20-22

Izzard, Ralph: MC 70; Abominable Snowman research of, MC 105

MY *The Mystical Year;* **PE** *Phantom Encounters;* **PH** *Powers of Healing;* **PP** *Psychic Powers;* **PS** *The Psychics;* **PV** *Psychic Voyages;* **SA** *Secrets of the Alchemists;* **SE** *Search for the Soul;* **SI** *Search for Immortality;* **SS** *Spirit Summonings;* **TN** *Transformations;* **TS** *Time and Space;* **UP** *The UFO Phenomenon;* **UV** *Utopian Visions;* **VP** *Visions and Prophecies;* **WW** *Witches and Witchcraft*

J

J, Mrs.: MA 123

Jackals: and transformation, TN 20-21, *22*

Jack and the Beanstalk (fairy tale): CD *43*

Jack-in-the-Green: EE *102,* MY *45*

Jacko (Sasquatch): MC 116. *See also* Sasquatch

Jack-o'-lanterns: MY *96, 97*

Jackson, Miss: PE 99

Jackson, Andrew: HN 93, *94;* ghost of, HN 108

Jackson, Rebecca: UV 68

Jack the Ripper: and Robert James Lees, PS 27-29, 31; and psychic detection, PS 27-28; and Scotland Yard, PS 27-29, 31; victims of, PS 27-28, *30-31*

Jacob (biblical figure): AE *45,* CD 58, DD 37

Jacob, Archibald: PE 8

Jacob of Nisibis, Saint: MQ 70; rel-

ic given to, reported, MQ 70, 77

Jacobs, David: UP 9; and investigation of abduction by aliens, AE 42, 102, UP 143; and UFOs, AE 42, UP 144

Jacobs, George: WW 74-75; as witch, WW 75

Jacob's Dream (Blake): PV *76*

Jacob's ladder: SA *70, 77*

Jacobson, Edmund: PH 137

Jacoby, Jensen: alleged reincarnation of, PV 119-122

Ja confession: WW *64*

Jade: MA 101, SA *111*

Jade Emperor: MY 126

Jaegers, Beverly: PS *20, 46;* business advice of, PP 136; and psychic detection, PS 45, 46, 48

Jagannath (god): MY 52-53

Jagger, Mick: CC 84, EM 122

Jaguar (empress): UV *141*

Jaguar cult: ML 113

Jaguars: Andean, ML *104;* and shamans, ML 105, TN 25; statuette of, TN *25*

Jahan, Shah: EM 35

Jahn, Robert G.: PS 88, SE 135, *136,* 139

Jain, Chandra Mohan: *See* Rajneesh, Bhagwan Shree

Jains and Jainism: SE 67; cosmogonies of, TS 25; icon of, SE *67;* and Kailas, TS 11; and reincarnation, PV 102, TS 25-27; and space, TS 26-27; and time, TS 25-26

James, David: Loch Ness monster research of, MC 73, 76, 77, 80

James, Henry: HN 112

James, Henry (the elder): psychic experience of, PP 21

James, William: AE 110, CD 128, DD 139-140, 141, PE 94, SE 62-63, 91-92, SS *83,* TS 95-97; and

American Society for Psychical Research, PP 24, SS 81; and mediums, PP 24; and mediumship, PP 36; and Frederic W. H. Myers, SS 77; and Leonora Piper, SS 81-82, 83; and pragmatism, SS 83; and psychic phenomena, PP 24; and psychic research, PP 48; and Jane Roberts, SS 136-137. *See also* MB *index*

James I (king of England): MA 115-116, PE 106, 109, WW 7, *8;* attempted murder of, WW 6, 7; and Agnes Sampson, WW 7; and Stonehenge, MP 84; and witches, WW 6, 7, 8, 62

James II (king of England): PE 106

James IV (king of Scotland): and alchemy, SA 56; and John Damian, SA 56; death of, SA 58

James VI (king of Scotland): *See* James I

AE Alien Encounters; AW Ancient Wisdom and Secret Sects; CC Cosmic Connections; CD Cosmic Duality; DD Dreams and Dreaming; EE Earth Energies; EM Eastern Mysteries; HN Hauntings; MA Magical Arts; MB The Mind and Beyond; MC Mysterious Creatures; ML Mysterious Lands and Peoples; MM Mind over Matter; MP Mystic Places; MQ Mystic Quests; MW The Mysterious World;

"Jameson Satellite, The" (Jones): SI 114

Jamnitzer, Wenzel: pitcher by, MA 105

Jampal: EM 50

Janet, Pierre: MB 78-79

Janmot, Louis: painting by, SE 69

Jansen, Olaf: and hollow earth theory, MP 150

Janus (god): MY 122, 123, TS 22-23

Japan: archery in, MM 121; fire walking in, MM 107; ghosts in, PE 34, 73-81; and paradise myths, UV 11; superstitions in, MA 8; tricksters in, TN 49, 54-55; volcanoes in, EE 69; Zen Buddhism in, EM 55

Japan Air Lines: MW 43

Japan Current: ML 120

Japanese: and America, discovery of, ML 117; cosmogonies of, TS 20-22; god of, ML 113; as stockbrokers, SI 44-45, TS 111; and stress, SI 45; and time, TS 97, 98, 99; and undernutrition, SI 81; and water, SI 131

Japanese healing: PH 60. See also Eastern healing

Jar: ML 109; ancient, Cyclops myth depicted on, MQ 53

Jaroslaw, Dan and Grant: and faked UFO photograph, UP 95

Jason (Greek hero): MW 13; father of, MQ 35; and Medea, WW 20, 22-23; trials of, WW 20-22

Jasper (Canada): MW 47

Jasper (stone): MA 101

Jat, Jasbir Lal: and reincarnation, PV 109-110

Jauk dancer: EM 66-67. See also Dances

Java: MW 59, 62; volcanoes on, EE 68-69

Jayatirtha: EM 127

Jaynes, Julian: and auditory hallucinations, MB 44-45; and consciousness, MB 14; and left brain/right brain, MB 44, 45

Jefferson, Thomas: AW 105-108, CC 80, MY 58; ghost of, HN 108

Jefferson Airplane: EM 125

Jelic, Luka: ML 130

Jenkins, Henry: SI 14

Jenkins, Stephen: and vision of medieval warriors, MP 104-105

Jenner, Edward: MA 136

Jensen, Wiers: PE 100

Jeremiah (biblical figure): VP 10

Jerusalem (Israel): MW 6-7, 99, 133

Jeshaele (language): MB 118

Jeshahr the Guide: MB 118; and out-of-body experiences, MB 118, 120, 121; and Telsen-Sao, MB 118, 120

Jessup, Morris: ML 29

Jesuits: MY 33

Jesus: DD 87, ML 29, MW 6-7, MY 26, 28, 30, 43, 46, 84, 86, 114, 120, 122, 123, 127, PH 17, 85, TS 37, 42, VP 41; out-of-body experiences of, PV 16. See also Christ

Jet (stone): MA 101

Jet lag: TS 84, 85-86

Jewelry, Babylonian: ML 22

Jewels: emerald of Lucifer, MQ 117; Treasure of Priam, MQ 36

Jews: and afterlife, CD 82; in Alexandria (Egypt), SA 19, 23; and Cyrus the Great, CD 80-82, and evil, CD 80-82, 93; and Gnostics, CD 29; and Nazis, CD 93, 128; persecution of, SA 46; and Persians, CD 82; and Raoul Wallenberg, CD 128

Jihad: MW 102

Jimmie (Korsakoff's syndrome victim): MB 60

"Jimmy Young Show" (radio program): and Uri Geller, MM 6-7

Jin-Fa Zhang: PS 98

Jingquan, Fan: MC 113

Jinner, Sarah: CC 107

Jiundu Swamp: MW 65, 70

Jiva: defined, SE 67

Jivaro Indians: MW 113, 117-119

Jnana-yoga: defined, EM 37, 117; and Swami Vivekananda, EM 117. See also Yoga

Jo (abductee): AE 123

Joan (pope): CD 64

Joan (psychic): clairvoyance of, PP 128

Joan of Arc, Saint: CC 89, DD 37, VP 14; clairaudience of, PP 17, 18-19

Job (biblical figure): CD 82

Johannes (monk): ML 61

Johannes (spirit): at Glastonbury Abbey, PP 120

Johann Georg II (prince-bishop of Bamberg): death of, WW 92; and Johannes Junius, WW 94; and witches, WW 90-91, 92; and witch hunts, WW 69-70

John (abductee): AE 39

John (apostle): MA 50, UV 23, 24-25

John (fictional character): AE 45

John (feral child): TN 69; autism of, TN 69; and Harlan Lane, TN 68, 69; and Richard Pillard, TN 68, 69

John, Apostle (spirit guide): SS 10; and Kevin Ryerson, SS 10, 146

John XXII (pope): HN 137, SA 34; and witches, WW 54

John Birch Society: AW 108

John Paul II (pope): CD 58, 110

Johnson, George: AW 86-89, 104, 108

Johnson, James: as exorcist, HN 93; and poltergeists, HN 93, 94

Johnson, Jesse: AE 83-84

Johnson, John: sketch by, AW 75

Johnson, Lyndon B.: MW 133, VP 26

Johnson, Marvin: MA 126-128

Johnson, Ronald: AE 76

Johnson, Samuel: CC 85, MA 137, SE 58; and creativity, MB 90; and depression, MB 88; and obsessive-compulsive disorder, MB 88; and séances, HN 64

Johnston, Jerry: CD 96

John the Baptist, Saint: MW 129, UV 35; and Muhammad, DD 50

John the French Leich: See Damian, John

Joint Air Reconnaissance Intelligence Centre (JARIC): MC 73

Joint Army-Navy-Air Force Publication (JANAP): and UFO secrecy, UP 70

Joke Fest: PH 133, 135

Jol: MY 121

Joller, Karoline: HN 71

Joller, Melchior: HN 71; and poltergeists, HN 70-72

Jolnir (god): MY 121

Jomard, Edmé-François: and Great Pyramid, MP 55-57, 63

63

Jomon: and Ainu, ML 30; potters of, ML 116-117

Jones (lieutenant): PS 70-71

Jones, Eryl Mai: MY *95;* clairvoyance of, PP *32-33,* 34

Jones, George Cecil: AW 128

Jones, Inigo: and Druids, MP 88; and Stonehenge, MP *84-85,* 86, 88, 92

Jones, John Paul: AW *80,* 81

Jones, Neil R.: SI 114

Jones, Nella: and Yorkshire Ripper case, PP 134, *136, 137*

Jong, Henk de: MC 34

Jonky, Dionizy: and psychometry, test of, PP 120-121

Jonsson, Olof: PS *112;* and stock market, PS 112, 113

Joplin, Janis: CC 89, EM 125

Jordan, biblical quests in: Ark of the Covenant dig, MQ 47-48; Dead Sea, MQ 43

Josef (possessed person): CD 88-90

Joseph (biblical figure, husband of Mary): DD 37

Joseph (biblical figure, son of Jacob): DD 26-29; as seer, VP 10, *15*

Joseph, John (a.k.a. Prince, or Archdeacon, of Nouri): MQ 79-80

Joseph, Saint: MY 23, 84, 95, 114

Joseph II (Holy Roman emperor): VP 69

Joseph d'Arimathie (Borron): MQ 118-120, 123

Josephine (empress of France): AW 103

Josephine (percipient of postmortem apparition): PE 58

Joseph of Arimathea: EE 88, MQ 110, 119, 123, *126;* and Glastonbury (England), ML 52; and Grail, ML 52, 56

Joseph of Copertino, Saint: CD 115-116; levitation of, MM *116*

Josephson, Brian: SE *137*

Josephus: MB 42; and Essenes, UV 33, 35

Jotunheim: WW 28

Jourdain, Eleanor: HN 39, MY *68,* PE *122;* handwriting of, HN *41;* music heard by, HN *48;* and retrocognition, HN *43-51*

Journal of Parapsychology: MM 62; founding of, PP 56

Journeys Out of the Body (Monroe): PV 30, 32

Journey to Ladakh (Harvey): EM 97-98

Journey to the Centre of the Earth (Verne): MP 146-147

Journey to the Earth's Interior, A (Gardner): MP 148-151

Jouvet, Michel: DD *103;* and sleep, DD 99

Joyce, James: CC 90, TS 66

JPF: SE 109, 110, 112

Juan, Don (magician): MA 115

Judaism: MW 99

Judas, seat of (Siege Perilous): MQ 118, 120

Judas Iscariot (biblical figure): EE 92, MY 97, SE 82

Judd, Neil M.: ML *129*

Jude, Saint: MY 97

Judeo-Christian tradition: and paradise myths, UV 6, *12-13, 14-15,* 18, 20

Judge, William Quan: AW 140, 141

Juggernaut: MY 53

Juggler, The (Chagall): DD 12, *13*

Ju-jus: MA 82

Julian calendar: MY 83, 125

Juliette (spirit communicator): SE 100, 102

Julius (emperor of Rome): MY 49

Julius Caesar (Shakespeare): VP 110

Jullian, Phillipe: HN 50

Jung, Carl Gustav: AW 49, CC 37, 84, 131, CD 29, 35, DD *59, 69, 79,* EM 35, MA 62, MM 72, MY 64, PE 117, PV 16, SA 132-133, SE 115-117, 139, TS *123,* UP *53,* VP *9, 122;* and alchemy, SA 115, 129-133; and aliens, AE 101; and androgyny, CD 70; and anima/animus, CD 70; and archetypes, AE 111, CD 42-43, DD 57, 71, 73, 81, 85, 87, 89, 91, WW 115; background of, DD 67-68, EE 50-51, 76; and Brahma, DD 71; and churingas, EE 50; and coincidences, TS 121; and collective unconscious, AE 101, 111, 120, DD 70, 73, 81, 153, EE 51, MB 20, 23, PP 21, SA 130, 132, TN 31, TS 121; depression of, DD 69-72; and dreams, DD 24, 56, 57-58, 59, 67, 68, 69-72, *70-71,* 73-74, 75, 78, 127, 153, MB 20, PP 66, SA 130-131, 132; and dualities, CD 35; and Albert Einstein, TS 121; and exploding knife, PP *57;* and Sigmund Freud, DD 56-57, 58, 59, 67, 68-69, 70, 72, 73, SA 129-130; and Budd Hopkins, AE 127; house of, DD *76-77;* and *I Ching,* TS 122, VP 119, 122; and individuation, DD 75; and kaabir, EE 50-51, 76; and mandala, AE 127, DD 75, MB *23,* UP 53; and mental illnesses, MB 79; and nirvana, CD 18; and Wolfgang Pauli, TS 121; and Philemon, DD 70; and Helene Preiswerk, MB 79; and primordial mind, MB 90; and psyche, DD 57; psychic beliefs of, PP 21; and psychic research, PP 56; and psychoanalysis, DD 60, 69, EE 50; and psychology of the medium, PP 21; and J. B. Rhine's experiments, PP 57; and séances, MB 79; and *spiritus mundi,* EE 51; and synchronicity, TS 121-122; as Tarot reader, VP 140; theories of, PV 125, VP 9, 122; and the unconscious, DD 73, MB 20; and UFOs, AE 111, 114, UP 53

Jung, Emilie: DD 69

Jung, Emma: DD 72

Jung, Paul: DD *69*

Jungle (Garber): MB 66

Jungle, The (Sinclair): UV 85

Junius, Johannes: WW 88-*89,* 90, 92-95

Junkanoo: MY 121

Junks: EM *8-9*

Juno (goddess): CC 43, MY 49, 50

Jupiter (god): CC *43,* MW 90, MY 24, 103. *See also* Zeus

Jupiter (planet): AE *90-93,* CC 16, 24, 36, 43, *57,* 98, *150,* MA *36,* 40, 41, MY 86, 103; background of, AE 92; symbol for, SA *25*

Jürgenson, Friedrich: PE 116-*117*

AE *Alien Encounters;* **AW** *Ancient Wisdom and Secret Sects;* **CC** *Cosmic Connections;* **CD** *Cosmic Duality;* **DD** *Dreams and Dreaming;* **EE** *Earth Energies;* **EM** *Eastern Mysteries;* **HN** *Hauntings;* **MA** *Magical Arts;* **MB** *The Mind and Beyond;* **MC** *Mysterious Creatures;* **ML** *Mysterious Lands and Peoples;* **MM** *Mind over Matter;* **MP** *Mystic Places;* **MQ** *Mystic Quests;* **MW** *The Mysterious World;*

K

KNIGHT. *The knight upon his mount symbolizes the spirit dominating matter in order to subdue evil. Saint George (left) was probably a third-century Christian martyr, although he became a dragon-slaying knight in medieval legend.*

K., Mr.: MW 34, 37-38; and transformations, TN 47-48
Ka: defined, CD 122
Kaabir: defined, EE 50; and Carl Jung, EE 50-51, 76
Ka'ba: CD *101,* EE 52, MY *90, 91*
Kabala: *See* Cabala and Cabalists
Kabbalah: *See* Cabala and Cabalists
Kabuki theater: PE 73, 77, 79, 81
Kachina dancers: MY *132-133*
Kachinas: MA 46, MY *64*
Kahan, Barry: PH 54
Kahn, Herman: VP 28
Kahuna ana'anas: MA 84-86, 90. *See also* Low magic
Kahuna la'au lapa'aus: MA 90, *91;* and folk medicine, MA 87, 90; and Julius Scammon Rodman, MA 90
Kahunas: MW 127; defined, MM 103; fire walking of, MM 103-104
Kaigh, Frederick: TN 20-21
Kaihogyo: EM 58
Kailas, Mount: EE *28,* EM *42-43,* MW 93, TS 6, *10-11*
Kaimakoi (king of Easter Island): ML 87
Kaiô Maru No. 5 (research vessel): MW 94
Kane: and folk medicine, MA 87-90
Kai tribe: DD 24
Kajintin: defined, MA 80
Kalacakra (Wheel of Time; Buddhist teachings): MQ 25-26
Kalapa (capital of Shambhala): MQ 25
Kalaripayit: EM *144-145*
Kalasasaya: MW *82*
Kalash (vessel): MY 104
Kalash people: SI *91*
Kali (decadent age): UV 23
Kali (goddess): AW *40,* CD *13,* EM 116, MY *134*

Kali Yuga: MY 134, UV 102
Kalki (incarnation of Vishnu): PV *98-99*
Kamala (feral child): TN *62, 63,* 64
Kamea: defined, MA 36, 41; and planets, MA *36, 37,* 41
Kami: defined, EE 57
Kammerer, Paul: TS 121, *122*
Kampman, Reima: and reincarnation research, PV *124-125*
Kan (god): TS 34
Kandinsky, Wassily: AW *162,* MY 115, UV *131;* and Bauhaus, UV 129, 131; and expressionists, UV 129; and Kazimir Malevich, UV 131; paintings by, AW *162-163;* UV *131;* and suprematists, UV 131; and utopia, UV 121
Kane: and folk medicine, MA 87-90
Kangyur (Tibetan holy book): MQ 23
Kanname-Sai: MY 94
Kant, Immanuel: CC 81, CD 107, 127-128, SE 58-59, TS 42; and Rudolf Steiner, UV 111, 114
Kanzi (chimpanzee): MB *43*
Kao, Johnny: EE 35
Kao Tsong: DD *27*
Kapha: PH 65, 66, 67
Kaplan, Stephen: and vampires, TN 136

Kaplan, Stuart R.: VP 134
Kapor, Mitchell: EM 142
Karakoram Mountains: SI *48-49*
Karate: EM *153,* MW 127
Kardec, Allan: SE 45, *91;* reincarnation beliefs of, PV 102
Karian (islet): ML 97
Karkom, Har (mesa; Israel): MQ *44-45*
Karma: PH 63; Edgar Cayce's beliefs in, PV 124; defined, CD 85, 111, EM 37, PV 99, 102, SE 45, 67, TS 25; and Milarepa, EM 50; Theosophical beliefs in, PV 103
Karma-yoga: and Mirra Alfassa, UV 147; and Auroville (India), UV 149; defined, EM 37; and Sri Aurobindo, UV 146. *See also* Yoga
Karnak (Egypt): MW 77, 99, 100-102
Karoshi: SI 45
Kashim: MY 117
Kashyapa: EM 55
Kassada: MY 126
Kauaua: EE *90*
Kaufman, Andy: PH 36, 37
Kaumualii (ruler of Kauai): MW 99
Kautz, William: PS *108-109,* 110, 130
Kaya Kulp: and alchemists, SI 34; defined, SI 32

Kaye, Violette: residence of, PS *36*
Kaygee (spirit guide): and Irene Hughes, PP 99
Kazhinsky, Bernard: PS 79
K-complexes: DD 97. *See also* Sleep
K. E. (hypnotist): PV 119
Kean, Charles: PE 119
Kebalananda: SI 8-9
Kecak dance: EM *67. See also* Dances
Kecksburg (Pennsylvania): UFOs in, AE *86-87*
Keel, John: MC 123
Keeler, William M.: spirit photography of, PP *44-45*
Keeler, William W.: PS 109
Keeley, Leslie: SA 116
Keeton, Joe: as hypnotherapist, PV 115
Kekule von Stradonitz, Friedrich August: DD *116;* and hypnagogic state, DD 116, 117
Keli Mutu, Mount (Indonesia): SE 24
Kellar, Harry: SS 101-102, 103
Keller, Helen: MB 54, PH 55
Kelley, Edward: SA *58-59;* and alchemy, SA 58; death of, SA 59-60; and John Dee, MA 45, 57, SA 58-59; as scryer, VP 46-47, 49; and séances, SA 59
Kelly, Aidan: WW 105, *113;* and Gerald Brosseau Gardner, WW 105-107, 113
Kelly, Edward: CC 74
Kelly, J. H.: PH 107
Kelly, Katherine: HN 114; and ghosts, HN 115, 117-118
Kelly, Maurice: and ghosts, HN 114-115, 117-118
Kelly, Patricia: and ghosts, HN 114
Kelly, Rose: AW 118, *119,* 120
Kelly-Hopkinsville event: and encounter with aliens, UP 64-65, *68*
Kelmscott Press: UV 85
Kelpius, Johannes: UV 60
Kelta Indians: SE 16
Kendo: EM *150-151*
Kenjutsu: EM 150
Kennedy, James: and psychic research test data, PP 60
Kennedy, John Fitzgerald: CC 82,

MY The Mystical Year; PE Phantom Encounters; PH Powers of Healing; PP Psychic Powers; PS The Psychics; PV Psychic Voyages; SA Secrets of the Alchemists; SE Search for the Soul; SI Search for Immortality; SS Spirit Summonings; TN Transformations; TS Time and Space; UP The UFO Phenomenon; UV Utopian Visions; VP Visions and Prophecies; WW Witches and Witchcraft

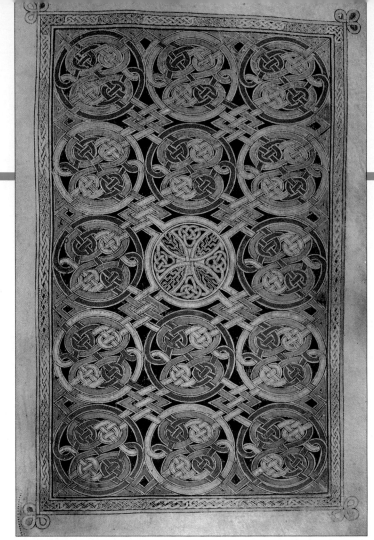

KNOT. *The pattern in this illumination from a medieval manuscript is based upon the knot, a symbol that can represent either a state of psychic bondage or, quite differently, the continuity of life.*

149, EE 67, MY 103, VP 23; assassination of, PS *8-9,* 121; and Jeane Dixon, PS 9; presidential election of, PS 121; and David Williams, PS 121

Kennedy, Robert F.: VP 25

Kensington Stone: ML *129;* and Hjalmar R. Holand, ML 126; and Olof Ohman, ML 126; and M. W. Stirling, ML 128

Kent, Dora: SI 123-128

Kent, Elizabeth: HN 63

Kent, Fanny: death of, HN 63, 64, 70; and poltergeists, HN 63

Kent, Saul: SI 123

Kent, William: HN 63; and séances, HN 64

Kenya: MW 65, 66-67, 75

Kenya, Mount: MW 133, 136, *137*

Kenyatta, Jomo: MW 136

Kepler, Johannes: AW 54, CC 25, 96-100, *98,* TS *52*

Kercado: MW 88

Keres: MY 19

Kerinci, Mount: MW 59

Ker-Is: MW 87

Kermario Alignment: MW *87,* 88

Kermesse: MY 91, 96

Kern babies: MY *73*

Kernbeis, Franz: art by, MB *66-67*

Kerner, Justinus A. C.: and ghosts, HN 129-130

Kerotakis: defined, SA 24

Kerouac, Jack: EM 137; and Zen Buddhism, EM 138

Kerr, Roy: and rotating black holes, TS 73

Ketchum, Wesley H.: PH 30

Ketieu plants: ML 97

Keuls, Eva: CD 55-56

Keyhoe, Donald E.: UP 56; and Condon committee, UP 116; and investigations of UFOs, UP 46, *47;* and National Investigations Committee on Aerial Phenomena, UP 69, 70

Key of Solomon (Anonymous): MA 54, 59, 62

Khakhlov, V. A.: MC 110; drawing by, MW *60*

Khazneh: ML *74-75*

Khembalung (legendary valley; Nepal): MQ 30; Bernbaum's quest for, MQ 30-31

Khmer: god-kings of, ML 70

Khodzko (Russian colonel): MQ 75

Khosrow II (Persian king): MQ 115

Khufu: MP 48. *See also* Great Pyramid of Cheops

Khunrath, Heinrich: SA 80, 81-82, 90

Khvit (Zana's son): MC 110. *See also* Almas; Zana

Kidd, James: MY 54, SE 6-12, *9,* 15-20, 32, 71, 139; claims to bequest of, SE 15, 18-20, 71; will of, SE *11,* 12, 15

Kidinnu: CC 24-26, 29

Kiecorius, Edith: disappearance of, and psychometry, PP 129-130

Kielar, Alan: MC 82

Kierkegaard, Søren: CC 81

Kiki-a-Ola: MW 96

Kikuno (ghost): PE *78-79*

Kikuyu people: MW 133, 136

Kilauea, Mount: MM 103-*104*

Kilburn, Steven: abduction by aliens, UP 58, 60-61

Kilimanjaro, Mount: MW 42

Kilindini: MW 75

Kimbrell, Andrew: SI 85

Kincaid, Charles: HN 107

Kinder, Gary: and Brit Elders, AE 105; and Eduard Meier, AE 104, 105

Kinetic hypothesis: defined, MM 64. *See also* Psychokinesis

King, Billie Jean: MM 126; visualization by, MM 126

King, Charlotte: PS *18*

King, Francis: and Gerald Brosseau Gardner, WW 105

King, George: PS 100; and Aetherius Society, UP 78-79

King, John (spirit guide): SS 52, 54-55, 59, 60

King, Katie: MY 68, SS *60,* SS 52, 53, 55, 56, *58,* 60

King, Martin Luther, Jr.: CC 89

King, Stephen: and vampires, TN 136

Kingfishers: MY 119

King's Bridge: MA 120

Kingsford, Anna: AW 128

King Solomon's Masonic lodge: monument erected by, AW 79

King Solomon's mines: MQ *42,* 43; search for, MQ 41-42

King Solomon's Mines (Haggard): ML 68, MQ 41

Kingu (satellite): AE *93;* background of, AE 92

Kino: and folk medicine, MA 87-90

Kipling, Rudyard: AW 98, 111, DD 131, EM 35, MB 90, WW 103

Kircher, Athanasius: drawings by, EM *29*

Kiribati Islands: ML 96-97

Kirkpatrick, John Simpson: MW 34, PE *136-137*

Kirlian, Semyon: and auras, PP 145; and Valentina, PH 78

Kirlian effects: on fruit juice, PP *150;* on humans, PP *146-147;* on metal, PP *151;* on plants, PP *148-149*

Kirlian photography: PH 75, *78-79,* 103; and auras, PP 145, *146-151*

Kirmes: MY 96

Kirtananda (a.k.a. Keith Ham): EM 127-130

Kissinger, Henry: MA 6, MM 36

Kitchener, Horatio Herbert: VP 81, 82

Kite, Charles: PH 88

Kites: MY *92*

Kittle, Ron: hypnosis of, MM *100*

Kitty (ghost): PE 10

Kitty's Steps: PE *10-11*

Kivas: MY 133; defined, ML 80

Kiyota, Masuaki: thoughtography of, MM 68

Klamath River: MW 47

Klass, Philip J.: AE 24, UP 127, 143; debunking UFOs at Exeter, UP 104-106, *105*

Klee, Paul: UV 129, 130; painting by, UV *130*

Klein, Martin: MC 78

Kleitman, Nathaniel: DD *100,* TS 81; and REM sleep, DD 96, 97

Klemme, Herbert L.: and time slips, TS 113

Kleopatra: and alchemy, SA 24; diagram by, SA *28*

Kline, Deborah Sue: disappearance of, PP 132, *133*

Kline, Jane: PP 132-133

Kloeckler, Herbert F. von: CC 131

Kmetz, John: and Cleve Backster, EE 108-109; and plant con-

AE Alien Encounters; AW Ancient Wisdom and Secret Sects; CC Cosmic Connections; CD Cosmic Duality; DD Dreams and Dreaming; EE Earth Energies; EM Eastern Mysteries; HN Hauntings; MA Magical Arts; MB The Mind and Beyond; MC Mysterious Creatures; ML Mysterious Lands and Peoples; MM Mind over Matter; MP Mystic Places; MQ Mystic Quests; MW The Mysterious World;

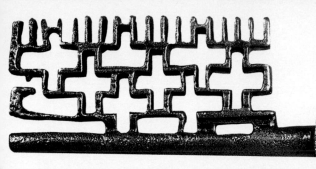

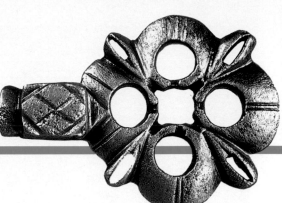

sciousness, EE 108-109

Knarr: ML 123

Kneipp, Sebastian: SI 28, 29; and Kneipp cure, SI 29

Kneipp cure: SI 28, 29; and Sebastian Kneipp, SI 29; and Nathaniel Rothschild, SI 29

Knievel, Evel: MM 125, 126; visualization by, MM 124, 126

Knight, Mrs.: and hauntings, HN 86-88

Knight, J. Hardwicke: MQ 84-85

Knight, J. Z.: SS 140-141; background of, SS 137-140; and Shirley MacLaine, SS 140; and Ramtha, SS 8-9, 137, 140-142; and Carl Raschke, SS 150

Knights: MQ 110, 111; of the Round Table, MQ 111, 119, 120-121; in Parzifal, MQ 111-112, 114, 117, 118

Knights Templars: AW 12, 36, HN 12, MA 50, MQ 118, 122, MY 21, PE 124; and Assassins, AW 39; decline of, AW 36-39; and Freemasons, AW 97, 98, 100; history of, AW 33-36; initiation of, AW 36, 38; and Muslims, AW 38-39; seal of, AW 36; and Sufis, AW 35. See also individual Knights Templars

Knipe, Ruth: MQ 40

"Knockers": defined, MA 129

Knoll, Joseph: SI 74

Knollys, William: MW 22

Knossos (Crete): MW 53

Koans: EM 97

Koch, Albert: MC 28, 30

Koch, Joseph Anton: mural by, CD 88-89

Koestler, Arthur: MB 117; out-of-body experiences of, PV 15

Koffmann, Marie-Jeanne: MC 112, MW 60

Kogan, Ippolite M.: psychokinesis research of, MM 79

Koguski, Felix: UV 112-113

Kohada Koheiji: PE 77

Koh-i-noor: MW 127, 129

Kohlberg, Kravis, Roberts: PS 119

Kolam: MY 101

Kolb, Fred: PS 20

Kolbe, Maximilian: CD 110

Kolff, Willem: SI 83

Kolisko, Lilly: SA 130-131

Koller, Fritz: art by, MB 66-67

Komodo dragon: MC 20-21

Kongamato: MW 65, 67-68, 70

Koniags: and amulets, MA 109

König, Wilhelm: ML 23

Kon-Tiki (raft): and Thor Heyerdahl, ML 93, 95, 120

Koor, Alexander: MQ 84

Kopp, Hermann: SA 114

Koran: MY 90-91; and paradise myths, UV 6, 7

Korea: Buddhism in, EM 100, 101, 104-105; dominoes in, VP 112; monks in, EM 104-105

Koreans: cosmogonies of, TS 20-22

Korein, Julius: SE 138

Koreshanity (religion): MP 148, 151

Korsakoff's syndrome: defined, MB 60

Koryak Indians: burial rituals of, PE 53; and sacrifices, MA 120-121

Koslov, Samuel: and psychic research, military applications of, PP 144

Kosmos: defined, TS 43

Kosok, Paul: and Nazca lines of Peru, MP 110-112

Kosrae Island: ML 102

Köthendörffer, Dr.: WW 92

Krafft, Karl Ernst: CC 132, 134-138, 135, 140, MY 99, PS 62-63

Krakatau: eruption of, EE 68

Kraken: MC 10, 11, MW 71, 73; characteristics of, MC 11, 45; history of, MC 22. See also Squid

Kramer, Gustav: and migration, TS 82

Kramer, Heinrich: 62-64; and Innocent VIII, WW 62-64

Kramer, Milton: DD 110-111

Krantz, Grover: MC 124, 125; Sasquatch research of, MC 124, 126

Krater (divine cup): MQ 109

Kresge, George (a.k.a. Kreskin; mentalist): mind-reading act of, PP 114, 115-117; powers of, PP 103, 115

Kreskin: See Kresge, George

Krieger, Dolores: PH 107

Krippner, Stanley: DD 119, 124, 146-149; and dream research, PP 66, 74

Krishna (god): DD 24, EM 124, MY 72, TS 23, 25; as Blue God, UV 9

Krishna, Gopal: EM 24

Krishnamurti, Jiddu: AW 143, SE 131, 134, UV 115-118. See also EM index

Krishnamurti, Nitya: EM 87-88

Krita Yuga: MY 134

Krivé, Taryn: SS 14-15, 148

Kriya-yoga: and Babaji, SI 10, 11; characteristics of, EM 118; defined, SI 10; and Lahiri Mahasaya, SI 10; and Paramahansa Yogananda, EM 118, 119; and Sri Yukteswar, EM 118. See also Yoga

Kroc, Ray: PS 104-105

Krueger, Myron: MB 130

Krupp, E. C.: and Nazca lines of Peru, MP 114

Ku: MA 90

Kuala Selangor (Malaysia): hauntings in, PE 138

Kubary, Johann Stanislaus: ML 98-100

Kubera (god): EM 16

Kubie, Lawrence S.: PH 127

Kublai Khan: ML 66; and Marco Polo, EM 27-28; residence of, EM 10

Kübler-Ross, Elisabeth: EM 139; and Jay Barham, PV 65; and near-death-experience research, PV 58, 64-65, 66; out-of-body experience of, PV 65

Kubota, Shiro: AE 61-62

Kubrick, Stanley: CC 84

Kudurru: CC 10

Kukulcan (god): MY 103

Kulagina, Nina (Nelya Mikhailova): MM 23, PS 78; lawsuit by, MM 26-27; psi phenomena of, MM 23, 26-27

Kuleshova, Rosa: MB 52

Kumade: MY 103

Kumbha Mela: SI 16-21; background of, SI 16; characteristics of, SI 20; and Hindus, SI 16-21; purification rites of, SI 21

Kundalini: PH 74

Kunegel, Gregor: CD 89

Kung: CD 109

Kung fu: visualization in, MM 128-129

Kunisada, Utagawa: print by, PE 78-79

Kuniyoshi, Utagawa: prints by, PE 74-75, 81

Kunkin, Art: SA 134-135

Kunlun, Mount: MW 128

Kunlun Mountains: SI 36

Kuntz, Otto: MP 23

Kupka, František: AW 164; paintings by, AW 164-167

Kurcsics, Michael: disappearance of, and clairvoyance, PP 132-133

Kuroshio Current: ML 120

Kurtz, Paul: CD 127

Kushi, Lawrence: PH 63

Kushi, Michio: PH 60, 61

Kutchin Indians: reincarnation beliefs of, PV 108

Kuwait: MW 43

Kuykendall, Karen: Tarot cards by, VP 138-139

Kvaran, Einar: SE 99

Kveldulf (berserker): transformations of, TN 36-37

Kwakiutl Indians: MA 70-71, MW 113; culture of, TN 6; masks of, TN 9, 13, 14-15

Kwearriburras: burial rituals of, PE 53

Kyot der Provenzal: Wolfram's citation of, MQ 117

Kyteler, Alice: excommunication of, WW 55; as witch, WW 54-55

Kyudo: EM 152; defined, MM 121

MY The Mystical Year; PE Phantom Encounters; PH Powers of Healing; PP Psychic Powers; PS The Psychics; PV Psychic Voyages; SA Secrets of the Alchemists; SE Search for the Soul; SI Search for Immortality; SS Spirit Summonings; TN Transformations; TS Time and Space; UP The UFO Phenomenon; UV Utopian Visions; VP Visions and Prophecies; WW Witches and Witchcraft

L

Laaber family: and ghosts, HN 15

LaBerge, Stephen: DD *112;* and lucid dreams, DD 110-113; and Mnemonic Induction of Lucid Dreams, DD 110; and out-of-body-experience research, PV 42-44

Labo, Ramon ("Junior"): PH 36-37

Laboratories: SA *36-41;* altars in, SA 35; characteristics of, SA 35; fire in, SA 35, *36-37, 38-39;* of Heinrich Khunrath, SA *81;* location of, SA 35; origins of term, SA 80

Laboratory of Biophysics: PS 84

Labrador (Canada): MW 42

Labrang monastery: EM *102-103*

Labyrinth: UV *61*

LaChapelle, Dolores: EE 62

Ladd, George Trumbull: DD 59

Ladders: MA 118

Lady (horse): AE *40*

Lady in Moscow (Kandinsky): AW *162*

Lady Wonder (horse): performance of, PP *110;* psychic abilities of, PP 57

Laestrygones: decimation of Ulysses' fleet by, possible setting for, MQ 55

Lafayette, Marie-Joseph de: AW 79, *80,* 82, 104-105; Masonic apron of, AW *81*

La Grua, Vincenzo: MW 36-37

La Harpe, Jean-François de: VP 6

Laila, Terfren: VP *21*

Laing, Ronald David: MB *76;* and ego, MB 92; and schizophrenia, MB 75-77

Lairre, Marie: casket of, HN *69;* ghost of, HN 68

Laithwaite, Eric: PE 113-114

Lake monsters: MW *map 46,* 49; Champ, MC 62, *63;* history of, MC 61-62; Loch Ness monster, MC 60-61, 63, 66-69, 71-73, *74-75,* 77-79, *80-81, 82-85,* 87-89; Morag, MC 62, 90; Naitaka, MC 62; Ogopogo, MC *62-63;* spirits, MC 61; water bulls, MC 61; water horses, MC 61; water kelpies, MC 61. *See also* Sea serpents; *specific lake monsters*

Lake of Gems: SI 36

Lakshmi (goddess): AE *44,* MY 101

Lalibela (Ethiopia): MW 99, 102, *103*

Lalibela (king of Ethiopia): MW 102

Lamas: MC *104,* MQ 23, 27, 30, PV 128, 132-133, *134-135, 136-137;* in China, EM *78, 79;* defined, PV 120; as fortunetellers, TS 95; In Tibet, EM *31, 82-83. See also* Dalai Lamas

Lamb, Lawrence: SI 88

Lambert, André: prints by, CD 87

Lambert, G. W.: HN *122,* PE 122; and ghosts, HN 122, 125; and retrocognition, 50

AE Alien Encounters; AW Ancient Wisdom and Secret Sects; CC Cosmic Connections; CD Cosmic Duality; DD Dreams and Dreaming; EE Earth Energies; EM Eastern Mysteries; HN Hauntings; MA Magical Arts; MB The Mind and Beyond; MC Mysterious Creatures; ML Mysterious Lands and Peoples; MM Mind over Matter; MP Mystic Places; MQ Mystic Quests; MW The Mysterious World;

LOTUS. *Dressed in lotuses, the Hindu deities Krishna (right) and Radha, his mistress, float upon more of the blossoms. The lotus is India's sacred flower, symbolic of creation, purity, and life everlasting.*

LAUREL. *Assisted by cherubs, a muse of poetry and the Greek god Apollo crown a poet with laurel leaves in the painting below. Laurel connotes poetic inspiration, perhaps because chewing its intoxicating leaves is said to rouse creativity.*

Lambert, Madame: out-of-body experience of, PV *26*

Lamb's heart: MA *22*

Lamech (biblical figure): SI 12

Lame Deer, John: MQ 6, 10, 12, 15, 17

La Mettrie, Julien Offroy de: MB 13, 19

Lamia (hill; Greece): cave chapel in, MQ 59

Lamia (mythical beast): MC *57*, MQ 58, 59; characteristics of, TN *110*, 111, 134; defined, TN 110. *See also* Human-beasts; Vampires

Lammas: MY 65, 73

Lammer, Arthur: and Edgar Cayce, PP 94

Lamon, Ward H.: and Abraham Lincoln, PP 17-18

Lamps: MA 82; oil, EM *52*

Lan Caihe: SA *113*

Lancaster, Maude (mentalist): mind-reading act of, PP 107

Lancelin, Charles: PV 25

Lancelot (character in Arthurian legend): ML 49, MQ 120

Lancre, Pierre de: and Jean Grenier, TN 86, 87; and witch hunts, WW 68-69

Landau, Lucian: PE 94, 95

Land mines: defined, PS 74; and dogs, PS 74, 76

Land of Room Enough and Time Enough: EE 40-41

Landolphia fruit: MC *95*

Landrum, Vickie: and UFO sighting, UP 8-9, *10-11*

Landscape Angel: EE 135

Lane, Harlan: and John, TN 68, 69

Lang, Mrs.: TS 131, 132

Lang, Andrew: and poltergeists, HN 72

Lang, David: TS 131-132

Lang, George: TS 131, 132

Lang, Sarah: TS 131, 132

Lang, William: PH 34, *35*

Langeville, Harcouët de: SI 34

Lang Pachaa: EM *52-53*

Langport (dog): ML 44-45

Lanier, Jaron: and computer clothing, MB 130; and Virtual Programming Languages, Inc., MB 130; and virtual reality, MB *130-*

131, 137

L'Anse aux Meadows (Canada): ML 124-126

Lansing, Jessica: SS 146-147

Lantern Festival: MY 128, 129

Lanyi, Monsignor de: DD 141, MY 57

Lanza, Cesare: MW 37

Lanza, Laura: MW 34, 36-37

Laozi (Lao-tzu): EM 51, 53, PH 53, TS 29

Laparoscopy: AE 36

Lapis lazuli: MA 101

Lapland: MW 119-*121*

Lapps: ML *30*, MW 119-*120*

Laramie, Treaty of: MW 79

Larbig, Wolfgang: self-mutilation research of, MM 108-112

Lares (ancestral spirits): MY *135*

Larkin (lieutenant): MY 116

Larsen, Caroline: out-of-body experience of, PV 14-15, *16*

Larsson, Rolf: MW 54-55

Lascaux Cave: painting in, SE 16, TN *26*

Laser puncture: PH 49, *50*

Laser treatment: SI *94*

Lashley, Karl: MB 58-59

Laski, Albert: VP 47

Last Days of Pompeii, The (Bulwer-Lytton): MP 146

Last Hope Inlet: MW 47, 50-*51*

Last Judgment: TS *41*

Last Supper: MA 119; chalice from, Holy Grail as, MQ 106, 119, 123, *126*; reenactments of, in grail legends, MQ 118, 119-120

Last Supper (Castagno): VP *109*

Lasuria, Khfaf: SI 41-43

Latané, Bibb: CD 111

Lateau, Louise: stigmata of, MM 113

Latihan: EM 121

Latimeria chalumnae: See Coelacanths

Laubheim, Alvin: MM 50

Laudanum: MA 63, SA 65

Laufer, Berthold: MQ 27

Laughing figurine: MQ *97*

Laughing gas: MB 102

Laugh therapy: PH 6-7

Laurel: MA 99

Laurelite: PS 130

Laurels: divination with, VP 40

Laurens, Henry: MY 116

Lavater, Johann Kaspar: as physiognomist, VP 67-69, *72*

Lavater, Ludwig: treatise of, PE *48*

Laveau, Marie: MA *81-82*

La Vey, Anton Szandor: CD *81;* and Michael Aquino, CD 78; and Church of Satan, CD 78, 80, 96

Law, William: drawing by, EE *96*

Lawden, D. F.: and ghosts, HN 85

''Lawless nights'': MY 98

Lawren, Bill: SI 85

Lawrence, D. H.: out-of-body experiences of, PV 15

Lawrence, T. E. D.: CC 84

Laws (Plato): UV 23

Lawson, Alvin: AE 111

Lawson, Joel S., Jr.: PS 90

Laxdaela (Anonymous): WW 30

Laying on of hands: MW 109, PH 83-87, *84-85. See also individual healers*

Laying the ghost: defined, HN 118

Lay monks: in Tibet, MA 18

Layne, Al C. (hypnotist): and Edgar Cayce, PH 31, PP 92

Lay of the Werewolf (France): TN 79

Lazaris (spirit guide): *See* Pursel, Jach

Lead: characteristics of, SA 21; symbol for, SA *25*

Leadbeater, Charles Webster: AW *136;* and auras, AW 144, *145;* and Annie Wood Besant, AW *142-143;* and *chakras*, AW *144;* and Jiddu Krishnamurti, AW 143; and Tantra, AW 139; and thought forms, AW 144, *145;* and werewolves, TN 89; and wound doubling, TN 89

Leaf, Alexander: and Miguel Carpio, SI 43; and Caucasus Mountains, SI 43; and Hunzakuts, SI 43, 49; and Khfaf Lasuria, SI 41; and longevity, SI 41, 43; and Vilcabamba (Ecuador), SI 43

Leaf, Horace: PS 29; and Arthur Conan Doyle, PS 32; and psychometry, PS 32

MY *The Mystical Year;* **PE** *Phantom Encounters;* **PH** *Powers of Healing;* **PP** *Psychic Powers;* **PS** *The Psychics;* **PV** *Psychic Voyages;* **SA** *Secrets of the Alchemists;* **SE** *Search for the Soul;* **SI** *Search for Immortality;* **SS** *Spirit Summonings;* **TN** *Transformations;* **TS** *Time and Space;* **UP** *The UFO Phenomenon;* **UV** *Utopian Visions;* **VP** *Visions and Prophecies;* **WW** *Witches and Witchcraft*

LILY. *German artist Franz von Stuck captures the symbolic meaning of this chaste flower in his 1889 painting Innocence, in which a young woman holds a lily bouquet. In many religions the flower represents a virgin goddess or matriarch.*

League of Nations: VP 20

Leahy, William: VP 27; and A-bomb, PP 144

Leander (brig): PS *129;* and Mobius Society, PS 128; and Stephan A. Schwartz, PS 128

Leap year: MY 137

Leary, Timothy: EM 138, MB 106-107, 112-114, *115-117*

Leaves of Grass (Whitman): VP 80

LeBlond, Paul H.: MC 38-39, 44

LeCron, Leslie M.: MM 122-123

Leda: TN *35*

Ledge: ancient, psychically detected, MQ *103*

Le Diable Amoureux (Cazotte): VP 6

Ledoux, A.: MW 69

Ledrede, Richard de: and Alice Kyteler, WW 55

Lee, Ann (a.k.a. Ann the Word, Mother Ann): UV *73*, 74; and Baptists, UV 65; and Calvinists, UV 65; and celibacy, UV 64, 65, 70; death of, UV 68; marriage of, UV 63; persecution of, UV 65-68; and Shakers, UV 56, 63-64; and transcendentalists, UV 81; and visions, UV 56, 63, 64, 69, 71

Lee, Bettina: and astrology, PP *94-95*

Lee, John: and dreams, TS 117

Lee, Marguerite Du Pont: and automatic writing, PP 44; and spirit photography, PP 44, *45*

Lee, Martin: MM 75

Leek, Sybil: WW *116, 117;* and Wicca, WW 108

Lees, Robert James: PS 27-29, *30-31;* and Jack the Ripper, PS 27-29, 31

Left brain/right brain: MB 41-44, 45, 47-49. *See also* Cerebral cortex; Split-brain operations

Legge, James: VP 117

Legionnaires' disease: MM 80

Legion of Honor: EM 84

LeGuin, Ursula K.: WW 122

Leg vises: WW *92*

Leibniz, Gottfried Wilhelm: MB 20, SA 88, SE *59*, TS 42

Leibo, Stanley: SE 132

Leidenfrost effect: and fire

walking, MM 105-106

Leiden papyrus: SA *19;* and gold, SA 18, 19

Leif Eriksson: ML 123-124

Leigh, Richard: MQ 125, 127

Leikind, Bernard J.: fire-walking research of, MM 106-107

Leland, Charles: and Wicca, WW 102

Leland, John: ML 51

Le Loyer, Pierre: PE 48

Lemaître, George: TS 60-61

LeMay, Curtis: AE 88

Lemke, Leslie: MB 62

Lemures: MY 35

Lemuria: MP 26-28, 30, MW 14, map 15. *See also* Mu; ML *index*

Lemurian Fellowship: MY 34; and Lemuria, ML 6, 14

Lemurs: ML 7, 28, MW 14

L'Enfant, Pierre: HN 105

Lenin, Vladimir Ilyich: CC 81

Lennox, Annie: CD *69*

Leno, Dan: PE 119

Lenox (Massachusetts): MW 25-27

Lent: MY 28, 136

Lenz, Hans Gerhard: PS *120-121;* and astro-economics, PS 121, 124; and astrology, PS 124; horoscopes by, PS 124

Leo (zodiac sign): CC 36, *57, 84,* 94, 139, ML *46*, MY 63

Leo, Alan: CC 116

Leo X (pope): CC 68, PH 87

Leon, Maximillian de (a.k.a. Bernhard Müller): UV 63

Leonard (demon): MA *95*

Leonard, Gladys Osborne (medium): PP 50, SS 81, *89,* 90-91

Leonard, Jim: PH 128

Leonardo da Vinci: VP 27, *28*

Leonie (multiple-personality patient): MB 78-79

Leopard-men: *borfimah* of, TN 44; garment of, TN *47;* killings by, TN 44-46; and transformations, TN 44; weapons of, TN *46*

Leopard seals: MC 44

Leopold I (Holy Roman emperor): SA 99

Leopold II (king of Belgium): VP 82

Le Pen, Jean-Marie: AW 112

Le Petit Inventeur (magazine): MB *24*

Le Plongeon, Augustus: ML 83; and Mu, MP *26*

Leptoquarks: EM 142

Le Rossignol, Ethel: SE 109-113; spirit art by, SE *109-113*

Leroy, Olivier: CD 118, MM 117

Le Serrec, Robert: MC 34, 37; sea serpent photograph by, MC *35;* sea serpent research of, MC 34-37

LeShan, Lawrence: TS 115

Leslie (postmortem apparition): PE 68-69, 72

Leslie, John: and hollow earth theory, MP 142, 146

Lester, David: VP 93

Lesueur, Charles-Alexandre: MC 28

Lethbridge, Mina: TS *130*

Lethbridge, Thomas C.: PE 128, TS *130;* and dowsing, TS 128, 129; and ley lines, TS 129; and pendulums, TS 129, 131; and "tape recording," TS 129, 130

Lethe (river): SE 45, 72, *86*

Lethe case: SE 95-98, 107

Leto (goddess): MW 104

Letters: MA *38*

Levelland (Texas): and UFO sighting, UP *67-69*

Levengood, W. C.: AE 75-76

Lévi, Éliphas (a.k.a. Abbé Constant, Alphonse Louis Constant): AW 65, 66, 68, MA *60*, VP 109-114; and magic, MA 60, 64; as Tarot reader, VP 127, 129; and werewolves, TN 88-89; and wound doubling, TN 89

Leviathan: and Mother Goddess, WW 15; and Yahweh, WW 15

Levigation: defined, SA 128

Levine, Ondrea: EM *139*

Levine, Robert: and monochronic cultures, TS 97-99; and polychronic cultures, TS 97-100

Levine, Stephen: EM *139*

Levingston, William: PH 27

Levitating Saint: EM 118

Levitation: and Clara Germana Celle, CD 75, *76-77;* hoaxes, SS *125;* and Daniel Dunglas Home, SS 37, 38, 41; and Joseph of Copertino, CD 115-116; at ley site, MP *106-107;* and Richard Mattuck, CD 118; and *munis,* EM 33; and Yogi Subbayah Pullavar, EM *33;* and Teresa of Ávila, CD 115, 117; Theosophical views of, PV 21; and Transcendental Meditation, EM 121, 122; and Evan Harris Walker, CD 118. *See also* MM *index*

Levitation (Leroy): MM 117

Levitation (Richards): MM 118

Levy, Jerre: CD 66

Lévy, M. Arthur: MM 15

Levy, Walter Jay: psychic experi-

AE *Alien Encounters;* **AW** *Ancient Wisdom and Secret Sects;* **CC** *Cosmic Connections;* **CD** *Cosmic Duality;* **DD** *Dreams and Dreaming;* **EE** *Earth Energies;* **EM** *Eastern Mysteries;* **HN** *Hauntings;* **MA** *Magical Arts;* **MB** *The Mind and Beyond;* **MC** *Mysterious Creatures;* **ML** *Mysterious Lands and Peoples;* **MM** *Mind over Matter;* **MP** *Mystic Places;* **MQ** *Mystic Quests;* **MW** *The Mysterious World;*

ments, falsification of, PP 57-60
Lewes, George Henry: PS 30
Lewes, Ludwig: treatise of, PE 48
Lewis, Danny: and Loring UFO sighting, UP 127-129
Lewis, David: ML 99
Lewis, E. E.: SS 21
Lewis, H. Spencer: AW 70-72
Lewis, Ioan: CD 86
Lewis, Isle of: MW 85
Lewis, Jim: CC 149, 154-155
Lewis, Larry: MM 74
Lewis, Leslie: PS 126
Lewis, Ralph: AW 72
Lex Salica: WW 30
Leyaks: defined, EM 61
Ley lines: TS 129; defined, EE 38, PE 123; and dowsing, MP 98; and earth energy, MP 96, 103; and Nazca lines of Peru, MP 98; and Old Straight Track Club, EE 38, MP 94-98; psychic episodes at, MP 103, 104-105, 106-107, 108-109; and Saint Peter's Church, EE 37; and taki'is of Bolivia, MP 98; and telluric currents, EE 38; theory of, MP 94-95, 98, 102, 103, 108; and Alfred Watkins, EE 36, 38. See also UFO sightings
Lhamo, Ahkön Norbu: EM 135
Lhamo Latso: VP 44
Lhas (gods): ML 12
Lhasa (Tibet): EM 14-15, MW 127
Lhote, Henri: ML 36, MW 100
Liana plant: MB 108
Lian chi Ba shi: DD 23
Liang Songzeng: VP 70
Libanius: MY 113
Liber (god): MY 25
Liberalia: MY 25
Liberia: MA 13, MW 133
Libi, John: MQ 89
Libra (zodiac sign): CC 21, 57, 86, 131, 139, MY 88-89
Libyans: ML 117
Li Chum: MY 131
Liddel, Moat of: MQ 132-133
Lie (spirit of dishonesty): CD 26
Liébeault, Ambroise August: PH 123; hypnosis research of, MM 94
Life: beginning and end of, SE 138
Life (magazine): and UFO possibil-

ities, UP 51, 109
Life after Life (Moody): PV 65, 73
Life at Death (Ring): PV 72-73, 77
Lifeboat dilemma: CD 128
Life lesson number: defined, VP 98. See also Numerologists; Numerology
Life line: VP 58-59, 85. See also Palmistry; Palmists
Life of Lycurgus (Plutarch): UV 33
Life of Merlin, The (Geoffrey of Monmouth): MQ 133

Life of St. Brendan (Anonymous): ML 122
Life span: length of, SI 59, 69; of men vs. women, SI 76
Life spirit: SA 92
Lifschutz, Joseph E.: stigmata research of, MM 113
Light: and Albert Einstein, TS 55-57; movement of, TS 53-54; and near-death experiences, PV 57, 59, 69, 70-71, 77, 82-83, 84
Light, Festival of: MY 92

Light-blasting: AE 68-69
Lightning: and Greta Alexander, PS 25, 26; and John Catchings, PS 49; causes of, EE 70; and Thomas-François D'Alibard, EE 70; effects of, EE 70; and Benjamin Franklin, EE 70; interpretation of, VP 33-34; mistaken for UFOs, UP 20, 21; and oaks, EE 92; and thunderstorms, EE 69-70
Lightning Bullets: MA 7-8
Lightning doctors: MA 13
Light of the Lord: WW 38
Light-years: AE 114
Likouala Swamp: MW 65
Lilies: MY 54; divination with, VP 40
Lilith: CD 80, TN 110, 111; and Adam, WW 15-16; and Lilitu, WW 19; and Mother Goddess, WW 15-16. See also Vampires
Lilitu (hag): WW 18, 19
Lilly, John: MB 116, 117-122
Lilly, William: CC 102-104, 105, 106-109
Li-Lung (dragon king): MW 94
Lily Dale Assembly: PS 28-29
Limbic system: and Pierre-Paul Broca, MB 50; and memory, MB 60; purposes of, MB 40, 50, 74; and schizophrenia, MB 74; and synesthesia, MB 52. See also Cerebellum
Lincoln, Abraham: CC 90, MW 27, 28, MY 31, PE 112, 113, SA 124, SS 22-23; ghost of, HN 108; psychic dream of, PP 22-23; psychic experiences of, PP 17-18
Lincoln, Henry: MQ 125, 127
Lincoln, Mary Todd: and ghosts, HN 108
Lindbergh, Charles A.: CC 90, MY 38, PV 7; out-of-body experience of, PV 8-9
Lindorm: MW 53, 55
Lindow Man: AW 10-11, 19
Lindsay, Elmer: HN 119
Lindsay, James Ludovic: MM 115, 116, SS 41, 42
Lindsay, John: palmistry, numerology, and tarot, use of, PP 96-97
Linear time: TS 42
Lines of palm: VP 58-59, 85. See

71

also Palmistry; Palmists

Linga: CD *6, 7*

Linger effect: defined, PE 128

Linnaean Society of New England: MC 28

Linnaeus, Carolus (a.k.a. Carl von Linné): EE 103, TN 56, VP 67; and kraken legend, MP 37

Linscott, Steve: PS 38-41

Lin Yung: EE 35

Linzmayer, Adam J.: telepathy of, PP 52

Lions: MW *10-11,* MY *63,* SA *51;* carved head of, at Chalice Well, MQ *116;* Gilgamesh and, MQ *33;* in grail legend, MQ *120*

''Lion's Sermon'': MY 94

Lipstick: and evil spirits, MA 118

Lissitzky, El: art by, UV *125*

Lister, Joseph: PH 33

Litany of Loreto (Anonymous): AW 49

Lithobolia: HN *59;* defined, HN 60. *See also* Poltergeists

Lithomancy: defined, VP 35

Lithuania: feral children in, TN 57-59, *58;* trees in, EE 91, 92; werewolves in, TN 75

Li Tieguai: SA *113*

Little Adolph (ghost): HN 32

Little Bighorn River: MY 56

Little Ice Age: EE 66. *See also* Ice ages

Little Men: MW 59, 60-*62*

Little Miss Muffet (nursery rhyme): CD *42-43*

Little Red Riding Hood (fairy tale): CD *46-47*

Little Stasia: *See* Tomczyk, Stanislawa

Litwak, Leo: UV 134-135

Liu, Robert: SI 103

Liu Sheng: burial suit of, SA *111*

Live burials: SI 99-100, 101, *102-103*

Liver: VP *32*

Livermore, Jesse: PS 105, *110,* 111-112

Livestock industry: SI 110

Livestock mutilations: *See* Animal mutilations

Living Longer, Growing Younger (Segall): SI 84-85, 123

Livonia: werewolves in, TN 75-78

Livre des Enfants Sauvages, Le (Demaison): TN 64

Li Yuan chuo: DD 23

Llorona, La: MW 27

Llull, Ramon: AW *27,* SA *32, 45;* and alchemy, SA 33; death of, SA 34; and Edward II, SA 33; and Muslims, SA 32; and philosophers' stone, SA 33; and visions, SA 33

Llyr (god): MQ 110

LNI: *See* Loch Ness Investigation

Loa: PH 25

Loa Danh: MW *113*

Loading hypothesis: defined, MM 64. *See also* Psychokinesis

Loaf Mass: MY 65, 73

Loas: CD 86; and voodoo, MA 83, 86

Lobenstein, Anneliese Hofer von: and hauntings, HN 32

Lobenstein, Maximilian Hofer von: and hauntings, HN 32

Localized psi effects: *See* Hauntings

Loch-mo-Naire: MY *66*

Loch Morar: MC 61-62, 90

Loch Ness: MC *64-65, map 67,* MW 17, 53; characteristics of, MC 60, 63-66, 67; deaths in, MC 66; ghost ship in, MC 84; sonar probes of, MC *78, 80, 86-87, 88,* 90

Loch Ness and Morar Project: MC 90

Loch Ness hoodoo: MC 84

Loch Ness Investigation (LNI): disbanding of, MC 89; Loch Ness monster research of, MC 73, 76-78, 83, 84, 85

Loch Ness monster: MW 17, 53, MY *63. See also* Lake monsters; Sea serpents; MC *index*

Loch Ness Monster and Others, The (Gould): MC 71

Loch Ness Phenomena Investigation Bureau: *See* Loch Ness Investigation

Locke, John: SA 98, SE 56

Lockyer, J. Norman: and megalithic monuments, astronomical alignments of, MP 91-92; and pyramids and archaeoastronomy, MP 65; and Stonehenge, MP 65, 110

Lodge, Oliver: HN 7, MM 15, PE 21, PP 24, PV 19, *20,* SE 97; and Arthur Conan Doyle, SS 100; and Gladys Osborne Leonard, SS 89, 90; and Eusapia Palladino, SS 60, 61, 62; and Leonora Piper, SS 86-87, *88;* and spiritualism, PP 50

AE Alien Encounters; AW Ancient Wisdom and Secret Sects; CC Cosmic Connections; CD Cosmic Duality; DD Dreams and Dreaming; EE Earth Energies; EM Eastern Mysteries; HN Hauntings; MA Magical Arts; MB The Mind and Beyond; MC Mysterious Creatures; ML Mysterious Lands and Peoples; MM Mind over Matter; MP Mystic Places; MQ Mystic Quests; MW The Mysterious World;

Lodge, Raymond: SS *88-89, 90*

Loeb, Jacques: SI 102-103

Loe Bar: vision at, MP *104-105*

Loehr, Franklin: EE 108

Loewi, Otto: DD 37

Loftus (colonel): MW 21

Logical atomism: SE 65

Logic vs. experience: SA 34

Logie family: MW 47-48

Löher, Hermann: and witch hunts, WW 72-78

Loki (god): MA 119, VP 108

Lombards: and witches, WW 30

Lombroso, Cesare: SS 59; and creativity, MB 87; and mental illnesses, MB 87; and outsider art, MB 63; psychokinesis research of, MM 12-13

London, Great Fire of: CC 107

London, Jack: out-of-body experiences of, PV 15

London, Tower of: MW 19

London Spiritual Alliance: SE 109

Long Ears, and Easter Island: ML 85, 86, 95

Longfellow, Henry Wadsworth: ML 130, SS 35, 83-86

Long houses: Iroquois, MQ *99;* site of, MQ 90, *99*

Longren, Sig: EE *136*

Long Salts: MA 78

Longship: MY *129*

Lono: MA 90

Lono (god): MY 102

Lonsdorf, Nancy: PH 68

Look (magazine): and Donald E. Keyhoe's UFO investigations, UP 56; and Donald H. Menzel's UFO theories, UP 51

Look into the Future, A (Ebertin): PS *58-59*

Loomis, Roger S. L.: MQ 108

Lo Pan compass: EE *113*

López Portillo, José: MM 36

Lorber, John: SE 129

Lord of the Animals (Cernunnos): MQ 136

Lord of the Forest: TN 86

Lord of the Universe: TS 23

Loren, Sophia: CC 85, MM 36

Lorenzen, Coral and Jim: and Aerial Phenomena Research Organization, UP 53

Loretto Chapel: ML 60

Loring Air Force Base (Maine): and UFO sighting, UP 127-129

Lorke, Gail: PS *52-53;* and John Catchings, PS 49-57; disappearance and murder of, PS 49, *57;* and Steven Lorke, PS 50, 53, *54-55,* 56; and square dancing, PS *50-51;* and Marty Wing, PS 50, 53, 56

Lorke, Steven: and Gail Lorke, PS 50, 53, *54-55,* 56; and Ronald Phillips, PS 56; and Marty Wing, PS 50, 53, 56

Lorrain, Pierre le: CC 68, PS 27

Losar: MY *107, 108-112,* 134

Lost-continent hypotheses: ML *6-15*

Lost Continent of Mu, The (Churchward): ML 8, MP 27, 28

Lost Horizon (Hilton): MQ 27, SI 39, 47

Lotorg: MW 61-62

Lotteries: MA 113

Lotus: MB *15*

Lotus 1-2-3: EM 142

Lotus Urn: UV *147*

Louis XIV (king of France): MW 129

Louis XV (king of France): MW 57

Louis XVI (king of France): MW 129, PH 90, SA 102

Louisiana: voodoo in, MA 80, 81

Louis the Pious (Holy Roman emperor): and witches, WW 44

Lounsbury, Floyd: CC 61

Lourdes (France): CD 119-120, *121,* MW 85, 91

Love: and black magic, MA 92-93, 99, 100; and magic, MA 20-21; and magicians, MA 20; and mandrake root, MA 100; and voodoo, MA 81

Love, Mike: EM 122

Love apples: WW 35

Loveday, Betty May and Raoul: AW 116, *117*

Love elixirs: herbs in, WW *34, 35*

Lovelock, James: EE *121;* and cryobiology, SI 109, 122; and cryopreservation, SI 109; and Daisyworld, EE *122-123;* and Gaia (theory), EE 118-119, 119-124, *122-123,* 137; and William Golding, EE 120; and hypothermia,

SI 109; and Mars, EE 119; and NASA, EE 119; and redwoods, EE 121; and Paul Segall, SI 122

Love potions: ginseng in, EE 100; mandrakes in, EE 96

Low, Robert: and Condon committee, UP 116

Lowe family: and poltergeists, HN 59

Lowell, James Russell: ML 130-131

Lowell, Percival: CC 47

Lowen, Alexander: PH *101*

Lower World: EM 63

Low magic: MA 15-17, 44, 61, 65, 76-80. *See also Kahuna ana'anas;* Magic; Voodoo

Lowrance, Darrell: MC 90

Loyer, Pierre Le: and ghosts, HN 24-25

Loy Krathong: MY *100*

Lozanov, Georgi: MB 125

LSD (lysergic acid diethylamide): EE 100; drawings made under influence of, MB *114-115;* and dreams, DD 114; effects of, MB 116-117; and hallucinations, MB 104, 106; and Albert Hofmann, MB 104; and John Lilly, MB 122. *See also* Hallucinogens

Lubbock (Texas): and UFO sighting, UP 49-50, *51*

Lucas (feral child): TN 66-67

Lucas, Paul: and alchemy, SA 42; and dervish, SA 42-43, 47

Lucerito (canary): VP *38-39*

Lucerne dragon stone: MA *107*

Lucia, Saint: MY *117*

Lucid dreams: *See* Dreams; DD *index*

Lucifer (demon): MA 94, UV *113. See also* Demons; Satan

Lucifer (journal): AW 137

Luciferans: CD 83

Lucifer legends: MQ 117

Lucretius: SE 46; and space, TS 42

Lucy and Nancy (ship): MY 134

Ludendorff, Erich: and Adolf Hitler, SA *120;* and Franz Tausend, SA 117

Lü Dongbin: SA *113*

Lug (god): MY *65*

Lugnasadh: MY 65, WW 123

Lugosi, Bela: as Count Dracula,

TN *137*

Luhrmann, Tanya M.: WW 110, 118-119, 122-124

Luke (biblical figure): PH 85

Lulus: AE *96-97*

Lumbini Gardens: EM *72-73*

Lumitron: MB 48

Luna (goddess): SA *73, 75*

Luna, Luis Eduardo: MB 108

Lunantishees: MY 100

Lunar essence: SA *73, 74, 75, 76, 84. See also* Moon

Lund, William: CC 104

Lung-gom: EM 75-76

Lunt, Alfred: MA 128-129

Lu Pan: MY 62

Lupercalia: MY 133

Luria, Aleksandr: MB 53-56

Lusk, Charles: and 1896 airship sighting, UP 18

Lust: CD *87*

Luther, Martin: CC 69, 74, UV 57; coat of arms of, AW *49;* and papal bull, SA 64; and theses, SA 63; and witches, TN 38, WW 66

Lutherus medicorum: See Paracelsus

Lutyens, Mary: FM 120

Lutz, George and Kathy: HN *100-101;* and hauntings, HN 100

Lutz, Kathy: levitation of, HN 100

Lycaeus, Mount: TN 74

Lycanthropy: defined, TN 21. *See also* Transformations; Vampires; Werewolves *in* TN *index*

Lycaon (king of Arcadia): as werewolf, TN 74, *78, 79*

Lychnomancy: defined, VP 35

Lydford Gorge: PE *10-11*

Lydia: gold in, SA 16

Lyell, Charles: MP 23

Lynn, Steven Jay: MB 92

Lyon, S. Silas: PH 27

Lyonnesse: MW 85, 86-87

Lyons, Arthur: CD 95

Lyons, Meg: HN 52

Lysergic acid diethylamide: *See* LSD

Lysis: UV 28-30

Lyttelton, Mary Catherine: SS *98;* and Arthur Balfour, SS 80-81, 92, 96-99

Lytton, Lord: and hollow earth theory, MP 146, 151

M

MASK. *Masks like this one from the Ivory Coast are powerful, active symbols of supernatural beings. The mask is said to submerge the wearer's identity, while the being manifests itself in a human body and voice.*

M., Dr. (colleague of Freud): DD 63

Maat (goddess): MC *58. See also* Human-beasts

Mab (queen of fairies): MY 88

Mabinogion, The (Welsh legends): MQ 109

Mabon: MY 88

Macanese: as fortunetellers, TS *94-95*

Macaque: EE *125;* hands of, MC *112,* 114. *See also* Animals

Macarius: PH 85, 87

MacArthur, Douglas: PE 138, PH 55

Macaulay, Thomas: MB 53

McBean, Monica: PP 34

Macbeth: MW 86

Macbeth (Shakespeare): MA 115-116, PE 37, WW 15. *See also* Curse of Macbeth

Maccabee, Bruce: AE 75, MW 40; and Fund for UFO Research, AE 71; investigation of abduction by aliens, UP 143; investigation of UFOs, UP 130-131; and SRS camera, AE 71-72; and Edward Walters, AE 71-73, 74

McCarley, Robert W.: DD 100

McCarrison, Robert: SI 43

McCarthy, William J.: fire-walking research of, MM 106

McCay, Clive: SI 78

Macchietti, Girolamo: painting by, SI *27*

McClelland, David: MB 107

MacCluiunn, Gaffer: MA 30

McConnel, David E. (postmortem apparition): PE 30

McConnell, David: MY 116

McCormick, Donna: and out-of-body-experience research, PV 40; and poltergeists, HN 74

McCreery, Charles: PE 95-97

AE *Alien Encounters;* AW *Ancient Wisdom and Secret Sects;* CC *Cosmic Connections;* CD *Cosmic Duality;* DD *Dreams and Dreaming;* EE *Earth Energies;* EM *Eastern Mysteries;* HN *Hauntings;* MA *Magical Arts;* MB *The Mind and Beyond;* MC *Mysterious Creatures;* ML *Mysterious Lands and Peoples;* MM *Mind over Matter;* MP *Mystic Places;* MQ *Mystic Quests;* MW *The Mysterious World;*

MYRTLE. Emblem of undying love, this fragrant plant was sacred to the Greek goddess Aphrodite, who used it to commune with her dead lover Adonis. Thereafter, wands of myrtle became a popular means of trying to contact the departed.

Tab.672.

Myrtus communis.
Gemeine Myrte.
Ok.1941.

McCulloch, Pat: UP 68-69
McDivitt, James: AE 85
Macdonald, Colin: and *Titanic* disaster, premonition of, PP 29
McDonald, Duncan: MC 61
McDonald, James E.: AE 88; investigation of UFOs, UP 115-117
McDonald, Maurice and Richard: PS 104-105
MacDonald family: and poltergeists, MW 25, 27
McDonnell, Duncan: MC 90
McDonnell, James: MM 78
MacDougall, John: MC 62
McDougall, William: EE 126, MM 57, 62; and Mina Crandon, SS 110; and extrasensory perception in animals, PP 57; and Eileen Garrett, SS 85; and psychic research, PP 48-49, 50
McDowell, Clayton: PS *126*
McEwan, Dorothy and Peter: HN 33, 34, *35*
McFarland, Morgan: WW 96-97, 99-100, 115
McGill, Ormond: EM 91-92
McGreevy, Michael: MB 137
McGregor (surgeon): SI 100
Macharomancy: defined, VP 35
Machu Picchu: ML *72-73*, MW 79
McIntyre, Leslie: MY 103
Mack, John: AE 110
McKaig, A. C.: PH 97
Mackal, Roy P.: MC 25, 77, 85, 91, *92-94*
Mackay, John: MC 66-67
Mackay, Mrs. John: MC 66-67
Mackenzie, Mrs. (ghost percipient): VP 30
MacKenzie, Andrew: HN *88*, *118-122*, PE 113; and hauntings, HN 33, 34, 35, 88-89; poltergeist research of, MM 49
Mackenzie, Kenneth: *See* Odhar, Coinneach
MacKenzies (ghost percipients): PE 43
Mackie, Andrew: HN 89-92
McKinley, William: AW 111
McKinnie, Ian: VP 43
McKinstry, John: AW *101*
McLaine, Patricia (psychic adviser): PP 97-98
MacLaine, Shirley: AE 99-101, PV

43; alleged previous incarnations of, PV 124; and J. Z. Knight, SS 140; out-of-body experiences of, PV *43,* 44; and Kevin Ryerson, SS 10, 145-146; seminars of, PV *43,* 44
MacLaines (ghost percipients): PE 45
McLaughlin, Corinne: UV 153
McLaughlin, Robert B.: UP 46-47
McLean, Adam: SA 70, 71, 76
Maclean, Charles: and Amala, TN 63; and Kamala, TN 63
Maclean, Dorothy: and devas, EE 134, 135, UV 143, 144; and Findhorn Foundation, EE 133, UV 142, 143, 144; and holism, UV 144; and Landscape Angel, EE 135
McLean, Evalyn Walsh: MW 129
MacLean, Paul D.: MB 40
MacLeod clan: MW 119, 120-121, 124
McMinnville (Oregon): and UFO sighting, UP 47-48, 138
McMullen, George (psychic): MQ *98, 102;* Egyptian structures psychically detected by, MQ 100, *101, 102-103;* and Iroquois sites, MQ 98, *99,* PP 125-126; and psychometry, PP 123-127; sketch by, MQ *102*
MacNab, P. A.: Loch Ness monster photograph by, MC *75*
MacQueen-Pope, Walter James: PE 119-121
McRae, Ron: PS 80, 90
Macrobiotics: PH 60, 61, 63
Macro-PK: defined, MM 7. *See also* Materializations; Poltergeists; Psychokinesis
M'Taggart, John M'Taggart Ellis: SE 63-65
Macumba: MW 113, PH 23
Madagascar: MW 14, 65, 69, 133; contagious magic in, MA 15; trees in, EE *93*
Maderna, Carlo: sculpture by, SI *26-27*
Madoc (prince of Wales): ML 125
Madonna, Black: CD *58. See also* Virgin Mary
Madrid Codex: VP *12-13*
Maenads: TN *34-36*

Mafu (spirit guide): *See* Rubin, Penny Torres
Magellan, Ferdinand: TS 84-85
Magen David: MA *38*
Magi: MA 25, 44-45, 48, 49, *58,* 59, MY 86, UV 25. *See also* Magicians
Magia Posthuma (Schertz): TN 116
Magic: black, SI 30; and Helena Petrovna Blavatsky, EM 84; and Buddhism, EM 40; and Alexandra David-Néel, EM 84; defined, WW 107; and Ormond McGill, EM 92; and Milarepa, EM 41, 49-50; and Padmasambhava, EM 41; and Taoism, EM 52; and trees, SI 13. *See also* Black magic; Contagious magic; High magic; Imitative magic; Low magic; White magic; MA *index*
Magical saining: WW 136
Magic and Mystery in Tibet (David-Néel): EM 75, 84, PE 98
Magic circles: MA 22, 54; and Cabala, MA 59; casting of, WW 128; defined, WW 107; in Egypt, MA 54
Magic Door: MW 119, 127
Magic Flute, The (Mozart): AW 90

"Magic helmet": MB *132*
Magician, The (Maugham): AW 122
Magician among the Spirits, A (Houdini): PP 108
Magicians: MA 20, 23, 25; in Hong Kong, MA *11;* and love, MA 20; and mandrake root, MA 99-100. *See also* Magi; Sorcerers
Magick: MY 93
Magic of Uri Geller, The (Randi): MM 34
Magic spells: WW *38, 39, 107*
Magic wands: MA *52,* WW *121;* and Aleister Crowley, MA *57;* history of, MA 21
Magill, John: MW 24
Magma: defined, EE 59
Magnetic field altering: of Ingo Swann, MM 27
Magnetic resonance imaging (MRI): MB 132
Magnetite: EE 61
Magnetoelectric machine: PH 89
Magnetometer: defined, MM 75
Magnusson, Eyolf: MW 35
Magnusson, Irene: MW 54-55
Magog (giant): MW *6-7*
Magpies: MY *59*

MY The Mystical Year; PE Phantom Encounters; PH Powers of Healing; PP Psychic Powers; PS The Psychics; PV Psychic Voyages; SA Secrets of the Alchemists; SE Search for the Soul; SI Search for Immortality; SS Spirit Summonings; TN Transformations; TS Time and Space; UP The UFO Phenomenon; UV Utopian Visions; VP Visions and Prophecies; WW Witches and Witchcraft

Magritte, René: and hypnagogic state, DD 16; paintings by, DD 16, 17
Magus, Simon: MA 24-25
Mahabharata: ML 32-33
Mahakala (god): MY 106
Maha Kumbh Mela: EM 36
Mahal, Mumtaz: EM 35
Mahamantra: EM 124
Mahan, Joseph: ML 134-135
Maharaja of Rewa: EM 30
Maharaja of Sikkim: EM 74
Maharishi: EM 90-91
Maharishi International University: EM 122, 125
Mahasaya, Lahiri: SI 9-11
Mahatmas: AW 136, EM 85-86, PV 22; and Annie Wood Besant, AW 140-141; and Helena Petrovna Blavatsky, AW 132-133, 134, 140; and William Quan Judge, AW 141
Mahd adh Dhahab (mine; Saudi Arabia): MQ 41-42
Maher, Michaeleen: PE 128; and ghosts, HN 136
Mahisasura (demon king): MY 88
Mah-to-toh-pa (chief of Mandans): ML 125
Maia (goddess): MY 17
Maidenhill Wicca: WW 112
Maier, Michael: AW 57-58, 59, SA 86
Maimonides Medical Center: DD 146-149, 153, PP 67, 74
Mairan, Jean Jacques d'Ortous de: TS 80
Maison Picassiette: UV 50-51
Maister John the French Leich: See Damian, John
Major Arcana: VP 132-133; contents of, VP 123; history of, VP 125; interpretation of, VP 124, 127, 129, 130. See also Tarot; Tarot readers
Makahiki: MY 102
Makara-Sankranti: MY 125
Makemake (god): ML 89
Makeup: SI 90-91
Mala: VP 114-115
Malaika: CD 122. See also Angels
Malaysia: TN 25
Malcolm II (king of Scotland): PE 37

Malea, Cape (Greece): MQ 50
Maleficium: defined, WW 9, 41
Male mythopoetic groups: CD 59-61, 60-61
Malevich, Kazimir: AW 168, UV 124; and Wassily Kandinsky, UV 131; paintings by, AW 168-169, UV 124; and suprematists, UV 124
Malibu Miniature Golf: PS 116-117
Malik (angel of death): DD 54-55
Malik Shah, ship of: See Phantom Ark
Malin, Michael: AE 104
Malinowski, Bronislaw: MA 128, 135
Malleus Maleficarum (Kramer and Sprenger): CD 59, 83, TN 111, WW 64, 99
Mallow: WW 39
Malmesbury, William of: MQ 123
Malmstrom Air Force Base (Montana): UP 129-130

Malocchio: See Evil eye
Malory, Thomas: ML 48-49, MQ 111, 120, 121, UV 36
Malphas (demon): MA 96
Malta: MW 85, 91; evil eye in, MA 124; temple on, SE 10
Maltais, L. W.: AE 82
Maltwood, Katherine: ML 46; and Glastonbury zodiac, ML 44-45
Mama Ocllo (goddess): TS 13
Mambos: MA 82, 83, 84
Mammalian brain: defined, TN 31
Mammone, Gaetano: as vampire, TN 123
Mammy Water (spirit): EE 53, MW 99
Mamun, Caliph al-: CC 52
Man, City of: UV 30, 39
Man, Isle of: MW 119
Mana: defined, ML 90, 95
Man and Law (journal): MM 27
Manasarowar, Lake: EM 44-45; and Sven Hedin, EM 83

Manatee: MW 73
Manco Capac (god): TS 13
Mandala: AW 139, DD 75, EM 122, MB 23, TS 30, 31; defined, DD 75; and Carl Jung, AE 127, DD 75, MB 23, UP 53; and UFOs, AE 127, UP 53
Mandan Indians: MA 74-75, ML 125
Mandell, Steven: SI 119
Mandeville, John: drawings by, ML 63
Mandlestam, Robert: PS 76
Mandrakes: WW 35; as anesthetics, EE 96; and Arabs, EE 96; and fertility symbols, EE 96; and Greeks, EE 96, MA 99; in love potions, EE 96; and murderers, EE 96; and Rachel, EE 96; and Romans, EE 96; roots, MA 99-100, 101, SI 67; and William Shakespeare, EE 96-99; in sleeping potions, EE 96; substi-

76

MANDALA. With counterbalanced geometric forms, the mandala stands for the melding of opposites, such as order and diversity. These Tibetan mandalas represent the spiritual path from the finite, material world to the infinite Center.

tute for, EE *101;* and witches, EE 96

Mango-tree trick: EM 90

Mangrove fox squirrel: MW 44

Mani (prince of Babylon): AW 20-22, CD 31, 122

Manic-depression: and Johann Hauser, MB 68, 69

Manicheans: AW 20-22, 28, CD 31-32, 122, UV 25; and Cathars, AW 26; and Catholicism, AW 26; cosmogonies of, TS 22-23; persecution of, AW 22. *See also* Cathars

Manifestation: UV 144

Manilius: CC 34

Man in gray (ghost): HN 31, PE *119-121*

Man in Relation to the Planets (Steiner): UV *113*

Manipogo: MW 47, 48-49

Manirung Pass: EM *16-17*

Manitoba, Lake: MW 47, 48

Manley, T. F.: PS 77

Mann, Horace: VP 75

Mann, Thomas: CC 82

Manning, Matthew: PH 99, 103; automatic painting of, SS 138

Mannor, Frank: UP 106, 109

Manor of Rillaton: PE *14-15*

Ma-no Umi: MW 93, 94

Mansfield, Katherine: UV *109*

Mansi, Sandra: Champ photograph by, MC *63*

Manson, Charles: TN 130

Mansur, Caliph al-: CC 52

Manta ray: MC *39*

Mantell, Thomas: MY 124; and UFO chase, UP 41

"Man That Broke the Bank at Monte Carlo, The" (song): MM 65

Manticores: MC *10*

Mantras: EM 122, MM 118, 119

Manual of Discipline: UV 34

Manual of Psychometry (Buchanan): PS 30

Manuel I Comnenus (Roman emperor): ML 64, MQ 122

Man Who Mistook His Wife for a Hat, The (Sacks): MB 38, 60

Manzini, Angelina: DD *143-144*

Manzini, Maria: DD *143-144*

Maori (country): ML 82

Maori (people): CD 24, SE 10; tribesmen, EE *55,* SE *11*

Mao Zedong: CC 89, EE 61

Map, thirteenth-century: MW *6-7*

Map, Walter: and witches, WW 49

Map dowsing: MQ *100,* PP 138, PS *122,* 124-126. *See also* Dowsing

Mara (god): EM 40

Marathon, Plains of: MW 34, PE 129

Marathon monks: EM *56, 57,* 58

Marble tiles: Egyptian, MQ *102*

Marcel, Jesse A.: AE 79, 81

Marcel, Sire: SA 47

Marco Polo: MQ 70

Mardi Gras: MY *136-137*

Marduk (god): CC 16, CD 24, 55, TS 20; and Tiamat, WW 15

Marea (buried city; Egypt): archaeological dig at, MQ *102-103*

Mare stones: EE *57*

Margaret (apparition): PE *40*

Margaret (fictional character): AE *45*

Margaret (queen of Navarre): VP 18

Margaret (witch): WW 72

Margaret, Saint: MY 62

Margaret Rose (princess of Great Britain): CC 132

Margaritomancy: defined, VP 35

Marge (percipient of postmortem apparition): PE 69-72

Margery (medium): *See* Crandon, Mina

Margins of Reality (Jahn and Dunne): SE 136

Mariah (ship): UV 56, 64

Maria K.: stigmata of, MM 113

Mariana, Nick: MY 66

Marianne (possessed person): CD 92-93

Maria the Jewess: SA 24

Maria Theresa (queen of Hungary and Bohemia): AW 102, TN *121*

Marie, Louis Ferdinand: SE 102

Marie, Robert: SE 100-102

Marie-Antoinette (queen of France): AW 103, HN 41, 48, *50,* MW 34, 129, MY 68, SA 100

Mariette, Auguste: ML 22-23

Marijuana: DD 114, MB 116

Marinatos, Spyridon: MP 35

Marine saurian: MW 72

Marinetti, Filippo (a.k.a. Caffeine of Europe): UV 122

Maringer, Johannes: TN 26

Marion, Frederick (mentalist): PP *110-111*

Marius Alterius: CC 69

Marjetica: MY *44-45*

Mark, Saint: MW *6-7,* MY 32

Markham, Ursula: VP 52

Marlowe, Christopher: CD 84, MA 45

Marmas: PH 66-67

Marmion (knight): PE 16

Maronia (Greece): MQ 50

Marpa: EM 50

Marquesans: SE 21

Marriage: and Gypsies, MA 102; and superstitions, MA 130

Marriage bed blessing: MY *50*

Marriage line: VP 85. *See also* Palmistry; Palmists

Marriage of Cupid (Raphael): SI *10-11*

Marriott, William: SS 125, 129

Marryat, Frederick: MW 21

Mars (god): CC 40, *41,* MY 17, 18, 19, 23, 40, 95

Mars (planet): AE 90-93, *94,* CC 16, *25,* 36, 41, 98, 104, 117, EE 119, MA *36,* MY 23; background of, AE 92; characteristics of, AE 114, SA 21; and *Phobos 2,* AE *118-119;* symbol for, SA *24;* and *Viking,* AE 114

Marsden, Simon: photographs by, PE *7-17*

Mars effect: CC 141-142

Marshall, Annie: SS 76-77, 92

Marshall, Mrs. Jack: and *Titanic* disaster, premonition of, PP 29

Marshall, Ninian: TS 118-120

Marshall, Walter: SS 77

Mars-Jupiter Conjunction: PS 120

Mars line: VP 85. *See also* Palmistry; Palmists

Marston Moor: battlefield of, PE 129

Marten, Maria: DD *136*

Martha of Bethany, Saint: MY 65

Martial arts: EM 55, 57, *143-153,* PH 52-53, SI *42*

Martians: AE *103*

Martin, Eddie Owens (a.k.a. St. EOM): art by, UV 43, *46-47*

Martin, John: painting by, UV *14-15*

Martin, Malachi: CD 91

Martin, Marlene: MC 16

Martin, Saint: MY 100

Martin, T. Henri: and Atlantis, MP 20-21

Martini (professor): MA 32-33

Martinmas: MY 100

Martino, Ernesto de: MA 33

Marto, Francisco: CD 120, MY 93

Marto, Jacinta: CD 120, MY *93*

Martyn, Michael: and hauntings, HN 89

Martyr, Deborah: MW 62

Martyrs: defined, CD 110

Marwa: MY 91

Marwick, M. G.: MA 11

Marx, Karl: CC 81, CD 40

Mary (biblical figure): DD 37, ML 29. *See also* Virgin Mary

Mary, Queen of Scots (Mary Stuart): HN 8, MW 19

Mary Celeste (ship): MP *38-39,* MY 99

Mary F. (sea serpent observer): photograph by, MC *36, 37*

Mary M.; and ectoplasm, PP *40*

Mary Magdalene: and grail, MQ 124, 125

Mary Tudor (queen of England): PE 106, SA 58, VP 20, 46

Marzenna: MY *24*

Masaccio, Tommaso: fresco by, TS 40

Maskelyne, John: SS 101-102

Masking rituals: MY 74-*80*

Masks: CD *32-33,* 95, EE *94,* MW 47, MY 25, *72-73, 74-80,* 81, *106,* SA 9, SE *13,* WW 65; in Bali, EM *66-67;* of Bon, TN *42;* of frog, TN *18;* for funerals, SI *100;* of the Inuit, TN *33;* of the Kwakiutl, TN *9, 13, 14-15;* of mud, SI *91;* of octopuses, TN *14;* of otters, TN *19;* of owls, TN *17;* of ravens, TN *12-13;* of shamans, TN *16, 18, 19;* of the Sisiutl, TN *14-15;* in Tibet, EM *79;* of the Tlingit, TN *16, 17;* of whales, TN *15;* of wolves, TN *16*

Masons: and Alessandro Cagliostro, MA 42-43, 44, SA 102; and Comte de Saint-Germain, SA

MY The Mystical Year; PE Phantom Encounters; PH Powers of Healing; PP Psychic Powers; PS The Psychics; PV Psychic Voyages; SA Secrets of the Alchemists; SE Search for the Soul; SI Search for Immortality; SS Spirit Summonings; TN Transformations; TS Time and Space; UP The UFO Phenomenon; UV Utopian Visions; VP Visions and Prophecies; WW Witches and Witchcraft

101. *See also* Freemasons

Masques: SA 90

Mass hysteria: MA 63

Massimo, Paolo: PV *61*

Mass wedding: MB *99*

Master Chuang: *See* Chuang Chou

Masters, R. E. L.: TN 46

Matacia, Louis: PS 77

Mata Hari: CC 84, VP 84

Materialism: CD 40, MB 9, 13, 14, 17-19, 26, SE 130. *See also* Materialistic monism

Materialistic monism: MB 13, *16, 17. See also* Materialism

Materializations: MW 106; of Florence Cook, SS 53; of Mrs. Samuel Guppy, SS 53-54; hoaxes, SS *129;* of Daniel Dunglas Home, SS 37, 38, 39, *40-41,* 53; of Elizabeth Hope, SS 55; of Carlos Mirabelli, SS 117, *118-119,* 120; of Eusapia Palladino, MM 13, 15. *See also* Macro-PK

Mathematics: and Maya, ML 19; and Pythagoras, SA 20, TS 43

Mather, Cotton: HN 58, PE 85, WW *76-77*

Mather, Increase: HN 58-60, WW 76, *80*

Mathers, Moina MacGregor (a.k.a. Vestigia): AW 148, *153,* 155, VP 137

Mathers, Samuel Liddell MacGregor: AW *149,* MA 64, SA 128, VP 127, 137; and Aleister Crowley, AW 114, 156; death of, AW 156; and Annie Horniman, AW 151-152, 156; and Secret Chiefs, AW 152-153; and William Wynn Westcott, AW 148; and William Butler Yeats, AW 148-150

Mathesis (Firmicus Maternus): CC 49-50

Mathews, Mrs.: and ghosts, HN 34

Mathews family: HN 33-34

Matin de Magicien, Le (Bergier and Pauwels): PS 70, 71

Matlock, James G.: PV 112

Matrimandir: UV *146,* 148, 149

Matronalia: MY 18

Matteson, T. H.: paintings by, WW *74-75, 76-77*

Matthew (biblical figure): DD 37, PH 85

Matthew, Saint: MY 87

Mattuck, Richard: CD 118

Mauch, Karl Gottlieb: MY 83; death of, ML 68; and Great Zimbabwe, ML 65, 68; and Ophir, ML 67, 68; and Adam Renders, ML 67; sketch by, ML *64*

Maud, Countess: PV 113, 124

Maugham, W. Somerset: EM 117

Mauna Kea: EE 67

Maupassant, Guy de: PE 97, 100, *101,* PV 15

Maurice (landgrave of Hesse): AW 57

Mauritius: fire walking in, MM *106*

Maury, Alfred: DD 58-59

Mavalankar, Damodar K.: AW 135

Mawnan (England): MW 53, 55-56, *57*

Max: and cloning, SI 56-57, 57-59, 85; and David M. Rorvik, SI 56-57, 85

Maxime (count): PH 90

Maxwell, Nicole: PH *19*

Maya (hypnosis): defined, EM 92

Maya (mother of Buddha): DD 37-39

Maya (people): CC 60-*61,* CD 102, MW 79; agriculture of, ML 19; almanac of, TS 102; arches of, ML 19; and astronomy, ML 19; and Atlantis, ML 28; background of, ML 19; and Charles-Étienne Brasseur de Bourbourg, ML 27; calendars of, ML 19, TS 34, VP 12; cities of, ML 19; codices of, ML 27, VP *12-13;* cosmogonies of, TS 19, 32-34; and Diego de Landa, ML 27; dentistry of, ML 22; and Egyptians, ML 83; and extraterrestrials, ML 32; gods of, ML *106;* and Lemuria, ML 83; and Augustus Le Plongeon, ML 83; and mathematics, ML 19; and Mu, MP 26; numerology of, VP 105; ornamentation of, ML 19; pyramids of, ML 19; and reincarnation, TS 36; and sacrifices, TS 37; seers, VP *12-13;* and space, TS 34, 36; and time, TS 32, 34-36; and Erich von Däniken, ML 32; writing system of, ML 19

May apple: MA 99

May Day: EE *102, MY 32, 33, 34, 36, 46,* UV *90-91;* in Portugal, MA *12. See also* Beltane

May Eve: MY 98

Maypoles: CD *55,* MY 17, 32, *33,* WW *134-135*

Mazdaznan: UV 130

Mazes: SE 10, *11*

Meacham, Joseph: UV 65, 68

Mead, Margaret: CD 61-62, MA 137, PP *27*

Meaden, Terence: EE 20

Meade-Waldo, E. G. B.: MC 32

Mean chance expectation (MCE): defined, MM 58

Meath, Petronilla de: WW 55

Mecca (Saudi Arabia): MW 99, MY *90-91*

Medea (sorceress): MQ *35,* SI *27,* WW 20-*23*

Medical examinations: *See* Physical examinations

Medici, Cosimo I de': CC *74,* MW 119, 122

Medici, Francesco I de': MW 119, 122, *123*

Medicine: bags, MA 80; clay as, EE 58; kit, PH *121;* mask, PH *14;* patent, SI *31;* sticks, PH *65. See also* Elixirs

Medicine men: PP 75, 78-79. *See also* Shamans

Medicine Wheel (Wyoming): MP *120*

Medicine Wolf (spirit): PS 77

Medina (Saudi Arabia): MY 91

Meditation: CD *103,* EE *106,* PH 73, *137,* SA *106;* advantages of, MB 117; and Richard Alpert, MB 117; and Buddha, EM 40; and Buddhism, EM *104-105,* MB 102; and Andrew Da Passano, SI *71;* and enlightenment, EM 37; and health, SI 23; and Aldous Huxley, MB 117; and hypothermia, SI 109; and longevity, SI 23, 109; and Milarepa, EM 50; purposes of, MB 117; and trances, MB 103; and Janwillem van de Wetering, EM 97; and Roy L. Walford, SI 109. *See also* Transcendental Meditation

Meditations on the First Philosophy (Descartes): SE 52, 55

Mediterranean Sea: MW *map 8-9*

Medium Coeli (MC): CC 118

Mediums: AW 129, 132, MW *107-109,* PP 35, 36, 88-89, SE 89-90, SS 7; cabinets of, SS *36,* 37; and channelers, SS 131-132; characteristics of, HN 118, MM 10; defined, SS 18, 130-131; demonstrations of, PP *36, 37, 38-39,* 40; hoaxes of, SS 101-102, *123-129;* and multiple-personality disorder, SS 84-85; powers of, PP 24. *See also individual mediums*

Mediums Night: MW 108

Medjugorje (Yugoslavia): CD 122, *123*

Medmenham Abbey: MW 121-125

Medoff, Marc: PP 101

Medrawt: *See* Mordred

Medusa: MC 22. *See also* Cephalopods *in MC index*

Medusa (queen of Gorgons): WW 17-19

Medvedev, Zhores: SI 43

Meenakshi (goddess): MY *36*

Meerloo, Joost: TS 124-126, 137

Megalithic Lunar Observatories (Thom): MP 94

Megalithic monuments: MP *69-79, 81,* MW 85, 90, MY 86; astronomical alignment of, MP 91-92; Avebury, MP *86-87,* MW 85; Callanish, CC *18-19,* MP *76-77,* MW 85; Carnac, MW *87,* MY 86; as observatories, MP 68, *93;* fertility rituals at, MP *86-87;* geomagnetism at, MP 97; as healing stones, MP *73, 93;* and ley theory, MP 94, 96, 97; powers of, MP 68, *73, 93;* and psychic emissions, MP 102; radiation levels at, MP *96-97;* types of, MP *81;* and UFO sightings, MP 98. *See also* Stonehenge

Megalithic Sites in Britain (Thom): MP 94

Megalithic yard: MP 94

Megamouth (shark): MC *20,* MW 71

Megatherium (dog): PE 32

Megavitamins: MA 114

Meh-teh: defined, MC 104

Meier, Eduard (Billy): and abductions by aliens, AE 104-105; and

MOON. Long hailed as queen of the night, the moon has generally been equated with feminine powers. Influencing covert forces of nature as well as the tides, it is also symbolic of the psychic, the occult, and the magical.

aliens, AE 98, 99, 100, 101; and Steve Ambrose, AE 104; and Asket, AE 99; audiotapes by, AE 99, 104; and Neil Davis, AE 104; and Brit Elders, AE 105; and Wally Gentleman, AE 104; and Ground Saucer Watch, AE 105; and Gary Kinder, AE 104, 105; and Shirley MacLaine, AE 99-101; and Michael Malin, AE 104; metallurgic samples found by, AE 99, 104; movies by, AE 99; photographs by, AE 98, 99, *100-101*, 102-104, UP *137*; and Bob Post, AE 104; psychic energy of, AE 105; and Semjase, AE 98, 99; and Sfath, AE 99; and Wendelle Stevens, AE *100-101*; and UFOs, AE 98, 99; and Marcel Vogel, AE 104; and Erich von Däniken, AE 99-101; and Louise Zinsstag, AE 101, 102

Meisenhelder, Thomas: TS 90
Meithe, Adolphe: SA 117, *118*
Mekriti people: EM *26*
Melanesia: MW 127, 130-133

Melba, Nellie: UV 96
Mellaart, James: CD 54
Melling, June: MW 55; sketch by, MW *56-57*
Melling, Vicky: MW 55
Meltemi (wind): MQ 55
Melton, J. Gordon: CD 96, WW 107, 108, 126
Melville, Herman: CC 84
Melville, John: VP 50
Melwas (king of Somerset): ML 56
Memories, Dreams, Reflections (Jung): CD 70, DD 24, 79
Memory: MB 58-60. *See also* Eidetic memory
Memory theater: MB 56-58
Men: aggression of, CD 68; brain organization of, CD 65-66; as hunters, CD 49-50, 55; and psi powers, CD 68; as warriors, CD 49, 55
Men-an-Tol: MA 118, *119*
Menard, H. William: PP 140
Mencken, H. L.: MB 90
Mendeiros, Marsha and William: MW 49-50

Mendeleyev, Dmitry: DD 44-45, VP 115
Menehune: MW 93, 96-99
Menehune Ditch: MW 96
Menelaus (king of Sparta): UV 23
Meneurs de loup: TN *90*
Menhirs: EE 16, 54, MW 87-88
Men in Black (MIB): UP *77*
Menninger Foundation: DD 146
Meno (Plato): SE 46
Menorah: AW *26*, MY 121
Menstrual cycles: TS 79, 80
Mental illnesses: MB 71-73, 74, 75, 79, 87, 88, PE 101. *See also* Multiple personality disorder; Outsider art; Psychoses; Schizophrenia
Mentalists: powers of, PP *103-117*
Mental Radio (Sinclair): PP 20, 25, 27
Mental suggestion: PP 140, 141. *See also* Telepathy
Menzel, Donald Howard: AE 101, UP 56; and alleged biblical UFO sightings, UP 14; debunking UFOs, UP 118, 122, 123, 131; and Lubbock UFO sighting, UP 50 51; and Norfolk UFO sighting, UP 52-53; and temperature inversion, UP 53, 55
Mephistopheles: *See* Satan
Mercator, Gerardus: CC 72
Mercedes, Joseph (mentalist): second-sight act of, PP *107*, 108
Mercure de France: AW 47
Mercurii, The: CC 113
Mercury (god): CC *42*, SA *74, 76*
Mercury (metallic element): MA 63, SA 21-23, 24
Mercury (planet): AE 90-93, 114, CC 17, 25, 42, 82, 98, MA *37*, MY 38, SA 21-23, 24, TS *102*
Mercury poisoning: SA 110
Meredith, Dennis: MC 89
Merhorse: MW 72, 75
Meridians: CC 118, PH *46*, 47, 54
Merlin (sorcerer): MQ 130, MW 86, SS *12*-13, VP 38; animals, associations with, MQ 136; as bard, MQ 133; battle site associated with, MQ *132-133;* cave of, ML *58-59;* and Geoffrey of Monmouth, ML 48; Hart Fell site associated with, MQ *134-135;* re-

treat to woods, MQ 133, 135; stag god identified with, images of, MQ *130, 133, 135, 136-137;* and Stonehenge, MP 82, 84, 85; youth, scene from, MQ *130-131*
Merlinus Anglicus Junior (Lilly): CC 107
Mermaids: MC *54, 55,* MW *73;* legends of, MP 37. *See also* Humanbeasts
Merman: MC *54. See also* Humanbeasts
Merodack, Sar: AW 68
Merovingian kings: MQ 125
Merton, Holmes Whittier: VP 74
Merton, Thomas: EM 139-142
Merton Institute for Vocational Guidance: VP 74
Meru, Mount: ML 70, TS 11, *31*
Mescaline: DD 114, MB 104-106. *See also* Hallucinogens
Mesmer, Franz Anton: PH 20, 87-90; criticism of, MM *92, 93;* death of, MM 92; and hypnosis, development of, PP 69; hypnosis research of, MM 92, *93;* pupils of, MM 94; and spiritualism, SS 26-27
Mesmerism: defined, HN 130. *See also* Hypnosis and hypnotic regression; Hypnotism
Mesopotamia: and metals, SA 21-23; numerology in, VP 105
Mesopotamians: CD 122, ML 117
Messadié, Gérald: and Jacques Bergier, PS 71; and *Nautilus,* PS 70
''Message to Garcia, A'' (Hubbard): UV 85
Messengers of Deception (Vallee): AE 120
Messiha, Khalil: ML 32
Messina, Strait of: EE *72-73*
Messing, Wolf (mentalist): PP 111-113, PS 66
Metal bending: MM 6-7, *27*-36, 78, *79, 86-87*
Metals: and Aristotle, SA 21; background of, SA 44; and Geber, SA 30; and Mesopotamia, SA 21-23; and planets, MA 36, 37
Metamorphoses: *See* Transformations

79

MY The Mystical Year; PE Phantom Encounters; PH Powers of Healing; PP Psychic Powers; PS The Psychics; PV Psychic Voyages; SA Secrets of the Alchemists; SE Search for the Soul; SI Search for Immortality; SS Spirit Summonings; TN Transformations; TS Time and Space; UP The UFO Phenomenon; UV Utopian Visions; VP Visions and Prophecies; WW Witches and Witchcraft

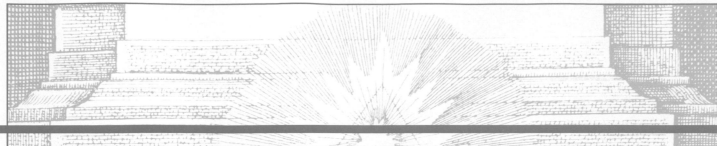

Metamorphoses (Apuleius): AW 16

Metamorphoses (Ovid): SE 97, SI 27, UV 23

Metaphysical evil: defined, CD 80

Metaphysics (Aristotle): SE 50

Metcalf, Manfred: ML 134, 135

Metcalf Stone: ML 134-135

Metempsychosis: UV 28. *See also* Reincarnation

Meteorology: EE 63-64. *See also* Weather

Meteor showers: MY 68, 101

Metetherial space: defined, PE 31

Methuselah (biblical figure): longevity of, SI 12, 13

Metoh-kangmi: See Abominable Snowman

Metopomancy: defined, VP 35

Métraux, Alfred: ML 87-89

Metteya, Bhikku Ananda (a.k.a. Allan Bennett): EM 92

Metz, Christian: UV 75

Mexico: biodynamic farming in, EE 131; giants in, ML 25; numerology in, VP 105; Tres Zapotes excavation in, MQ *96-97*

Mexico City (Mexico): MW 113, 115

Meyer, Silvio: metal bending by, MM 34

Meyerson, Blanche: PH 95-96

Mezapos (Greece): MQ *55*

MIB: UP 77

Mibu Ohana-taue: MY *46-47*

Mice: mummies of, WW 12

Michael (archangel): CD 132, *133*, EE 32, MW 85, 91-93, MY 35, 89

Michael (spirit guide): SS 146-147

Michaelmas: MY 35, 89

Michalak, Stephen: AE *60-61*

Michals, Duane: photographs by, PV *33-35*

Michaux, Charles: HN 36, 37

Michel, Anneliese: CD 91

Michell, John: and black holes, TS 63; and Stonehenge as UFO representation, MP 98-99

Michelson, Albert: TS 54, *55*

Michon, Jean-Hippolyte: VP 92

Microawakening: DD 110

Microcosm/macrocosm: CC *109*, MA 26; and Robert Fludd, SA 90; and Carl Jung, SA 132-133; and Heinrich Khunrath, SA 82;

and *Mutus Liber*, SA *71*; and Paracelsus, SA 64, 80. *See also* Correspondences theory

Microlaser scanner glasses: MB *132-133*

Micro-PK: MM 7-8, 70, *71*, 72-73, 85. *See also* Psychokinesis; Thoughtography

Microwave radiation: MM 79-80

Middle East: MW *maps 34-35*, 64, 98, 132; evil eye in, MA 127

Middleton, J. Connon: DD 132; and *Titanic* disaster, premonition of, PP 29

"Middle way": EM 40

Middle World: EM 63

Midgard: EE 92

Midnight sun: MY 37

Mid-ocean ridge: defined, EE 59

Midsummer: WW 123

Midsummer Eve: MY 49, 56

Midsummer Night's Dream, A (Shakespeare): MA 92, MB 87, UV 96, *97*

Midwest: superstitions in, MA 135

Midwives: CD 59, PH 40, WW 19

Mighty Atom: MB 96

Migration: TS *82-83*

Mihalasky, John: PS *106-107*

Mikakunin hiko-buttai: MW 94. *See also* UFOs

Mikesell, Mike: ML 21-22

Mikhailova, Nelya: *See* Kulagina, Nina

Milan Commission: MM 13

Milarepa, Saint: EM 41, 49, 50, 138-139, TS 11

Mila-Sherab-Gyaltsen: EM 41

Milbanke, Annabella: PE 39

MILD: *See* Mnemonic Induction of Lucid Dreams

Milden, Mrs. C.: PP 33, 34

Miles (beagle): SE *132;* and Paul Segall, SI 122-123, *129*

Milgram, Stanley: CD 94-95

Milioni, Il: *See* Polo, Marco

Milky Way: AE 114

Millennialists: MY 122; defined, UV 57; and Golden Age, UV 24-25; and Harmony Society, UV 63; and William Miller, UV 57, 60; and John Humphrey Noyes, UV 77; and George Rapp, UV 61, 62; and Jemima Wilkinson,

UV 74; and Woman in the Wilderness, UV 60

Millennium: defined, UV 57, VP 14

Miller, David C.: AW 84-85

Miller, Hamish: EE *91*

Miller, William: UV 57, 60

Milligan, Billy: MB 70-71, 77, 80, *84-85*, 87

Millikan, Robert: TS 65

Millman, Robert: PP 99

Mills, Clarissa: TS 113-114

Milne, Ian: MC 66

Milne, Robert Duncan: UP 19

Milton, John: CD 93, 130, MB 53, 89

Miming: MY 120

Mind: defined, MB 39. *See also specific headings*

Mindanao trench: MC 18

Mind and Its Brain, The (Eccles and Popper): MB 19

Mind at Large: MB 106

Mind-body problem: PV 78

Mind-brain identity theory: MB 17-18

Mind Children: The Future of Robot and Human Intelligence (Moravec): SI 88

Mindi: MW 63

Mind of a Mnemonist, The (Luria): MB 56

Mind of My Own, A (Sizemore): MB 79

Mind prints: PS *132-137*; defined, PS 132

Mind readers: *See* Psychics

Mind reading: *See* Telepathy

Mind Science Foundation: MM 70

Mind Wars (McRae): PS 82

Mineiri: EM 59

Mineral waters: EE 76

Miner's disease: SA 65

Mines, King Solomon's: ML 19, 47, MQ 41-*42*, 43

Mining: and Paul Clement Brown, PS 128-130; and dowsing, PS 122-123, *125*, 128-130; and Uri Geller, PS 122-123; and Clayton McDowell, PS *126;* and J. W. Young, PS 128

Minister of God (ghost): HN 103, 104

Mink, Everglades: MW 44

Minkowski, Hermann: TS 54

Minnesota Center for Twin and Adoption Research: CD 109

Minnesota Multiphasic Personality Inventory: VP 93

Minney, Johnny: PE 114, *115*

Minoan civilization: EE 74, MP 34-35, 36, MW 85

Minor Arcana: VP 123, 125, 130. *See also* Tarot; Tarot readers

Minos (character in *Divine Comedy):* SE *72-73*

Minos (king of Crete): MC 56

Minotaur (mythical beast): MC *56*, MW 53, SE 10. *See also* Humanbeasts

Minozzi, Renato: *See* Jeshahr the Guide

Min River: EM *12-13*

Minsky, Marvin: SE 123

Mir (space station): EE 112

Mirabelli, Carlos: SS 117-120

Mirabila: defined, ML 47

Miracles: CD 114-116, *117*

Mirage: mistaken for UFOs, UP 14

Miraj: DD 47, *50-55*

Miramar, Maria de: AW 118, *119*

Miriam (biblical figure): SA 24

Mirror, cosmic: SA *110*

Mirror-image reversal: PS 17

Mirror of Life and Death, The (engraving): CD *38*

Mirrors: and John Dee, MA 21-22, *57;* and Ferdinand of Tyrol, MA *56-57;* history of, MA 21; and superstitions, MA 118, 137

Mirville, Marquis de: MM 37-38

Mischief Night: MY 98

Misel, Harvey: MM *100*

Missing Time (Hopkins): UP 141-143

Missionaries: MQ 26-27

Mississippian culture: earthen mounds of, MP 123

Mississippi River region: giants in, ML 25

Miss J. K.: hypnosis of, PP 64

Misskelley, Darleen: MW *109*

Mistletoe: EE 95-96, MY 97

Mitchell, Edgar D.: EE 124, MM 28, PP 54-55

Mitchell, Janet: PV 36

Mitchison, Graeme: DD 100

Mithraism: AW 16, *17*

Mithras (god): AW *16-17*, CC 36,

MAN. *As exemplified in this 17th-century drawing, Western theories have held that a human is the universe in microcosm. The Chinese have said the universe is like an immense human being. Either way, mankind symbolizes the unity of the cosmos.*

MANDRAKE. *An embodiment of Satan but with great healing powers, mandrake when uprooted was said to emit a shriek that killed all who heard it. Here, a peasant covers his ears before an unwitting dog pulls up the root to which it is tethered.*

MY 120, *121,* VP 107
Mitochondrial DNA: CD 60
Mitsukini: PE *80-81*
Mixtecs: TS 37
Mnemonic devices: MB *58-59*
Mnemonic Induction of Lucid Dreams (MILD): DD 110, 113
Mnemonists: defined, MB 53. *See also* Eidetic memory
Mnemosyne (goddess): MB 56
Mo (divination system): VP 114
Moai kavakava: ML *96*
Moat of Liddel: MQ *132-133*
Moberly, Anne: HN 39, MY 68, PE *122;* handwriting of, HN *41;* map by, HN *43;* and retrocognition, HN *43-48, 50-51;* sketch by, HN *45*
Mobius Society: Egyptian expedition of, MQ *100-103;* and *Leander,* PS 128; and parapsychology, PS 89; and psychic archaeology, PP 124; and Stephan A. Schwartz, PS 89, 128
Mochras fault: AE 106
Modern Astrology (Leo): CC 116
Mohave Indians: CD 65
Mohenjo-Daro: ML 20 21, *70-79*
Mohican Indians: ML 115-116
Mohs, Gordon: MW 76
Moi, Stephen: and aliens, UP 70
Mokele-mbembe: MC 77, *91-97,* MW 65
Molay, Jacques de: AW *38, 39, 97,* MY *21*
Moleoscopists: VP 66, *68*
Moly: WW 20
Momaday, N. Scott: EE 39
Mombasa: MW 75
Mompesson, John: HN *56-57*
Monads: SE 59
Monasteries: EM 57, 58, *82,* TS *106,* 109
Mondeville, Henri de: SI 89
Mondragon, Carlos: SI *120-121,* 130
Mondrian, Piet: AW 158, UV *132;* paintings by, AW *158-161*
Monica (past-life therapy patient): PV *88-95*
Monism: SE 50. *See also* Materialistic monism
Monkey-boys: TN *66-69. See also* Feral children
Monkey gland treatment: SI 62
Monkeys: TN 68; macaque, MC *112,* 114; vervet, CD 109
Monk-fish: MC *54. See also* Human-beasts
Monks: CD *104-105,* EM *80-81, 102-103,* MA *18;* and Antony, CD 82; Buddhist, PH *137;* Franciscan, PS *97;* in Korea, EM *104-105;* of Shingon sect, EM *112-113;* in Thailand, EM *108-109;* and trances, MB *96-97;* and tulpa, MB 85; and women, CD 58; and yoga, MB *96-97. See also* Lamas
Monkshood: WW *32*
Monochord: defined, VP 105
Monochronic cultures: TS 97-99
Monod, Théodore: TN 66
Monroe, Marilyn: CC 82, VP 104
Monroe, Robert: PV *27-32, 33, 34,* 35
Monroe Institute for Applied Sciences: *See* Monroe, Robert
Monsters: MW *6-7, 10-13,* map 46, *47,* maps 52, 58, 64; in films, MC *127-137. See also specific creatures*
Montagu, Mary Wortley: SA 98-100
Montague, Nell St. John: as crystallomancer, VP 49-50
Montaire, Rinoir: VP 40
Montecatini Spa: SI *91. See also* Spas
Montefeltro, Guido de: CC 48
Montego Bay: MW 27
Monteil, Doctor: beauty devices

MY The Mystical Year; PE Phantom Encounters; PH Powers of Healing; PP Psychic Powers; PS The Psychics; PV Psychic Voyages; SA Secrets of the Alchemists; SE Search for the Soul; SI Search for Immortality; SS Spirit Summonings; TN Transformations; TS Time and Space; UP The UFO Phenomenon; UV Utopian Visions; VP Visions and Prophecies; WW Witches and Witchcraft

by, SI 95

Montesquiou, Robert de: HN 50

Montezuma: VP 34

Montezuma II: UV 24

Montfort, Pierre Denys de: octopus drawing by, MC 24; sea serpent research of, MC 22

Montgomery (Alabama): and UFO sighting, UP 42

Montgomery, Gabriel de: VP 18

Montgomery, Ruth: PS 18, SS 121

Montgomery, William: TN 41

Montpellier, University of: SA 31, 33

Montrose Aerodrome: MW 19-21

Mont-Saint-Michel: MW 85, 91

Montségur (Cathar fortress): AW 30, CD 33, MQ 118, 124, 127, 129, PV 101, SE 45. See also Cathars

Monumenta Britannica (Aubrey): MP 88-89

Monument Valley: EE 40-41

Moo, Queen (goddess): MA 52

Moody, Raymond A., Jr.: background of, PV 65-66; and near-death-experience research, PV 58, 66-72, 73

Moon: CC 9, 10, 38, 39, 71, 117, MA 37, MW 119, TN 92; characteristics of, SA 23; marriage of, CD 37; research on, TN 92; symbol for, SA 24; and theory of twelfth planet, AE 90-93. See also Lunar essence

Moon, Edward Gibson: psychic experience of, PP 10-11

Moon, Sun Myung: MB 99

"Mooncakes": MY 89

Moon god: MY 116

Moon Hare: MY 89

Moon madness: TN 92

Moon Trail: and Horace S. Hambling, SE 99

Moon watching: and biodynamic farming, EE 130-131

Moore, Alice: UV 84

Moore, Constance: HN 122; and ghosts, HN 124, 125

Moore, Francis: CC 112, 113

Moore, James: PS 47

Moore, John: and poltergeists, HN 64; and séances, HN 64

Moore, Robert: MQ 81

Moore, Robert Y.: TS 87

Moore, William: and Roswell UFO crash, UP 74-75

Moorman, Jack: CD 124

Moose: CD 109

Morag (lake monster): sightings of, MC 62, 90. See also Lake monsters

Moral evil: defined, CD 79

Moravec, Hans: SI 88

Moravia, vampires in: TN 121

Mordred: and Arthur, ML 48; battles of, ML 47

More, Thomas: UV 18; and Augustine, UV 39; background of, UV 39; and Plato, UV 39; and Reformation, UV 17; and utopia, UV 58

More than a Legend (Whyte): MC 72

More than an Ark on Ararat (Irwin): MQ 94

Morgan, J. P.: CC 7, 132, 139; and Evangeline Adams, PS 120-121; and astrology, PS 120-121; and clairvoyance, PS 111; and fortune-telling, PS 111; and stock market, PS 121

Morgan, Robert: SI 45-46

Morgan, William: AW 84-86, 105

Morgan le Fay: and Arthur, ML 48; and Avalon, ML 48, 52

Morgawr (sea serpent): MC 36, MW 75; history of, MC 37; sightings of, MC 37-38. See also Sea serpents

Morgenstern, Christian: CD 136

Morgenthau, Henry, Jr.: MQ 20

Morgner, A. V. (medium): spirit photograph of, PP 45

Morgue: in Vienna, design for, PE 92-93

Morial the Mahatma (Collins): AW 141

Mori cemetery (Japan): SE 30-31

Morley, Edward: TS 54, 55

Morley Hall: and ghosts, HN 128

Mormons: trek of, UV 58-59

"Morning after" abortion pill: See RU-486

Morning-glory seeds: EE 101

Morning Star (god): MA 68

Morocco: MW 65, 66; evil eye in, MA 127

Morpheus (god): DD 24, 29

Morphic fields: and biodynamic farming, EE 128; characteristics of, EE 128; and Alan Pickering, EE 128; and Gary Schwartz, EE 128; and Rupert Sheldrake, EE 124-126, 127-128

Morris, Desmond: MC 123

Morris, Grace: PS 118-119, 123-124

Morris, Henry M.: MQ 72

Morris, L.: and hauntings, HN 25-28

Morris, Michael S.: AE 116, TS 75

Morris, Robert: SE 88; and ghosts, HN 133; and out-of-body-experience research, PV 40, 41-42

Morris, William: UV 36-37, 85

Morris dancers: MY 36

Morrison, Richard James: CC 113-116

Morrison, Tony: and Nazca lines of Peru, MP 119; and taki'is of Bolivia, MP 98

Morrison, William: and ghosts, HN 35

Mortar: ML 104, SA 41

Morte d'Arthur, Le (Malory): ML 48, MQ 111, 120, 121, UV 36

Mosaic: Romanesque, Noah and animals depicted in, MQ 82

Moselle River: MY 27

Moses (biblical figure): AW 23, MY 39, SA 19, SI 13; and Ark of the Covenant, MQ 46; and earthquakes, EE 59; and golden calf, MQ 48; and sacred places, EE 30; on Sinai, MQ 45

Moses de Leon: AW 24

Moslems: See Muslims

Mosque of Abraham: MY 91

Mosque of the Prophet: MY 91

Moss, Thelma: PH 78, 103

Mossman, Tam: SS 147-148

Most Notable Antiquity of Great Britain, The, Vulgarly Called Stone-Heng, on Salisbury Plain. Restored (Webb): MP 85, 86

Most Pressing Humble Complaint of the Pious Innocents (Löher): WW 78

Mother: as archetype, DD 82-83. See also Alfassa, Mirra

Mother Ann: See Lee, Ann

Mother Dragon (goddess): TS 20

Mother Earth: CD 11

Mother Goddess: CD 23, 50, 51, 52, EE 22-23, MW 85, MY 20, 42, 51, 130, WW 17; in Africa, EE 27; and Aztecs, EE 26; and Joseph Campbell, EE 26, WW 13; characteristics of, EE 17, WW 13, 17, 115-116; and Chinese, CD 50; and Cretans, CD 54; decline of, CD 54, 55; and Delphic oracle, EE 29; and Egyptians, CD 50, 56; and Mircea Eliade, EE 24-26; and Eve, CD 59; and Germanic folklore, WW 27-28; and Ggantija, CD 52, 54; and Greeks, EE 29, WW 17; growth of interest in, CD 59; and Ruth Gruhn, CD 50; and Jane Ellen Harrison, WW 17; and Hesiod, CD 24; history of, WW 10-17, 97; and Hopi, EE 26; in Ice Age, CD 50; in India, EE 26; and Isis, WW 13; and Leviathan, WW 15; and Lilith, WW 15-16; and Maori, CD 24; and James Mellaart, CD 54; and mythologies, WW 13, 15-17; names of, WW 13; and Navajo, EE 24; in Neolithic period, CD 50, 54, WW 11-13; and Nut, WW 13; in Paleolithic period, CD 50, 54, 61; and Pelasgians, CD 23-24; and Romans, EE 26; and sacrifices, CD 54; and Semites, WW 13-16; and sexual equality, CD 54; and Slavs, EE 26-27; and Smohalla, EE 24; son and lover of, CD 50; and spirals, EE 17; and Starhawk, WW 115; and Sumerians, CD 50, 55, WW 13; symbols of, ML 54; and Tammuz, WW 16-17; temple of, CD 52-53; and toads, WW 14; and Virgin Mary, CD 58, 59; and Wicca, WW 10, 115-116, 131; and Donna Wilshire, CD 51; and Zuni, EE 24. See also Gaia (goddess)

Mothers: schizophrenogenic, MB 74

Mother Teresa: CD 107, 126

Mouhot, Henri: ML 70

Mould, Andy: AW 10

AE Alien Encounters; AW Ancient Wisdom and Secret Sects; CC Cosmic Connections; CD Cosmic Duality; DD Dreams and Dreaming; EE Earth Energies; EM Eastern Mysteries; HN Hauntings; MA Magical Arts; MB The Mind and Beyond; MC Mysterious Creatures; ML Mysterious Lands and Peoples; MM Mind over Matter; MP Mystic Places; MQ Mystic Quests; MW The Mysterious World;

MIRROR. *Considered a medium of communication between this world and the spirit realm, the mirror symbolizes ineluctable mortality and the futility of self-love. This one reflects the chalky visage of death against the image of youthful beauty.*

Mount, The: MW 25-*28*

Mountain, Edward: MC 71, 85

Mountain Giants, Norse: ML 25

Mountain lion, Eastern: MW 50. *See also* Beast of Truro

Mountain men: PS 77

Mountains of the Moon: MW *map 8-9*

Mountbatten, Earl: MC 70

Mountford, Rev. W.: PE 86

Mount Fuji: EM *20-21*

Mount Hiei: monastery on, EM 57, 58

Mount Kailas: EM *42-43*

Mounts of palm: VP *56-57. See also* Palmistry; Palmists

Moxibustion: PH *49,* 54, 55, 58

Moya, Miguel Angel: AE 60

Moya, Remedios: PH *39*

Moyset: and Pierre Burgot, TN 82

Mozambique: MW 65, 67-68

Mozart, Constanze: MB 89

Mozart, Wolfgang Amadeus: AW 90, *94-95,* 111, CC 90, DD 46, MM 92, PV 118, *122;* manuscript by, MB *89*

MPD: *See* Multiple personality disorder

M'Quhae, Peter: MC 31

MRI (magnetic resonance imaging): MB 132

Mr. K's (restaurant): EE 35

''Mr. Sludge, the Medium'' (Browning): SS 39, 50

''MS. Found in a Bottle'' (Poe): MP 145-146

Mu: MP 26-*27,* 28, MW 14, *map 15,* MY 34; Elders of, ML 14; people of, UV *46-47. See also* Lemuria

Muck Olla (god): MY 97

Mud mask: SI *91*

Mudra: EM *112-113*

Muezzin: TS 96

MUFON: *See* Mutual UFO Network

Mugwort: WW *39*

Muhammad (prophet): AW *34,* 36, 38, CC *54,* CD 18, 122, MY 33, 90, 91, SA 25, UV 24; and *adhan,* DD 39; and Buraq, DD *48, 49, 50, 55;* and dreams, DD 39, *47-55;* and Eve, CD 58; and Gabriel, DD 39, 47, 48, 50, 53, 55; and John the Baptist, DD 50; and Malik, DD *54-55;* and Zacharias, DD 50

Muharram: MY *137*

Muisak: MW 117-119

Mukti: defined, TS 93

Mukti Bhavan: TS *93*

Mukulian Empire: ML 14, MY 34

Mu Kung (god): SI 36

Muldoon, Sylvan Joseph: out-of-body experiences of, PV 25-27, *28-29,* 33

Mulhatten, Joe: TS 132

Mulholland, John (illusionist): UP *56*

Mullein: WW *38*

Müller, Bernhard (a.k.a. Maximillian de Leon): UV 63

Multidimensional geometry: and psychic phenomena, PP 70, *72*

Multiple Man (Crabtree): SS 152

Multiple personality disorder: and channeling, SS 150-152; characteristics of, SS 84; and coconsciousness, SS 152; and Adam Crabtree, SS 152-153; and mediums, SS 84, 85. *See also* MB *index*

Multiple universe theory: UP *150-151*

Multispectral image analyzer station: PS 84, 90

Mumford, Lewis: SI 23

Mumler, William: and ghosts, HN 26

Mummies: ML *22, 29,* MY 26-27; of cats, SE 28-29, SI 70, WW *12;* of Egyptians, SI 23, 99, *100;* embalming of, SI *100;* and immortality, SI 99, 100; of mice, WW 12; of pharaohs, SI 23; purposes of, SI 23, 99

Mummification: SE 24-25, *28-29*

Mummu (planet-god): AE 92, *93*

Mundugumor: CD 62

Munis: characteristics of, EM 33-37; defined, EM 33; and levitation, EM 33; and transmigration, EM 37

Munro, Daniel Colin: SI 13

Munsalvaesche (fictional castle): Montségur identified as, MQ 118, 124, 127

Mural: Roman, MQ 55

Murderers: and mandrakes, EE 96

Murphy, Bridget (Bridey): MY 102; reincarnation of, PV 114-118

Murphy, Gardner: DD 146, SE 17, 18, 98, TS 113; and psychic research, PP 49, 56

Murphy, Michael: and Esalen Institute, UV 135, 137; and Sri Au-

robindo, UV 135, 145

Murphy, Peggy: MM 67

Murray, Gilbert: MY 106

Murray, Margaret A.: WW 101-102, *103,* 112

Murray River: MW 59, 62-63

Muscarello, Norman J.: and Exeter UFO sighting, UP 99-102, *103*

Muscle reading: PP 105, PS 27

Muses, Charles: TS 127

Mushroom ring: AE *50*

Mushrooms: EE 102; and Frank Barron, MB 107; and Timothy Leary, MB 107-112. *See also* Hallucinogens

Music: and Geoffrey Hodson, TS *118-119;* and Pythagoras, TS 43, 47

Musical intervals: defined, TS 47

Music of the spheres: CC 23

Musk ox: TN *77*

Muslims: AW 38-39, CC 52-53, *54, 55,* SI 114; and Abraham, EE 52; and afterlife, CD 99, 126; and alchemy, SA 29-30; and angels, CD 122; conquests of, SA 25, 30, and evil, CD 80; and fig trees, EE 77, and hajj, EE 52; and Ka'ba, CD *101,* EE 52; and Ramon Llull, SA 32; and Muhammad, SA 25; and paradise myths, UV *6, 7;* and prayer, TS *96*

Mussolini, Benito: CC 84, PS 65

Mustangs (airplanes): MY *124*

Musteros: AE *102-103*

Mutations, The (film): MC *134-135*

Mutilation: *See* Animal mutilations; Scars; Self-mutilation

Mutual UFO Network (MUFON): and aliens, AE 62; background of, AE 24; and Philip J. Imbrogno, AE 59; and investigation of Rendlesham Forest UFO sighting, UP 136, 141; questionnaires published by, AE *70-71;* and Edward Walters, AE 70, 71

Mutus Liber (Anonymous): and Armand Barbault, SA 132; and Bible, SA 70, *77;* and Adam McLean, SA 70, 71, 76; and microcosm/macrocosm, SA *71;* and philosophers' stone, SA 70

Myers, Frederic W. H.: DD 107,

83

MOUNTAIN. *Though believed to be created by the devil chewing up the smooth earth and spitting it out in mounds, majestic peaks such as Japan's Mount Fuji (below) are widely revered as symbols of spiritual loftiness and oneness with God.*

NAVEL. *Just as the navel at the center of the body links unborn child to mother, this marble omphalos—Greek for navel—in the Temple of Apollo at Delphi was emblematic of the center of the world and the passageway to the domain of the gods.*

MM 15, PE 19, 23-24, 36, PS 27, SE 95, *96*, 97, 98, 107, VP 50; and Rosina Despard, PE 111; ghost research of, PE 31, 47, 91, 100; and ghosts, HN 30; and out-of-body experience research, PV 19, 20. *See also* SS *index*

Myers, Leo: SE *96*

Myers, Robert: SE 15-17, 18, 19

My Life (Wagner): DD 46

Mylodon: MW 50-*51. See also* Su monster

Myomancy: defined, VP 35

Myrial, Mademoiselle: *See* David-Néel, Alexandra

Mystère des Cathédrales, Le (Fulcanelli): MW 127, SA 119-120, 123

Mysteries of Magic, The (Lévi): TN 88

Mysterium Coniunctionis (Jung): SA 132

Mysterium Cosmographicum (Kepler): CC 98

Mystery cults: AW 13, SA 23

Mystery Hill: ML 131-133

Mystery of the Hereafter, The (Saint-Gaudens): HN *112-113*

Mystery of the Mind, The (Penfield): MB 8

Mystery plays: UV 115, *118-119*

Mystical: defined, MB 94

Mysticism: CD 111-114

Mystic Night (Sheets): DD 147

Mystic Order of Veiled Prophets of the Enchanted Realm: AW 109

Mystics: and chakras, MB 15; characteristics of, MB 117; Christian, near-death experiences of, PV 59; and consciousness, MB 101; and mind, MB 10; and trances, MB 93

My Story (Geller): MM 27

Mythic Tarot: VP *140-41. See also* Tarot; Tarot readers

Mythology: Greek, VP 108; and Mother Goddess, WW 13, 15-17, Norse, VP 106, 108; and witches, WW 10

Myths: child in, DD 87; defined, DD 29; feral children in, TN *56-57;* and fire, DD 34; hero in, DD 93; transformations in, TN 34-36; werewolves in, TN 74

84

AE Alien Encounters; AW Ancient Wisdom and Secret Sects; CC Cosmic Connections; CD Cosmic Duality; DD Dreams and Dreaming; EE Earth Energies; EM Eastern Mysteries; HN Hauntings; MA Magical Arts; MB The Mind and Beyond; MC Mysterious Creatures; ML Mysterious Lands and Peoples; MM Mind over Matter; MP Mystic Places; MQ Mystic Quests; MW The Mysterious World;

N

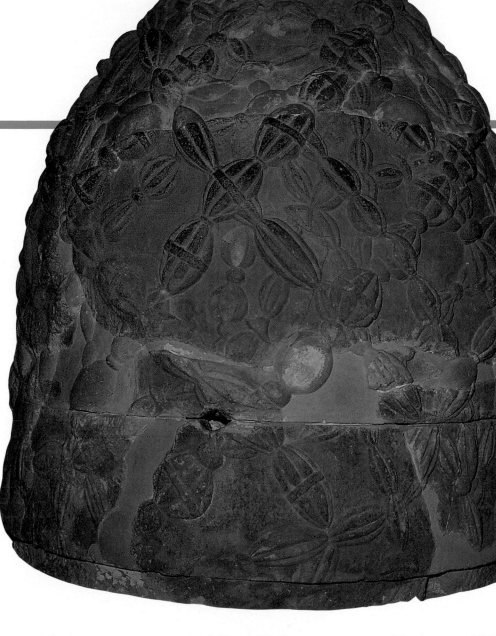

Naacal: ML 8
Nabataeans: ML 75
Nabhi: VP 10. *See also* Seers
Naciketas: SE 43
Nadia (autistic): drawing by, MB *61*
Nadia-Nadyr: MM *97*
Nadis: PH 72, 74
Nagadevta (god): EM 39
Nagaoka, Hantaro: SA 117
Naga Panchami: EM *38-39,* MY *58-59*
Nagas (gods): MY 58
Nagas (holy men): CD *14,* SI 18-20. *See also* Sadhus
Nagloper: AE *46*
Nagualism: defined, TN 30. *See also* Transformations
Nagy, Ivan. PH *55*
Nagyvary, Joseph: SA 128
Nahnmwarkis: ML 102
Nahua Indians: MW 115-116, TS 32, 36
Nails, bed of: EM *32-33*
Naitaka (demon god): MC 62. *See also* Lake monsters
Naive visionaries: defined, UV 43; works by, UV *44-55*
Nakamura, Toshio: AE 61-62
Nakedness: dreams of, DD *122-123*
Namahage: MY *122*
Name amnesia: defined, MB 49
Namgyal, Thondup (prince of Sikkim): CC 7
Naming ceremony: EE 26
Nammu (goddess): CD 50
Nanautzin (god): TS 37
Nandi Bear: MW 65, 66-67
Nan Douwas tomb: ML *100-101*
Nan Madol: ML 97-98, *100-101,* 102
Nanotechnology: SI 128-130
Nansen, Fridtjof: MP 148

Nantag: defined, MA 80
Napier, John: MC 123, 124
Napoleon Bonaparte: CC 84, DD 42-43, PS 75; armies of, MQ 122, SI 15
Napoleon III: MM 115, SS 22, 39
Nara (Japan): MW 59, 61
Narcisse, Clairvius: MA *88*
Narcisse, Marie Claire: MA 88
Narcolepsy: DD 110, 116
Narcotics: and psychokinesis, MM 61
Nari Valaya Yantra: CC *111*
Naropa Institute: EM 134
Narrative of Arthur Gordon Pym of Nantucket, The (Poe): MP 145-146

Narwhal (boat): MC 78
NASA: EE 119; satellite, photograph by, MQ 64, *66;* scientists, MB *132-133,* PE 117
Nasca: *See* Nazca; Nazca lines of Peru
Naseby: battlefield of, PE 129
Nash, John A.: PS 34
Nash, Lonson: MC 28
Nash, William B.: UP 52, 53
Nashe, Thomas: CC 104
Nasik (India): SI 16
Natal (South Africa): MW 133, 135
Natal charts: PS *118-119*
Nataska (ogre): MA *46*
Nathael (sun spirit): MA 62, 63
National Academy of Sciences:

and Condon report, UP 118
National Aeronautics and Space Administration: *See* NASA
National Airport (Washington, D.C.): MW 42
National Enquirer (tabloid): AE 38, 88
National Geographic (magazine): and Loch Ness expedition, MC *86-87*
National Investigations Committee on Aerial Phenomena (NICAP): background of, AE 24; and Condon committee, UP 116; and Exeter UFO sighting, UP 103, 105; and Richard Hall, AE 85
National Laboratory of Psychical

MY The Mystical Year; PE Phantom Encounters; PH Powers of Healing; PP Psychic Powers; PS The Psychics; PV Psychic Voyages; SA Secrets of the Alchemists; SE Search for the Soul; SI Search for Immortality; SS Spirit Summonings; TN Transformations; TS Time and Space; UP The UFO Phenomenon; UV Utopian Visions; VP Visions and Prophecies; WW Witches and Witchcraft

Research: MM 19, PE *126,* PP 87; founding of, HN 65

National Maritime Museum: HN *27*

National Opinion Research Center: survey by, HN 128

National Secular Society: AW 140

National Security Council: PS 91

Native Americans: *See* Indians, American

NATO: MW 42

Natron: SI *100*

Nats (spirits): SE 25

Natural evil: defined, CD 79

Natural History of Norway (Pontoppidan): MC 22

Natural History of Religion, The (Hume): AW 90-91

Natural Law of Vibration: PS 119

Natural phenomena: mistaken for UFOs, UP *18, 20, 21. See also individual phenomena*

Natural selection: SI 47; and Charles Darwin, MB 13, 14, 21; and Alfred Russel Wallace, MB 13, 14. *See also* Evolution

Nature: SA *91*

Nature (Emerson): SE 61-62

Nature (journal): EE 127, MM 29-30

Nature's Explication and Helmont's Vindication (Starkey): SA 96

Naudé, Gabriel: WW 72

Naughty little girl theory: defined, HN 72. *See also* Poltergeists

Naumov, Eduard: PS 79, 80, 84, 142

Nausea (Sartre): SE 71

Naushon Island (Massachusetts): SE *93*

Nautilus (submarine): PP 140-141, PS 70-71, *72-73,* 78, 79. *See also* Submarines

Nauvoo (Illinois): UV 59

Navajo Indians: MA 72, MW 79, 81-83, PH 15, *41;* astral body beliefs of, PV *18;* and Canyon de Chelly, TS 7; cosmogonies of, EE 24, TS 30; and directions, TS 30; and Glen Canyon Dam, EE 48; and holy people, EE 19; and Monument Valley, EE 40; and Mother Goddess, EE 24; and Rainbow Bridge, EE 48; sand

paintings of, CD *11,* DD *30,* TS 30, *31,* 95; and San Francisco Peaks, EE 39; and Ship Rock, EE 42; and Spider Rock, EE 43; and Spider Woman, EE 43; and time, TS 97; and transformations, TN 43; tunic of, DD *31;* and Window Rock, EE 49; and witches, TN 43

Navajo Mountain: MW 83

Naval Aviation News (magazine):

and UFO sightings, UP 48-49

"Naval Treaty, The" (Doyle): SS 101

Navarra, Fernand: MQ *85,* 86, *87;* ark expedition, MQ *85-87,* 86-89

Navarra, Raphael: MQ *86,* 87-88

Navel of the World: TS 6

Navigatio Sancti Brendani (Anonymous): ML 122, 123

Navratil, Leo: MB 65, 67, 69

Navratilova, Martina: MA 128

Navy, U.S.: PS 84-90

Naylor, R. H.: CC 132

Nazca (Peru): ML 32, MW 79

Nazca culture: MP 112

Nazca lines of Peru: MP 15, 110 119, *113, 115, 118-119,* SE 11; astronomical alignments of, MP 110-113; construction of, MP 111; and ley theory, MP 98; purpose of, MP 111, 119, *129-133;* summer solstice at, MP 112;

AE Alien Encounters; AW Ancient Wisdom and Secret Sects; CC Cosmic Connections; CD Cosmic Duality; DD Dreams and Dreaming; EE Earth Energies; EM Eastern Mysteries; HN Hauntings; MA Magical Arts; MB The Mind and Beyond; MC Mysterious Creatures; ML Mysterious Lands and Peoples; MM Mind over Matter; MP Mystic Places; MQ Mystic Quests; MW The Mysterious World;

NIMBUS. In cultures both East and West, the nimbus, or halo, signifies divinity, saintliness, enlightenment, or other extraordinary virtue. These Buddhist divinities grace a silk tapestry depicting the "Pure Land of the Western Paradise."

winter solstice at, MP 110. *See also* Earth drawings

Nazis: CD 93-94, 128; and astrology, PS *69;* and Beer Hall Putsch, PS 58; and dowsing, PS 59, 68; and dreams, DD 41; and Ian Fleming, PS 68; and fortunetelling, PS 59; and Sigmund Freud, DD *67;* and Erik Jan Hanussen, PS 60-61; interest of, in Holy Grail, MQ 127-128; and Stefan Ossowiecki, PS 66, 67; and psi powers, PS 58-69; and psi-warfare experiments, PS 68-69. *See also* SS

NDEs: *See* Near-death experiences

Neanderthals: MC 111, 112, MW 60, SE 20

Near-death experiences (NDEs): AE 53; defined, PE 35. *See also* PV *index*

Nebel, Long John: and alien spacecraft, UP 74

Nebraska Wesleyan University: MW 27

Nebu (god): CC 17

Nebuchadnezzar (king of Babylon): CC 17, DD 29

Necho (pharaoh): ML 119

Necklaces, charm: MW 127

Necromancers: MA 22

Necromancy: SA 59; defined, VP 46

Necromanteion (Oracle of the Dead; Greece): site of, MQ *57*

Nectar: SI *10-11*

Needham, Joseph: PH 51, 106-107

Needleman, Jacob: PP 101

Néel, Philippe: and Alexandra David-Néel, EM 73-74

Neff, Wilbur L.: and Ravenna UFO sighting, UP 111-115

Negev Desert (Israel): Har Karkom site in, MQ *44-45*

Neglect syndrome: defined, MB 50

Nehru, Jawaharlal: AW 142

Neihardt, John G.: and Oglala Sioux Indian spirit visions, PP 78

Neil, Graham: MA 128

Neill, Patrick: MC 42

Nelson, Robert: SI 118-122

Nelson, Roger: PS 88

Nematodes: SI 72-73

Nemesis (goddess): MC 14-15

Nennius: ML 47

Neolithic period: CD 50, 54; Mother Goddess in, WW 11-13; women in, WW 11

Neopaganism: and Margot Adler, WW 97-98, 119; characteristics of, WW 119; defined, WW 107; festivals of, WW 97; members of, WW 97-98. *See also* Paganism

Neoplasticism: AW 161

Neoplatonism: SE 49

Neo-Pythagoreans: UV 33

Nepal: burial rituals in, PE *54;* haruspicy in, VP *33;* shamans in, EM 42

Nepal, legendary valley of (Khembalung): quest for, MQ 30-31

Nephelomancy: defined, VP 35

Nepthys (goddess): MY *85*

Neptune (god): CC 40, *46,* MY 134, SA *71*

Neptune (planet): AE *90-93,* CC 46, 139; background of, AE 92; characteristics of, AE 114

Neresheimer, E. August: UV 90

Nergal (god): CC 16-17, 41

Neri, Filippo: PV *61*

Nero (Roman emperor): CC 34, VP 40, 109; ghost of, HN 131

Nerve auras: PS 30

Nessie: MW 17, 53, MY 63

Nessie: Seven Years in Search of the Monster (Searle): MC 84

Nessiteras rhombopteryx: See Loch Ness monster

Nestorian Church: ML 63

Netherlands: biodynamic farming in, EE 130

Netsuke: EM *49*

Netto, Ladislau: ML 136-137

Neuberg, Victor: AW 116, *117*

Neural networks: PS 132-137

Neuroglia: defined, MB 39

Neurons: SE *116,* 118, 128, SI 83; defined, MB 39

Neuropsychiatric Institute: SE 126

Neuroscience: MB 9

Neurosuspension: SI 116-118, 119

Neutral monism: SE 62

Neutron star: TS 64

New, Reformed, Orthodox Order of the Golden Dawn: and Aidan Kelly, WW 105

New Age movement: AW 125, 126, PP 84, 95, 99, SS 7, 18; and Age of Aquarius, UV 138; beliefs of, PP 96; and Pierre Teilhard de Chardin, UV 138-139; criticisms of, PP 101; defined, PV 43, 44; and Georgei Ivanovitch Gurdjieff, UV 102-105; and human-potential movement, UV 142; and intentional communities, UV 138, 139; publications of, PP 96-97; and Rudolf Steiner, UV 102-105; and Arnold Toynbee, UV 139

New Alchemy Institute: SA 135-136

New Atlantis (Bacon): MP 20, UV 42, VP 27

New Caledonians: SE 21

New Eden (magazine): article in, MQ 81, 83

Newell, Tricia: Tarot cards by, VP *140-141*

New England Antiquities Research Association: ML 131

Newgrange (Ireland): MW 85, MY 9, *15;* characteristics of, EE 16, 17; enclosing of, EE 30; and fertility symbols, EE 17-19; and spirals, EE 17; as sun temple, MP *99;* and winter solstice, EE 16-17, *18,* MP *99*

New Guinea: CD 61-62, MW 42; Asmat warrior of, SE *14;* burial rituals in, PE 53

New Hall Tavern: MW *24*

Newhouse, Sewell: UV 80

New Jerusalem: UV 23, 25

New Jerusalem church: UV 34

New mammalian brain: *See* Cerebral cortex

New Man, The (Lissitzky): UV *125*

Newmann, C. A. George (mentalist): PP 107-108

"New Mental Battlefield, The" (J. Alexander): PS 90-91

"New religions": MW 127, 129-130

New Science of Life, A: The Hypothesis of Formative Causation (Sheldrake): EE 127

New Scientist (journal): EE 127

Newstead Abbey: PE 39

New Stone Age: CD 50, 54

Newton, Isaac: AE 115, CC 96, 100-101, 148, CD 38, SE 50, UV 32, VP 8; and alchemy, SA 80, 97-98, 102; background of, MB 87-88; and Robert Boyle, SA 98; and calculus, MB 20; and Great Pyramid, MP 54; and Hermes Trismegistus, SA 98; and homosexuality, MB 87; and John Locke, SA 98; and paranoia, MB 87; and physics, MB 25; as scientist, SA 97, 98; and Anthony Storr, MB 87-88; theories of, MB 9, 10

Newton, J. R.: PH 90-91

New Vrindaban: EM 127-130

New Year, Buddhist: EM *51, 52*

New Year festivals: MY 20, 21, 23, 25, 26, 29, *32,* 58, 63, 89, 96-97, 101, *106-112,* 123, 124-125

New Zealand: volcanoes in, EE 69

Nez Percé Indians: and Coyote, TN *52-53;* and tricksters, TN 49, *52-53*

Ngai (god): MW 137

N'ha-a-itk: MW 47

Niall: and witches, WW 29-30

Ni''alnii'gi: EE *49*

Nias, D. K. B.: CC 142

Nibiru (planet-god): AE *90-93,* 94-95, 97

NICAP: *See* National Investigations Committee on Aerial Phenomena

Niceros: TN 75

Nichiren: MY 85

Nichol, Agnes: *See* Guppy, Mrs. Samuel

Nicholas, Saint: MY *116*

Nicholas II (czar of Russia): MB 98, MQ 83, PH 86

Nicholas IV (pope): SA 34

Nicias: CC 20, VP 33

Nickell, Molli: SS *149*

Nicklaus, Jack: DD 115-116

Nicolai, Renato: and UFO sighting in France, UP 121-122

Nicoll, Michael J.: MC 32, 33

Nider, Johannes: and witches, WW 62

Nidhögg: EE 93

Niehans, Paul: SI *64-65,* 66

Nielson, Bob: AE 33

Nietzsche, Friedrich: EM 85

Niflheim: EE 92

87

MY The Mystical Year; PE Phantom Encounters; PH Powers of Healing; PP Psychic Powers; PS The Psychics; PV Psychic Voyages; SA Secrets of the Alchemists; SE Search for the Soul; SI Search for Immortality; SS Spirit Summonings; TN Transformations; TS Time and Space; UP The UFO Phenomenon; UV Utopian Visions; VP Visions and Prophecies; WW Witches and Witchcraft

Nigg, Walter: CD 129
Night-force: CD 36-37
Night Journey, Muhammad's: AW 34
Nightmare, The (Fuseli): CD 84
Nightmares: DD 102-106, 114, 115. *See also* Dreams
Nightshade: MA 99, TN 73-74, WW 32
Night terrors: DD 106. *See also* Dreams
Night Way: DD 30
Nigredo: MW 127
Nijinsky, Vaslav: MQ 19
Nile River: MY 62, 67
Nim (chimpanzee): MB 42-43
Niman dance: MY 64
Nine: in dice, VP 111; in numerology, VP 103, 108, 114-115
Nine Sisters Masonic lodge: AW 80
Nineveh (ancient Mesopotamian city): tablets from, MQ 80
Nin-Gilbert, Margaret: TN 41
Ninhursag (goddess): AE 96, 97, UV 18-20
Nintzel, Hans: SA 127
Ninurta (god): CC 17
Nirvan (Telsen-Sao participant): MB 118
Nirvana: CD 18, 99, MY 41; and Buddha, EM 40, 101; and Buddhism, EM 101; Buddhist beliefs in, PV 127; characteristics of, SI 16; and Alexandra David-Néel, EM 81; defined, EM 101, MB 101, PV 102, 120, 127; and Hindus, SI 16, 18; and Milarepa, EM 50-51. *See also* Paradise
Nisbet, John: MB 87
Nisi: evil eye on, MA 11-13
Nisir, Mount: ML 34
Nissan: employee of, SI 45
Nitrous oxide: MB 102
Nixon, Richard M.: CC 89, VP 23
Nizam al-Mülk: AW 33
Nkisi figure: MA 83
Nkrumah, Kwame: PS 76
N. N. (magician): MA 52-53
Noah (biblical figure): CD 132, MW 99, MY 35, 99, SI 12-13; and Ararat, ML 22, 34; and flood stories, EE 74, ML 33-34; and olive trees, EE 79; as patriarch,

ML 24
Noah's Ark: *See* MQ *index*
Nobel Peace Prize: EM 130
Noel, Madame: SS 66, 67
Noise Intoners: UV 123
Nolan, Finbarr: PS 103
Nolen, William: PH 36, 104-107
Nomads: Golok, EM 80-81
"No-men": Scythian, CD 63
Nonquase (Xhosa): MW 135-136
Non-REM sleep: DD 96, 97, 99, 100. *See also* REM sleep; Sleep
Noorbergen, Rene: and flood stories, ML 33, 34
Noosphere: UV 139
Nootka: culture of the, TN 6; shamans of the, TN 11
Norepinephrine: MB 106
Norfolk (Virginia): and UFO sighting, UP 52
Noriega, Manuel: MA 6-7, 8, 92
Norman, Harold: MA 110-111
Norman, Ruth (a.k.a. Uriel): SS 148-150, 151; and Unarius Foundation, UP 78, 79
Norse mythology: CD 24, VP 106, 108; witches in, WW 27, 28-29

North America: MW *maps* 10-11, 15, 26, 34-35, 46, 78, 112; wolves in, TN 76
North Berwick (Scotland): witches in, WW 6-8, 9
North Equatorial Current: ML 120
Northern Hemisphere, skies of: MW *map* 12
Northern lights: EE 70-71
Northern Pacific Railroad: MW 80
Northern Way: WW 112
North Pole: MP 148
Northrop, John: SI 102-103
North Star: EM 10
Northumberland (England): church archaeology in, MQ 105
North Wind (satellite): AE 93
Norton, Thomas: SA 36, 45
No Ruz: MY 26
Norway: arrival apparitions in, PE 100
Norwegian Society for Psychical Research: PE 100
Nosferat: TN 134-136. *See also* Vampires
Nostradamus (Nostredame, Michel de): AW 72, CC 69-72, 73, 135,

136, 153; and Joseph Goebbels, PS 62; and Karl Ernst Krafft, PS 62, 63; as scryer, VP 47; as seer, VP 16, 17-20, 19, 28; and Louis de Wohl, PS 68
"Nostradamus Predicts the Course of the War" (Anonymous): VP 20
Notarikon: MA 55
Notes & Queries: VP 16
Notre Dame Cathedral: MA 92, 93, MW 119, 125-127, SA 119, 124-125
Nouri, Prince or Archdeacon of (John Joseph): MQ 79-80
Nourlangie Rock: ML 40-41
Nova Wicca: WW 112
Novomeysky, Abram: MB 52
Noyes, John Humphrey: UV 76, 77-78, 80
Noyes, Russell, Jr.: PV 63-64, 78
NSC: PS 91
Nubaigai: MY 91
Nuclear holocaust: ML 32-33
Nudists: EM 122
Nugua (goddess): CD 50, TS 27
Nü Kwa (goddess): *See* Nugua
Numa (king of Rome): MY 37
Numbakulla (god): EE 90
Numbers: characteristics of, TS 44-45; and Gnosticism, MA 60-61; and Greeks, TS 45; and Last Supper, MA 119; and Pythagoras, MA 26, 60, TS 44; and Pythagoreanism, MA 54, 60, TS 43, 44-45, 49; and superstitions, MA 119, 121, 129; and talismans, MA 41
Numerologists: VP 105-109, 115. *See also* Numerology
Numerology: PS 75; use of, PP 96-97. *See also* Numerologists; VP *index*
Nuns: Buddhist, PV 130-131; Tibetan, EM 30
Nut (goddess): CC 29, 31, CD 50, TS 20, WW 16; and Mother Goddess, WW 13
Nuwah (progenitor of Chinese race): ML 34
Nyambi (god): UV 20
Nyon (Switzerland): MW 34
Nystagmus: defined, MB 85
Nyx (goddess): TS 19-20

OWL. *Depicted here in an Etruscan carving, the owl represents evil in many cultures and is often linked with sorcery. In Botswana, the bird is so dreaded that if one alights on a home, a witch doctor is called in to perform purification rites.*

Oakley, Annie: CC 84
Oakley, Antony: MA 110, 111
Oaks: EE *80-81*, 92. *See also* Trees
Oannes (god): EE 72
Oarfish: MC *39*, 44
Oaxacan Indians: and time, TS 100
Obelisks: Egyptian, MP 57, *60-61*
OBEs: *See* Out-of-body experiences
Objective consciousness: UV 107
Object reading: *See* Psychometry
Obol: TN *113;* defined, TN 113
O'Brien, Lady Honora: PE 38
O'Brien, Thomas P.: and Boston Strangler case, PP 131-132
Observation theories: MM 71, TS 120
Observatories: CC *97, 110, 111,* MY *12-13,* 28
Obsession: PP 42, 43
Obsessive-compulsive disorder: causes of, MB 71; and Samuel Johnson, MB 88. *See also* Mental illnesses
Occam's Razor: MP 36
Occipital lobe: MB 50-51
Occult: defined, MA 45
Occult places: MW *maps* 112, 118, 126, 132
Occult World, The (Sinnett): EM 89
Ocean People: defined, TN 15
Oceans: EM *62-63;* and Babylonians, EE 72; and Greeks, EE 72-74
Och (god): MA 62-63
Ochorowicz, Julien: MM 13, *14,* 17-18, SS 61
O'Connell, James: ML 98
O'Connor, John: CD 96
Octagon House: HN *112*
Octopuses, giant: MC 19, *24, 25,* MW 75; habitat of, MC 25-26; sightings of, MC 24-26. *See also*

Cephalopods *in* MC *index*
Octopus mask: TN *14*
"Ode to Spurzheim" (Pierpont): VP 75
Odhar, Coinneach: VP 30-32, 45
Odin (god): EE 93, MA *27*, MY 121, SE 13, TN 36, WW 28; and runes, MA 27, 28. *See also* Zeus
O'Donnell, Elliott: PE 41, 62
O'Driscoll, Monique: AE 54
Odysseus: AE *47*, SE 27-28; and Circe, MQ *56*, WW 19-20; voyage of, MQ *49-61*
Odyssey (Homer): MC 22, SE 27-28, UV 23, WW 19-20, 35; retracing voyage in, MQ *49-61*
Oedipus complex: CD 60-61; defined, SA 129
Oenomancy: defined, VP 35
Ogburn, William F.: TN 63
Oghams: ML *132-135*
Oglala Sioux Indians: PP 75, 78-79
Ogopogo (Lake Okanagan monster): MC 62-63, 77, MW 47-48. *See also* Lake monsters
Ohashi, Wataru: PH 55
Ohio: MW 79
Oh-mah-ah (hominoid): MC 116
Ohman, Olof: ML 126
Ohrmazd (god): CD 26-28, *28-29,* 82, 122, MW 102, MY 82, TS 22
Ohsawa, George: PH 61
Oil lamps: EM *52*
Oiwa: MW 34, *36,* 38; shrine to, MW *37,* 38
Okanagan, Lake: MW 47
Okanagan monster: *See* Ogopogo
Okapi: MC *21*
O'Keefe, Daniel Lawrence: MA 10-11
Okiku (ghost): PE *76*
Okinawa: MW 127
Okiyome: MW 130
Olcott, Henry Steel: AW 126, 131,

CC 116, EM *86-87*, MY *84;* and Annie Wood Besant, AW 141; and Helena Petrovna Blavatsky, AW 124-125, 129-130, EM 84; death of, AW 141; in India, AW 132, 133, PV 21-22; at Society for Psychical Research, PV 22; Theosophical beliefs of, PV 20, 22; and Theosophical Society, AW 126, CC 116, EM 85, MY 84
Old Griet: MW 34, 37-38
Old mammalian brain: *See* Limbic system
Old Man (sea serpent): MC 33. *See also* Sea serpents
Old Man of the North: SI 14
Old Ones: defined, WW 107
Old Stone Age: CD 50, 54, 61
Old Straight Track, The (Watkins): MP 94, 98
Old Straight Track Club: EE 38
Old Vic: and ghosts, HN 31
Old Woman: MY 91
Olga, Mount: MW *97*
Oliphant, Pat: cartoon by, UP *117*
Olitiau: MW 65, 70
Olivero, Count Augusto: PE 124
Olive trees: EE *78-79*. *See also* Trees
Olivier, Laurence: MA 116
Olmec: ML 115-116
Olmolungring (sacred land of Bön religion): MQ *25*
Olsihpa and Olsohpa (founders of Nan Madol): ML 101-102
Olympic Games: MY *72*
Olympus, Mount: CD 23-24
Omah (hominoid): MC 116
Omand, Donald: MC 84
Ometeotl (god): TS 36
Omphalomancy: defined, VP 35
Omphalos: EE *30, 31,* TS 9; char-

acteristics of, EE 32-33; and Charlemagne, EE 33; defined, EE 32; and Eleusinian mysteries, EE 54; and Forbidden City (China), EE 33; and geomancy, EE 32; importance of, EE 52; Ka'ba as, EE 52
Onassis, Aristotle: TS 117
Onassis, Jacqueline Kennedy: CC 84
On Death and Dying (Kübler-Ross): PV 64
On Divination (Aristotle): DD 34
On Dreams (Aristotle): DD 34, 107
One: in dice, VP 111; in dominoes, VP 112, 113; in numerology, VP 99, 108, 109
Oneida community: UV *76;* and Sewell Newhouse, UV 80; and John Humphrey Noyes, UV 77-78; and sex, UV 75, 78, 80; and silverware, UV 80; and steel traps, UV 80; and stirpiculture, UV 80; success of, UV 78-80
Oneirocritica (Artemidorus Daldianus): DD 35, 37
Oneiromancy: DD 26, VP 35
"1000 Airplanes on the Roof" (Hwang): AE *112-113*
On Instruments and Furnaces (Zosimus of Panopolis): SA *29*
Onions: MY 21, 114
On Prophecy in Sleep (Aristotle): DD 34
On Sleep and Waking (Aristotle): DD 34
Ontake, Mount: CD *100-101*
Ontario (province; Canada): Iroquois Indian site in, MQ 98, *99*
On the Origin of Species by Means of Natural Selection (Darwin): AW 127, CD 93, 109, MQ 74, SS 23, 73
On the Track of Unknown Animals

MY *The Mystical Year;* **PE** *Phantom Encounters;* **PH** *Powers of Healing;* **PP** *Psychic Powers;* **PS** *The Psychics;* **PV** *Psychic Voyages;* **SA** *Secrets of the Alchemists;* **SE** *Search for the Soul;* **SI** *Search for Immortality;* **SS** *Spirit Summonings;* **TN** *Transformations;* **TS** *Time and Space;* **UP** *The UFO Phenomenon;* **UV** *Utopian Visions;* **VP** *Visions and Prophecies;* **WW** *Witches and Witchcraft*

OVEN. *To those who used them, alchemical ovens such as the one below were seen as being analogous to the human body: Just as the soul was purified within the body, so would metals be transformed from base to noble in the oven.*

OLIVE. *In this fragment of an Egyptian stone carving (right), a hand holds out an olive branch as an offering to the sun god. Besides its common use as a sign of peace and friendship, the olive has been a symbol of protection against witchcraft.*

(Heuvelmans): MW 65-66

Onychomancy: defined, VP 35

Onyx: MA 101

Oonark, Jessie, astral body as viewed by: PV *19*

Opalia: MY 119

Opening of the Mouth: MA *50-51*

Open universe: TS 62

Opera Chemica (Llull): AW 28-*29*

Operational Thetans: PS 84

Operation Deepscan: MC *88;* Loch Ness monster research of, MC 89, 90. *See also* Sonar probes

Ophiomancy: defined, VP 35

Ophion (serpent): CD 23-24

Ophir (site of King Solomon's mines): ML 47, 66-68, MQ 41-*42, 43*

Opium den: MB *112*

Opium poppy: WW *34*

Oppenheim, Garrett: PV 88, *89*

Ops (goddess): MY 119

Optical disk: MY *70*

Optics: SA 34

Oracle bone divination: VP 117, *119*

Oracle of the Dead (Necromanteion; Greece): site of, MQ *57*

Oracles: EE 54, MB 93, PP 7, 17; Bin, VP 119; Claros, MW 99, 104, VP 11-14; Floral, VP 40; Sabu, EM 98; Tibetan, EM *51. See also* Delphic Oracle; Seers; *specific types of divination and oracles*

Orang-Dalam (hominoid): MC 100

Orang Pendeks: MW 59, 60-*62*

Orangutans: MW 60

Order of Builders: AW 109

Order of DeMolay: AW 109

Order of Job's Daughters: AW 109

Order of Rainbow: AW 109

Order of the Dragon: TN 104

Order of the Eastern Star: AW 103, 109

Order of the Golden Dawn: *See* Hermetic Order of the Golden Dawn

Order of the Illuminati: AW 101-104, *105,* 108, 112, MY 33

Order of the Rose-Croix of the Temple and of the Grail: AW 68

Order of the Rose of Ruby and the Cross of Gold: AW 153, 156

Order of the Silver Star: MA 65

Order of the Star in the East: AW 143, EM 87, 88

Order of the Templars of the East: AW 114, *115,* 139

Order of the Temple of the Orient: MA 64

Ordo Rosae Rubeae et Aurea Crucis: AW 153, 156

Ordo Templi Orientis: AW 114, *115,* 139

Ordre Kabbalistique de la Rose-Croix: AW 68

Organic farming: EE 129. *See also* Biodynamic farming; Farming

Organology: *See* Phrenologists; Phrenology

Organ stones: MA *106*

Orgone: EE *127,* UP 52; boxes, PH *100,* 101; energy, PH 100, 101

Orgone energy accumulator: EE *126*

Origen: CD 82, PV 99, SE 45; reincarnation as viewed by, PV 99

Original Plant (Steiner): UV *112*

Orion the Hunter: MW *13*

Orishas: MW 113-115

Orkney Islands: MW *85*

Orléans, duke of: AW 104-105

Ormond, Ron: and buried-alive trick, EM 92; and Ormond McGill, EM 92; and *vipassana,*

EM 92-95

Orpheus: AW *15,* SE 32; and hollow earth theory, MP 139

Orphists: AW 14, 16, 58; and Orphism, AW 167

Orthodox Church: MY 30

Orthon (alleged alien): UP 76

Orvius, Ludovicus: AW 55

Osborn, H. C. (Buz): MW 44-45

Osborne (British frigate): MC 32

Osborne, David: MW 29

Osborne, Sarah: as witch, WW 74

Oscar II (king of Sweden): MW 54

Oshun (orisha): MW 113

Osirion: PV *107*

Osiris (god): CC 29, MA 52, MY *88,* PV 98, SE 25, 26, *27, 28-29,* VP 106; death of, WW 13

Osis, Karlis: PE 35, 68, 69-72, PV 62-63, *64;* and near-death-experience research, PV 62, *64;* and out-of-body-experience research, PV 36, 39-40, 41; and poltergeists, HN 74

Osnato, Rosemary: and abduction by aliens, AE 133; painting by, AE *132-133*

Ossowiecki, Stefan (psychic): PP 120-*123,* 127, PS 66, *67*

Ostade, Adriaen van: painting by, SA *36-37*

Ostanes: SA 23

Ostman, Albert: MC *116,* 118-119

Ostrander, Sheila: PP 141-142

Osty, Eugène: psychokinesis research of, MM 21

Osty, Marcel: MM 21

Oswald, Ian: DD 100

Oswald, Lee Harvey: CC 149

"Other realities": EM 115-116

Otia Imperialia (Gervase of Tilbury): TN 78-79

OTO: AW 114, *115,* 139

Otters: and Loch Ness monster sightings, MC 80-81, 83, 85; mask of, TN *19;* as spirits of the dead, TN 6

Otto (doctor): DD 63, 66

Otto, Rudolph: MB 25

Ouija board: PP 42, SE *100-101,* SS *107;* and William Fuld, SS 107; and Jane Roberts, SS 134

Our Inheritance in the Great Pyramid (Smyth): MP 58-62

Our Lady of Czestochowa: CD *58*

Our Lady of Guadalupe: Basilica of, CD 119

Ouroborus: AE 111

Ouspensky, Peter D.: AW 168, DD 116, EM *85,* UV 98, *100*

Outback: MW 34, 38

Outer personality number: defined, VP 98. *See also* Numerologists; Numerology

Outer Santa Barbara Channel: MW 75

Outlawe, William: WW 54, 55

Out-of-body experiences (OBEs): CD 116, MY 38, PE 94-95, PV *15,* SE 28-31, 88; of Ambrose, PV 17; American Society of Psychical Research's research on, PV 20, 36; anesthetics' effect on, PV 16, 36; and animals, PV 40, *41,* 42; of Anthony of Padua, PV 16-17; astral body in, PV 16, 25, 34-35, *46-55;* Eugene E. Barnard's research on, PV 16; and Susan Blackmore, PV 36-37, 44; Helena Petrovna Blavatsky's views of, PV 21; and body double, PV 17; of Emily Brontë, PV 15; of Hugh G. Calloway, PV 22-25, 27, 33; Hereward Carrington's research on, PV 25, 27; of Clement of Rome, PV 17; cord

in, PV *8-9, 22-23, 25-26, 33, 43, 16 17, 40 49, 52-53, 54-55;* Robert Crookall's research on, PV 33-34, 35; Adolphe d'Assier's theory of, PV 20; defined, PV 7; and dreams, DD 127, PV 16, 42, 44; Egyptian beliefs in, PV *16-17;* of Elisha, PV 16; extrasensory perception compared with, PV 36, 39, 40, 42; Glen Gabbard's research on, PV 44; of Johann Wolfgang von Goethe, PV 15; Celia Green's research on, PV 33-35; Edmund Gurney's research on, PV 19; hallucinogens' effect on, PV 16; of Keith Harary, PV *40,* 41-42; of Hermotimus of Clazomene, PV 16; history of, PV 15-17; Richard Hodgson's research on, PV 22; of Aldous Huxley, PV 15; as hypnagogic images, PV 44; illnesses' effect on, PV 16; immobility and rigidity in, PV 24, 25, 46; inducing of, PV 25, 27, 31, 32, 65; and Jeshahr the Guide, MB 118, 120, *121;* of Jesus, PV 16; of Arthur

Koestler, PV 15; of Elisabeth Kubler-Ross, PV 65; Stephen LaBerge's research on, PV 42-44; of Madame Lambert, PV *26;* of Caroline Larsen, PV 14-15, 16; of D. H. Lawrence, PV 15; of Alphonsus Liguori, PV 17; of Charles A. Lindbergh, PV *8-9;* of Jack London, PV 15; Donna McCormick's research on, PV 40; of Shirley MacLaine, PV *43,* 44; of Guy de Maupassant, PV 15; Duane Michals's views of, PV *33-35;* Janet Mitchell's research on, PV 36; of Robert Monroe, PV 27-32, 33, 34, 35; Robert Morris's research on, PV 40, *41-42;* of Sylvan Joseph Muldoon, PV 25-27, *28-29,* 33; Frederic W. H. Myers's research on, PV 19, 20; in near-death experiences, PV 16, 56-57, 59, 63-64, 67, *74-75,* 77, *80-81;* Karlis Osis's research on, PV 36, 39-40, 41; penetration of solids in, PV 26, 28, *50-51;* pineal gland's effect on, PV 22-23, 25; Frank Podmore's re-

search on, PV 19; and Graham Potentializer, MB 48; serenity of, PV 45; of Severns of Ravenna, PV 17; Dean Sheils's research on, PV 42; sleep's effect on, PV 16, 17, 42, 44; spirit in, PV 7; and Ingo Swann, PP 82-83, PV 36-39; of Alex Tanous, PV 40-41; Charles T. Tart's research on, PV 16, 35-36; telepathy compared to, PV 19, 42; and Telsen-Sao, MB 118, *120-121;* unpleasantness of, PV 45; Graham Watkins's research on, PV 42; and werewolves, TN 89; of Miss Z., PV 35-36

Out-of-body travel: and Church of Scientology, PS 84; and Ingo Swann, PS 85; and warriormonks, PS 94

Out on a Limb (MacLaine): PV 44, SS 10, 146

Outrigger canoes: ML 99

Outsider art: MB *63-69. See also* Mental illnesses

Ouwens, P. A.: MC 20

Oval Composition (Mondrian): AW

160

Overlay: MB *32-33*

Overlord (code name): MY 34

Oversoul: SE 62

Ovid: MY 18, SI 27, TN 74, UV 23, WW 15, 23

Oviedo, Gonzalo Fernández de: MQ 29

Ovomancy: defined, VP 35

Owen, Alan R. G.: MM 41, 42, 54

Owen, George: MM 25

Owen, Iris: MM 25

Owen, Richard: MW 63

Owen, Robert: DD 150, 152

Owlman of Mawnan: MW 53, 55-57

Owls: MA 101, ML *127,* WW *15;* mask of, TN *17;* and Ovid, WW 15; and Pliny the Elder, WW 15; as spirits of the dead, TN 6; and witches, WW 12, 15

Oxenby (manor house): PE 41

Oxenham, Margaret and James: PF 44

Ozarks: superstitions in, MA 130

Oz factor: UP 71

Ozone layer: thinning of, EE 19

MY The Mystical Year; PE Phantom Encounters; PH Powers of Healing; PP Psychic Powers; PS The Psychics; PV Psychic Voyages; SA Secrets of the Alchemists; SE Search for the Soul; SI Search for Immortality; SS Spirit Summonings; TN Transformations; TS Time and Space; UP The UFO Phenomenon; UV Utopian Visions; VP Visions and Prophecies; WW Witches and Witchcraft

P

Pacifica: *See* Lemuria

Pacific Northwest: MC *115*

Pacific region: MW *maps 34-35,* 58, 92, 126

Pacioli, Fra Luca: TS *39*

Padmasambhava: EM 41, 133

Paganism: WW 42-44, 107. *See also* Neopaganism

Page, Thornton: UP 122

Paha Sapa: MW 79-80

Pahnke, Walter: MB 114

Pain, treatment of: MM 98, *99, 134-135*

Painting, automatic: of Luiz Antonio Gasparetto, SS 138-*139;* of Matthew Manning, SS 138

Paiute Indians: MW 110

Palace of Gold: EM *126,* 127

Palace of Minos (Evans): ML 135

Palace of the Occult: and Erik Jan Hanussen, PS 60, *61*

Palatine (ghost ship): HN *76-77*

Palazzo Vecchio: MW *122*

Palenque: MW 79

Paleolithic period: CD 50, 54, 61

Pales (gods): MY 31

Palestine: trees in, EE 91

Palisade: Iroquois, site of, MQ 98, *99*

Palitayan, Placido: PS *102,* 103

Palladino, Eusapia: MM 12-17, MY 37, SS 64. *See also* SS *index*

Palmelo Group: PH *84-85*

Palmer, Annie: HN 132, 133

Palmer, Austin N.: VP 94

Palmer, John Rose: HN 132

Palmer, Nelson: PS 35-36, 37, *39*

Palmer, Ray: MP 152-153

Palmer Method: VP 94

Palmerston, Lord: SA 78

Palmistry: CC *chart* 63, MA 26, MW 119, TS 95; air hand, VP *54, 60;* Chinese, VP 81; dominant hand, VP 53; earth hand, VP *54,*

PEACH. *A symbol of longevity in ancient China, the peach later came to represent female sexuality. In this painting on a leaf from a bo tree—the kind under which Buddha reached enlightenment—a monkey tempts an ascetic with a peach.*

92

PELICAN. *This 13th-century painting depicts the notion that pelicans tear open their own breasts to feed their blood to their young. Though later debunked, this belief led medieval Christians to see the bird as a symbol of Christ's self-sacrifice.*

61; fate line, VP *58-59,* 85; fire hand, VP *54, 63;* Greek, VP 81; head line, VP *58-59,* 85; health line, VP 85; heart line, VP *58-59,* 85; Indian, VP 81; intuition line, VP 85; life line, VP *58-59,* 85; marriage line, VP 85; Mars line, VP 85; mounts of palm, VP *56-57;* passive hand, VP 53; relationship lines, VP *58-59;* sun line, VP 85; techniques, VP *53-63, 85-86;* use of, PP *96-97, 98-99;* Venus line, VP 85; water hand, VP *54, 62. See also* Palmists

Palmists: Nathaniel Altman, VP 60-63; Aristotle, VP 81; Cheiro, VP 64-65, 66, 81-85, *84;* Galen, VP 81; Gypsies, VP *87-91;* Hippocrates, VP 81; Johann Hortlich, VP 81; Plato, VP 81. *See also* Palmistry

Palm Sunday: MY 28

Palm Sunday case: SS 96-99. *See also* Cross-Correspondences

Palmyra (Syria): MW 125

Palombara (marquis): MW 119, 127

Palombo, Stanley. DD 102

Palongawhoya (spirit): CD 39

Pamir Mountains: MW 59-60

Pampini (Geller): MM 36

Pan (god): MQ *56;* and Horned God, WW 107

Panathenaea: MY 60

Panda, giant: MC *21,* 114

Pandits: EM 29-33

Pangaea: EE 58; and continental drift, theory of, MP 33

Pangi (god): CD 24

Pan Ku: TS 27

Pan Lu: MW 93-94, *95*

Pantaleon, Saint: MY 64

Pantheism: MA 83; defined, WW 115; and Wicca, WW 115

Panther, Florida: MW 44

Panzenella, Frank: UP 113

Paole, Arnold: TN 116, 118-120

Papa (goddess): CD 24

Papago Indians: MA 70

Papal bull: SA 64, TS *105*

Paper boats: MW 34

Paper magic: MW 113, 115-*116, 117*

Papua New Guinea: and UFO sighting, UP 70, 72-73

Papuans: SE *19,* 24

Papus: VP 127

Parabolic diffusion effect: HN *136-137*

Paracelsus (a.k.a. Philippus Aureolus Theophrastus Bombast von Hohenheim): AW 53, 57, CC *78,* MB 29, PH *119-122,* SA 116, SE 54, SI 32; and herbs, MA 63; name of, MA 50. *See also* SA *index*

Paracelsus Research Society: and Albert Riedel, SA 133, 134, 135

Parachemy (journal): SA 134

Paradise: CD 18, 111. *See also* Nirvana

Paradise Garden: UV *48-49*

Paradise Lost (Milton): CD 93, 130, MB 53

Paradise myths: UV 6-15, 18-20, 20-22

Paraíba Stone: ML 135-137

Parallel universe: AE *122-123,* UP 148-149; defined, AE 123; and Jacques Vallee, AE 120, 121

Paramecia: SI 23

Paramuktas: SI 9

Paranoia: MB 87. *See also* Mental illnesses

Paranoid schizophrenia: MB 73-74. *See also* Schizophrenia

Paranormal, The (Gooch): MB 41

Paranormal dreams: *See* Psychic dreams

Paranormal phenomena: MB 41, 54, 83-85, 87, 92. *See also* Precognitive visions; *specific phenomena*

Parapsychological Association: PP 27, 60-61, 74; founding of, PP 57

Parapsychology: CD 68, PP 17; and CIA, PS 80, 91; defining the study of, PP 70; and Sigmund Freud, PP 21; and Mobius Society, PS 89; and Eduard Naumov, PS 79; and psi-warfare experiments, PS 79; and Charles Rose, PS 80; science of, PP 16; and Soviet Union, PS 78-79; study of, PP 24-26, 61. *See also* Psychic archaeology

Parapsychology Foundation: PP 86, 91, PV 62, SE 18; founding of, HN 130

Parathyroid glands: SI 64

Parentalia: MY *133,* 135

Parhelion: mistaken for UFOs, UP 14

Paris (France): PS *62-63*

Paris, Vampire of: *See* Bertrand, Victor

Parise, Felicia: DD 148, MM 27

Parker, Calvin: MY 92

Parker, Cozet: PH 44

Parker, Dorothy: CC 84

Parker, Gilbert: PE 83-85, *86-87*

Parkes, Alan: SI 109, 122

Parkinson's disease: SI 74, 82-83

Parkman, Francis: MQ 34

Parks, Lillian Rogers: HN 108

Parmenides: and time, TS 38

Parnell, Charles Stewart: VP 82

Parr, Thomas: SI 14, *15*

Parris, Elizabeth: WW 73, 74, 75-76

Parris, Samuel: and witches, WW 73

Parrot, J. J. Friedrich W.: Ararat ascent of, MQ 71, 74

Parsees: *See* Zoroastrians

Parshva, Lord: TS 27

Parsimony, law of: defined, MM 7

Parsley: WW *37*

Parsons, Elizabeth: HN 63-70

Parsons, John Whiteside: MA 48

Parsons, Richard: HN 63, 64

Parthenon: CD 56

Particle accelerators: TS 57-58, 66

Particle-collision experiments: SA 136

Partridge, John: CC 109

Parvis, Sarah: WW 80

Parzifal (Wolfram von Eschenbach): MQ 111-112, 114, 117-118, 124, 125, 127

Pasaquan: UV 43, *46-47*

Pasaquoyan: defined, UV 47

Pascagoula (Mississippi): and aliens, MW 43, UP *69,* 141

Pascal, Blaise: PV *123,* SE 55

Paschal II: HN *131*

Passive hand: VP 53. *See also* Palmistry; Palmists

Passover: MY 24, 30

Passport to Magonia (Vallee): AE 120

Pasteur, Louis: AW 128, PH 33

Past-life regression: MY 102. *See also* Past-life therapy

Past-life therapy: PV 88-*95,* 112, SE 45. *See also* Cryptomnesia; Hypnosis and hypnotic regression; Reincarnation

Past lives: *See* Reincarnation

Patakas: SI *20-21*

Patanjali: PH 72

Patent medicines: SI *31. See also* Elixirs

Path of destiny number: defined, VP 98. *See also* Numerologists; Numerology

Path of Genius, The (Hablik): UV *120*

Patrick, Saint: ML 121, MW 85, MY 19, 22, TN 78, VP 45, WW 42; and Glastonbury (England), ML 52-56

Pattee's Caves: ML 131

Patterson, Roger: MY 95; Bigfoot film by, MC 98, 99, *118, 119,* 120, 124; Bigfoot research of, MC 98-99

Patton, George S.: PV *7;* alleged previous incarnations of, PV *12-13,* 106

MY The Mystical Year; PE Phantom Encounters; PH Powers of Healing; PP Psychic Powers; PS The Psychics; PV Psychic Voyages; SA Secrets of the Alchemists; SE Search for the Soul; SI Search for Immortality; SS Spirit Summonings; TN Transformations; TS Time and Space; UP The UFO Phenomenon; UV Utopian Visions; VP Visions and Prophecies; WW Witches and Witchcraft

Paul (apostle): CD 56, MA *24-25;* and exorcism, CD 88; and stigmata, CD 116

Paul (split-brain patient): MB 47-49

Paul II (pope): CC 68

Paul III (pope): CC 69, 93

Pauli, Wolfgang: MM 72, SE 136, TS *122;* and Carl Jung, TS 121; and quantum mechanics, TS 122; and synchronicity, TS 122

Paulicians: heresies of, WW 49

Pauling, Linus: SI 75

Paulus, Joseph: MB 82

Pausanias: ghost of, HN 24

Pawnee Indians: EE 100, MA 68

Paxos (island; Greece): MQ 56

Payns, Hugues de: AW 33

Pazder, Larry: CD 95

Peabody, Elizabeth Palmer: UV *81*

Peace, City of: EM 27

Peace, John: MC 40-42

Peaceable Kingdom, The (Hicks): UV *40-41*

Peace celebration: MY *104*

Peace symbol: MY *104*

Peach banquets: SI 6, 36, *37*

Peach Blossom Spring: UV *10-11*

Peaches: SA 108, 113, SI 6, 36

Peacocks: MA 101, MC 20; as symbol, SE *16*

Peale, Norman Vincent: MB *124,* MM 103

Peale, Rembrandt: VP 75

Peanuts: EE 105

Pearce, Hubert E., Jr.: telepathy of, PP 53

Pearce, Joseph: MB 85

Pearson, Durk: SI 75-76, *80*

Peary, Robert: AW *111*

Pease Air Force Base (New Hampshire): and UFO sighting, UP 102

Peccaries: MC 20

Peck, August: TS 131, 132

Peckham, Rufus W.: PH 107

Pecoraro, Nino: PP *36, 37*

Pecti-Wita: WW 112

Pectoral: SA *13*

Pedler, Christopher: PE 21

Pedler, Kit: PH 103

Pedro, Don (voodoo priest): MA 83

Pedro II (emperor of Brazil): ML 136

Pegler, Westbrook: MQ 18

Peiffer, Kenneth: PP 132-133

Péladan, Joséphin (a.k.a. Sar Merodack): AW 66, *67,* 68

Pelasgians: CD 23-24

Pelasgus: CD 24

Pele (goddess): EE 67

Pelée, Mount: DD *134,* MY 35

"Pelican": SA *39*

Pellegrini, Marquis di: *See* Cagliostro, Alessandro di Conte

Pelletier, Kenneth: MB 10

Pellew, George (GP): SS 87

Peloponnese (Greece): MQ 50

Penal code: of Brandenburg (Germany), WW *82*

Pendragon, Uther: and Stonehenge, MP 82, 84

Pendulums: MM *101,* TS 129, *131, 132,* VP *51. See also* Hypnosis and hypnotic regression

Penelope (Delvaux): DD *14,* 15

Penetralia, The: Being Harmonial Answers to Important Questions (Davis): VP 22

Penfield, Wilder: MB 8-9, *26,* 59-60

Penis envy: CD 60. *See also* Phallus

Penises, of tigers: SI *67*

Penn, William: UV 40-41

Pennsylvania: MW 113; founding of, UV 40-41

Penny-dreadful novels: TN 133

Penrose, Roger: TS 63

Pentacles: VP 130, *144-145. See also* Tarot; Tarot readers

Pentagrams: MA *39,* 54, TS *46, 47;* defined, TS 47; in Egypt, MA 54

Pentecost: MY 43, 50

Peonies: SA *108-109*

People of the Sky: TN 51

Pepper, John Henry: PE *96*

Pepys, Samuel: MP 102

Perceval (character in grail legends): MQ 33, 111, 120, *121;* nephew, Prester John as, MQ *127;* as Parzifal, MQ 111-112, 114, 117; source of name, MQ 118

Perchta (goddess): WW 27. *See also* Holda

Percipient: defined, PE 83

Percy, Henry (ninth earl of Northumberland): PE 109

Perdurabo, Frater: *See* Crowley, Aleister

Pereira, Maria Gomez: HN *96-97*

Perella, Angelina: MA 122-124

Perennial Philosophy, The (Huxley): UV 142

Perfect: CD 33. *See also* Cathars

Perfect and True Perfection of the Philosophical Stone, A (Richter): AW 62

Perfecti (Cathar priests): MQ 124

Perfectionists: UV 57, *76, 77-78*

Perfumes: MA 22-23

Perfume Saint: EM 118

Pericles: UV 96

Periodic table of elements: SA 116, VP 115

Periwinkle: WW *34*

Perkins, Joseph: PS 45

Perkunas (god): EE 92

Perls, Frederick (Fritz): DD 74-76, *80*

Permanent Peace Congress: UV *93*

Pernety, Antoine Joseph: VP 72; treatise by, VP *73*

Perot, H. Ross: PS 105

Perot, Rebecca: UV *68*

Perpetual-motion machines: SA *94-95*

Perry, Nicholas: CD 121

Perseids: MY 68

Persephone (goddess): CC *47,* MY *86,* 130, TN 34

Perseus (constellation): MY 68

Perseus (warrior): WW 17

Persian Gulf war: PS 111

Persian legends: of flood, MQ *78;* of Lucifer, MQ 117

Persians: CD 82, 122, TS 30

Persinger, Michael A.: DD 149, MM 79, UP 134

Personal power: defined, WW 107

"Personal-Year Cycles": defined, VP 98. *See also* Numerologists; Numerology

Perspectives (Dali): DD *19-21*

Persuasions of the Witch's Craft (Luhrmann): WW 110, 119

Peru: god of, ML *112;* search for King Solomon's mines in, MQ 42, 43

Perun (god): EE 92

Pesticides: EE 131

Pestle: SA *41*

Peter (American soldier): EM 97

Peter (apostle): MA *24-25,* MY 105, PH 85

Peter (priest): CD 91, 92-93

Peter Martyr d'Anghiera: MQ 34

Peter of Hamelin (feral child): TN *58,* 59

Peters, John: TS 116-117

Peterson, Mark: MB 82-83

Petit Trianon: HN *map 51,* PE *122;* and retrocognition, HN *46-51. See also* Hameau; Versailles

Petra: ML *74-75*

Petracca, Richie: AE 57

Petrie, William Matthew Flinders: MP 62, 63

Petro: MA 83

Petroglyphs: ML *42-43, 88-89, 127*

Petronius: TN 75

Petukhov, Valery G.: PS 84, 144

Peyote: EE *100;* and Brulé Sioux, EE 101; and Comanche, EE 101; and dreams, DD 114; effects of, EE 101; and Huichol, EE 100; psychic uses of, PP 80

Phaedo (Plato): SE 43, 44, 46

Phaedrus (Plato): PV 98, SE 44

Phalanxes: defined, UV 82

Phallus: CD *54, 67;* symbolism of, CD 55-56

Phantasms of the Living (Gurney, Myers, and Podmore): PE 23-25, 47, 85-86, 89, PV 19, SS 78

Phantom Ark (rock formation; Turkey): MQ 90-91, 92-94

Phantom leaf effect: and psychic auras, PP *148-149*

Phantom of the Poles, The (Reed): MP 148-150

Phanuel (angel): EE 32

Pharaohs: MA 50, 51, SA 16-17, SI 23

"Pharaoh's curse": MY 27

Pharmacy: and Paracelsus, SA 63, 65

Phenomena of Materialization (Schrenck-Notzing): SS 68

Phi Beta Kappa: medal of, AW *100*

Philadelphia Flyers: MA 128

Philalethes: SA 55

Philatheles, Eirenaeus: SA 96

Philemon (fantasy guide): DD *70*

Philip (fictional spirit): MM 25

94

Philip, Saint: MW *6-7*

Philip II (king of Spain): VP 18

Philip IV (king of France): AW 38, *39, 97,* MY 21, PE 124, SI 89

Philip of Flanders, Count: MQ 111

Philips, Pauline: HN 36, 37

Philip the Bold (duke of Burgundy): MA 49

Philistine, The (magazine): UV 85

Phillips, Jerry: and Blythe Giant, MP 119, 121

Phillips, Karen: PS 38-40

Phillips, Robert: and Truddi Chase, MB 83, 87

Phillips, Ronald: PS 56

Phillips, Ted, Jr.: AE 76

Philo Judaeus: CD 63, UV 35

Philolaus: CC 23, VP 107

Philosophers' stone: AW 54, 57, *59,* 66, MA 31, 32, MY 126, SA *52, 54,* SI 32; and Thomas Aquinas, SA 32; and Avicenna, SA 31; and Alessandro Cagliostro, SA 102; characteristics of, SA 44-45; creation of, SA 41, 55, *77, 87;* and Nicholas Flamel, SA 42, 45; grail compared to, MQ 117; and Jan Baptista van Helmont, SA 93; and James IV, SA 56; and Heinrich Khunrath, SA 82; and Ramon Llull, SA 33; and Albertus Magnus, SA 32; and *Mutus Liber,* SA 70; and prima materia, SA 45; and George Ripley, SA 47-55, *52;* symbol for, SA *75;* and transmutation, SA 45; and Arnau de Villanova, SA 33; and Zosimus of Panopolis, SA 25, 44. *See also* Elixirs

Philosophiae Naturalis Principia Mathematica (Newton): CC 100-101, SA 98

Philosophy: TS 38-43

Philosophy of Right (Hegel): SE 59

Philosophy of Spiritual Activity (Steiner): UV 114

Philters: MA *117. See also* Potions

Phiney, J. N.: DD 117

Phinuit, Dr.: SS 86-87

Phips, William: WW 74, 76

Phobos (satellite of Mars): CC 41

Phobos 2 (spacecraft): photograph by, AE *118-119*

Phoenicians: ML *66,* 117, 119, *137*

Phoenix (Arizona): and UFO sighting, UP 40-41

Phoenixes: CD *12,* MY 95, SA *52;* marrow of, SI 36, 37; as sacred animal, EE *113,* 114, 115; and Xi Wang Mu, SI *37. See also* Animals

Phony Turk: MB *18-19*

Photodynamism of Boccioni (Bisi): UV *123*

Photoelectric effect: TS 65

Photographic memory: *See* Eidetic memory

Photography: of psychic auras, PP 145, *146-151. See also* Kirlian photography

Photons: AE 107, SE 131, TS 65

Photosynthesis: defined, EE 89

Phrenological Cabinet: VP 76, 79

Phrenologists: MB *41;* George Combe, VP 72, 75; Jessie Fowler, VP 76; Lorenzo Fowler, VP 76, 78, 80, 81; Lydia Folger Fowler, VP 78, 81; Orson Fowler, VP 76, 78, 80, 81; Franz Joseph Gall, VP 69-72, *75;* Nelson Sizer, VP 79-81; Johann Kaspar Spurzheim, VP 72-75; Charlotte Fowler Wells, VP 76, 78; Samuel Robert Wells, VP 76, 78. *See also* Phrenology

Phrenology: MB 40, VP *chart 76,* 79; bust, VP *77;* defined, VP 72. *See also* Phrenologists

Phrenometer: VP *83*

Phrygians: and Cybele, WW 23

Phurba: defined, EM 76

Phyllorhodomancy: defined, VP 35

Physical examinations: AE *29;* of Betty Andreasson, AE 13, 15; characteristics of, AE 27-28, 35-36, 50; effects of, AE 35, 112-114; of Charlie Foltz, AE *19,* 20; of Carl Higdon, AE 9, 10; of Barney Hill, AE 21, 27; of Betty Hill, AE 21, 27, 35; of Budd Hopkins, AE 28, 35-36; of John, AE 39; purposes of, AE 35-36; of Chuck Rak, AE *19,* 20; of Susan Ramstead, AE 36; of Sara Shaw, AE

95

PENTAGRAM. *Widely viewed as a magical emblem, the pentagram—upright—also represents the human body, the upper triangle being the divinely inspirited head. Inverted, the figure symbolizes evil, the two points being the horns of the devil.*

23, 27-28; of Louise Smith, AE 22; of Mona Stafford, AE 22; of Whitley Strieber, AE 24; of Elaine Thomas, AE 22; of Travis Walton, AE 9, 23; of Jack Weiner, AE *19,* 20; of Jim Weiner, AE *19,* 20. *See also* UFOs

Physicians: CC 65, 76-78

Physics: CC 145-148, SA 23; and Niels Bohr, MB 25; and Fritjof Capra, MB 25; and Albert Einstein, MB 25; and Shakti Gawain, MB 123; and Werner Heisenberg, MB 25; and mind, MB 9-10, 25-26; and Isaac Newton, MB 25; and Rudolph Otto, MB 25; quantum, SE 108, 130-139. *See also* Quantum mechanics

Physiognomists: VP 66, 67-69, *70, 72, 74. See also* Physiognomy

Physiognomy: TN *89;* Chinese, VP *70-71;* defined, VP 66, 70; history of, VP 66-67; as sign of lycanthropy, TN 89; techniques, VP *74;* treatise on, VP *73. See also* Physiognomists

Physiology: experimental, SI 24

Piaget, Jean: MA 136

Pianco, Magister: AW 64

Piano Keys—Lake (Kupka): AW *166*

Piazza Vittorio: MW 119, 127

Picasso, Pablo: CC 87

Piccot, Theophilus and Tom: giant squid attack on, MC *46-51*

Piccus, Jules: ML 136

Pickering, Alan: EE 128

Pickford, Mary: CC 132

Pico della Mirandola, Giovanni: AW 24, 26, CC 64-67

Pictographs: ML 134, MQ *45*

Picts: ML *50*

Picture of Dorian Gray, The (film): CD *82*

Picture of Dorian Gray, The (Wilde): AW 127

Piddington, James G.: SE 95-97

Piddington, Leslie and Sydney: thought-transference act of, PP 117

Pidgeon, William: MP 98, 122, 123

Piedmont (Missouri): and UFO in-

vestigation, UP 134, *135*

Pied Piper of Hamelin: MY 56, TN 116, 117

Pierpont, Rev. John: VP 75

Pietists: UV 75

Pietrelcina, Pio da: CD 116-*118*

Piezoelectricity: EE 61, UP 134

Pifferari: MY 114

Pigafetta, Antonio: TS 85

Pigeons: PS 74

Pigs: and Agnes Brown, WW *61;* as criminals, TN 40; divination with, VP *42*

Pig whale: MC *19*

Pike, Albert: AW *105*

Pike, James: SS *121*

Pilgrimage of Grace: HN 90

Pilgrims: CD *121, 123*

Pilgrim's Progress (Bunyan): SE 60; illustration from, SE *60*

Pilgrim Way: MW 93-94, *95*

Pillard, Richard: TN 68, 69

Pillars of Hercules: *See* Strait of Gibraltar

Pima Indians: EE 76

Pindar: CC 20, SA 16

Pineal gland: MB *12,* ML 12, SE 15, *53,* 123; and René Des-

cartes, MB 11-13, 19; and mind, MB 11; and out-of-body experiences, PV 22-*23,* 25; purposes of, MB 11, 12; symbol of, MB *14*

Pines, bristlecone: SI *72;* longevity of, SI 23, 72

Pines, Isle of: ML 96

Pine tree: SA 108

Pingala: PH 74

Pinjrapole: defined, EM 39

Pinturicchio: fresco by, PE *84*

Pioneer 10 (spacecraft): UP 126; inscription on, MY *19;* message carried by, AE 108, *109,* UP 124

Pioneer 11 (spacecraft): AE 108; message carried by, UP 124

Piper, Leonora (medium): SE 95, 97, SS *82-83;* automatic writing of, SS 87, 92; and Chlorine, SS 83-86; and Elizabeth Webb Gibbens, SS 83; and Richard Hodgson, SS 82, 86, 87; and William James, SS 81-82, 83; and Oliver Lodge, SS 86-87, *87-88;* methods of, PP *36;* and Frederic W. H. Myers, SS 86, 87, 93-94; and George Pellew, SS 87; and Dr. Phinuit, SS 86-87; and

J. G. Piddington, SS 93-94; and William Piper, SS 82; possible telepathy of, PP *36;* and Society for Psychical Research, SS 86; trances of, SS 83, 86

Piprahwa (India): MQ 40-41

Pique-assiette, Le: *See* Isidore, Raymond

Piri Re'is map: ML *21*

Pisces (constellation): MY 86

Pisces (zodiac sign): CC 36, *50, 91,* 139, MY 134

Pisces, Age of: CC 145

Pitcairn Island: ML 95

Pitcher: MA *105*

Pitenius, Titus: CC 26

Pitjantjatjara Aborigines: TS 15

Pitman, C. R. S.: MW 70

Pitta: PH 65, 66, 67

Pituitary gland: ML 10, SI 71; and out-of-body experiences, PV 22-23

Pius II (pope): TN 105

Pius XII (pope): CD 121, SI 65

Pixies: AE 114

PK: *See* Psychokinesis

Placebo effect: SI 62

Placebos: PH 6, 122-125

96

AE Alien Encounters; AW Ancient Wisdom and Secret Sects; CC Cosmic Connections; CD Cosmic Duality; DD Dreams and Dreaming; EE Earth Energies; EM Eastern Mysteries; HN Hauntings; MA Magical Arts; MB The Mind and Beyond; MC Mysterious Creatures; ML Mysterious Lands and Peoples; MM Mind over Matter; MP Mystic Places; MQ Mystic Quests; MW The Mysterious World;

Plach family: and poltergeists, MM *42-44*

Plague: TN 117

Plains Dwellers: ML 14

Plains Indians: MA 78, 80. *See also* Vision quest

Plains of Arafat: MY 91

Plains of Heaven, The (Martin): UV *14-15*

Plains of Marathon: MW 34, PE 129

Planchette: HN 68, SS *106,* 107

Planck, Max: TS *68;* and atoms, TS 55; and Albert Einstein, TS 65; and quantum mechanics, TS 64

Planck constant: TS 64

Plancy, Collin de: engraving by, WW *14*

Planetary aspects: CC *124-125*

Planets: CC 37-47, *68-69, 99;* and archangels, MA 36; barrenness of, AE 7; and colors, MA 36, 37; and intelligence, MA *36, 37, 40;* and *kamea*, MA *36, 37, 41;* and metals, MA 36, 37; mistaken for UFOs, UP *20;* retrograde, CC *25,* 125, 139; and sigils, MA *36, 37, 40;* and talismans, MA *35, 36-37,* 40, 41. *See also individual planets*

Plant consciousness: EE 107-110

Plant harmonics: EE 110-112

Plants, divination with: VP 40

Plant stone: SA 134

Plasmas: UP 104-105

Plasma vortex theory: EE 20

Plas Teg: MW 19

Plastic surgery: *See* Cosmetic surgery

Plate, earthenware: ML *110*

Plate tectonics: EE 59, MP 33

Plato: CC 23, CD 34, 37, 38, 48, 49, DD 34, MQ 109, SE 42, 43-44, 46, *47,* 50, UV 23, VP 81; and Academy, SE 42, *47,* UV 31; and Atlantis, ML 26, 27, MP 7, 8, *10-13,* 15-17, 23, 26, 31, 36; background of, UV 17; characteristics of, SA 18-19; and dialectic, TS 41; and dualism, MB 10; and dualities, CD 34; and elements, SA 21; and ethical objectivism, CD 127; and ghosts,

HN 24; and hollow earth theory, MP 139; and mind, MB 10, 11; and Thomas More, UV 39; near-death experience beliefs of, PV 59; and Pythagorean Society, UV 30-31, 33; reincarnation as viewed by, PV 98; and space, TS 40, 41; and time, TS 40-41, 101

Plattes, Gabriel: SA 98

Playfair, Guy Lyon: TS 136

Pleiades (stars): EM 95, MY 102

Plesiosaurs: MC *42, 43,* MW 49, MY *28;* and Loch Ness monster sightings, MC 69, 71, *82-83,* 84; and sea serpent sightings, MC 43, 44

Plessis, Armand-Jean du: *See* Richelieu, Cardinal

Plethysmograph: PS *106*

Pliny the Elder: AW 18, EE 95, MC 45, SA 16, WW 14, 15

Plogojowitz, Peter: TN 108-109

Plosky, Joyce: DD 147

Plotinus: SE 49

Plough Monday: MY 124

Plowing season: MY 24

Plowman, Etruscan: EE *26-27*

Plunkett, P. T.: EM 33

Plutarch: MA 52, MY 22, UV 33; and Delphic oracle, EE 29; and Eleusinian mysteries, EE 54; and trees, EE 91

Pluto (god): CC 47, MY 95

Pluto (planet): AE *90-93,* 114, CC 47, 149

Plutonion: EE 54. *See also* Caves

Plymouth Brethren: AW 113

Pneuma: defined, CD 29, EE 29

Podmore, Frank: PE 21, 23, 34, 47; and hauntings, HN 28; and out-of-body-experience research, PV 19; and poltergeist research, HN 72, MM 38

Podomancy: defined, VP 35

Poe, Edgar Allan: CC 89, MY 127, PE 93, VP 22; and graphology, VP 86-92; and hollow earth theory, MP 145-*146;* and transatlantic balloon flight, story of, UP 22-23

"Poème de l'Ame": SE *69*

Pogroff, Ira: SS 85

Pohnpei: ML 101-102

Point Loma Universal Brotherhood

and Theosophical Society: UV *86-97*

Poisoning: mercury, SA 110

Polackin, Rosina: TN 121

Poland: werewolves in, TN 75

Polaris (star): EM 10

Polarity therapy: PH 100

Polar Light (Magritte): DD 16, *17*

Pole, Margaret (countess of Salisbury): PE 106

Polgar, Franz J. (mentalist): mind-reading act of, PP 114-*115*

Polge, Christopher: SI 111-113

Police investigations: and clairvoyance, use of, PP *126-137*

Polidori, John: MY 30; and George Gordon Byron, TN 132-133; and vampires, TN 132-133

Pollock, Gillian and Jennifer: PV 105-106, *110-111*

Pollock, John: PV 105-106, 111

Polo (sport): SI *55*

Polo, Marco (a.k.a. Il Milioni): AW 32, 33, MC 57, ML 66, MQ 70, MW 60, SI 24-26; and Kublai Khan, EM 27-28; travels of, EM 25, 26, 27-28

Poltergeist effects: defined, PE 126

Poltergeists: HN 57, MW 24-25, 27, 32, 37-38; and adolescents, HN *54,* 55, 58, 72; characteristics of, HN 24, 54-55, 58, *59,* 60, 73, 74, 86; and hoaxes, HN 72, 74; and lithobolia, HN *59,* 60; and psychokinesis, HN 73, 74. *See also* Ghosts; Hauntings; Macro-PK; MM *index*

Polybius: TN 72

Polychronic cultures: TS 97-100

Polyembryony: AE 78-*79*

Polygraph machines: and Cleve Backster, EE 107-*109*

Polynesians: and America, discovery of, ML 117; and Thor Heyerdahl, ML 91, *92;* migration of, ML 120

Polysomnograph: DD 111

Polytheism: WW 115

Pomeroy, Margaret: PE *40*

Pomo Indians: MA 66

Pompeia: MY 115

Ponape: *See* Pohnpei

Ponca Indians: MW 79

Ponce de León, Juan: EE 76, MQ

34, *38,* 39-40, SI 24-*25;* end of life, MQ 40; Fountain of Youth quest, MQ 34, 39

Pongal: MY 125

Poniatowski, Stanislaw: PP 121-122, 123

Ponomareff, Nicholas (post-mortem apparition): PE 61

Pons Sublicius: MY 37

Ponte Rotto: MY *37*

Pontifex Maximus (priest): MY 18, 37

Pontoppidan, Eric Ludvigsen: MC 22

Poor Richard's Almanack (Franklin): AW 80

Poor Robin: CC 75-76

Popa, Mount (Burma): SE *25*

Poplars: EE 96. *See also* Trees

Popper, Karl: MB 19, SE 124

Poppies: MA 99; opium, WW *34*

Porcelain-making: SA 88

Porphyria: TN 93-94, 125. *See also* Hypertrichosis

Porphyrin: defined, TN 94

Porphyry: CC 36, EE 89-90

Porpoises: and sea serpent sightings, MC 44

Porshnev, Boris: MC 110-112, MW 60

Portal dolmens: MP *72*

Portals of Light: AE 124

Porter, George: MM *8*

Porter, William: HN 94

Portman, Dora: MM *8*

Portraits: MA 118

Portugal: effigies in, MA *12*

Poseidon (god): CC 46; characteristics of, EE 72-74; and olive trees, EE 79; temple of, Cape Sounion, Greece, MQ *51;* temple of, in Atlantis, MP 7, 8-9, *10-11,* 16, 19

Posidonius: CC 32-34

Position effect: defined, MM 61-62

Possession: MB 116, MW 133, MY 59; and Catholics, CD 90; and Clara Germana Celle, CD 71-77; and Christians, CD 86-88; decline of, CD 96; defined, PV 108; and Josef, CD 88-90; and Ioan Lewis, CD 86; and Marianne, CD 92-93; reincarnation compared with, PV 108, 110, 125; and

97

Saul, CD 86; and Somalians, CD
86; by spirit, SE 90-95; surveys
about, CD 85-86; and Theobald,
CD 88-90; and voodoo, CD 86,
MA 83; in Zimbabwe, MA 13-15
Possessors of the Orb (painting):
SE *112*
Post, Bob: AE 104
Post, Wiley: TS 85
Post-biological competence: MB
125-126
Posthumous Humanity (Assier): TN
121
Posthypnotic amnesia: defined,
MM 94. *See also* Hypnosis and
hypnotic regression
Postmortem apparitions: PE *59;*
defined, PE 49, 111; of family
members, PE 52, 58, 59, 61, 63-
72; hauntings compared with,
PE 111, 119. *See also individual
postmortem apparitions*
Post-traumatic stress disorder
(PTSD): AE 34
Potala: EM *14-15,* MW 93, MY
134, PV *120-121,* UV *26-27. See
also* Buddhists and Buddhism;
Tibet
Potentialities: defined, MB 20
Potentization, law of: PH 120-121
Potions: and black magic, MA 92,
99. *See also* Philters
Potlatches: defined, TN 8
Pots: ML *108, 109, 111*
Potters: MA 121, ML 116-117
Pottery Jar, Festival of the: *See*
Kumbha Mela
Pouches: for talismans, MA 35,
40-41
Poughkeepsie Seer: *See* Davis, An-
drew Jackson
Powamu: MY 133
Powell, James: MC 91
Power, Tony: MB 53
Power bands: MB *32-33*
Power of Positive Thinking, The
(Peale): MB 124, MM 103
Power of Thought, The (drawing):
SE *110*
Power places: MW *maps* 78, 84,
92, 98
Powers: CD *131*
Prabhupada, A. C. Bhaktivedanta
Swami (a.k.a. Abhay Charan

98

De): EM 124-127

Practical ESP and Clairvoyance (Jaegers): PS 46

Prague (Czechoslovakia): MW 119, PS *12-13*

Prana: PH 72-74

Pranayama: MM 118, PH 72-74

Pratt, Joseph Gaither: MM 46, 51, SE 17-18; and poltergeists, HN 73, MM 46, 50; and recurrent spontaneous psychokinesis, HN 55; and J. B. Rhine's telepathic tests, PP 53

Prayer: and Muslims, TS *96*

Prayer beads: VP *114-115*

Prayer flags: CD *98*, MY *112*, PV *130*. *See also* Buddhists and Buddhism; Tibet

Prayers: MA 85

Prayer stations: EE *132*

Prayer wheel: PV *130-131*. *See also* Buddhists and Buddhism; Tibet

Precession of the equinoxes: CC 11-13, 32, 138

Precognition: MM 57, PP 69; and Weston Agor, PS 130; and causality, TS 120; and Douglas Dean, PS 107; defined, PP 16, PS 7, 25, SE 115-117, TS 17; demonstration of, PP 10-11; description of, PP 7; and ESP, PS 113; examples of, PS *8-23*; and executive ESP, PS 107, 130; and Gerald Feinberg, TS 120; and Eileen Garrett, PP 88-90; and John Gribbin, TS 117-118; and Keith Harary, PS 116-117; and Irene Hughes, PP 98-99; and intuition, PS 109; and Eryl Mai Jones, PP *32-33*; and William W. Keeler, PS 109; and Robert James Lees, PS 27-28; and Jesse Livermore, PS 110, 112; and Ninian Marshall, TS 118-120; and Joost Meerloo, TS 124-126; and John Mihalasky, PS 107; and mirror-image reversal, PS 17; and John Peters, TS 116-117; and physical laws, PP 70; and psychokinesis, MM 81; and Harold Puthoff, PS 83; and short-term memory, TS 120; and W. T. Stead, PP 27-32; and stock market, PS 113, 115,

116-117; and Alex Tanous, TS 115; and Russell Targ, PS 83; testing of, PP 62; and *Titanic,* PP *30-31;* and Alan Vaughan, PS 14; and Evan Harris Walker, TS 120; and Danah Zohar, TS 116, 118. *See also* Fortunetelling

Precognitive dream: *See* Dreams; Psychic dreams; DD *index*

Precognitive dreaming: demonstration of, PP 74

Precognitive visions: MB 85-87. *See also* Paranormal phenomena

Pre-Columbians: ML 137

Predestination: defined, SE 70

Predictions: *See* Seers; *specific types of predictions*

Prehoda, Robert W.: SI 115

Preiswerk, Helene: MB 79

Preliminary Studies of a Vaudeville Telepathist (Soal): PP 111

"Premature Burial, The" (Poe): PE 93

Prentice, Joan: and toads, WW *60*

Preordained physiological obsolescence theory: SI 69, 71

Pre-Raphaelite Brotherhood: UV 35, 36

Presbyter: defined, ML 63

Present Age and Inner Life, The (Davis): SS 29

Presley, Elvis: CC 89, MY 124

Pressing: WW *86*

Prester: defined, ML 63

Prester John: ML 47, *62,* 63-64, 66, MQ *127;* empire of, MW *map 8-9*

Previn, Dory: EE 108

Priam (Trojan king): MQ *36*

Pribram, Karl: DD 152, MB 26, 28, SE 129-130, *131*

Price, Harry: HN *69,* MM *18, 20,* PE *126-127;* and ghosts, HN 68; and hoaxes of mediums, SS *127;* as inventor, MM *18,* 19-20; and National Laboratory of Psychic Research, PP 87; and poltergeists, HN 56, 65, 66, 68, 70, MM 39, 40; psychokinesis research of, MM 19-20, 21-22; séance research of, MM *20,* 21

Price, Henry Habberley: HN *23,* 25, 33

Price, James: and alchemy, SA 78-

79, 95, 102

Price, Margaret: MM 61

Price, Pat: PS 81-82, 84; and remote viewing, PP 60-61, 63-67, 142-144

Price, Richard: UV 135, 137

Price, William: AW *21*

Pride: CD *87*

Priestley, J. B.: TS *126,* UV 109, VP 8; and dreams, TS 117; and John William Dunne, TS 124; and time, TS 124

Priestley, Joseph: HN 61

Priests: MY *34,* WW *106;* Etruscan, EE *26;* Indian, CC *141;* Shinto, SE 30-31; Tibetan, TN *42*

Prieuré, Le: UV *108*

Prima materia: SA *49;* and Aristotle, SA 21; defined, EE 70, SA 21, 44, 70, 115; and Nicholas Flamel, SA 46; and Robert Fludd, SA 90; and philosophers' stone, SA 45; and Zosimus of Panopolis, SA 24-25

Primavera (Botticelli): UV *12,* VP *106*

Primordial atom: TS 61. *See also* Atoms

Primordial mind: defined, MB 90

Prince, Lydia: CD 122-124

Prince, Morton: MB 78

Prince, Richard: HN 31

Prince, Walter Franklin: and co-consciousness, SS 152; and Mina Crandon, SS 110, 116-117; and Pearl Curran, PP 42, SS 85; psychic investigations of, PP 44-45; and *Scientific American's* tests of mediums, PP 38-39

Prince Hall Masonry: AW *104*

Princeton Engineering Anomalies Research (PEAR): SE 135-136

Principalities: CD *131*

Principles of Geology (Lyell): MP 23

Principles of Nature, Her Divine Revelations, and a Voice to Mankind, The (Davis): SS 27, VP 22

Principles of Psychology, The (James): SE 62, TS 95-97

"Principles of Wiccan Belief" (Council of American Witches): WW 113

Prisoners: and time dilation, TS 90-91

Priulus, Franciscus: CC 68

Probability theory: defined, MM 65

Probability value: defined, MM 58

Problems of Mysticism and Its Symbolism (Silberer): SA 129

Process-oriented research: PP 62-63, 67

Process philosophy: MB 20-22

Processus pyramidalis: defined, VP 35. *See also* Haruspicy

Procris: SE *16*

Proctor, Richard: and Great Pyramid, astronomical alignment of, MP 63, 65

Procter family: HN 29

Prodigies: PV 118, *122, 123. See also* Children

Progeria: SI 71

Progressive relaxation: MM 100, PH 137-138

Project Blue Book: AE 21, 78, UP 87, *88-97,* 98, 110, 111, 115, 118, 120; activation of, UP 49; and Ann Arbor UFO sighting, UP 107; disbanding of, AE 78, UP 119; and Lubbock UFO sighting, UP 51; and Norfolk UFO sighting, UP 52, and Ravenna UFO sighting, UP 113-115

Project Cyclops: UP *126*

Project Grudge: UP 44, 46, 47, 49, 87

Project Hessdalen: UP *133-134*

Project Identification: UP 134, *135*

Projection: defined, SA 41. *See also* Transmutation

Projection of the Astral Body, The (Muldoon and Carrington): PV 25

Project Ozma: MY 28

Project Scanate: PP 142-144, PS 81-82

Project Sign: UP 38, 41, 42, 44, 87

Project Skyhook: UP 41, 47

Project Twinkle: UP 46

Proletariat: defined, CD 40

Prometheus (god): MA 131, WW 20

Promised Land of Saints: ML 122

Pronin, Alexander G.: MW 60

Proofs of a Conspiracy (Anonymous): AW 105, 108

Prophecies: dreams as, DD 42-44. *See also* Seers; *specific types of*

POMEGRANATE. As birds and beasts feed, a young woman gathers pomegranates in the 14th-century illustration below. The fruit's many seeds and blood-red juice lend it a symbolic association with fecundity and menstruation. Brides in clas- sical Rome wore wreaths of pomegranate blossoms as a fertility charm, and Turkish brides use the fruit for divination. Dashing one to the ground, a bride counts the number of seeds scattered to foretell how many children she will bear.

prophecies

Prophecy (film): MC *136-137*

Prophetic Messenger, The (Smith): CC 113

Prophets: *See* Seers; *specific types of prophecies*

Proportion: and Pythagoreans, TS 47

Proprioception: defined, MB 51

Prosopagnosia: defined, MB 50

Prospect of Immortality, The (Ettinger): SI 113, 114, 115, 116

Proteins: SI 66

Proteus (god): UV 23

Proust, Marcel: CC 83, MB 87, 90

Provand (captain): MW 21-22

Proxy sittings: SS 90, 91

Prytz, John: AE 115, 116-118

Przewalski, Nikolai: MC 107

Przewalski's horse: MC 107, 112

Pseudopods: SS 61, 104. *See also* Ectoplasm

Psi: PP 56, 74

Psi component: SE 66-68

Psilocybin: and hallucinations, MB 104; and Arthur Koestler, MB 117; and Timothy Leary, MB 112, 114, 117. *See also* Hallucinogens

Psi-missing: defined, MM 60. *See also* Psychokinesis

Psi phenomena: defined, MM 8, 63; of Nina Kulagina, MM 23, 26-27; Michael A. Persinger's research on, MM 79; Zdeněk Rejdák's research on, MM 26; Leonid Vasiliev's research on, MM 23. *See also* Extrasensory perception; Psychokinesis

Psi powers: CD 68; and computers, PS 131; and Nazis, PS 58-69; and psychic detection, PS 7; and telecommunications, PS *134-135;* types of, PS 7

Psi research: *See* Psychic research

Psi Squad: *See* Psychic Detective Bureau

Psi Tech: PS 90

Psi-warfare experiments: *See* PS *index*

Psiwork: PS 94

PSR 1257+12 (neutron star): AE 115

Psyche: DD 57, SE 43, 118

Psyche (witch): MC 37

Psychedelic Journey, The (Leary and Alpert): MB 114

Psychedelics: *See* Hallucinogens

Psychic abilities: PP 15-16; and Altered States Research, PP 69; and decline effect, PP 53; motivation of, PP 53; and sleep, PP 69-74. *See also individual psychics and types of ability*

Psychic advisers: PP 84, *92-99*

Psychical Research Foundation: HN 36, PV 40, 41, SE 19, 88, 89

Psychic archaeology: MQ *95-105;* churches, dowsing at, MQ *104-105;* demonstration of, PP 124; Egyptian expedition, Mobius Society's, MQ 100-103; at Iroquois Indian village, MQ 98, 99; Tres Zapotes, Mexico, excavation, MQ *96-97*

Psychic attack: MA 62

Psychic auras: PP *86;* photography of, PP 145, 146-151

Psychic detection: *See* PS *index*

Psychic Detective Bureau: PS 45, *46,* 48

Psychic Discoveries behind the Iron Curtain (Ostrander and Schroeder): PP 121, 122

Psychic dreams: DD 131, 133-135. *See also* DD *index*

Psychic emissions: at megalithic monuments, MP 102

Psychic energy: AE 105

Psychic ether theory: HN *23. See also* Ghosts

Psychic farming: EE *136. See also* Farming

Psychic healing: and Edgar Cayce, PP *90-91;* defined, MM 8; and touch, PS *95-103*

Psychic phenomena: acceptance of, PP 17; and electromagne- tism, PP *70-71;* and multidimensional geometry, PP 70, *72;* and quantum mechanics, PP 70, *73;* and scientific research, PP 84. *See also specific types of psychic phenomena*

Psychic readings: PP 102; and Edgar Cayce, PP *90-91;* and Patricia McLaine, PP 97-98

Psychic research: PP 48-74, 103; and Margaret Mead, PP *27;* military applications of, PP 140-144, *141;* in Soviet Union, PP 141-142; at SRI, PP 142

Psychics: PS 46; characteristics of, PS 24-25, 37, 41. *See also individual psychics*

Psychic Self-Defense (Firth): MA 62

Psychic split: PS 48

Psychic spying: *See* Psi-warfare experiments in PS *index*

Psychic vampires: TN 135

Psychic voyages: *See* Near-death experiences; Out-of-body experiences; Reincarnation

Psychoanalysis: EE 50, EM 142; background of, DD 57, 60; defined, CD 60; and Sigmund Freud, DD 60, 61; and Carl Jung, DD 60, 69

Psychoanalytic Congress, Fourth International: DD 69

Psychogony (Plato): MQ 109

Psychographology: VP 92. *See also* Graphologists and graphology

Psychokinesis (PK): CD 118, PP 83, SS 64; and alcohol, MM 61; Kenneth Batcheldor's research on, MM 25; John Beloff's theory about, MM 8; Sigurd Binski's research on, MM 62-63, 64; and caffeine, MM 61; causes of, MM 82-89; characteristics of, PS 134; and computers, PS 131; William Cox's research on, MM 64, 66; William Crookes's research on, MM 12; defined, MM 7, 56, 83; dice experiments and, MM 58-66, *58, 59,* 60, 63, 67; and emotions, MM 60-61, 72; and extrasensory perception, MM 8; faking, MM 78; Haakon Forwald's research on, MM 66-70, *67,* 71; and Uri Geller, PS

AE Alien Encounters; AW Ancient Wisdom and Secret Sects; CC Cosmic Connections; CD Cosmic Duality; DD Dreams and Dreaming; EE Earth Energies; EM Eastern Mysteries; HN Hauntings; MA Magical Arts; MB The Mind and Beyond; MC Mysterious Creatures; ML Mysterious Lands and Peoples; MM Mind over Matter; MP Mystic Places; MQ Mystic Quests; MW The Mysterious World;

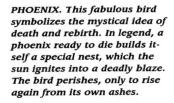

PHOENIX. *This fabulous bird symbolizes the mystical idea of death and rebirth. In legend, a phoenix ready to die builds itself a special nest, which the sun ignites into a deadly blaze. The bird perishes, only to rise again from its own ashes.*

124; by group, MM 24-25; Arthur Hebard's research on, MM 75; of D. D. Home, MM 11-12; kinetic hypothesis of, MM 64; Ippolite Kogan's research on, MM 79; loading hypothesis of, MM 64; Cesare Lombroso's research on, MM 12-13; and narcotics, MM 61; Julien Ochorowicz's research on, MM 13, 17-18; Eugène Osty's research on, MM 21; of Eusapia Palladino, MM 12-17; of Felicia Parise, MM 27; and poltergeists, HN 73, 74; and precognition, MM 81; Harry Price's research on, MM 19-20, 21-22; Harold Puthoff's research on, MM 75; and quantum mechanics, MM 70, 71; and Dean Radin, PS 131; and J. B. Rhine, MM 57, 58 61, 59, 62, 73, PS 130; Louisa Weckesser Rhine's research on, MM 57, 62; Charles Richet's research on, MM 13-15; Gertrude Schmeidler's research on, MM 76-77; Helmut Schmidt's research on, MM 72-73; of Rudi Schneider, MM 21-22; of Willi Schneider, MM 20-21; of Kastor Seibel, MM 63, 64; in Soviet Union, MM 75-81; and spying, MM 75-81; and Ingo Swann, MM 73-75, 76-77; Robert Thouless's research on, MM 63-64; uses of, MM 81; of Alla Vinogradova, MM 27. *See also* Extrasensory perception; Psi phenomena; Psychotronics; Recurrent spontaneous psychokinesis; *specific types of psychokinesis*

Psychological Survival (Cohen and Taylor): TS 90

Psychological warfare: *See* Psi-warfare experiments *in* PS *index*

Psychology: and alchemy, SA 115, 128-133

Psychology and Alchemy (Jung): SA 132

Psychology of the Unconscious, The (Jung): PP 21, SA 130

Psychometry: PS 33; and Joseph Rodes Buchanan, PS 30; defined, HN 30, PS 7, 29, 30, 33;

demonstration of, PP 92-93; and William Denton, PS 30-33; and Arthur Conan Doyle, PS 29; and Beverly Jaegers, PS 46; and Horace Leaf, PS 32; and George Henry Lewes, PS 30; and nerve auras, PS 30; and Stefan Ossowiecki, PP 121-122; and Nelson Palmer, PS 35-36, 37, 39; and psychic detection, PS 29-30, 32, 33; and Psychic Detective Bureau, PS 46; purposes of, PS 46; and Florence Sternfels, PS 33; and telepathy, PS 30; tests of, PP 121-127; use in police investigations, PP 127, 129-132, 133; and Dixie Yeterian, PS 47-48. *See also* Clairvoyance

Psychoneuroimmunology (PNI): PH 129-133; defined, MM 136

Psychophysical Research Laboratory (Princeton, N.J.): and extrasensory perception, testing of, PP 62; and ganzfeld research, PP 68-69

Psychoses: and hallucinogens, MB 104, 116. *See also* Mental illnesses

Psychosomatic illnesses: PH 126-129

Psychotherapy: MM 98, PS 123

Psychotronic equipment: PS 84

Psychotronics: Victor Adamenko's research on, MM 76, 79; and John B. Alexander, PS 90-91; Thomas Bearden's research on, MM 80; conference on, PS 81; defined, MM 76, 80, 81; and Zdeněk Rejdák, PS 80, 81; and Soviet Union, PS 90-91. *See also* Psychokinesis

Pterodactyls: MW 67-68, 70

Pterosaurs: MW 70

Ptolemy: CC 25, 34-36, 94, MW 133, 134, TS 51

PTSD: AE 34

P-2: AW 112

Puberty: and poltergeists, MM 41, 44, 48, 49

Public baths: in Baden-Baden (Germany), SI 131-137

Puccini, Giacomo: DD 117

Pudeator, Ann: WW 73

Pueblo Bonito: ML 80, MY 14

Pueblo Indians: and rituals, MA 68-69; and shamans, MA 68, 72-73; and time, TS 100

Pueblos: MW 80

Puffer fish: MA 88, 89

Puffers: defined, SA 55

Puget Sound: MW 75

Puglia (Italy): MW 119

Puharich, Andrija: MM 28, 35

Pukao: ML 95; defined, ML 84, 95

Pulcer, Publius Claudius: VP 39-40

Pullavar, Subbayah (yogi): EM 33; levitation of, MM 119

Pulsarium Coya (queen): MB 110-111

Pulsars: AE 109

Pulses: evaluation of, PH 56

Pulsing: MB 110-111

Pulvermacher Electric Belt: PH 88

Punya: defined, EE 82

Puppets: EM 60-61, MY 37

Purdy, Henry J.: PE 83

Pure Land: CD 126

Pure Land Buddhism: EM 23. *See also* Buddhism

Purification rites: CD 99, 102, MQ 8-9, MY 37, 40, 54, 107, 108, 117, 131, SI 21

Purkinje, Jan Evangelista: DD 58

Purple basilisk: EM 49

Purple Luminous constellation: EM 10

Pursel, Jach: SS 143-145, 146, 153

Pursuit: dreams of, DD 124-125

Pushkin, Alexander: MY 117

Pust (spirit): MY 44

Puthoff, Harold: and Church of Scientology, PS 84; and CIA, PS 81; and clairvoyance, MM 29-30, PS 80; criticism of, MM 35; and ELF waves, PS 86; photograph by, PS 86; and precognition, PS 83; and Pat Price, PS 81-82; and psychokinesis, MM 75; and remote viewing, PP 63-67, 142-144; and SRI International, PS 81, 83; and Ingo Swann, PS 85; and telepathy, MM 29-30; and John Wilhelm, PS 84

Putnam, Frank: MB 80-82

Puyo (Ecuador): MW 113

P-value: defined, MM 58

Pygmy hippopotamus: MW 47

Pygmy hunters: AE 102-103

Pyramid inch: EE 25

Pyramid Odyssey (Fix): MP 67

Pyramid power: MP 47, 65-66

Pyramids: EE 25, MP 46, 47, 48-67, MW 99, MY 8-9, 11, 55, SI 23-24; of Cheops, ML 116; on dollar bill, MQ 20; of Maya, ML 19; of the Sun, ML 116. *See also* Giza; Great Pyramid of Cheops

Pyramids and Temples of Gizeh, The (Flinders Petrie): MP 62-63

Pyromancy: defined, VP 38

Pyrrhus (king of Epirus): PH 85

Pythagoras: AW 14-16, 98, CC 23, 36, 98, SA 20, SE 32, TS 43; alleged previous incarnations of, PV 98; characteristics of, UV 25-26; and Iamblichus, UV 25, 26, 30; and magi, UV 25; as magician, MA 26; and music, TS 43, 47; and numbers, MA 26, 60, TS 44; as numerologist, VP 105-109, 115; and Pythagorean Society, UV 17, 26

Pythagoreans and Pythagoreanism: AW 16, 35, CD 34; and astronomy, TS 47; and ceremonial magic, MA 54, 60; and Freemasons, AW 98; and gnomonic expansion, TS 49; and golden mean, TS 47; and golden section, TS 47, 49; and harmony, TS 47, 49; initiation of, AW 58; and numbers, TS 43, 44-45, 49; and proportion, TS 47; and ratios, TS 47. *See also* Pythagorean Society

Pythagorean Society: characteristics of, UV 26-28; and Council of Three Hundred, UV 26; decline of, UV 30, 35; and Essenes, UV 33, 35; and Golden Age, UV 28; initiation into, UV 28; and metempsychosis, UV 28; and Plato, UV 30-31, 33; and Plutarch, UV 33; and Pythagoras, UV 17, 26; and Virgil, UV 33

Pythagorean theorem: TS 43, 49

Pytheas of Massilia: ML 119-120

Pythia (prophetess): TS 9, VP 10-11; defined, VP 10

Pytho: MW 85

Pythons: MC 44

MY The Mystical Year; **PE** Phantom Encounters; **PH** Powers of Healing; **PP** Psychic Powers; **PS** The Psychics; **PV** Psychic Voyages; **SA** Secrets of the Alchemists; **SE** Search for the Soul; **SI** Search for Immortality; **SS** Spirit Summonings; **TN** Transformations; **TS** Time and Space; **UP** The UFO Phenomenon; **UV** Utopian Visions; **VP** Visions and Prophecies; **WW** Witches and Witchcraft

QUADRIGA. *As with many subjects involving the number four, in a quadriga, or four-horse chariot, the horses symbolize fire, air, water, and earth, the building blocks of the cosmos. On this Greek vase, the team is led by the sun god Helios.*

Q

Qagyuhl Indians: CC 20
Qatwan: battle of, ML 63
Qi: MW *127,* 128, PH 46, 47, 49, 53, 72; and breath control, SA 106; characteristics of, EM 52, SA 104, 106; and ch'i kung, EE 106; circulation of, SA *104;* defined, CD 35, EE 33, 36, 106, 113, EM 52, 143, PS 73, 98, SA 104, TS 34, 35; effects of, SA 108; and feng shui, EE 33, 36, 113, 114-*115,* 116; and psi-warfare experiments, PS 73; and Sun Tzu, PS 73; and trees, EE 106; and yang dwellings, EE 114-*115, 116-117;* and Yang Lu Chan, EM 143; and *ying qigong,* EM 55; and yin/yang, SA 104
Qiang Shi: TN 110. *See also* Vampires
Qigong: PH *52-53;* therapy, PS 98
Quadriplegics: PS *136-137;* and virtual reality, MB *135*
Quadriplicities: CC 122
Quaife, Arthur: SI 116, *118,* 119
Quanta: defined, TS 64
Quantum leap: TS 65-66
Quantum mechanics: SE 108, 130, 139, TS 65-66, 68, 118, 120, 122; and Niels Bohr, TS 65, 68; characteristics of, MM 71-72, TS 51, 64; defined, MM 71, TS 67; and Albert Einstein, TS 65, 68; and Max Planck, TS 64; and psychic phenomena, PP 70, *73,* 74; and psychokinesis, MM 70, 71
Quarks: SA 136, TS 66
Quartz, beads made of: ML *24*
Quazgaa (alleged alien): and Betty Andreasson, UP 86
Queen, Richard: PS 91
Queen Elizabeth II (ship): CC 152
Queen Guinevere (Morris): UV *37*
Queen Lily of the Conjugal

Angels: UV 79
Queen Mary (ship): and ghosts, HN *82-83;* and poltergeists, HN 73
Queen of Sheba: ML 68, MY 136, SI 12
Queen's Bedroom: HN *108;* and ghosts, HN 108
Queste del Saint Graal (medieval narrative): MQ 118, 120, 121
Queste du Graal, La (Péladan):

AW *67*
Quest for Camelot: ML 51-52
Quest for Merlin, The (Tolstoy): MQ 130
Quetzalcoatl (god): ML 137, UV 24
Quiche Maya: DD 26
Quicksilver: *See* Mercury (metal)
Quigley, Joan: CC 129, 152
Quimby, Phineas Parkhurst: PH 91, 124

Quinerolane: SI 67
Quinones: SI 75
Quinta essentia: See Philosophers' stone
Quintanilla, Hector, Jr.: and Project Blue Book, UP 110, 111, 114
Quintiscence: *See* Philosophers' stone
Qu Yuan: MY 54

AE Alien Encounters; AW Ancient Wisdom and Secret Sects; CC Cosmic Connections; CD Cosmic Duality; DD Dreams and Dreaming; EE Earth Energies; EM Eastern Mysteries; HN Hauntings; MA Magical Arts; MB The Mind and Beyond; MC Mysterious Creatures; ML Mysterious Lands and Peoples; MM Mind over Matter; MP Mystic Places; MQ Mystic Quests; MW The Mysterious World;

ROUND TABLE. *Supposedly created by Merlin for King Arthur (portrayed at top), the round table is a symbol of harmony and egalitarianism. All the knights who sat at it were the same distance from the central rose, a symbol of concord.*

Ra (god): CC 29, *30-31*, 38, CD *14*

Ra II (boat): ML 117-119

Rabbits: and witches, WW 12

Rabbit's foot: MA 118, SI 67

Rabies: TN 93

Race, Victor: hypnosis of, MM *95*

Rachel (biblical figure): EE 96

Rack: WW *86-87*

Racquetball: MB *135*

Radar: and UFOs, UP *54*

Radar studies: of Phantom Ark site, MQ 93

Radescock, Paul: DD 61; and Sigmund Freud, DD 61

Radford, Ralegh: ML 59

Radiation sickness: AE 42

Radin, Dean: PS *131*

Radiocarbon dating: in ark study, MQ 88-89; of Shroud of Turin, MQ 108

Radionics: PH 75, *80-81*

Radio receiver: MB *24*

Radio station: and ghosts, HN 36-37

Radio transmissions: and search for extraterrestrial intelligence, UP 124, *127*

Radishes: MY 94

Radner, Gilda: PH 138

Radulphus Cancellarius: ML 61

Rafn, Carl: ML 130-131

Raft, David: and near-death-experience research, PV 78

Ragnarok: EE 93

Rahman, Abd el-: CC 55

Rahn, Otto: MQ 127, *128*

Raiders of the Lost Ark (film): MQ *47*

Railway Workers' House of Culture: PS *81*

Raimbaud of Auvergne: TN 78

Rain: collecting of, SA 74, *76*

Rainbow Bridge: EE *48*

Rain god: MY 34

Rain goddess ritual: MY 34

Rain-making ceremony: of Huichol Indians, PP *80-81*

Rain People: MY 51

"Rains": TS *134-135*

Raising the Cone of Power: WW *132-133;* and Andras Corban Arthen, WW 133. *See also* Cone of power

Raj: *See* Rajneesh, Bhagwan Shree

Raja-yoga: defined, EM 37, 117; and Swami Vivekenanda, EM 117. *See also* Yoga

Raja Yoga Academy: UV *90, 91, 94*

Raja-yoga school: UV *94, 95;* and Katherine Tingley, UV 95. *See also* Education

Rajneesh, Bhagwan Shree (a.k.a. Chandra Mohan Jain, Raj): EM 128-*129*, 130-131, 133, MB *99*

Rajneesh (Oregon): EM 131

Raju, Satyanarayana Ratnakara Raju: *See* Baba, Satya Sai

Rak, Chuck: AE 16, *18*, 28; and abduction by aliens, AE 17-20

Raknes, Ola: PH *100*

Raleigh, Walter: CD 64, MQ 29, MW 19, MY 39, PE 106, 109, SA 58, SI 14

Ram: MY *23*, SA 72, *74, 76*

Rama (god): EM 124, MY *30*

Rama III (king of Siam): MW 128-129

Ramadan: MY 69

Ramakrishna: EM 116-*117*

Ramanga: MA 15

Ramaswami: SI 99

Ramaswamier: AW 133, 135

Ramayana (Sanskrit text): EM 43, ML 32

Ramey, Roger: and crash retrievals, AE 79, 85; and Jesse A. Marcel, AE 81; and Roswell UFO sighting, UP 39

Ram Navami: MY 30

Ramsay, Andrew Michael: AW 98

Ramsay, William: and alchemy, SA 115, 123

Ramses II (king of Egypt): MW 100, PV 104

Ramses III (king of Egypt): MW 101

Ramsey, William: CC 102

Ramstead, Susan: AE 36-38

Ramtha (spirit guide): *See* Knight, J. Z.

Randall, Shawn: SS *152-153*

Randi, James (magician): MM *78*, PS 44-45, SS 131; and criticism of psychokinesis, MM 78; and criticism of thoughtography, MM 68; and Uri Geller, MM *32*, 34-35, PP *117;* poltergeist research of, MM 54

Randle, Kevin D.: and crash retrievals, AE 81-82, 83; and Glenn Dennis, AE 83; and Arthur E. Exon, AE 84

Randles, Jenny: AE 106; and Oz factor, UP 71; and radar evidence of UFOs, UP 54

Random bits: PS 131

Random event generators (REGs): MM 70, PP 62. *See also* Micro-PK

Random number generators: *See* RNGs

Rangda (demon): EM 69, TN *112*. *See also* Vampires

Rano Raraku (volcano): ML 87

Rao, Hatayogi Sandra: fire walking of, MM *106*

Raoul (spirit): PS 26

Raphael (archangel): CD *132*, EE 32

Raphael (artist): CC 113; engraving of painting by, VP *15;* painting by, SI *10-11*

Raphaell, Katrina: PH *110*

Rapid eye movements (REMs): defined, PV 35; and dream research, PP 66. *See also* REM sleep

Rapp, George: UV *61, 62, 63*

Rappites: *See* Harmony Society

"Raptures": MY 25

Rapunzel (fairy tale): CD *45*

Rasayana: SI 32

Raschke, Carl: SS 150

Rashid, Harun al-: CC 52

Rasi Valaya Yantra: CC *110*

Rasmussen, Knud: Eskimo studies of, PP 76

Rasputin, Grigory: MB 98, PH *86*, VP 84

Rassam, Hormuzd: CC 8

Rast, Walter: MQ 43

Ratatosk: EE 93

Ratcatcher: TN *116*

Rationalism: SE 118

Ratios: and Pythagoreans, TS 47

Ratnoff, Oscar: stigmata research of, MM 113-115

Rato Machhendranath (god): EM 52

Rats: MA 100-101, TN *117;* experiments with, EE 126-127; and plague, TN 117. *See also* Animals

Rattle: MA *105;* shamans', TN *11*

Ratto, Matt: MC 16, 17

Raudive, Konstantin: PE 116, *117*

Ravel, Maurice: CC 91, MB 49

Raven (trickster): TN 49-51

Ravenna (Ohio): and UFO sightings, UP 111-115

Ravens: MA 101, VP 40; mask of, TN *12-13;* as totems, TN 9

Rawlinson, Mr.: PE 23

Raymond VI (count of Toulouse): AW 31

Raynham Hall: MW 19, 21-22, *23*

Razdan, Rikki: MC 82

R-complex brain: MB 40

Reagan, Nancy: CC 6, 129, 130,

103

152

Reagan, Ronald: CC 6, 90, 128, 129-130, DD 137, MA 6, MY *122*

Realgar: defined, SA 24

Reality of the Rulers (Gnostic text): CD 59

Realm of spirit: UV 109

Realm of the Immortals: SA *112*

Rebecca the Jewess: TS 126

Rebirth: EE 26

Rebirthing: PH 128

Rebus (hermaphrodite): CD *36*

Recipes: for philters, MA *117*

Reciprocal dreams: DD 149-152. *See also* Dreams; Psychic dreams

Recordi, Pierre: witch trial of, WW 56

Recurrent localized apparitions: *See* Ghosts

Recurrent spontaneous psychokinesis (RSPK): defined, HN 55, 73. *See also* Poltergeists; Psychokinesis

Red Book (Jung): DD *70-71*

Red Brigades: PS 91-92

Redcap, Robin: HN 11

Redshift: TS 58-60

Red stage: SA 48, 51

Redwoods: EE *86-87,* SI 72; and American Indians, EE 87; and James Lovelock, EE 121. *See also* Trees

Reed, Graham: MB 71

Reed, William: and hollow earth theory, MP 148-150, 155

Rees, W. Dewi: PE 65-66

Reeves, John: MY 18

Reflexology: PH *55*

Reformation: SA 43; effects of, WW 64-66; and Martin Luther, UV 57; and Thomas More, UV 17

REG: MM 70. *See also* Micro-PK

Regan, Donald T.: CC 129

Regardie, Israel: Tarot cards by, VP *136-137*

Regelson, William: SI 74

Regeneration: SI 81-*82;* ritual, MY *46*

Regression: *See* Hypnosis and hypnotic regression

Regression therapy: *See* Past-life therapy

Regular haunters: MW 22

"Reguli": SA *88*

Rehmeyer, Nelson: as witch, WW 98

Reich, Wilhelm: PH *100*-101; and orgone, EE 126, 127, UP *52*

Reiche, Maria: MP 127; and Nazca lines of Peru, MP 111-*113,* 114, 117

Reichenberg Castle: MW 35-36

Reichenberg Protocol: MW 36

Reichstag: burning of, PS *60;* and Erik Jan Hanussen, PS 60, 61

Reid, C. S.: archaeological site studied by, MQ 98, *99*

Reid, Dan: EM 130

Reid, Gladys: MW *109*

Reid, Thomas: DD 114

Reidel, Walter: and UFOs, UP 52

Reign of the Phallus (Keuls): CD 55-56

Reincarnation: AW 16, 28, 132, MY 41, 102, PV *97,* SE 32, 45, 46, 67; in a group, PV 101; in Bali, PV *102;* of Ben, PV 114; of Bentreshyt, PV 104; and birthmarks, PV 108-109; Helena Petrovna Blavatsky's beliefs in, PV 22, 103; and Ray Bryant, PV *115;* and Buddhists, CD 99, 111, PV 102, 120, 127; Burmese beliefs in, PV 108; of Cathars, PV 99, 101; and Edgar Cayce, PP 94, PV 122-124; and channeling, PV 103; C. T. K. Chari's research on, PV 110; and children, PV 96-98, 103, 105-106, 106-110, 111, 118; and Chuang Chou, CD 12; Christianity's views of, PV 98, 101; and Mary Cohen, PV 113-114; cryptomnesia's effect on, PV 112-113, 115, 124, 125; of the Dalai Lama, PV 120; defined, PV 7, 96, SE 45; Druse beliefs in, PV 108; and Dorothy Eady, PV 104-105, 107; Eastern views of, PV 99-102; Thomas A. Edison's beliefs in, PV 103, *105;* Egyptian beliefs in, PV 98; extrasensory perception compared with, PV 108, 125; of Roger-Isarn de Fanjeaux, PV 101; of Sammy Fernando, PV 96-98; Henry Ford's beliefs in, PV *105;* Benjamin Franklin's purported beliefs in, PV *104,* Alan Gauld's views of, PV 112; Arthur Guirdham's research on, PV 101; of Naomi Henry, PV 113-114; Herodotus's views of, PV 98; and Hindus, CD 111, PV 99, 102, 120, SI 16; history of, PV 98-103; of Graham Huxtable, PV 114; and hypnotic regression, PV *88-95,* 103, 112, 113; Indian beliefs in, PV 108; of Jensen Jacoby, PV 119-122; and Jains, PV 102, TS 25-27; of Jasbir Lal Jat, PV 109-110; Reima Kampman's research on, PV 124-*125;* Allan Kardec's beliefs in, PV 102; Kutchin Indian beliefs in, PV 108; and Lahiri Mahasaya, SI 9; and Shirley MacLaine, PV 124; James G. Matlock's views of, PV 112; and Maya, TS 36; and Monica, PV 88-95; of Bridey Murphy, PV 114-118; Origen's views of, PV 99; and paramuktas, SI 9; of George S. Patton, PV *12-13,* 106; Plato's views of, PV 98; of Gillian Pollock, PV 105-106; of Jennifer Pollock, PV 105-106; John Pollock's beliefs in, PV 105-106, 111; possession compared with, PV 108, 110, 125; and prodigies, PV 118; of Pythagoras, PV 98; and retrocognition, TS 126; D. Scott Rogo's research on, PV 106, 110, 122; and Ravi Shankar, PV 109, 110; of Mrs. Smith, PV 101; Society for Psychical Research's research on, PV 113; sociocultural aspects of, PV 108; of spirit, PV 7, 99-102; of Reuben John

AE Alien Encounters; AW Ancient Wisdom and Secret Sects; CC Cosmic Connections; CD Cosmic Duality; DD Dreams and Dreaming; EE Earth Energies; EM Eastern Mysteries; HN Hauntings; MA Magical Arts; MB The Mind and Beyond; MC Mysterious Creatures; ML Mysterious Lands and Peoples; MM Mind over Matter; MP Mystic Places; MQ Mystic Quests; MW The Mysterious World;

RING. On the hand of a monarch, a ring was traditionally a symbol of great power, both worldly and supernatural. When given in marriage, as in the painting at left, the unbroken circular band stands for a vow of fidelity that has no end.

ROSE. Though at times emblematic of secrecy and death, roses such as those below, bearing the names of Muhammad (top left) and Allah (top right), are also symbols of divine love and perfection long associated with conceptions of paradise.

Stafford, PV 115; Ian Stevenson's research on, PV 97-98, 103, 106-112, 118, 125; and Sujith, PV 96-98, 108, 110; and T. E., PV 119-122; Alfred Tennyson's belief in, PV 103; Theosophical beliefs in, PV 22, 103; Tibetan beliefs in, PV 108, 120, 127-137; and Virginia Tighe, PV 114-118; of Tlingit Indians, PV 108-109; of Sobha Ram Tyagi, PV 110; types of, PV 103; of John Ralph Wainwright, PV 90-95; Ian Wilson's views of, PV 105-106, 110-112, 118, 122; and xenoglossy, PV 118-119; Edwin Zolik's research on, PV 124

Reinhard, Johan: and Nazca lines of Peru, MP 119

Reisenbauer, Heinrich: art by, MB 67

Rejdák, Zdeněk: PS 81; psi research of, MM 26; and psi-warfare experiments, PS 74; and psychotronics, PS 80

Rejoicing Day: MY 26

Rejuvenation: fountain of youth, theme of, MQ 34, 35, 39-40

Rejuvenation through the Experimental Revitalization of the Aging Puberty Gland (Steinach): SI 62

Relationship lines: VP 58-59. *See also* Palmistry; Palmists

Relativity theory: SE 130; characteristics of, AE 115, 118; and Frank Dyson, TS 50-51; and Arthur Eddington, TS 50-51, 58; and Albert Einstein, AE 115, 118, TS 50, 51, 54, 55-57, 58, 59, 60, 75; and time travel, TS 71, 73; and Frank Tipler, TS 77

Relaxation: MB 96

Relics: from Noah's Ark, supposed, MQ 70, 71, 76, 77, 79, 81, 84, 86, 87, 88-89; Shroud of Turin, MQ 108-109, 122. *See also* Artifacts, ancient; Holy Grail

Religion: and fire, MA 131; and magic, MA 9-10, 113; and superstitions, MA 113-114, 116, 118

Rembrandt: etching by, CD 27

"Remembrance of Things Future, The" (Feinberg): TS 120

Remembrance of Things Past (Proust): CC 83

Remote viewing: defined, TS 17; examples of, PP 60-63, 85; and Hella Hammid, PP 67; map dowsing, findings of, MQ 100; military applications of, PP 142-144; and Pat Price, PP 60-61, 63-67; testing of, PP 63-67. *See also* Extrasensory perception

REMs (rapid eye movements): defined, PV 35; and dream research, PP 66

REM sleep: DD 96, 97-99, 102, 107; and animals, DD 105; and Eugene Aserinsky, DD 96, 97; deprivation of, DD 102, 114; and J. Allan Hobson, DD 108; and Nathaniel Kleitman, DD 96, 97. *See also* Dreams; Non-REM sleep; Sleep

Remus: MY 133; and wolves, TN 56-57, 72

Remy, Nicholas: WW 78; and witch hunts, WW 66-68, 78

Renaissance: and alchemy, SA 34, 43; characteristics of, SA 43

Renaissance Tarot: VP 132-133. *See also* Tarot; Tarot readers

Renan, Ernest: and Paraíba Stone, ML 136, 137

Renders, Adam: ML 67

Rendlesham Forest (England): and UFO sighting, UP 132-141

Renfrew, Colin: ML 35

Renner, John: SI 76

Renz (priest): CD 91

Repa: defined, EM 50

Repercussion: TN 89

Reptilian brain: MB 40

Republic (Plato): MP 15, PV 59, SE 45, UV 16, 31-33, 39, 95

Resch, Tina: MM 54

Resch family: and poltergeists, MM 54-55

Res cogitans: defined, CD 38

Res extensa: defined, CD 38

Resonance phenomena: defined, TS 120

Resurrection: SE 50, 51, SI 12

Retallack, Dorothy: and plant harmonics, EE 110, 111-112

Retin-A: SI 90

Retrocognition: PS 7; and Arnall

Bloxham, TS 126; and Laura Jean Daniels, TS 16, 17; defined, HN 39, PE 122, 129, TS 17, 126; demonstration of, PP 10-11; description of, PP 7; and Rebecca the Jewess, TS 126; and reincarnation, TS 126; and Alex Tanous, PP 99, TS 115

Retrocognitive haunting: MW 34

Retrograde amnesia: defined, MB 60

Retropsychokinesis: defined, MM 72; Helmut Schmidt's research on, MM 72-73

Reuchlin, Johannes: AW 26

Revenants: defined, TN 113, 122-123; deterring of, TN 118; vampire bats compared with, TN 129

Revere, Paul: AW 74, 76, 77, 78; metalwork by, AW 73, 76, 77, 82

Reverie: defined, MB 90

Reverse connection: PS 103

Revival meetings: MB 116

Rewa: maharaja of, EM 30

Rex Nemorensis (god): MY 69

Reynolds, Jeremiah: and hollow earth theory, MP 144-145, 146

Rhasis of Persia (a.k.a. Abu Bakr Muhammad ibn Zakariya ar

105

MY The Mystical Year; PE Phantom Encounters; PH Powers of Healing; PP Psychic Powers; PS The Psychics; PV Psychic Voyages; SA Secrets of the Alchemists; SE Search for the Soul; SI Search for Immortality; SS Spirit Summonings; TN Transformations; TS Time and Space; UP The UFO Phenomenon; UV Utopian Visions; VP Visions and Prophecies; WW Witches and Witchcraft

Razi): SA 30

Rhea (goddess): CC 44

Rhea, Kay: clairvoyance of, PP *128, 129*

Rhedosaurus: MC *130-131*

Rheumatoid arthritis: SA 116

Rhine, Joseph Banks: CD 68, PE 128, SE 17, SS 85, 116; criticism of, MM 62; and dogs, PS 76; and ESP, PS 130; and extrasensory perception in animals, PP 57; extrasensory perception research of, MM 56, 57-58, 61-62; and Eileen Garrett, PP 86; and hypnotism, PP 69; and *Journal of Parapsychology,* founding of, PP 56; and Lady Wonder, PP 110; and Walter Jay Levy, PP 57-60; and Joseph Gaither Pratt, PP 53; and psi-warfare experiments, PS 74-76; and psychic research, PP 49-61; and psychokinesis, MM 57, 58-61, *59,* 62, 72, PS 130; as researcher, HN 118, 133; and Karl Zener, PP 52

Rhine, Louisa Weckesser: CD 68, PE 21, 35, 47, 128, PP 49, 50; and psychic research, PP 69; and psychokinesis research, MM 57, 62

Rhinoceroses: horns of, SI *67*

Rhodes, William A.: and Phoenix UFO sighting, UP 40-41

Rhodesia: *See* Zimbabwe

Rhu (Plains Dweller): ML 14

Rhydderch (champion of Christianity): MQ 133

Ribesal (demon): MA *98*

Riccardo, Martin: and vampires, TN 136

Rice, Anne: and vampires, TN 136

Rice farming: EE *132. See also* Farming

Rice festivals: MY *52,* 53, 54

Rich, Lady Diana: PE 85

Rich, Valentin: ML 33

Richard (duke of Gloucester): *See* Richard III

Richard (duke of York): PE 104

Richard, Paul: and Mirra Alfassa, UV 145, 146; and Sri Aurobindo, UV 145, 146

Richard II (king of England), huntsman of: MW *24*

Richard III (king of England): MY 59, PE 104

Richards, Steve: levitation research of, MM 118

Richardson, Bruce: TS 81

Richardson, George F.: PS 33

Richelieu, Cardinal: and Urbain Grandier, WW 48

Richet, Charles: SS *64;* and Eva C., SS 64-66, 68, 70; and Eusapia Palladino, SS 60, 61, 62, 64, 66, 67; psychic research of, PP 40; psychokinesis research of, MM 13-15

Richmond, Clara and William: PE 115-118

Richmond, Cora L. V.: SS *30-31*

Richter, Sigmund (pseud. Sincerus Renatus): AW 62-63

Rickenbacker, Edward V.: near-death experience of, PV 58

Ricky (postmortem apparition): PE 69, 72

Rider-Waite Tarot: VP *142-143, 146-149. See also* Tarot

Ridpath, Ian: and investigation of Rendlesham Forest UFO sighting, UP 136, 141

Riedel, Albert (a.k.a. Frater Albertus): SA 133-135

Rietveld, Gerrit: architecture by, UV *132;* chair by, UV *133;* and de Stijl, UV 133

Right brain: *See* Left brain/right brain

Rig Veda: EE 101-102, ML 20; and pandits, EM 29-33

Riley, Ethel Beresford (a.k.a. Ethel Le Rossignol): SE 112

Rimland, Bernard: MB 62

Rimsky-Korsakov, Nikolay: MQ 19

Rines, Robert: MC *78, 80;* Loch Ness monster photographs by, MC 78, *79, 80, 81,* 82, 85, 90; Loch Ness monster research of, MC 77, 78, 79, 85, 89

Ring, Floyd O.: PH 127-129

Ring, Kenneth: and near-death-experience research, PV 58, 72-73, 77

Ring of Brodgar (Scotland): and earth energy, MP *70-71*

Ring of the Nibelung, The (Wagner): DD 46

Rinpoche, Chogyam Trungpa: EM 132-134

Rinpoche, Lama Yeshe Dorje: as exorcist, HN *126-127*

Rinpoche, Penor: EM 135

Rio de Janeiro (Brazil): MW 113

Rio Santa Cruz: MW 47

Ripley, George: and alchemy, SA 47-55; and Brook Farm, UV 81, 82; death of, SA 55; and philosophers' stone, SA 47-55, *52;* religious beliefs of, SA 47; scroll

AE Alien Encounters; AW Ancient Wisdom and Secret Sects; CC Cosmic Connections; CD Cosmic Duality; DD Dreams and Dreaming; EE Earth Energies; EM Eastern Mysteries; HN Hauntings; MA Magical Arts; MB The Mind and Beyond; MC Mysterious Creatures; ML Mysterious Lands and Peoples; MM Mind over Matter; MP Mystic Places; MQ Mystic Quests; MW The Mysterious World;

by, SA 48-54
Rishi Valley School: EM 120
Ristori, Giuliano: CC 74
Ritchie, George: near-death experience of, PV 56-58, 65-66
Rite of Spring, The (ballet; Stravinsky): MQ 19
Rites of Eleusis: AW 117
Rituale Romanum: CD 90
Ritual magic: defined, WW 41
Rituals: and Aborigines, MA 21; and Comanche, MA 68; and Gessner, MA 62, 63; and hernias, MA 125; and Hopi, MA 68; and Kwakiutl, MA 70-71; and magi, MA 49; and Mandans, MA 74-75; and Pawnee, MA 68; and Pueblo, MA 68-69; and shamans, MA 66, 68, 70-71; and sickness, MA 72, 135; in Spain, MA 125, 134-135; and spirits, MA 125; and Weber, MA 61-62, 63; and Wicca, MA 64-65; and Zenner, MA 62, 63
Ritual sex: and Gerald Brosseau Gardner, WW 104
Rivail, Hippolyte (a.k.a. Allan Kardec): SE 91
Rivera, Rita: AE 54-55
Rivers, L. Mendel: and UFO investigations, UP 109, 110
River Styx: MW 125
RNA: SI 66
RNGs (random number generators): and mind prints, PS 132-133; and quadriplegics, PS 136-137; and telecommunications, PS 134-135. See also T7001
Roark, Ronald: PS 49
Robat: See Buckland, Raymond
Robbins, Shawn: and advertising campaigns, PS 127; and stock market, PS 113; visions of, PS 127-128
Robbins, Tony: fire walking of, MM 102-103, 105, 106
Robert (king of France): CD 83
Robert I (king of Scotland): HN 11
Robert-Houdin, Jean Eugène (mentalist): PP 104-105, 108
Robert of Saint Albans: AW 39
Roberts, Eleanor: PH 95
Roberts, Jane: SS 133-137
Roberts, J. M.: AW 89

Roberts, Susan: and witches, WW 118
Robertson, Cloretta: stigmata of, MM 113
Robertson, Morgan: MY 29, PP 28; Titan and Titanic, similarities of, PP 28, 30-31
Robertson report: and H. P. Robertson, UP 55-56
Robert the Pious (king of France): PH 87
Robigus (god): MY 32
Robin (demon): and Alice Kyteler, WW 55
Robinson, Ann: and hoaxes, HN 70; and poltergeists, HN 70
Robots: AE 90, MY 18, SA 32-33; and immortality, SI 6, 86-87, 88; and Hans Moravec, SI 88
Roc: MW 65, 69
Rochester Creek: ML 127
Rock: as object of worship, EM 48-49
Rock, Joseph: photograph by, EM 80-81
Rock alignments (North America): MP 121
Rock carving: Italian, ML 40
Rock Creek Cemetery: and ghosts, HN 112-113
Rock drawings: Israeli, MQ 45
Rockefeller, John D.: CC 83
Rocket ship: AE 94. See also specific rocket ships
Rock garden: EM 110-111
Rock paintings, prehistoric: ML 36-37
Rock shelter: MY 15
Rocky Mountains: MW 40-41
Rodegast, Pat: SS 148
Rodenstein (duke): MW 35-36, 39
Rodenstein Castle: MW 34, 35-36, 39
Rodman, Julius Scammon: MA 90
Roe, William: MC 117-118; Sasquatch drawing by, MC 114
Roerich, Nikolay Konstantinovich: MQ 19, 21, MW 42; and Theosophists, MQ 19, 27; and Wallace, MQ 19-20, 22; wife, MQ 20
Roerich Pact and Banner of Peace: MQ 19; emblem of, MQ 20; signing of, MQ 19, 20
Roff, Mary: SE 93, 94-95

Rogation Days: MY 39
Roger of Hereford: CC 57-59
Roggeveen, Jacob: ML 84-85
Rogo, D. Scott: AE 121, MB 87, PE 128; and reincarnation research, PV 106, 110, 122
Rohan, cardinal prince de: SA 102
Rok (Sweden): MW 119
Roland, Per: MB 19
Roll, William G.: HN 73, SE 17, 89, 108; and ghosts, HN 23, 83, 104; and hauntings, HN 35-36, 37; and poltergeists, HN 55, 73, 104, MM 38, 46, 50, 54; and Psychical Research Foundation, HN 36; and recurrent spontaneous psychokinesis, HN 55
Rollet, Jacques: as werewolf, TN 86
Rollright Stones (England): psychic episodes at, MP 96-97
ROLOR talisman: MA 38
Romains, Jules: MB 52
Roman amphitheater: at Hissarlik site, Turkey, MQ 37
Roman calendar: MY 123
Roman catacomb: Christian painting from, MQ 72
Roman Catholicism: See Catholics and Catholicism
Romances: werewolves in, TN 79
Romanes, Professor: PE 33
Romanesque mosaic: Noah and animals depicted in, MQ 82
Romanies: See Gypsies
Roman-Irish bath: SI 134
Roman mural: MQ 55
Romanos, Del: PS 48
Romans: TS 107; and Hecate, WW 19; and hot springs, SI 24, 131; longevity of, SI 22; and mandrakes, EE 96; and Mother Goddess, EE 26; and oracles, EE 54; and Tellus, EE 26; and trees, EE 91; and water, SI 131
Romberch, Johannes: mnemonic devices of, MB 58-59
Rome (Italy): MW 119; alectryomancy in, VP 34; augury in, VP 33-34; dice in, VP 110; haruspicy in, VP 34, 35; seers in, VP 14
Rome International Airport: PS 87
Romulus: MY 31, 133; and wolves,

TN 56-57, 72
Rongorongo boards: on Easter Island, ML 90-95, 97; and Guillaume de Hevesy, ML 95; and Hotu Matua, ML 90
Röntgen, Wilhelm Conrad: PH 75
Ronwe (demon): MA 96-97
Roosevelt, Eleanor: CC 86, 138
Roosevelt, Franklin Delano: CC 135, MQ 18, 30, PE 112; at signing of Roerich Pact, MQ 19, 20
Roosevelt, Theodore: AW 110
Roosters: MA 135
Rope trick: East Indian, EM 92
Rorschach inkblots: VP 93, 129
Rorvik, David M.: and J. Derek Bromhall, SI 57; and cloning, SI 56-57, 85; and Max, SI 56-57, 85
Rose: WW 35; Christmas, WW 34
Rose, Mr.: PE 91-94
Rose, Charles: PS 80
Rose, Elliot: and Gerald Brosseau Gardner, WW 104
Rose Hall: HN 134-135, MW 27; and ghosts, HN 132-133
Rosenberg (count of Bohemia): SA 59
Rosenberg, Samuel: and legends of alien visitors, UP 16
Rosenberg, Terry, sculpture by: AE 130
Rosenkreutz, Christian: AW 48, 153, SA 84; life of, AW 50-51; and Rosicrucianism, SA 83; tomb of, AW 51-53, 54
Roseto (Pennsylvania): PH 133-134
Rosetta Stone: MP 57
Rosh Hashanah: MY 89
Roshi: defined, EM 95; and Janwillem van de Wetering, EM 95, 97
Rosicrucian Fellowship: AW 68
Rosicrucians and Rosicrucianism: CC 101, MA 64, MY 71, UV 60; alchemy of, AW 50, 54, 55-56, 61, 70-72; and Johann Valentin Andreae, SA 85; artwork by, AW 66; background of, SA 83, 84, 85; and Francis Bacon, SA 83-85; and Christoph Besold, SA 85; branches of, AW 63, 67-72; as brotherhood, AW 12; and Cabala, AW 66-67; and Catholi-

RABBIT. *The symbol of a soul reborn, through death, to life eternal, the rabbit in this eighth-century mosaic feasts on the fruit of paradise. Prolific breeders, rabbits also are commonly associated with fertility and the generation of new life.*

cism, AW 46-48; characteristics of, SA 83, 85, 90; and Comte de Saint-Germain, SA 101; decline of, AW 60, 61, 66; and John Dee, SA 83; and René Descartes, SA 85; emblems of, AW *48, 58;* in England, SA 86; and Robert Fludd, SA 86, 90, *91;* and Freemasons, AW 60-62, 66; in Germany, SA 83, 85-86; growth of, SA 85-86; history of, AW 48-49, 51-53; hoaxes of, AW 55-56, 63-64, 66; initiation of, AW 58, 63; and Lemuria, ML 6, 10; and magic, AW 66-67; and Michael Maier, SA 86; manuscript about, AW *62;* name of, AW 49; and Paracelsus, SA 83; philosophers' stone of, AW *59;* revival of, AW 61-62, 66-67, 68; and Christian Rosenkreutz, SA 83; and royal scientific brotherhoods, AW 60-61; rules of, AW 62-63; symbols for, SA *91;* telepathy of, AW 48; temple of, AW *52. See also individual Rosicrucians*

Roskovitsky, Vladimir: account by, MQ 81, 83-84

Ross, Balthasar: and witch hunts, WW 69

Rossetti, Dante Gabriel: SS 39, UV *38;* and Jane Burden, UV 36; and William Morris, UV 36; painting by, UV *38;* and Pre-Raphaelite Brotherhood, UV 36

Roswell (New Mexico): MW 42; briefing paper on UFOs, UP 144; crash retrievals in, AE 78-*85,* UP 74-75; UFOs in, AE 78-85, UP 38-*40*

Roszak, Theodore: WW 97

Rotating black holes: and Roy Kerr, TS 73; and time travel, TS *72-73,* 77. *See also* Black holes

Rothbaum, Susan: SS 142

Rothe, Friedel: and Fritz Haarmann, TN 129-130

Rothschild, David: MQ 47

Rothschild, Nathaniel: SI 29

Round Table, Knights of the: MQ 111, *119,* 120-*121*

Round Trip (Vaterlaus): AE *133*

Roundworms: SI 73. *See also* Nematodes

Rousseau, Henri: paintings by, DD *6, 8-9;* and surrealism, DD 7

Roving Rocks in *Odyssey:* MQ 59; site associated with, MQ *58*

Rowan, Roy: PS 130

Rowan berries: WW *38*

Rowe, Neville: and dolphins, SS *16-17,* 148

Rowen, Lady: *See* Buckland, Rosemary

Royal Australian Air force: and Papua (New Guinea), UFO sighting, UP 72

Royal Fire: MW 102

Royal Institution of Great Britain: PE 113-114

Royal Society of London for Improving Natural Knowledge: and Robert Boyle, SA 95, 96; and James Price, SA 78, 79, 95

Roycroft Printing Shop: UV 85

Royer, Daniel: MW 111

RR et AC: AW 153, 156

RSPK: *See* Poltergeists; Recurrent spontaneous psychokinesis

Rubedo: MW 127

Rubies: MA 101

Rubin, Penny Torres: SS 142-*143*

Rudbeck, Olof: and Atlantis, MP 20

Rude Man of Cerne: MA *122-123. See also* Cerne Giant

Rudhyar, Dane: CC 88, *148, 150,* CD 36-37

Rudman, Daniel: SI 73

Rudolf II (Holy Roman emperor): CC 95, MW 119, SA *60-61,* 86, VP 47; and alchemy, SA 60-61, 63; bell of, SA *61;* and John Dee, SA 59, 60; and Gustenhover, SA 60-61; and Edward Kelley, SA 59, 60

Rudolph II (emperor of Hungary): AW 57

Rudra (god): MY 25

Rue: MW 30

RU-486: and Étienne Baulieu, SI *74-75;* and longevity, SI 74, 75

Rugg, Harold: MB 90

Ruhl, Dick: AE 57

Ruilly, Jehan de: WW 57

Ruilly, Macette de: execution of, WW 57

Ruiz, Graciela: MW 32

Rujanksy, Boris V.: MQ 84

Rukh: MW 65, *69*

Ruler, House of the: MW *79*

Rumania: vampires in, TN 113, 134

Runes: MA 27, *28, 29, 30,* MW *54,* 119

Runolfsson, Runolfur (spirit): SE 99, 100

Ruppelt, Edward J.: UP 49, 51, 52, 87

Rushton, J. Philippe: CD 109

Ruskin, John: UV *35,* 36, 85; and arts and crafts movement, UV 35; and Pre-Raphaelite Brotherhood, UV 35

Russell, Bertrand: SE 32, *64,* 65, 66, SS 153, UV 25

Russell, George William (pseud. AE): SE 104-*105;* astral body as viewed by, PV *18-19;* mural by, SE *105*

Russell, Jeffrey: MA 15-17

Russia: Tibetans and, MQ 26

Russian Imperial Air Force: Noah's Ark find by, alleged, MQ 81, 83-84

Russians: SI 114

Russolo, Luigi: and Noise Intoners, UV *123;* painting by, UV *122*

Ruth (doubles percipient): PE 100-101

Rutherford, Ernest: SA 115-116

Rutherford, Lord: HN 16

Rutherford, Margaret: and ghosts, HN 31

Rutledge, Harley D.: and Project Identification, UP 134, *135*

Ryals, Jim: ML 25

Ryan, Lee: PS 37

Ryback, David: DD 138

Ryckaert, David: painting by, SA *40-41*

Ryerson, Kevin: SS *10-11;* and Apostle John, SS 10, 146; and Shirley MacLaine, SS 10, 145-146

Ryle, Gilbert: SE 68-69, 124

Rymer, Mrs.: and Daniel Dunglas Home, SS 43, 44, *46-47*

Rymer, John S.: and Daniel Dunglas Home, MY 63, SS 38, 39, 43, 44, 46

Ryoanji temple: EM *110-111*

Ryzl, Milan: and hypnotism, tests of, PP *64-65,* 69

AE Alien Encounters; AW Ancient Wisdom and Secret Sects; CC Cosmic Connections; CD Cosmic Duality; DD Dreams and Dreaming; EE Earth Energies; EM Eastern Mysteries; HN Hauntings; MA Magical Arts; MB The Mind and Beyond; MC Mysterious Creatures; ML Mysterious Lands and Peoples; MM Mind over Matter; MP Mystic Places; MQ Mystic Quests; MW The Mysterious World;

SUN. *In this Egyptian carving, Pharaoh Akhenaton and his queen Nefertiti worship the sun, who reaches down with beneficent hands, some holding life-bestowing ankhs. Throughout the world, the sun long represented an all-seeing god.*

S. (mnemonist): MB 53-56

Sabbath: UV 34

Sabbats: MY 32, *33*, 65; characteristics of, WW 49; defined, WW 107, 123; purposes of, WW 135; and witches, WW 9-10

Saber-toothed tiger: ML *10-11*

Sabine, W. H. W.: and retrocognition, HN 39

Sabom, Michael B.: PV 73-77, *78*

Sabu oracle: EM 98

Sacks, Oliver: MB *51;* and autism, MB 62; and Korsakoff's syndrome, MB 60; and neglect syndrome, MB 50; and Tourette's syndrome, MB 90

Sacrament desecration: and Jean Gehauds, WW 83; punishment for, WW *82-83*

Sacred art: UV 49

Sacred calendars: MY *63*

Sacred earth: EE 39

Sacred Furrow Day: MY 39

Sacred places: TS 6, *7-15;* and Mircea Eliade, EE 27-29, 30

Sacred Time: *See* Dreamtime

Sacred trees: in India, EE *94, 95*. *See also* Trees

Sacrifices: AW 17, *18-19, 20,* CD 54, EM 33, MA 120, MW 79, 99, 113-114, 115, 116-117, SE 20, 21, TS 37; in Africa, EE 27; of animals, MA *120-121;* and Aztecs, EE 26, TS *37;* by Druids, VP 38; and Hecate, WW 19; of humans, MA 120; in India, EE 26; and the Koryak, MA 120-121; and oaks, EE 92; and sinkholes, EE 74; and volcanoes, EE 67; and voodoo, MA 83

Sacro Catino (Holy Bowl): MQ 121-122, *125*

Sada: MY 117

Sadat, Anwar: assassination of, DD 137, *138-139*

Sadhus: EM *36,* MB *97;* defined, SI 17, 18; and Kumbha Mela, SI *16-17, 19. See also* Nagas

Sadism: of Elizabeth Báthory, TN 123-126, *127;* of Dracula, TN 105-*107;* of Ferencz Nádasdy, TN 123

Safa: MY 91

Sagan, Carl: CC 128-129, MM 34; and American Association for the Advancement of Science symposium, UP 122-123; and congressional symposium, UP 117; and Marjorie Fish, AE 29; and Betty Hill, AE 29; and message to alien civilizations, AE 108, *109,* UP 124; Sagan's para-

MY The Mystical Year; PE Phantom Encounters; PH Powers of Healing; PP Psychic Powers; PS The Psychics; PV Psychic Voyages; SA Secrets of the Alchemists; SE Search for the Soul; SI Search for Immortality; SS Spirit Summonings; TN Transformations; TS Time and Space; UP The UFO Phenomenon; UV Utopian Visions; VP Visions and Prophecies; WW Witches and Witchcraft

SNAKE. Because it regularly sloughs its old skin, the snake is a symbol of renewal and longevity. Yet as shown in this painting of the serpent tempting Eve in the Garden of Eden, it also represents evil and guile.

dox, UP 123

Sagas: Icelandic, MQ 78, SI 26; transformations in, TN 36-37

Sagée, Emilie: PE 82-83, 94

Sagittarius (zodiac sign): CC 36, *88*, MY 103

Sagrada Familia Church: UV *117*

Sahara Desert: MW 99-100

Saicho: EM 57

Sailors: MA 129

Saining: WW 136; magical, WW 136

Saint Andrew's Eve: MA 102

St. Andrew's Masonic lodge: AW 74, 76; invitation to, AW *77*

Saint Brendan, Isle of: ML 122

St. Clair, Sheila: MW 24-25

Saint-Denis, Marquis Hervey de: drawings by, DD *115*; and lucid dreams, DD 107

Saint Donat's Castle: MW 19, PE 42

Saint Elmo's fire: EE 70; defined, HN 75; and ghost ships, HN 75; mistaken for UFOs, UP 69. *See also* Lightning

Saint-Gaudens, Augustus: sculpture by, HN *112-113*

St. George's Church: MW *103*

Saint George's Eve: MA 102

Saint-Germain, Comte de: AW 64-66, MY 136, SI *14*; as alchemist, SI 12; immortality of, SI 12, 14; and Sheba, SI 12; and Solomon, SI 12. *See also* SA *index*

Saint Helens, Mount: PS *18-19*

St. Leger, Elizabeth: AW *102-103*

St. Mary and the Martyrs, Church of: illustration from Bible, MQ *46-47*

Saint Michael: church of, ML *54-55, 56*

Saint Michael's Mount: MW 87

Saint Paul's Cord: *See* Out-of-body experiences

Saint Peter's Church: EE *37*

Saint-Quentin (France): MW 34

Saints: CD 110, PP 7, 18; out-of-body experiences of, PV 16-17. *See also individual saints*

Saki: CD 125. *See also* Angels

Sakura Sōgorō: PE *74-75*

Salako Taka (cloud spirit): MA *47*

Salat: MY 33

Salazar de Frias, Alonzo: and witch hunts, WW 72

Salem (Massachusetts): witchcraft trials in, WW 73-77

Salerno-Sonnenberg, Nadja: MB 90

Salesian Order: DD 36

Salian Franks: and witches, WW 30

Salii: MY 19

Salish Indians: MC 116

Salmon: human soul of, TN *10*; rituals regarding, TN 10. *See also* Fish

Salt: tossing of, MA 118, 137

Salter, W. H.: SE 102-106, *107*

Salt Lake City (Utah): UV 59

Saltmarsh, H. E.: and dreams, TS 128

Saltpeter: SA 34

Salves: of werewolves, TN 73-74, *95, 98-99*; of witches, TN 38

Salyut-6 (space station): EE 112

Salyut-7 (space station): EE 112

Salzburg Cube: ML 21

Samadhi: PH 74; defined, CD 36

Samding monastery: abbess of, EM *78*

Samford, John A.: and Washington, D.C., UFO sightings, UP 55

Samhain: MY 81, *96-97*, WW 43, 123

Sami: MW 119-*120*

Samlesbury Hall: MW 19, 22-24

Samoans: cosmogonies of, TS 20

Samorani, Antonio: MW 59

Sampson, Agnes: as witch, WW 7

Samrat Yantra: CC 110, 111

Samsara: defined, EM 37, PV 127

Samson (biblical figure): SI 93

Samudra: EM 41

Samuel (biblical figure): and Saul, PS 27, *29*

Samurai: and Zen Buddhism, EM 55, 57

San Andrés Island: PS *86*

Sanbai-sama (god): MY 47

San Clemente monster: MC 33-34. *See also* Sea serpents

Sanders, Alexander: WW *114*; and Alexandrian tradition, WW 108; and Gerald Brosseau Gardner, WW 114; and Wicca, WW 108

Sanderson, Ivan T.: MC 111, MW 70; and Bermuda Triangle mystery, MP 37; sea serpent research of, MC 37

Sand foxes: divination with, VP *37*

Sandglass: TS *107*, 109

Sand paintings: CD *11*, DD *30*, PH *15*; in England, MA *14*; and the Navajo, MA 72, TS 30, *31, 95*; purposes of, MA 14

Sandunov Baths: SI 114

San Francisco earthquake: PS 105

San Francisco Peaks: EE 39

Sangam: importance of, SI 16, 18; and nagas, SI *19, 20*

Sangre de Cristo Mountains: EE *46-47*

Sanichar (feral child): TN *61;* and C. S. Valentine, TN 60-61

San Juan Capistrano mission: MY 23, 95

Sankaku-nami: MW 93

San Lorenzo: cathedral of, Genoa, Italy, MQ 122

San people: DD 26

Sanrinbo: MA 8

Sansanvi (angel): and Lilith, WW 16

Sanskrit: numerology in, VP 107

Santa Claus: MY 116

Santa Fe River: MW 27

Santa Maria del Popolo (church): HN *131*

Santayana, George: SE 46

Santería: MW 113-115, PH 23

Santeros: MW 113-115

Santiago (Chile): MW 113, 116

Santô Kyôden (artist): PE 77

Santorin (island): eruption of, EE 74; vampires on, TN 112-113

Santos, Lucia dos: CD 120-121, MY 93

Sanvi (angel): and Lilith, WW 16

Sanyo Chemical Industries: PS 107

Sapiens Dominabitur Astris: AW 146

Sapolsky, Robert M.: SI 22-23

Sapphires: MA 101

Sarah (housekeeper): HN 123

Sarah (multiple personality): MB 82-83

Sarasvati (goddess): MY 130

Saraswati River: SI 18

Sargasso Sea: MW 79, 83; Christopher Columbus's crew and fears of, MP 37

Sarras (legendary city): MQ 121

Sarsen: and Stonehenge, MP 82

Sartre, Jean-Paul: SE *69-71*

Sasquatch: MC 98, *114*, 116, 117, 120-126, MW 47. *See also* Hominoids *in* MC *index*

Satan: CD 82-85, 88, 131, UV *23*, 24-25; and Elizabeth Sawyer, WW 61; and Set, CD 78; survey

AE Alien Encounters; AW Ancient Wisdom and Secret Sects; CC Cosmic Connections; CD Cosmic Duality; DD Dreams and Dreaming; EE Earth Energies; EM Eastern Mysteries; HN Hauntings; MA Magical Arts; MB The Mind and Beyond; MC Mysterious Creatures; ML Mysterious Lands and Peoples; MM Mind over Matter; MP Mystic Places; MQ Mystic Quests; MW The Mysterious World;

SPIRAL. *A symbol of eternity similar to a circle or a mandala, the spiral, such as the one below from a Cornish church, represents the development of the universe from an infinitely distant, central point of absolute beginning.*

about, CD 96; and Theophilus, WW 45-46, *47;* and Waldensians, WW *59;* and witches, WW 8-9, 10, *44, 45, 46-47,* 49, *56-57.* *See also* Demons

Satan, slaves of: *See* Werewolves

Satanael (devil): CD 32

Satanism: CD 78-79, *95-96;* and Wicca, WW 126

Satellite photograph as evidence for Noah's Ark: MQ 64, *66*

Sathan (cat): WW 12

Satori: defined, EM 110; and Zen Buddhism, EM 97

SATOR square: MA *38*

Saturn (god): CC *44,* MY *118-119,* 121, SA *72, 73,* TS *21*

Saturn (planet): AE *90-93,* CC 17, 24, 36, 44, 104, 139, *150,* MA *36,* MY 86, 119, 127; characteristics of, SA 21; symbol for, SA *25*

Saturnalia: MY 18, 119, 121, 136, WW 43

Satyr: MC *57,* 100. *See also* Human-beasts

Saudeleur: defined, ML 101-102

Saudi Arabia: search for King Solomon's mines in, MQ 41-42

Saul (biblical figure): CD 86; and Samuel, PS 27, *29*

Saunas: SI *114, 134*

Saunders, David R.: and the Condon report, UP 119

Saunders, Richard: CC 102; as moleoscopist, VP 66, 68

Saurian, marine: MW 72

Sauropods: MC *95-96,* MW 65; characteristics of, MC 90; as Mokele-mbembe, MC 77, 90, 96

Saut d'Eau: MY *61*

Savant syndrome: MB 7, 38-39, 62

Savoy, Gene: MQ *42,* 43

Sawyer, Elizabeth: WW *61;* and Satan, WW 61

Saxe, Arthur: ML 102

Saxer, Hilde: PE 36

Scacciadiavoli (grenade): MW 123

Scales: MY *88,* SA *41*

SCANATE: PP 142, 144, PS 81-82

Scandinavians: cosmogonies of, TS 20

Scapegoats: MY 69, 89

Scapulomancy: defined, VP 35

Scarab: CD *12,* SA *8*

Scars, allegedly alien-inflicted: AE *34,* 112

Scene from the Inquisition, A (Goya): WW *52-53*

Sceptical Chymist, The (Boyle): SA *96, 97*

Schatzman, Morton: PE 100, 101

Schaub, Thomas: MQ 43

Scheerbart, Paul: UV 126

Scheid, Barbara: MM *8*

Schemenlauf: MY *123*

Schemit, Jean: SA 120; as publisher, SA 119

Schermann, Raphael: VP 92

Scherner, Karl Albert: DD 59; and Sigmund Freud, DD 61

Schertz, Charles Ferdinand de: TN 116

Schiller, J. C. Friedrich von: MB 90

Schilling, Leonetta: PS 46-47

Schiltberger, Hans: MC 107

Schirmer, Herbert: AE 29-30

Schizophrenia: MB 67, 71-77, 88. *See also* Mental illnesses

Schizophrenogenic mothers: MB 74

Schlater, Philip: ML 28-29

Schlemmer, Oskar: UV 131

Schliemann, Heinrich: MQ 36, 61; Troy discovered by, MP 18-*19,* MQ *36-37,* 40, 49

Schlitz, Marilyn: PS 87

Schloss Belle Vue: DD *62,* 63

Schmeidler, Gertrude R.: MM 74, PE 127, 128; and ghosts, HN 133-136; and process-oriented research, PP 62-63; psychokinesis research of, MM *76-77;* and Ingo Swann, PP 83

Schmid, William: SI 107

Schmidt, Clarence: art by, UV *52-53*

Schmidt, Helmut: MM *73;* criticism of, MM 70, 73; micro-PK research of, MM 70, *71, 72-73,* 85; and precognition, tests of, PP 62; retropsychokinesis research of, MM 72-73

Schmiechen, Hermann: paintings by, AW *132, 133*

Schmitt, Donald R.: and crash retrievals, AE 81-82, 83; and Glenn Dennis, AE 83; and Arthur E. Exon, AE 84

Schmitz, Oskar A. H.: CC 131

Schneider, Annemarie: and poltergeists, MM 51, 52-53

Schneider, Rudi: MM *20;* accused of hoaxes, MM 21, *22;* psychokinesis of, MM 21-22

Schneider, Willi: psychokinesis of, MM 20-21

School of the Dance (Degas): DD 147

Schöpke, Philipp: art by, MB *66*

Schreiber, Flora Rheta: MB 79-80

Schreiber, Karin: SS *144*

Schreiber, Klaus: SS *144*

Schrenck-Notzing, Baron Albert von: MM 20, SS *64;* and Eva C., SS 64, 68-70; and Eusapia Palladino, SS *62,* 63, 64; photograph by, SS *65,* 69

Schrey family: and poltergeists, MM 40-42, *41*

Schrödinger, Erwin: MM 72, TS 68

Schroeder, Lynn: and Soviet psychic research, PP 141-142

Schrum, Donald: AE 63

Schultheis, Heinrich von: and witch hunts, WW 78

Schultz, Dutch: murder of, PS 33, *35;* and Florence Sternfels, PS 33, 35

Schultz, J. H.: PH 138

Schumann, Robert: DD 46

Schutzstaffel (SS): MQ 127, 128

Schwagel, Anna Maria: witch trial of, WW 80

Schwartz, Mrs.: near-death experience of, PV 65

Schwartz, Gary: EE 128

Schwartz, Stephan A.: MQ 95, *100, 101, 102,* PS 129, SS 133; Egyptian expedition, MQ *100-103;* and ESP, PS 89; and *Leander,* PS 128; and Mobius Society, PS 89, 128; and psychic archaeology, PP 124

Schwarz, Jack: self-mutilation of, MM 112, 124

Schweitzer, Albert: PH 139

Schweitzer, John Frederick: *See* Helvetius

Schweizer-Reneke (South Africa): MW 34, 37-38

Schwinghammer, Gregor: ark sighting, report of, MQ 89-90

Sciater, Philip: and Lemuria, MP 26, 28

Science: and magic, MA 114, 135;

111

MY *The Mystical Year;* **PE** *Phantom Encounters;* **PH** *Powers of Healing;* **PP** *Psychic Powers;* **PS** *The Psychics;* **PV** *Psychic Voyages;* **SA** *Secrets of the Alchemists;* **SE** *Search for the Soul;* **SI** *Search for Immortality;* **SS** *Spirit Summonings;* **TN** *Transformations;* **TS** *Time and Space;* **UP** *The UFO Phenomenon;* **UV** *Utopian Visions;* **VP** *Visions and Prophecies;* **WW** *Witches and Witchcraft*

SHELL. This work by Botticelli shows Venus arriving newborn on a scallop shell, a symbol of fertility and conception. Like the goddess, whose Greek name, Aphrodite, means "foam born," the shell is associated with the seas, source of all life.

and superstitions, MA 114, 135-136

Science of spirit: UV 102

Science Unlimited Research Foundation (SURF): PS 81

Scientific American (journal): SA 117; and mediums, studies of, PP 36, 38-39

Scientology: PS 84

Sciomancy: defined, VP 35

Sciopedi: AE *102-103*

Scoliophis atlanticus: MC 28. *See also* Sea serpents

Scorer, Richard: cloud-busting research of, MM 17

Scorpio (zodiac sign): CC 36, *53, 87,* 139, MY 95

Scorpion: MY *94-95*

Scot, Michael: CC 64, HN 11

Scot, Reginald: WW 78

Scotland: sites in, associated with Merlin, MQ *132-135;* superstitions in, MA *113,* 134; witches in, WW 6-8, *9*

Scotland Yard: and Agatha Christie, PS 29; and Jack the Ripper, PS 27-29, 31; and Robert James Lees, PS 27-28, 31; and psychic detection, PS 27

Scott, Dr.: advertisement, PH 89

Scott, Peter: and Loch Ness monster research, MC 76, 80, 89; painting by, MC 80, *82-83*

Scott, Stuart: and Pyramid power, MP 66

Scott-Elliot, William: and Atlantis, MP 30; and Lemuria, ML 6, 12

Scottish Rite Masonry: AW 105

Scourges: WW *83*

Scratching Fanny (poltergeist): HN 64

Scrofula: PS 95

Scroll: by George Ripley, SA *48-54*

Scryers: VP 30-32, 45-*49, 47,* 50. *See also* Crystallomancy; Scrying

Scrying: CC 70, MY *39;* characteristics of, VP 32, 52; defined, VP 31, 45; techniques, VP 45, 50. *See also* Crystallomancy; Scryers

Scylla (Greek monster): MC 22, MQ 58, 59

Scythians: CD 63

SDA: AW 146

Seaborn, Adam: *See* Symmes, John Cleves

Seabrook, William: and voodoo, MA 81, 84

Sea cows: MC 85

Sea devil: MC 18

Sea dragon: MC *18, 19*

Seal of Solomon: AW 65

Seals: MC 44, 85, MY *55*

Séances: MM *11,* MW 106, PV 18, 21, SA 59, SE 99-107, *100-101;* Agénor de Gasparin's research on, MM 11, 13, *24,* 25; characteristics of, MB 17; of Eusapia Palladino, MM *13,* 15; and Stan Gooch, MB 41; and Erik Jan Hanussen, PS 60, *61;* Harry Price's research on, MM 19-20, 21; and Carl Jung, MB 79; and Helene Preiswerk, MB 79; and Society for Research on Rapport and Telekinesis, MM 25; and Alfred Russel Wallace, MB 17

Sea of the Devil: MW 93, 94

Sea People: TN 51. *See also* Fish; Whales

Search for extraterrestrial intelligence (SETI): AE 108-109, UP 124-126, *127*

Searle, Frank: Loch Ness monster research of, MC 83-84

Sea serpents: MC *18-19, 26, 27, 29, 31, 33, 35,* MW 10, *71-75,* map 74-75, MY 38, *63, 67,* 134. *See also* Lake monsters; MC *index*

Seax-Wica: and Raymond Buckland, WW 112

Sechrist, William: PP 134-135

Second Beast: *See* Aquino, Michael

Second Coming of Christ: MW 105; and Shambhala, belief in, MQ 20

Second Council of Constantinople: SE 45

Second Goetheanum: UV *114-115*

Second International Congress of Psychotronic Research: MM 76

Second sight: MA 101-102, PP 7, 16; defined, MM 63. *See also* Clairvoyance; Thought transference

Secret arrows: defined, EE 115

Secret Chiefs: AW 152-153, 155

Secret Doctrine, The (Blavatsky): AW 135, 137, 157, EM 86, ML 12, 28, MP 28-29, PV 22, UP 16

Secret societies: *See specific secret societies*

Sects: defined, AW 11; history of,

AW 11-12, 13; initiation into, AW 12-13. *See also specific sects*

Secular humanism: CD 127

Sedatives: and dreams, DD 114

Seder: MY 24

Sedona (Arizona): EE 65, MW 79

Seed-sowing ceremony: MY *32*

Seeress of Prevorst: *See* Hauffe, Friederike

Seers: *See* Psychic archaeology; Shamans; *specific types of seers;* VP *index*

Sefirot: defined, MA 26

Segall, Paul: SI 80, 83-85, 119, 122-123, *129*

Segerberg, Osborn, Jr.: SI 46

Seibel, Kastor: psychokinesis of, MM 63, 64

Seidr: characteristics of, WW 29; defined, WW 28

Seiokona: defined, WW 28

Seior: defined, WW 28

Seismic tomography: and earth's interior, MP 154

Seiss, Joseph: and Great Pyramid, MP 62, 63

Seiwa (emperor of Japan): MY 62

Selene (goddess): CC 39

Selenomancy: defined, VP 35

Self-consciousness: UV 107

Self-hypnosis: MM 101. *See also* Hypnosis and hypnotic regression

Selfishness: CD 109-110. *See also* Altruism *in* CD *index*

Self-mutilation: MM 107-112, 124

Self-projection: defined, PV 20. *See also* Out-of-body experiences

Self-Realization Fellowship: EM 119, SI 8

Self-referencing stereo (SRS) camera: AE 71-72

Sellers, Sean: CD 96

Semangelaf (angel): and Lilith, WW 16

Semen: SI *113*

Seminole Indians: MW 44

Semites: and Mother Goddess, WW 13-16

Semjase (alien): AE 98, 99

Senareus, Philip: airship stories of, UP 19

Seneca (spirit): MW 106

AE *Alien Encounters;* **AW** *Ancient Wisdom and Secret Sects;* **CC** *Cosmic Connections;* **CD** *Cosmic Duality;* **DD** *Dreams and Dreaming;* **EE** *Earth Energies;* **EM** *Eastern Mysteries;* **HN** *Hauntings;* **MA** *Magical Arts;* **MB** *The Mind and Beyond;* **MC** *Mysterious Creatures;* **ML** *Mysterious Lands and Peoples;* **MM** *Mind over Matter;* **MP** *Mystic Places;* **MQ** *Mystic Quests;* **MW** *The Mysterious World;*

SWAN. *Because the swan's inverted reflection—an emblem of death—is often seen in calm waters, the bird is associated with mortality. Yet when paired with eggs, like the ones that fill this 19th-century ceramic figure, the swan represents rebirth.*

Senescence: defined, SI 23

Sengen-Sama (goddess): MW 93

Senses: MB 54-55

Sensitives: *See* Psychics

Sensitivity: HN 129; suggestibility compared with, HN 129

Sensory deprivation: PP 67

Sensory-deprivation tank: and John Lilly, MB *116*, 117-122

Sequoias: EE 87. *See also* Trees

Serailian, Mihran K.: painting by, PV *23*

Seralung Gompa: EM *44-45*

Seraphim: CD *131*

Serapis (ship): AW *80-81*

Serbia: vampires in, TN 108, 113

Serialism: defined, VP 10; and John William Dunne, TS 123-124, 127. *See also* Dunne, John William

Seriality law: defined, TS 121

Serios, Ted: criticism of, MM 68; thoughtography of, MM *68-69*

Serotonin: MB 106, TS 79

Serow: defined, MC 104; scalp of, MC *104*, 106

Serpent god, Teotihuacán: ML *104*

Serpents: ML *127*, MY *8-9*, 29, SA *25*, *28*, SI *16*; and alchemy, SA 24, 25, 29; and Gnosticism, SA 25

Sesajen: MA *130*

Sesola Island (Greece): tunnel on, MQ *58*

Set: defined, MB 112; effects of, MB 116

Set (god): CC 29, CD 78, 80, MA 52, SE 25, 26

Seth (biblical figure): EE 95

Seth (god): CD 80

SETI: *See* Search for extraterrestrial intelligence

Seti I (king of Egypt): MW 100, PV 104, *107*

Seton, Alexander: MA 33

Setsubun: MY *131*

Setting: defined, MB 112; effects of, MB 116

Sety, Omm: *See* Eady, Dorothy

Seva Foundation: EM 138

Seveerns of Ravenna, Saint: out-of-body experience of, PV 17

Seven: in dice, VP 111; in numerology, VP 102, 107, 108

Seven Cities of Cibola: MW 79, 80

Seven Stones: MW 85, *86-87*

Seventeen: in dice, VP 111

Severin, Timothy: ML *121*, MQ *49*; voyage of Ulysses retraced by, MQ *49-61*

Severinus, Peter: and alchemy, SA 93; and Frederick II, SA 82; and Paracelsus, SA 81-82

Seward, Anna: DD 140

Sewell, Charlie: AW 154

Sex: and black magic, MA 92, 93-99; and Aleister Crowley, MA 65; and Alexandra David-Néel, EM 73-74; and Gerald Brosseau Gardner, WW 104; and gender, CD 49; and Haridas, SI 101; and Thomas Lake Harris, UV 79; and Hindus, CD 114; and immortality, SI 34, 39; and magic, MA 63-64; and John Humphrey Noyes, UV 77-78, 80; and Oneida community, UV 75, 78, 80; and Bhagwan Shree Rajneesh, EM 131; ritual, WW 104; and Shakers, SI 39; and Tantra, CD *66*, 69-70, 114; and Tantrism, MA 64, SI 39; and Taoism, CD 114, EM 52, SI *39*

Seylaz, Louis: MQ 80

Seyle, Hans: PH 6

Seyler von Reinburg, Johann Wenzel: plate by, SA *99*

Seymour, Jane: PE 106

Sha: defined, EE 115, 137

Shackelford, Joe C.: AE 83

Shackleton, Ernest: PE 71

Shadow: DD *71*; as archetype, DD 42-43, *94-95*; defined, DD 71; and Carl Jung, DD 71

Shadow play: EM *60-61*

Shah, Nadir: MW 129

Shaka (king of Zulu nation): MW 135

Shakers: MW 105, SI 39, SS *24-25*. *See also* UV *index*

Shakespeare & Company: MW 28

Shakespeare, William: CC 78, HN 22, MA 92, 115-116, MB 87, MY 22, PE 37, 48, SE 68, SI 67, UV 96, 97, VP 49; and mandrakes, EE 96-99

Shakleton, Ernest: VP 82

Shakti (goddess): CD 35, 69, MA 64

Shaku, Soyen: and Paul Carus, EM 136; and Teitaro Suzuki, EM 136; and Swami Vivekananda, EM 135-136

Shalett, Sydney: debunking UFOs, UP 44

Shalikula (Zana's grandson): MC 112. *See also* Almas; Zana

Shamans: CD 111, *114*, EM 42, MA *66-75*, MB 108, MW 79, 113, 115-116, *117*, 119, *120*, MY 28, *13*, PH 8, 10-15, *11*, *12-13*, *16*, *18*, PP 7, SE 13, 21, 24, VP 32-*33*; and the Apache, MA 74; carvings used by, TN *10*; characteristics of, MA 70; defined, TN 10, 25; and the Hopi, MA 68; and hunting, MA *74-75*; and American Indians, MA 77-78; initiation of, MA 66; and jaguars, TN 25; and Kwakiutls, MA *70-71*; and magic, MA 115; masks of, TN *16*, *18*, *19*; and the Navajo, MA 72; of the Nootka, TN 11; and the Papago, MA 70; pectoral of, SA *13*; powers of, PP *75-77*, *80-81*; and Pueblo Indians, MA 68, *72-73*; rattle of, TN *11*; and rituals, MA 66, 68, *70-71*, 72, 74; and sickness, MA *72-73*; and the Tlingit, MA 74, TN *16*, 18, *19*; tools of, MA 70; and transformations, TN 25; of the Tsimshian, TN 10

Shambhala: UV 26. *See also* MQ *index*

Shamdeo (feral child): TN *67*

Shame masks: WW *65*

113

MY The Mystical Year; PE Phantom Encounters; PH Powers of Healing; PP Psychic Powers; PS The Psychics; PV Psychic Voyages; SA Secrets of the Alchemists; SE Search for the Soul; SI Search for Immortality; SS Spirit Summonings; TN Transformations; TS Time and Space; UP The UFO Phenomenon; UV Utopian Visions; VP Visions and Prophecies; WW Witches and Witchcraft

Shangri-la (fictional place): MQ
27, 30; longevity in, SI 39, 47
Shankar, Ravi: reincarnation of,
PV 109, 110
Shankara: EM 142
Shaolin monastery: EM 55, *146,
147*
Shapeshifting: defined, TN 30. *See
also* Transformations
Shaposhnikov, Helena Ivanovna:
MQ 20
Sharks: MY *28;* basking, MC *42,
43;* Megamouth, MC *20,* MW 71;
whale, MC *39*
Sharman-Burke, Juliet: Tarot cards
by, VP *140-141*
Shasta, Mount: ML 10
Shaver, Richard S.: and hollow
earth dwellers, MP 153
Shavuoth: MY 39
Shaw, George Bernard: AW 140,
151, CC 84, DD 129, SA 126
Shaw, Sandy: SI 75-76, *80*
Shaw, Sara: and abduction by
aliens, AE 22, 23, 26, 121; and
Ann Druffel, AE 123; hypnosis
and hypnotic regression of, AE
23, 26, 123; physical examina-
tion of, AE 23, 27-28
Sheba, Queen of: ML 68, MY 136,
SI 12
Shebbear Stone: MA *13*
Shedūr: HN 126-127. *See also* Ex-
orcism
Sheela, Ma Anand: EM 131-133
Sheelah-na-gig (goddess): MY *22*
Sheep: in Greek mythology, arti-
facts depicting, MQ *35, 53*
Sheils, Dean: and out-of-body-
experience research, PV 42
Sheldon, H. H.: SA 117
Sheldrake, Rupert: EE 124-126,
127-128
Shelley, Mary Wollstonecraft: DD
117, MB *88,* MY 30, TN 133
Shelley, Percy Bysshe: CC 84, MB
89, PE 85, *91,* SE 63, TN 133
Shellfish: as aphrodisiacs, SI 67;
frozen-hibernator phenomenon
of, SI 107
Shennongjia (China): MW 59
Sheol: CD 82. *See also* Afterlife
Shepherd, John: AE *116-117*
Shepherd, Sarah: MM 49

Shepherds: MA 20
Sherr, Rubby: SA 114
"Shew stones": *See* Crystal balls
Shey Mountain: EM 98-99
Shiatsu: PH *55*
Shichi-Go-San: MY *101*
Shields: MY 19, *118*
Shiels, Anthony (Doc): MC *36,* 37
Shiels, Kate: MC 37
Shine, Adrian: MC *89;* Loch Ness
monster research of, MC 85;
Morag research of, MC 89, 90
Shingon sect: EM *112-113. See
also* Zen Buddhism
Shinkō shūkyō: MW 127, 129-130
Shinto: MW 93, PE 73, SE 31; and
feng shui, EE 36; and Fuji, EM
20; shrine for, EE *56-57;* and
sumo, EM 148
Ship graves: MW 85
Ship of the Prophet Noah (stone
structure; Turkey): MQ *74*
Ship Rock: EE *42*
Ships: and ghosts, HN *75-83*

Shipton, Eric: Abominable Snowman photographs by, MC *102,*
116, 123; Abominable Snowman
research of, MC 104-105
Shipton, Mother (seer): VP 14-16
Shipwreck sites: and psychic archaeology, PP 124
Shira, Indre: MW 21-22
Shirodhara: PH *69*
Shiva (god): CD 6, *9,* EE 93, MA
64, ML 70, MY *36, 136,* SA 127,
SI 114; and Amarnath Cave, EM
43, 47; and Benares (India), EM
19; characteristics of, CD 9, 80;
as dancer, TS 19, 25, *26-27;* and
dualities, CD 6, 9, 35; and
Ganges River, TS 11; and Himalayas, EM 16; and Hindus, CD
80; and Kālī, CD *13;* statue of,
CD *67;* symbolism of, CD 66;
and Tantra, CD 69; and Varanasi (India), TS 93; and Swami
Vivekenanda, EM 115
Shivaji, Mahatma Guru Sri Para-

mahansa (a.k.a. Aleister Crow-
ley): EM 93
Shivaratri: MY 136
Shofar: MY 89
Shogun: MY 84
Short Ears, and Easter Island: ML
85-86, 89, 95
Short-term memory: TS 120
Shott, H. H.: and transformations,
TN 24
Shou-lao (god): SI *36*
Shrine, Celtic: ML *50*
Shriners: AW *108-109*
Shri yantra: AW *139*
Shroud of Turin: MQ *108-109,* 122
Shrove Tuesday: MY 45, 136
Shtrang, Hanna: MM 36
Shtrang, Shipi: MM 28, 35
Shu (god): TS 20
Shugendo sect: CD 99, 100-101,
103
Shumway, Ninette: AW 118
Shun (emperor of China): MW 93
Shupe, Anson: CD 95-96

*AE Alien Encounters; AW Ancient Wisdom and Secret Sects; CC Cosmic Connections; CD Cosmic Duality; DD Dreams and Dreaming; EE Earth
Energies; EM Eastern Mysteries; HN Hauntings; MA Magical Arts; MB The Mind and Beyond; MC Mysterious Creatures; ML Mysterious Lands and
Peoples; MM Mind over Matter; MP Mystic Places; MQ Mystic Quests; MW The Mysterious World;*

Siberians: EE 102

Sibert, John: MC 38-39, 44

Sibley, Ebenezer: CC 112

Sibylline Books: MY 27, VP 33

Sibyl of Cumae: MW 85, *90*

Sicard, Claude: MW 102

Sickness: causes of, MA 72, PS 95; curing of, PS 90, *95-103;* and gold, SA 116; and Gypsies, MA 100; and Men-an-Tol, MA 118; and multispectral image analyzer station, PS 90; and rituals, MA 135; and shamans, MA *72-73;* and superstitions, MA 114, 130, 134. *See also* Doctors

Siculus, Diodorus: MP 88

Siddhārtha, Prince (Buddha): search for burial site of, MQ 40-41

Siddhartha Gautama: MY *29, 41,* 115

Siddhis: defined, EM 24, MM 117; and Satya Sai Baba, EM 24-25. *See also* Levitation

Sidereal zodiac: CC 138

Sideromancy: defined, VP 35

Sidgwick, Eleanor: PE 89, 122, PV 19, SS 61 62, 71, 74, 91, 92; and ghosts, HN *23,* 29 30, 33

Sidgwick, Henry: PE 21, 24-25, PV 19, SS *72-73,* 74, 78; and society for Psychical Research, PP 24; as spirit guide, SS 81, 92

Sidicus: defined, ML 66

Siduri (character in Gilgamesh epic): MQ 32

Siegel, Bernard S.: PH *127*

Siegel, Ronald K.: SE 126

Siege Perilous (seat of Judas): MQ 118, 120

Siemens, Werner von: and pyramid power, MP 65

Sierra de Perija: MW 47

Sight, sense of: MB 55. *See also* Blind persons

Sightings: *See* UFO sightings; MC *index*

Sigils: MA 36, 37, *40*

Signatures: doctrine of, EE 96

Significator: defined, VP 123. *See also* Tarot; Tarot readers

Signorelli, Luca: fresco by, SE *51*

Sikkim: maharaja of, EM *74*

Silberer, Herbert: and alchemy, SA

128-129, 131; death of, SA 129; and Sigmund Freud, SA 129

Silbury Hill (England): ML *54,* MP 81, MY *61*

Silicosis: SA 65

"Silly season": MY 49

Silva, Edivaldo: PH *37*

Silva Mind Control: MM 119-122

Silvanus (bishop): CD 83

Silver: SA 23, 24

Silver Star: MY 93. *See also* Argentinum Astrum

Silvester, Saint: MY *125*

Simeon Stylites, Saint: MY 63

Similarities law: MA 15

Simmons, Ruth: *See* Murphy, Bridget; Tighe, Virginia

Simms (physiognomist): VP 69

Simon, Benjamin: and Hill abduction story, UP 82-84

Simon, Saint: MY 97

Simpson, William: MC 90

Sims, Lida: UV 143

Sin (god): CC 10, 14

Sinai, Mount: MY 39; theorized location of, MQ *44-45*

Sinclair, Cindy: and poltergeists, HN 74

Sinclair, Mary Craig: *See* Craig, Mary

Sinclair, Ted: and poltergeists, HN 74

Sinclair, Upton: PP 27, UV 85; and cosmic consciousness, PP 21; telepathic tests of, PP 20-21, *24-25*

Singh, Arjun: SI 99

Singh, Jai: CC 110-111

Singh, J. A. L.: TN *62, 63;* and Amala, TN 62-63; and Kamala, TN 62-63

Singh, Mrs. J. A. L.: TN 63

Singh, Maharaja Ranjit: EM 40

Singh, Raja Dhyan: SI 99

Singh, T. C.: and Dan Carlson, EE 132; and plant harmonics, EE 110-111

Singularity: defined, TS 61, 73

Sinkholes: EE *75;* and sacrifices, EE 74

Sinnett, Alfred Percy: AW 133-134, EM *89*

Sins: CD *87. See also* Evil

Sioux Indians: MA 78-80, ML 25,

MW 79-80, 110-111, 113, *114-115,* MY 56, UV 23. *See also* Vision quest

Sirens: AE *47;* Ulysses and, Greek vase depicting, MQ 59

Sirius (star): MY 67

Sirlin, Jerome: AE 112

Sisiutl: mask of, TN *14-15*

Sistine Chapel: MW 124

Sita (goddess): MW 129, MY 30

Sitchin: AE 89-97, 119

Sitka (Alaska): MW 113

Sitting Bull: MY 56; and visions, MA 78, 80

Situa: MY 84

Siva (god): VP 106

Siva Samhita: MM 118. *See also* Levitation

Six: in dice, VP 111; in dominoes, VP 112; in numerology, VP 102, 108

Sixteen: in dice, VP 111

Sixth sense: MB 54, PP 7. *See also* Executive ESP

Sixtus V (pope): CC 104, HN 131, VP 17

Sizdar-Bedah: MY 26

Sizemore, Chris: and multiple personality disorder, MB 79; and precognitive visions, MB 85-87

Sizer, Nelson: as phrenologist, VP 79-81

Skallagrim: TN 37

Skeletons: DD *15;* in copper mine, ML *23;* dream symbols, DD 15

Skelking (god): WW 27

Skerflod-Mori: MW 32-35

Skidi Pawnee Indians: CC *117*

Skies: MW *maps* 12-13

Skillen, Robert: PS 90

Skin sight: MB 52, PP *143*

Skin vision: *See* Skin sight

Skrabanek, Petr: PH 51

Skraelings: ML 124

Skrying: defined, PV 25. *See also* Calloway, Hugh G.; Out-of-body experiences

Skulls: CD *97;* as dream symbols, DD 57; of Inca, ML *22*

Skunk Ape: MC 120, MW 44-45, 47, *48*

Sky Chief: TN 50-51

Skye: MW 119, 120

Sky Heroes (gods): MW 95, 96

Sky World: TN 50

Slag heap: MY *94-95*

Slater, Elizabeth: AE 38-40

Slate writing: PP 42, *43*

Slavery: MW 44, MY 119, 121, UV 35; and Easter Island, ML 87, 90

Slaves of Satan: *See* Werewolves

Slavs: and Mother Goddess, EE 26-27

Slee, Wimpie: disappearance of, PP *126*

Sleeman, William: AW *44*

Sleep: SI 97-99; and astral body, PV 21; and out-of-body experiences, PV 16, 17, 42, 44; and psychic abilities, PP 69-74; stages of, PP 66-67. *See also* DD *index*

Sleep (Dali): DD *20-21*

Sleep Disorder Service and Research Center: DD 114-115

Sleeping Beauty: SI 99

Sleeping Gypsy, The (Rousseau): DD *6, 7*

Sleeping potions: EE 96

"Sleeping prophet": *See* Cayce, Edgar

Sleep laboratory: DD *98*

Sleep learning: MB 125. *See also* Hypnopedia

Sleep of Reason Brings Forth Monsters, The (Goya): MB *73*

Sleepwalkers: MB 116

Slick, Tom: MC 105, 120, MM 70

Slipping the silver lining: PS 94

Sloth (sin): CD *87*

Sloth, giant ground: MW *50-51. See also* Su monster

Sma:alt Xath'aq: MW 76-77, 79, *81*

Smallage: WW *37*

Smallpox: MA 136; on Easter Island, ML 87, 90

SMA (supplementary motor area): MB 19

Smell, sense of: MB 54

Smith (telepathic sender): PS 70

Smith, Mrs. (alleged Cathar): previous incarnation of, PV 101

Smith, Alexander: HN 8

Smith, Anita: PS *114-115*

Smith, Audrey: and cryobiology, SI 109, 122; and cryopreservation, SI 109; and hypothermia, SI 109;

MY The Mystical Year; PE Phantom Encounters; PH Powers of Healing; PP Psychic Powers; PS The Psychics; PV Psychic Voyages; SA Secrets of the Alchemists; SE Search for the Soul; SI Search for Immortality; SS Spirit Summonings; TN Transformations; TS Time and Space; UP The UFO Phenomenon; UV Utopian Visions; VP Visions and Prophecies; WW Witches and Witchcraft

SALAMANDER. *The salamander symbolizes fire, one of the four elemental spirits of alchemy. As seen in this 17th-century engraving, the element fire is said to protect and nourish the creature that represents it.*

and Paul Segall, SI 122

Smith, E. F.: PE 132

Smith, Etta Louise: PS 37-38

Smith, G. A. (hypnotist): PP 27; and hauntings, HN 25, 28-29; telepathic tests, PP *28-29;* and thought transference, PP 26-27

Smith, George: MQ *80;* tablet translated by, MQ *80*

Smith, George E. (botanist): EE 111

Smith, Gibson: PH 27

Smith, Guy: and ghosts, HN 66; and poltergeists, HN 66

Smith, Hélène: SS 84-*85*

Smith, James Fairbairn: AW 86

Smith, J. L. B.: MC 18-19

Smith, John: and ghosts, HN 83

Smith, Joseph: UV *58,* 59

Smith, Justa: PH 102, 103

Smith, Louise: AE *22;* and abduction by aliens, AE 22, 23, 34; hypnotic regression of, AE 22; physical examination of, AE 22

Smith, Margaret Court: MM 126

Smith, Michelle: CD 95

Smith, Pamela Colman: Tarot cards by, VP *142-143, 146-149*

Smith, Richard Lee: MW 45

Smith, Robert (priest): CD 115

Smith, Robert Cross (astrologer):

CC 113

Smith, Robert T.: MA 126

Smith, Rev. Msgr. William B.: and New Age movement, PP 101

Smithsonian Institution: MW 129

Smohalla: EE 24

Smyth, Charles Piazzi: and Great Pyramid, MP 58-62

Smythe, Francis Sydney: CD 134-135

Snake dance: Hopi, TN 28-29

Snake god: MW 93

Snake-handling ceremony: MB *94*

Snakes: CD *14,* DD *32,* MC 44, MY 58-59, *91,* SA *108;* and alchemists, SI 34; and Chinese, SI *35;* as dream symbol, DD *32-33;* and Egyptians, CD 14; and Eve, CD 14, 26, 56; and Greeks, CD 14; and Hindus, CD 14; and Harcouët de Langeville, SI 34; and longevity, SI 34, 35; and physicians, SI 34; symbolism of, CD 6, 14, 56; and wine, SI *35*

Snake Society: MA 68

Sneider, Jack: and ghosts, HN 36-37

Snow Festival: MY 131

Snow White: EE 92

Soal, Samuel George: SE 98-99; and Frederick Marion, PP 110-

111; and psychic research, PP 56; and thought transference, PP *110, 111*

Societas Rosicruciana in America: AW 70

Societas Rosicruciana in Anglia: AW 67-68

Société Spirite: AW 129

Society for Cryobiology: SI 113

Society for Psychical Research (SPR; British): DD 107, PP 35, 48; and William Barrett, SS 71; and Helena Petrovna Blavatsky, AW 134-135, 141, PV 22; and Eva C., SS 64, 70; and Arthur Conan Doyle, SS 100, 101; founding of, HN 25, 72, 86, MM 15, 57, MY 135, PE 21-23, 85, 111, PP 24, 35, SS 60-61, 71; and ghosts, HN 25, 84, 123-124; and Edmond Gibson, PE 49; and Edmund Gurney, PE 21, SS 71; and hauntings, HN 86; journal of, PP 48; and Gladys Osborne Leonard, SS 90; and mediumship, PP 36; members of, PV 19; and Frederic W. H. Myers, DD 107, PE 21, SS 71; and Henry Steel Olcott, AW 134, PV 22; and Eusapia Palladino, SS 62, 63-64; and Leonora Piper, SS 86; and poltergeists, HN 86; purpose of, MM 15, PV 18-19; and reincarnation research, PV 102-103, 113; and Eleanor Sidgwick, SS 71; and Henry Sidgwick, SS 71, 73; survey by, HN 25; and thought transference, PP 26-27. *See also* American Society for Psychical Research

Society for Research on Rapport and Telekinesis (SORRAT): séance research of, MM 25

Society of Freemasons: EE 25

Sociobiology: CD 62

Socorro (New Mexico): MW 43; and alien encounter, UP 73

Socrates: CD 34, DD 24, PH 117, SA 18-19, SE 42-43, 44-46, TS 41, UV 31, VP 67; and oracles, PP 17

Soddy, Frederick: and alchemy, SA 115, 123

Sodom and Gomorrah: ML 33, MQ

43

Sofaer, Anna: ML 119

Sohei: EM 57-58

Sokeian: EM 137

Solar calendars: MY *8-16, 63*

Solar essence: SA *73, 74, 75, 84. See also* Sun

Solar system: AE *90-93,* VP *107,* TS 51-53

Solar temple: MY *11*

Solier, Poncet de: MA 49

Solomon (king of Israel): AW 97, SA 19, SI 12; mines of, ML 19, 47, MQ 41-*42,* 43; and Ophir, ML 47, 66-67, 68; in Sacro Catino legend, MQ 121

Solomon's Temple: MW 133

Solon: ML 26

Solstice, summer: ML *118,* MY 9, *10, 11,* 54, *55,* 123; at Callanish Circle, MP *76-77;* at Great Sphinx, MP *67;* at Medicine Wheel, MP *120;* at Nazca lines of Peru, MP *112;* at Stonehenge, MP 68, 90, *100-101*

Solstice, winter: ML *118,* MP 99, MY 9, *14, 15, 16,* 56, 119, 120, 121, 123, 125; at Egyptian pyramids, MP *67;* at Great Sphinx, MP *66;* at Nazca lines of Peru, MP 110, *130;* and Newgrange, EE 16-17, *18*

Soma: defined, SI 32; effects of, EE 102, EM 33, SI 33-34; and Hindus, MB 102, 104; and longevity, SI 34; and rasayana, SI 32; recipes for, SI 32-33; and *Sushruta Samhita,* SI 33. *See also* Hallucinogens

Soma (god): SI *33*

Somalians: CD 86, SI 22

Somatic dramas: PE 33-35

Somerton (England): maze, SE *11*

Sommer, Elke: HN *20;* and ghosts, HN 18-20, 21, 24

Sonar probes: of Loch Morar, MC 90; of Loch Ness, MC 78, *80, 86-87, 88,* 90. *See also* Operation Deepscan

Son of Sun: MY 83

Sons of Belial: MP 33

Sophocles: EE 54

Sorcerers: MW 133; and black magic, MA 25; in United States,

AE Alien Encounters; AW Ancient Wisdom and Secret Sects; CC Cosmic Connections; CD Cosmic Duality; DD Dreams and Dreaming; EE Earth Energies; EM Eastern Mysteries; HN Hauntings; MA Magical Arts; MB The Mind and Beyond; MC Mysterious Creatures; ML Mysterious Lands and Peoples; MM Mind over Matter; MP Mystic Places; MQ Mystic Quests; MW The Mysterious World;

SCARAB. *Scarab beetles were believed by ancient Egyptians to be all males, reproducing within the tiny balls of dung they rolled up, and thus self-generating, like the sun. This breastplate suggests a scarab rolling the winged sun across the sky.*

MA 9. *See also* Magicians; Witch doctors; Witches

Sorcerer's violet: WW *34*

Sotukhang (god): and Spider Woman, TS 7

Soubirous, Bernadette: CD 119-120, MY 132

Soudinos: VP 35

Soul: AE *52-53,* MY 19, 54, 78; depictions of, SE *16, 45, 48, 72-87;* psyche as, SE 118; "soul body," PE 35; survival of, PE 47, 68. *See also* Spirit

"Soul catcher," Tlingit Indian: PH *9*

Souling: MY 98

Soulis, Nicholas de: HN 11

Soulis, William de: and black magic, HN 11; ghost of, HN 11

Soul loss: defined, MA 11

Soul number: defined, VP 98. *See also* Numerologists; Numerology

Sound irradiation: *See* Plant harmonics

Sounion, Cape (Greece): MQ *50-51*

Souquat (priest): CD 89-90

South, Mary Anne (a.k.a. Mary Anne Atwood): SA 129; and al-

chemy, SA 126

South, Thomas: SA 126

South America: MW *maps 8, 15, 26, 34-35, 46, 78,* 112

Southern Cassadaga Spiritualist Camp Meeting Association: MW *105-109,* 113

Southern Hemisphere, skies of: MW *map 13*

South Wonston (England): crop circles in, EE *11*

Southworth, Dorothy: MW 22, *24*

Soviet-American exchange program: UV 137

Soviet Union: MA 8; aliens in, AE *62-63;* and ELF waves, PS 86; ginseng in, EE 100; and *Nautilus,* PS 71-72, 79; oaks in, EE 92; and parapsychology, PS 78-79; and psi-warfare experiments, PS 78, 79-80, 84; psychic research in, PP 141-142, 144; psychokinesis in, MM 23-26, 27, 75-81; and psychotronics, PS 90-91; and telepathy, PS 78, 79; UFOs in, AE *62-63*

Soyal: MY 118

Space: *See* TS *index*

Space Brothers: AE 21. *See also* Aliens

Spacecraft: AE *94,* VP 28. *See also specific spacecraft*

Space People (alien group): and George Van Tassel, UP 78

Space-time: *See* TS *index*

Space-time foam: and Alexander Vilenkin, TS 67; and John Wheeler, TS 66

Spagna, Theodore: photographs by, DD *108-109*

Spain: giants in, ML 25; gold in, SA 16, 17; Inquisition in, WW 79; rituals in, MA *125, 134-135;* witch hunts in, WW 79

Spalding, Albert and Katherine: UV 90

Spallanzani, Lazzaro: SI 82

Spangler, David: EE 135-137, UV 143-144

Spanish Armada: WW 104

Spanish fly: SI 67

Sparrow, Margaret: MM 25

Spas: SI 24. *See also* Fountain of Youth; Montecatini Spa

Spaulding, William H.: and Ground Saucer Watch, Inc., computerized analysis of UFO photographs by, UP *138-140*

Spaur, Dale: sketch by, UP *115;* and UFO sighting, UP 111, 113-115

Speaking Rock: EE *43*

Spectral evidence: defined, WW 75; and Cotton Mather, WW 76

Spee, Friedrich von: and torture, WW 83; witch hunts, WW 72

Speed, Steve: and psychometry, PP *92-93*

Spells: MA 49-50; antidotes to, WW *38, 39;* and black magic, MA 92, 93, 100; defined, WW 107; and mandrake root, MA 100; and superstitions, MA 126. *See also* Incantations

Sperring, Stephen: MC 23

Sperry, Roger: MB 47, SE 119, 120, *121,* 123, 125

Sphinx: CC 85, MC 53, *58-59,* MW 53. *See also* Great Sphinx; Human-beasts

Spicer, George: MC 67

Spicer, Mrs. George: MC 67

Spider Rock: EE *43,* MW 79, TS 6, 7

Spiders: CD *42;* and fortunetellers, TS 95

Spider Woman (goddess): EE *43,* MW 79, MY 118, TS 7

Spiegel, David: SS 150

Spiess, Johann: CD 84

Spine: SA 104

Spinning black holes: *See* Rotating black holes

Spinoza, Baruch: PS 108, SE 70

Spirals: EE 55, ML 110, *111;* and Mother Goddess, EE 17; and Newgrange, EE 17; purposes of, EE 55; as symbols, SE *10, 11, 60*

Spirit: Buddhist beliefs in, PV 102; defined, PV 54; in near-death experiences, PV 7; in out-of-body experiences, PV 7; reincarnation of, PV 7, 99-102. *See also* Astral body

Spirit art: SE *109-113*

Spirit bird in vision quest: MQ *14-15;* representation on shield, MQ *16-17*

Spirit guides: *See specific spirit guides*

Spiritism: defined, SE 91

Spiritistic theory: HN *22*

117

MY The Mystical Year; PE Phantom Encounters; PH Powers of Healing; PP Psychic Powers; PS The Psychics; PV Psychic Voyages; SA Secrets of the Alchemists; SE Search for the Soul; SI Search for Immortality; SS Spirit Summonings; TN Transformations; TS Time and Space; UP The UFO Phenomenon; UV Utopian Visions; VP Visions and Prophecies; WW Witches and Witchcraft

Spirit Leaving the Body (Michals):
  PV 33-35
Spirit masters: MY 65
Spirit monsters: MY 48
Spirit photography: PP 44-47; and
  Marguerite Du Pont Lee, PP 44,
  45; and William Crookes, SS 57;
  and Mrs. Samuel Guppy, SS 54;
  of William Hope, MY 20; of John
  King, SS 60
Spirit Pond: MW 108, 109
Spirit Pond Stones: ML 128-129
Spirit possession: MW 133
Spirit Rock (Wisconsin): WW 100-
  101
Spirits: MC 61; communication
  with, PP 75-77, 78-81, 120-122;
  guardian, MW 127; and Gypsies,
  MA 100; in Hawaii, MA 86-87;
  herbs for conjuring, WW 35; and
  rituals, MA 125; and superstitions, MA 120-121; vehicles of,
  PP 42; and witches, WW 35. See
  also Ghosts; Lake monsters
Spirit trap: MA 19
Spiritual development class: MW
  108-109
Spiritual Frontiers Fellowship: PP
  96
Spiritualism: EM 84, MB 17, MW
  105-109, MY 26, PH 20, PP 16-
  17, 48, 50, 104, PS 28-29, SE 45,
  62, 90, 91; background of, PS
  27; characteristics of, HN 130,
  MM 10, PV 17-18; decline of,
  MM 22; defined, MM 57, PP 35;
  and Kate and Maggie Fox, HN
  130; ghost theories of, HN 22,
  30; history of, PV 17-19; and
  Robert James Lees, PS 27; and
  Witchcraft Acts of 1735, WW
  103. See also SS index
Spiritualists: UV 69-70
Spirituality band: MB 32-33
Spiritual Regeneration Movement:
  and Maharishi Mahesh Yogi, EM
  121, 122
Spiritual Science: EE 130

Spiritual symbols: of Oglala Sioux
  Indians, PP 78
Spiritus mundi: defined, EE 51
Splanchomancy: defined, VP 35
Splendor Solis (Anonymous): AW
  56
Splicing: AE 36
Split-brain operations: effects of,
  MB 44, 45, 47, 49; research, SE
  119-120
Spoilt Dyke, Battle of the: MW 121
Spontaneous generation: SA 90
Spook bombs: UP 27
Sports: and superstitions, MA 126-
  128, 136-137
Spotted Elk: MW 111
SPR: See Society for Psychical
  Research
SPR Cross-Correspondences: See
  Cross-Correspondences
Sprengel, Anna: AW 146, SA 127
Sprenger, Jakob: and Innocent
  VIII, WW 62-64; and witches,
  WW 62-64
Spring Equinox: See Equinoxes
Spring festivals: MY 27, 39
Sprinkle, Leo: and abductions by
  aliens, AE 25; and Christy Dennis, AE 38

Spurzheim, Johann Kaspar: as
  phrenologist, VP 72-75
Spying: and psychokinesis, MM
  75-81. See also Psi-warfare experiments in PS index
Squid, giant (Architeuthis dux): MC
  11, 19, 22-23, 45-51, MW 71, 73
Squires, Daniel: giant squid attack
  on, MC 46-51
Squirrel, mangrove fox: MW 44
Squirting whale: MC 18
SRIA: AW 67-68
Sri Aurobindo (a.k.a. Aurobindo
  Ghose): UV 135, 145-146, 147,
  148
SRI International: and Uri Geller,
  PP 117; and psychic research,
  PP 142; and remote viewing, PP
  63-67. See also PS index
Sri Lanka: self-mutilation in, MM
  107-108
Srotas: PH 65
SRS camera: AE 71-72
SS (Schutzstaffel; Security Service): MQ 127, 128, PS 64. See
  also Nazis
Staff: WW 120
Stafford, Mona: and abduction by
  aliens, AE 22, 23, 34

Stafford, Reuben John: alleged reincarnation of, PV 115
Stag: in grail legend, MQ 120
Stag (Kernbeis): MB 66-67
Stage mentalists: performances
  of, PP 103-117
Stager, Lawrence: MQ 48
Stages of Dramatic Gesture
  (Schlemmer): UV 131
Stag god: Celtic, images of, MQ
  130, 133, 135, 136-137
Stahl, George Ernst: SE 118, 119
Stalin, Joseph: CC 47, 89, CD 80,
  PS 66; and Wolf Messing, PP
  113
Stalker, Douglas: PH 118
Standerin, Abraham: UV 63
Stanford Research Institute: See
  SRI International
Stanford Sleep Research center:
  PV 42-44
Stangl, Josef: CD 91
Stanhope, R. Spencer: painting by,
  SE 45
Stanton, William: and investigations of UFOs, UP 114
Stantone, Mademoiselle: secondsight act of, PP 107, 108
Stanzas of Dzyan, The (Anonymous): AW 135, ML 28; and
  alien visitors, UP 16
Stapleton, Ruth Carter: PH 95
Star festivals: MY 59, 132
Starhawk (witch): WW 98; and
  Mother Goddess, WW 115; and
  Wicca, WW 115
Stark, Rachel: MQ 48
Starkey, George: SA 96-97
Starkweather, Charles: TN 130
Starlady (Woldman): AE 131
Star of Bethlehem: MY 86
Star of David: MA 38
Star people: characteristics of, AE

118

AE Alien Encounters; AW Ancient Wisdom and Secret Sects; CC Cosmic Connections; CD Cosmic Duality; DD Dreams and Dreaming; EE Earth
Energies; EM Eastern Mysteries; HN Hauntings; MA Magical Arts; MB The Mind and Beyond; MC Mysterious Creatures; ML Mysterious Lands and
Peoples; MM Mind over Matter; MP Mystic Places; MQ Mystic Quests; MW The Mysterious World;

SWASTIKA. Though reviled in this century as the emblem of Nazi Germany, the swastika is an age-old symbol of infinity and good fortune. The design at far left, for example, decorates an eighth-century-BC Greek pot. Swastikas depicting the daily path of the sun, the rotation of the seasons, and other mystical concepts have been found worldwide. The one at center, whose arms are formed by whirling logs symbolic of the cardinal directions, is a reproduction of a sacred sand picture from a Navaho healing ceremony. The relief at near left, believed cast in the second millennium BC, is hallowed as well: Far from symbolizing evil, it is associated with Ganesh the pathfinder, Hindu god of wisdom, prudence, and learning.

126; defined, AE 102, 126; and Brad Steiger, AE 126

Stars: mistaken for UFOs, UP 20; and Raven, TN 50-51

Stars, Temple of the: ML 46

Star trails: CC 33

State Control Institute of Medical Biological Preparations: PS 84

Statues, on Easter Island: ML 83, 84-85, 86, 87-90, 94, 95, 96

Statuettes: Etruscan, EE 26-27

Stead, W. T.: and Titanic disaster, precognition of, PP 27-32

Stecchini, Livic: and pyramids, archaeoastronomy of, MP 65

Steele, Richard: AW 61-62

Steenstrup, Johan Japetus: MC 22

Stefanska, Bogna: and dermo-optical perception, PP 143

Steiger, Brad: and aliens, AE 126; and star people, AE 126; and UFOs, AE 124

Stein, Aurel: ML 83

Steinach, Eugen: SI 60, 62

Steinach rejuvenation operations: See Vasectomies

Steiner, George: SS 131

Steiner, Rudolf: AW 143, 157, MY 115, 136, SA 130-131, SE 103; and Anthroposophical Society, EE 130, MP 30; and biodynamic farming, EE 128-129, 129-130, 131; and birds, EE 131; and Spiritual Science, EE 130; and Theosophical Society, EE 129. See also UV index

Steinschneider, Hermann: PS 60-61

Stella Matutina: AW 156

Stepanek, Pavel: PP 69

Stephanos: SA 25

Stephen (UFO and Sasquatch observer): MC 120-122

Stephens, David: and encounter with aliens, UP 129

Stern, Frances Meritt: MM 126

Sternberg, Hal: SI 129

Sternfels, Florence: PS 33-34, 35

Steuart family: and hauntings, HN 123-125

Stevens, Anne: MA 85

Stevens, E. Winchester: SE 93

Stevens, Wendelle: AE 100-101

Stevens, William Oliver: DD 139, 149

Stevens Corporation: PS 105

Stevenson, Adlai: CC 90

Stevenson, Ian: PE 36, PV 113, SE 17-18, 45, 99-100, 102, 107; and poltergeists, HN 74; and reincarnation research, PV 97-98, 103, 106-112, 118, 124, 125; and xenoglossy research, PV 119-122

Stevenson, Judy: MB 84

Stevenson, Robert Louis: DD 23, 42, 46, TN 46

Stewart, Gary: AW 72

Stigmata: CD 116, 118-119, MM 112-113, 114, 115; defined, MB 95

Stijl, de (artistic movement): UV 121, 132, 133

Stinking rose: SI 78-79

Stinson, Walter: and Mina Crandon, SS 109-110, 113, 114, 115, 116; fingerprint, alleged, SS 116

Stirland, Clive: and father's ghost, PE 64-65

Stirling, M. W.: ML 128

Stirling Castle: HN 8-9, MW 19; and ghosts, HN 8

Stirpiculture: UV 80

Stock market: MA 121; in Japan, SI 44-45, TS 111. See also PS index

Stock market crash (1929): MY 96-97; and Evangeline Adams, PS 121; and astrology, PS 120. See also Black Tuesday

Stock market crash (1987): CC 139, PS 123

Stocks (torture device): WW 82

Stöffler, Johannes: VP 41

Stoics: CC 32

Stoker, Bram: MA 64, TN 104, 109, 111, 133-134, VP 127; background of, TN 134; and Arminius Vämbery, TN 134; and vampires, TN 134

Stokes, Doris: clairaudience of, PP 133-134

Stokkseyri (Iceland): MW 32, 34

Stolas (demon): MA 96

Sto:lo Indians: MW 76-77

Stomata: defined, EE 111

Stone, Irwin: SI 75

Stone, Randolph: PH 100

Stone, Robert: ML 131

Stoneham, Charles T.: MW 66

Stonehenge: AW 20, ML 119, MP 15, 80-102, 84-85, MW 85, 90, MY 11, 55, TS 103, VP 38; Altar Stone at, MP 80; astronomical alignment of, MP 90, 91, 92, 94, 119; as astronomical observatory, EE 54, MP 68; atmospheric halos at, MP 102; Aubrey Holes at, MP 88; chronology of, MP 82; and crop circles, EE 6; as Danish construction, MP 85-86; and Druids, EE 54, MP 86, 88-89, 90, 91, 100-101; and earth energy, MP 80; enclosing of, EE 30; and leys, theory of, MP 102; origin of, MP 78-79, 80, 82, 102; purpose of, MP 81, 83; as Roman temple, MP 85; Slaughter Stone at, MP 80; summer solstice at, MP 68, 90, 100-101; as UFO representation, MP 98-99; vortices in, EE 65

Stone of Petty: VP 32

Stones: as ancient anchors, MQ 91, 92, 94; calendar, Aztec, MQ 78; near Phantom Ark, MQ 94; Holy Grail as, MQ 117; Peruvian tablets, Savoy's find of, MQ 42, 43

Stone tower: ML 130-131

Stonor, Charles: MC 70

Storey, Janet and Kenneth: SI 107

Storms: ionospheric, PS 122

Stormville Flyers: AE 57, 58-59

Storr, Anthony: MB 87-88

Storsjon, Lake: MW 53-55

Storsjoodjuret: MW 53-55

Stout, Mrs. E.: MC 38-39

Stowe, Harriet Beecher: VP 78

Strabo: ML 33

Stradivari, Antonio: violin by, SA 128

Stradlings (ghost percipients): PE 42

Strahl, Lotte von: HN 21; as exorcist, HN 20

Strait of Georgia: MW 75

Strait of Gibraltar: MP 16, 20, 36, MW map 15

Strangeness-probability chart: and UFO investigations, UP 122

Strappado: WW 69, 82, 93

Stress: of Hunzakuts, SI 47; of Japanese, SI 45; and visualization, MM 130-131; and water, SI 136

Stress hormones: SI 74

Stressors: PH 126

Strieber, Whitley: and abduction by aliens, AE 24, 120, UP 62, 143

Strigae: WW 23

Strigoi: See Vampires

Stringer family: and poltergeists, MM 46, 47

Stringfield, Leonard: AE 83

Strings: defined, TS 70

Stromberg, Russ: TS 88-89

Stronsa beast (Halsydrus pontoppidani): sighting of, MC 40-43. See also Sea serpents

Strumpell, Ludwig: DD 59

Strutt, John William: SS 54

Struys, Jans Janszoon: MQ 70-71

Stuart, Robert: MQ 75-76

Stubbe, Peter: as werewolf, TN 70, 71-73, 72, 74, 75. See also Werewolves

Stuck, Franz: painting by, CD 57

Stukeley, William: and Stonehenge, MP 88-89, 90

Stumpf, Peter: See Stubbe, Peter

Stupas: CD 98, 99, HN 127; defined, EM 41, HN 127

Sturtz, Roseanne Michele: PS 40-41

Styx, River: MW 125

Subatomic particles: MM 82, 85, SA 115; tracks of, TS 68-69

Subconscious: See Unconscious

Subjective validation: PP 103

Subjectivism: CD 127-128

Submarines: and Ian Fleming, PS 68, 69; and Madame Zodiac, PS 90; and multispectral image analyzer station, PS 84-90; sinking of, PS 68-69; and telecommunications, PS 134-135. See also Nautilus; Taurus

Subtle body: PH 72; defined, AW 138

Subud: EM 121

Subuh, Ibu: EM 121

Subuh, Muhammad: EM 121

Succubi: characteristics of, WW 47-49; defined, CD 83, 84, TN 134, WW 15-16, 94

119

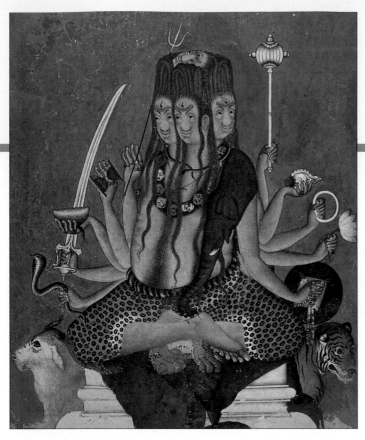

Sufis: AW *35;* dance of, CD *112-113, 114*

Suggestibility: sensitivity compared with, HN 129

Suggestion: and hypnotic regression, PV 112, 113

Sugrue, Thomas: and Edgar Cayce, PP 95

Suigyo: defined, EM 113; and Zen Buddhism, EM *112-113*

Suinn, Richard M.: MM 126

Sujith: and reincarnation, PV 96-98, 108, 110

Sukarno, Achmed: PS 76-77

Sukkoth: MY 91

Sukyo Mahikari: MW 130

Sulawesi (Indonesia): SE 21

Süleyman the Magnificent (sultan of Ottoman Empire): TN 111

Sullivan, Walter: and Condon report, UP 118

Sully, James: DD 60

Sumatra: MW 59, 60-62

Sumer: AE 89

Sumerians: AE 89-97, CC 10-14, CD 50, 55, ML 117, UV 18-20; cosmogonies of, TS 20; and fertility symbols, EE 76; and floods, EE 74; and Lilitu, WW 19; and Mother Goddess, WW 13

Summers, Diane: photograph by, EM *98-99*

Summers, Montague: TN 121-124, 127, 130, 135

Summer solstice: *See* Solstice, summer

Sumo: EM *148-149*

Su monster: MW 47, 50-*51*

Sun: CC 38, 39, *57, 70,* MA *37,* MW *119,* MY *6-7, 9, 23, 49, 56, 63, 87, 120,* SA *6-7, 23, 53, 76;* Dagger of the, ML *118-119;* Gateway of the, MW *82;* marriage of, CD *37;* Pyramid of the, ML *116;* symbol for, SA *24;* Temple of the, MW 124-125; and theory of twelfth planet, AE *90-93;* Virgins of the, ML *73. See also* Solar essence

Sunbeam (spirit): SE 92

Sun Dance: MA 78, MY 56-*57*

Sundials: TS *101,* 107

Sunflowers: EE 107

Sung dynasty: EE 36

Sun god: MY *87;* Egyptian, MQ 78

Sunlight, artificial: TS *84*

Sun line: VP 85. *See also* Palmistry; Palmists

Sunrise Ceremony: MY *82-83*

Sunscreens: SI 91. *See also* Complexion

Sun shield: MY *118*

Sun signs: CC *79-91. See also* individual zodiac signs

Sunspots: EE 66; and Arch Crawford, PS 122; and stock market,

PS 119-120, 122; and David Williams, PS 119-120

Sun Tzu: PS 73

Sun worship: in Egypt, MP *66-67*

Sunya: TS 29

Superconductivity: SE 137

Superconscious: defined, PS 109; and William Kautz, PS 109; and Masatoshi Yoshimura, PS 108, 109-110

Supereel: MW 72

Superego: defined, DD 64, 73; and Sigmund Freud, DD 64, 66, 73

Super-ESP: PE 69-72, SE 92, 108

Superior, Lake: ML 126-128

Supernatural Beings, Land of: TN 50

Supernova: SA *137*

Superotter: MW 72

Superstition Mountains: EE 52-54

Superstitions: UV 60. *See also* MA *index*

Supplementary motor area (SMA): MB 19, SE 123-124

Supply (ship): MW 42

Support groups: PH *132, 133, 134-*135; for alien abductees, AE 25, *35*

Suprachiasmatic nucleus: TS 87-88

Suprematism: AW 168-169

Suprematist Painting (Malevich): AW *168*

Suprematists: and Wassily Kandinsky, UV 131; and El Lissitzky, UV 125; and Kazimir Malevich, UV 124

Supreme Harmony, Hall of: MW 128

Supreme Self: CD 25

SURF: PS 81

Surfaces of action: defined, MM 86. *See also* Metal bending

Surgeon's Photograph: MC 71, *74,* 81, 83. *See also* Loch Ness monster; Wilson, Robert Kenneth

Surgery: etheric, PH 34; psychic, PH 36; tools of, PH *9*

Surratt, Mary: MW 27, 28-*29*

Surrealism: DD *6-9, 14-21*

Survivalists: SE 90, 107-108; defined, PE 68

Survival-of-fragments model: PE 69-72

Survival-of-personality model: PE 69-72

Survival suit: SI *111*

Surya (god): MY 125

Surya Siddhanta: CC 26

Susan B. Anthony Coven Number One: and Z Budapest, WW 108

Susila: defined, EM 121

Suspended animation: AE 28; defined, SI 97; and Benjamin Franklin, SI 97; and frozen-hibernator phenomenon, SI 107; purposes of, SI 123; and Paul Segall, SI 123. *See also* Cryonic suspension

Sussex Ghost Hunters: TS *132*

Susumna: PH 74

Sutcliffe, Peter: and Yorkshire Ripper case, PP 134, *136*

Sutphen, Dick: EE 65

Sutton, James and Rosa: PE 66-68

Sutton, Lucky: and aliens, UP 64-65

Sutton, Mary: and "swimming," WW 63

Suzuki, Teitaro (a.k.a. Daisetsu): EM *136,* 137, 139, MB 104

Svengali: MM 96

Svinka-Zielinski, Ludmila: and Wolf Messing, PP 113

Svyadoshch, Abram Moiseyevich: and hypnopedia, DD 117-118

Swami, Narasingha: EM 90

Swami Purna: SA *127*

Swamis: defined, EM 24

Swamp creatures: MC 70. *See also* Burus

Swamp gas: mistaken for UFOs, UP 108-109

Swan, John: ML 27

Swann, Ingo (psychic): PP 84, PS *23, 85,* PV 38-39; and astral travel, PP 82-83; and Berlin Wall, PS 23; and Church of Scientology, PS 84; criticism of, MM 75; experiments on, PP 85, PV 39, 44, PS 83, 85; and Iran hostage crisis, PS 91; magnetic field altering of, MM 27; and National Security Council, PS 91; and out-of-body experiences, PP 82-83, PV 36-39; and out-of-body travel, PS 85; and psychic auras, PP *86;* and psychokinesis,

SPHINX. *With a mighty lion's body and the head and intellect of a young pharaoh, this three-thousand-year-old sphinx is a symbol of earthly power and divine wisdom. The creature's wide-open, all-seeing eyes connote its otherworldly ken.*

MM 73-75, *76-77*, PP 83; and Harold Puthoff, PS 85; and remote viewing, PP 83, *85*, 142, PS 85; and SCANATE, PS 81, 82; and SRI International, PP 142, PS 85; and Russell Targ, PS 85; and *Taurus*, PS 83; temperature altering of, MM 27, 75, *76-77*; and John Wilhelm, PS 84

Swan on a Black Sea: SE 102-107

Swans: EM 119

Swanson, Erik: MW 29

Swastika: MA *39*, MY 110

Sweat bath (purification rite): MQ *8-9*, MY 117

Sweat house: PH *41*

Sweating: SI 114

Sweden: witch hunts in, WW 79

Swedenborg, Emanuel (mystic): CD 126-*127*, EM 72-73, MA 60, MY *129*, PH 27, SE 62, UV *34*,

VP 22; clairvoyance of, PP *8-9*; and Andrew Jackson Davis, SS 27; and spiritualism, SS 26, *27*; and Wilson Van Dusen, SS 152; visions of, SS 152

Sweet potatoes: EE 105

Swensen, Clifford: MA 137

Swetland, David: SS 148

Swieten, Gerard van: TN 121; and vampires, TN 121

Swift, Geraldine: SE 6-12, 15

Swift, Jonathan: CC 88, 101, 109, SI 26, VP 67

Swifte, Edmund Lenthal: PE 109

Swimmers: ML *36*, SI *76-77*, 114-*115*

"Swimming" (trial by water): and Matthew Hopkins, WW 78-79; and Mary Sutton, WW *63*; and witches, WW *62-63*, 78-79

Swinhoe, Imogen: PE 110-111,

112

Swinside Circle (England): legend of, MP *74-75*

Swithin, Saint: MY 61

Switzerland: witch trials in, WW 56

Swords: VP 130, *142-143*, WW *120*. *See also* Tarot

Swords, Michael: AE 102, 106; and aliens, AE 116-120

Sycomancy: defined, VP 35

Sylvester (pope): and clocks, TS 109

Sylvester II (pope): CC 55

Symbionese Liberation Army: symbol of, MB *98-99*

Symbolization: defined, MB 67

Symbols: and talismans, MA *38-39*

Symmes, John Cleves: and hollow earth theory, MP 142-144

Symmes's Hole: MP 143-144

Sympathetic action: SA 92

Sympathetic hunting magic: and Cro-Magnons, TN 26-27

Sympathetic magic: MY 120. *See also* Imitative magic

"Sympathetic powders": defined, SA 14

Synapses: SE 123

Synchro-Energizer: MB *48*

Synchronicity: CC 131; defined, TS 121, VP 9, 122; and Carl Jung, TS 121-122; and Wolfgang Pauli, TS 122. *See also* Jung, Carl Gustav

Synesthesia: AW 163; characteristics of, MB 7; defined, MB 52, 56

Synge, Richard L. M.: MC 61

Syphilis: SA 65

Szentágothai, János: MB 18-19

Szilard, Leo: VP 28

121

MY *The Mystical Year; PE Phantom Encounters; PH Powers of Healing; PP Psychic Powers; PS The Psychics; PV Psychic Voyages; SA Secrets of the Alchemists; SE Search for the Soul; SI Search for Immortality; SS Spirit Summonings; TN Transformations; TS Time and Space; UP The UFO Phenomenon; UV Utopian Visions; VP Visions and Prophecies; WW Witches and Witchcraft*

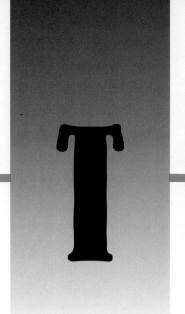

T

Tables: levitation of, MM *13, 15, 20, 25, 88-89. See also* Levitation

Tablet: Babylonian, TS *114*

Table turning: SS *19;* of Mina Crandon, SS 108, 109; defined, SS 22; and Michael Faraday, SS 33; of Leah Fox Fish, SS 32; of Kathleen Goligher, SS 104; hoaxes in, SS *125;* of Daniel Dunglas Home, SS 37, 38, 39, *44-45,* 50; of William Marriott, SS *125;* of Eusapia Palladino, SS 59-60, *62,* 63

Tablet Without Inscription: MW 94

Tabuariki (giant): ML 97

Ta Chiu: MY 121

Tachycardia: defined, MM 124

Tachyonic antitelephone: TS 70

Tachyons: TS 70

Tacitus, Publius Cornelius: and Druids, AW 19, MP 88

Tadzhikistan (former Soviet Union): MW 59

Tagore, Rabindranath: MQ 19

T'ai chi ch'uan: EM *147,* PH *52-53,* SI *42,* TS *34-35*

T'ai chi master: TS *34-35*

Tai Shan: MW 93-94, *95*

Taj Mahal: EM *34-35;* and Peter D. Ouspensky, EM 85

Takemikazuchi (god): EM 148

Taki'is of Bolivia: and ley theory, MP 98

Takt-i-Suleiman (temple; Iran): MW 99, 102-104; ruins, MQ *114;* tray depicting, MQ *115*

Takt-i-Taqdis: MW 102

Taliesin East: UV *104*

Talismans: MA 35, 82, VP *48;* and Cabala, MA 35, 39; consecration of, MA 41; creation of, MA *35,* 40-41; and Gypsies, MA 101; and Hebrew alphabet, MA 39, 41; and letters, MA *38;* and numbers, MA *41;* and planets, MA *35, 36-37,* 40, 41; pouches for, MA 35, *40-41;* purification of, MA 41; and symbols, MA *38-39;* Taoist, SI *38;* and voodoo, MA 82; and words, MA *38, 39. See also* Amulets; Charms

Talking boards: *See* Rongorongo boards

Tall Cedars of Lebanon: AW 109

Talmud: and dreams, DD 23

Tamar of Hang: MC *70*

Tambora: eruption of, EE 68

Tammen, Ann and Harry: MW 30

Tammuz (god): CC 14; and Horned God, WW 16-17; and Mother Goddess, WW 16-17

Tanabata Star Festival: MY 59

Tanah Lot: EM *62-63*

Tana Toraja: funerals, SE 33, *38-41*

Tancia, Mount: MW 91

Tane-mahuta (god): CD 24

Tangata manus: ML *88-89*

Tanka (Buddhist religious art): MQ *24,* PV *133*

Tanous, Alex (psychic): TS *115;* body double of, PV 40-41; experiments on, PV 41; out-of-body experiences of, PV 40-41; and retrocognition, PP 99

Tan Tan (aphasiac): MB 45

Tantra: AW 138-139, CD 35; artworks of, AW *139;* and chakras, CD 69; and enlightenment, CD 69, 70; and mysticism, CD 114; and sex, CD *66,* 69-70, 114; and Shakti, CD 69; and Shiva, CD 69; and yantra, CD 11

Tantric Buddhism: and dances, EM *103. See also* Buddhists and Buddhism; Tibetan Buddhism

Tantric yoga: EM 131. *See also* Yoga

Tantrism: SI 39; and chakras, MA 64; and Aleister Crowley, MA 65; and sex, MA 64

Tantrists: UV *29;* defined, MA 64

Tanzania: MW 65, 67-68

Tao: SE 131, SI 34; and change, TS 29-32; defined, TS 27-29; and *I Ching,* TS 32; and Laozi, TS 29

T'ao Ch'ien: UV 11

Taoists and Taoism: DD 35, MB 25, MW 93, PH 45-46, 63; and alchemists, SI 34; and alchemy, EM 52-53; background of, EM 51; and Buddhism, EM 53, 55; characteristics of, EM 51-52; and ching, SI 39; and cinnabar, SI 34; and coitus reservatus, SI 39; and Confucianism, EM 53; and death, CD 12; and elixirs, SI 34; and gold, SI 34; and immortality, EM 52-53, SI 34, 36, 39; and magic, EM 52; and mysticism, CD 114; and peach banquets, SI 36; and qi, CD 35; and sex, CD 114, EM 52, SI *39;* talisman of, SI *38;* and Tao, SI 34; and *Tao Te Ching,* EM 51, 52; and xian, EM 52, SI 34

Tao of Physics, The (Capra): MB 25

Taos Indians: EE 46

Tao-te ching (Laozi): MB 25; and t'ai chi ch'uan, EM 147; and Taoism, EM 51, 52

T'ao Yuan-Ming: MY 84

Tapas: defined, EM 37

"Tape recording": and Thomas Lethbridge, TS 129, 130

Tapir: MC 114

Taraka mantra: defined, TS 93

Tarasque: MY *65*

Targ, Russell: MM *28;* and Church of Scientology, PS 84; and CIA, PS 81; and clairvoyance, MM 29-30, PS 80, 81; criticism of, MM 35; and Delphi Associates, PS 83, 113, 116; and ELF waves, PS 86; and ESP, PP 136-140, PS 81, 83, 89, 113; and Keith Harary, PS 113-115; and precognition, PS 83; and remote viewing, PP 63-67, 142-144; and SRI International, PS 81, 83, 94; and stock market, PS 113, 115, 116-117; and Ingo Swann, PS 85; and *Taurus,* PS 83; telepathy research of, MM 29-30

Tari Pennu (goddess): MY 73

Tarot: MA 27; and Cabala, VP 27, 137; cards, CC *62,* MY *21,* VP *124, 125,* 130-149; of the Cat People, VP *138-139;* characteristics of, VP 104-105; Cups, VP 130, *140-141;* and executive ESP, PS 115; Golden Dawn Tarot, VP *136-137;* history of, VP 123-129; layouts of, VP 123, *146-149;* learning to use, VP 7, 110; Major Arcana, VP 123, 124, 125, 127, 129, 130, *132-133;* Minor Arcana, VP 123, 125, 130; Mythic Tarot, VP *140-141;* Pentacles, VP 130; *140-145;* Renaissance, VP *132-133;* research, VP 129; Rider-Waite, VP *142-143, 146-149;* significator, VP 123; and Anita Smith, PS *114-115;*

AE Alien Encounters; AW Ancient Wisdom and Secret Sects; CC Cosmic Connections; CD Cosmic Duality; DD Dreams and Dreaming; EE Earth Energies; EM Eastern Mysteries; HN Hauntings; MA Magical Arts; MB The Mind and Beyond; MC Mysterious Creatures; ML Mysterious Lands and Peoples; MM Mind over Matter; MP Mystic Places; MQ Mystic Quests; MW The Mysterious World;

TORTOISE. Although tortoises are emblems of immortality and perseverance, the one below also symbolizes nonviolent stalemate: The advantages and constraints of the tortoise's armor mean that neither it nor the snake can harm the other.

and stock market, PS 115, 116, 117; suits of, VP *138-145;* Swords, VP 130, *142-143;* techniques of, VP 122-123; Thoth, VP *144-145;* use of, PP 96-97, 98, 100-101; Wands, VP 130, *138-139;* of the Witches, VP *134-135. See also* Tarot readers

Tarot readers: Alliette, VP 125-127; Aleister Crowley, VP *126,* 129; Fredrick Davies, VP 146-149; Carl Jung, VP 140; Éliphas Lévi, VP 127, 129. *See also* Tarot

Tarrytown Group: and Rupert Sheldrake, EE 127-128

Tarshish: ML 119, 136

Tart, Charles T.: and out-of-body-experience research, PV 16, 35-36

Tartini, Giuseppi: DD *45,* 46

Tarxlen, Hal: temple of, SE *10*

Tashi Lama: EM 83

Tasmania: MW 59, 65

Tasseography: VP 42-45; defined, VP 42; techniques, VP 43

Tassili n'Ajjer: MW 99-100

Taste, sense of: MB 55

Tatin, Liseron: UV *54, 55*

Tatin, Robert: art by, UV *54-55*

Tattoos: EE *55,* EM *31,* MA 129, MW 127

Tatzelwurm: MW 53

Tau Ceti (star system): AE 88

Taulbee, William: bloodstains of, HN *107*

Taurus (submarine): PP 124, PS 82-83. *See also* Submarines

Taurus (zodiac sign): CC 32, *81,* 139, MY 31, 38, 55

Tausend, Franz: SA *121;* and alchemy, SA 117-119, 121; and Erich Ludendorff, SA 117

Taut, Bruno: architecture by, UV *126*

Taut, Max: architecture by, UV *127*

Tau-tau: SE *33,* 39

Tayloe, John: HN 112

Taylor, Billy Ray: and encounter with aliens, UP 64-65

Taylor, Daniel B.: AW 86

Taylor, Granger: house of, AE *33*

Taylor, John: MM *29;* and Great Pyramid, MP 57-58

Taylor, Leila S.: UV 69

Taylor, Lemesurier: and ghosts, HN 123, 124, 128

Taylor, Philip: AE 106

Tchaikovsky, Peter Ilyich: MB 89

Tchambuli: CD 62

Te Aba-n-Anti: ML 96-97

Tea-leaf reading: *See* Tasseography

Technical remote viewing: PS 90. *See also* Extrasensory perception; Remote viewing

Tectonic plates: ML 29

Tectonic strain theory: AE *map* 107; and abductions by aliens, AE 107-110; defined, AE 106-107

Teed, Cyrus Read (pseud. Koresh): MW 105; and concave earth theory, MP 147-148, *149*

Tefenet (goddess): TS 20

Tegesta: Ponce de León's travels to, MQ 39

Tegoma, Emilio: MQ *96;* dig aided by, MQ *96-97*

Teh: defined, MC 104

Tehuelche Indians: MW 50, 51

Teilhard de Chardin, Pierre: UV 138-139, 142

Te i-matang: defined, ML 97

Tek-'ic (shaman): MA *67*

Telecommunications: PS *134-135*

Telekinesis: PS 78; defined, ML 28

Telekinetoscope: MM *18-19,* 20

Telemark (Norway): MW 34

Telepathic dreams: *See* Dreams; Psychic dreams; DD *index*

Telepathic projection: PP 111, 113

Telepathy: MB 22, PE 24, 31, 88, 89; and Edgar Cayce, PP 95; and Church of Scientology, PS 84; and Mary Craig, PP 20-21; and

Douglas Dean, PS 106; defined, DD 147, MM 57, PP 16, PS 25, 27; demonstration of, PP *12-13,* 35, 36; and William Denton, PS 30; description of, PP 7; Einstein's opinion of, PP *26;* and electromagnetic radiation, PP 140; of Uri Geller, MM 29; and Lieutenant Jones, PS 70-71; and Bernard Kazhinsky, PS 79; and Adam J. Linzmayer, PP 52; and John Mihalasky, PS 106; military applications of, PP 141-144; and Frederic W. H. Myers, PS 27; and Eduard Naumov, PS 79; and *Nautilus,* PS 70-71; out-of-body experiences compared to, PV 19, 42; and Hubert E. Pearce, Jr., PP 53; and Valery G. Petukhov, PS 84; and physical laws, PP 70; and psychometry, PS 30; Harold

123

MY The Mystical Year; PE Phantom Encounters; PH Powers of Healing; PP Psychic Powers; PS The Psychics; PV Psychic Voyages; SA Secrets of the Alchemists; SE Search for the Soul; SI Search for Immortality; SS Spirit Summonings; TN Transformations; TS Time and Space; UP The UFO Phenomenon; UV Utopian Visions; VP Visions and Prophecies; WW Witches and Witchcraft

TREE OF LIFE. *An age-old symbol of the cosmos, the tree of life is said to pass through the center of the world and bloom in realms such as this one, an Aztec paradise presided over by a rain god. The tree's fruit are said to confer immortality.*

Puthoff's research on, MM 29-30; and Smith, PS 70; and Soviet Union, PS 78, 79; Russell Targ's research on, MM 29-30; tests of, PP 24-25, 28-29, 54-55; and T. O. Tulley, PS 113; and Leonid Vasiliev, PS 78; and Zener cards, PP *51-52*, 53. *See also* Dream-telepathy research; Intuition

Teleportation: MM *84-85*, TS 134; defined, MM 85

Telepresence: *See* Virtual reality

Telescope: CC *100-101*, SA 34; and Galileo Galilei, TS 51-53

Telfair, Alexander: as exorcist, HN 92; and hauntings, HN 92; levitation of, HN 92

Tellem tribe: ML 76

Telluric currents: defined, EE 38, 39; and ley lines, EE 38; and San Francisco Peaks, EE 39

Tellus (goddess): EE 26, MY 29, 129

Telsen-Sao: courses taught at, MB *118-119*; defined, MB 118; and Jeshahr the Guide, MB 118, 120; and Nirvan, MB 118; and out-of-body experiences, MB 118, *120-121*

Temay, Ulu (shaman): and Huichol Indians, PP 80-81

Temne: CD 65

Temperature altering: of Ingo Swann, MM 27, 75, *76-77*

Temperature inversions: and ghost ships, HN 75; as possible explanation for UFOs, UP 53, *55*

Tempestarii: and Agobard, WW 40-41; defined, WW 40. *See also* Witches

Templars: HN 12, MQ 118, 122, MY 21. *See also* Knights Templars

Templeisen (fictional knights): MQ 118

Temple of Bacchus: MW 125

Temple of Confucius: MW *93*

Temple of Peace: UV 90, *91, 92-93*

Temple of Set: CD 96

Temple of Solomon: MW 133, MY 21

Temple of the Rosy Cross: AW *52*

Temple of the Stars: ML *46*

Temple of the Sun: MW 124-125

Temples: EM *18-19*

Temporal cortex: MB 59-60

Temporal-lobe epilepsy: *See* Epilepsy

Temptation of Saint Anthony, The (Grünewald): MB *91*

Temura: MA 55

Ten: in dice, VP 111

Ten Commandments: MY 39; ark holding, MQ 46-48, *46-47*; Moses and, MQ 45, 48

Tendai school: EM 57. *See also* Tendai Shugendo

Tendai Shugendo: EM 58. *See also* Marathon monks; Tendai school

Tengyur (Tibetan holy book): MQ 23, *26*

Tenhaeff, Willem: and Gerard Croiset, PP 127-129, 130

Tenjin: MY 64

Tennant, Anne: as witch, WW 80

Tennant, Edward Wyndham: SS *90-91*

Tennant, Henry: SE 102-104, 106, 107

Tennyson, Alfred: MB 93, MM 118, MW 87; Theosophical beliefs of, PV 103

Tenochtitlán: MW 113, 115

Tension in Red (Kandinsky): AW *163*

Teonanactl: EE 101

Teotihuacán (Mexico): MW 79; design of, EE 33

Teotihuacán serpent god: ML *104*

T. E. (past-life therapy patient): and hypnotic regression, PV 119-122; and reincarnation, PV 119-122; xenoglossy of, PV 119-122

Tepes, Vlad: *See* Dracula

Teratorns: MW 50. *See also* Thunderbird

Terauchi, Kenju: and Japan Air Lines UFO sighting, UP *123*

Teresa of Ávila, Saint: CD 115, *117*, MY 25; and levitation, MM 116-117

Terminalia: MY 135

Terminus (god): MY 135

Terrace, Herb: MB 42

Terra Mater (goddess): EE 26

Terra repromissionis sanctorum: ML 122

Terriss, William: ghost of, HN 31

Tertiary period: ML 21

Tertullian: CD 58

Tesla, Nikola: and alternating-current generator, MB *57*; and eidetic memory, MB 53, 56; and trances, MB 53

Testosterone: CD 68, 69, MB 54, SI 62

Tet: MY 128

Teteoinnan (goddess): SE 21

Teton Indians: and amulets, MA *107*; song of, DD 30

Tetrabiblos (Ptolemy): CC 36, MW 133

Tetractys: defined, TS 44, VP 106-107

Tetragrammaton: MA 62; defined, MA 55; pronunciation of, MA 55-59

Tetrahydrocannabinol (THC): SI 104

Tetrodotoxin poisoning: MA 88

Teudt, Wilhelm: MW 90; and ley theory, MP 98

Teutonic tribes: WW 25

Tewnion, Alexander: MW 16

Texas: giants in, ML 25, *26*

Thackeray, William: MB 89

Thailand: Buddhism in, EM *108-109*; monks in, EM *108-109*; superstitions in, MA *129*

Thalamus: MB 60

Thales of Miletus: CC 21, SA 20

Thalestris (queen of Amazons): CD 64

Thatcher, David: UV 152

Theaters: and ghosts, HN *31*

AE *Alien Encounters;* **AW** *Ancient Wisdom and Secret Sects;* **CC** *Cosmic Connections;* **CD** *Cosmic Duality;* **DD** *Dreams and Dreaming;* **EE** *Earth Energies;* **EM** *Eastern Mysteries;* **HN** *Hauntings;* **MA** *Magical Arts;* **MB** *The Mind and Beyond;* **MC** *Mysterious Creatures;* **ML** *Mysterious Lands and Peoples;* **MM** *Mind over Matter;* **MP** *Mystic Places;* **MQ** *Mystic Quests;* **MW** *The Mysterious World;*

Theatre Royal: PE 119-*121;* and ghosts, HN 31

Thebes (Greece): MW 53

Thelema: defined, MA 65

Themis (goddess): VP 10

Theobald (possessed person): CD 88-90

Theophany: of Betty Andreasson, AE 30-32, *31;* defined, AE 27

Theophilus (priest): and Satan, WW 45-46, *47*

Theory of relativity: *See* Relativity theory

Theos, Lady: and *Handbook for Chaplains,* WW 99

Theosophical Society: AW 12, 157-160, 162, 164, 166, EE 129, MQ 19, 27, MY 84, SE 45, 103, 105; in America, AW 141; and Annie Wood Besant, EM 86, 87; and Helena Petrovna Blavatsky, EM 84, 85; branches of, AW 141, 143, 155-156; characteristics of, EM 85; and Alexandra David-Néel, EM 84; emblem of, AW *130;* Esoteric Section of, AW 137, 140; founding of, AW 125, 126, PV 20, 22, 103; growth of, EM 88; headquarters of, AW *136-137;* and Hermetic Order of the Golden Dawn, AW 146; and Jiddu Krishnamurti, EM 87-88, 119, 120; and Henry Steel Olcott, EM 85; and Peter D. Ouspensky, EM 85; purposes of, AW 125-126, EM 84, 88; revival of, AW 141; and Alfred Percy Sinnett, EM 89; and Tantra, AW 139; and Katherine Tingley, EM 88. *See also specific members*

Theosophic Order of Service: AW 141

Theosophists and Theosophy: CC 116, 130, SE 45, 103, 104; astral body beliefs of, PV 21; and avatars, UV 115; background of, PV 22, 103; and Helena Petrovna Blavatsky, UV 87, 115; Hugh G. Calloway's beliefs in, PV 25; defined, PV 20, UV 87; Thomas A. Edison's beliefs in, PV 103; and karma, PV 103; and levitation, PV 21; and Piet Mondrian, UV 132; Henry Steel Olcott's beliefs

in, PV 20, 22; purposes of, PV 20; reincarnation beliefs of, PV 22, 103; Alfred Tennyson's beliefs in, PV 103; and werewolves, TN 89; William Butler Yeats's beliefs in, PV 103

Thera: MW 85; and Atlantis legend, MP *34;* and Minoan civilization, MP 35

Therapeutic touch: PH 107

Thermal noise theory: CD 118

Thermistors: MM *76-77;* defined, HN 133

Thermodynamics: SA 94; second law of, TS 59

Thermography: PH 76, *77*

Theseus: MC *56,* SE 10

Thesmophoria: MY 94

Theta waves: DD 97, 98, MB 90; characteristics of, MM *82-83,* 108, 109; and fire walking, MM 105; and self-mutilation, MM 109. *See also* Sleep

Thévet, André: MW 50; sketch by, MW *51*

Thigpen, Corbett: MB 79

Third eye: PP 7. *See also* Pineal gland

Third mind: PP 24

Thirteen: in dice, VP 111; in numerology, VP 108

Thirteenth Annual Spacecraft Convention: UP *112*

Thirty Years' War: WW 91

Thom, Alexander: and megalithic monuments, MP 94; and Stonehenge, MP 94

Thomas (earl of Arundel and Surrey): SI 14

Thomas, Cyrus: and earthen mounds of North America, MP 123

Thomas, Elaine: AE *22;* and abduction by aliens, AE 22, 23, 34; death of, AE 22; hypnotic regression of, AE 22; illnesses of, AE 22; physical examination of, AE 22

Thomas, Saint: MW *6-7*

Thomas Aquinas, Saint: CC 62, CD 130, DD 107, SE 50, SS 18, TN 88; and alchemy, SA 33; and Aristotle, SA 31; and Albertus Magnus, SA 31, 32, 33; and Montpellier, University of, SA 31; and philosophers' stone, SA 32; and robot, SA 32

Thomas of Celano: CD 116

Thompson, Frederick: SE 90-92, 93; obsession of, PP 43, 93; painting by, SE *93,* sketch by, PP *43*

Thomson, John: photograph by, EM *8-9*

Thopaga: *See* Milarepa

Thor (god): MA 28, MY 64, VP 125; hammer, MA 30; and oaks, EE 80, 92; rites honoring, WW 43

Thoreau, Henry David: EM 71, UV *80,* 84; and Bronson Alcott, UV 82; and transcendentalists, UV 81

Thorel, Felix: and poltergeists, MM 37, 38

Thorir (berserker): TN 36

Thorne, Kip S.: AE 116; and wormholes, TS 75

Thornton Road residents: and poltergeists, MM *52-53,* 54

Thoth (god): CC *31,* MA 52, *53,* 61, SA *22,* VP 125; and Hermes, SA 20; and Hermes Trismegistus, SA 19-20, 23

Thoth Tarot: VP *144-145. See also* Tarot; Tarot readers

Thought forms: AW 144, *145*

Thoughtography: criticism of, MM 68; defined, MM 68; of Masuaki

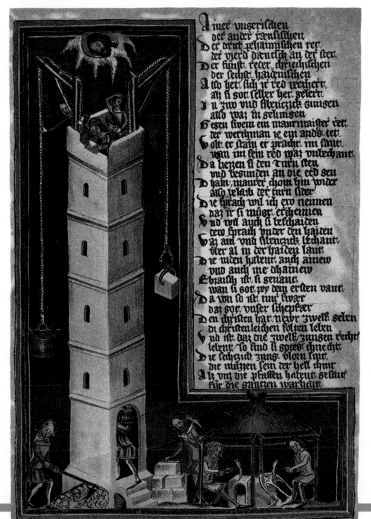

Kiyota, MM 68; of Ted Serios, MM *68-69. See also* Micro-PK

Thought transference: PP 24, 108; and Douglas Blackburn and G. A. Smith, PP 26-27; and stage mentalists, PP 104-109

Thouless, Robert H.: psychokinesis research of, MM 63-64

Thrasyllus: CC 34

Thread crosses: defined, HN 127

Three: in dice, VP 110, 111; in dominoes, VP 112, 113; in numerology, VP 100, 106, 108, 109-114

Three Faces of Eve, The (Thigpen and Cleckley): MB 77, 79

Threefold law: and Wicca, WW 114

Three Mile Island: TS *86-87;* and biological rhythms, TS 86, 87

Three-Pound Universe, The (Hooper and Teresi): MB 77

Threshing: SI *50*

Thugs: AW 40, *41;* decline of, AW 44-45; initiation of, AW 40; killings by, AW *41, 42-43;* rehabilitated, AW *44-45*

Thumb: VP *55. See also* Palmistry; Palmists

Thumbscrews: WW *92*

Thumo reskiang: and Alexandra David-Néel, EM 81-83; defined, EM 81

Thun, Maria: charts by, EE *130, 131*

Thunderbird: MW 47, 50

Thunderstorms: EE 69-70

Thurston, Herbert: CD 118-119; and exorcism, HN 137

Thury, Marc: telekinesis research of, MM 11

Thurzo, György: and Elizabeth Báthory, TN 125

Thutmose I (pharaoh): MW 100

Thutmose III (pharaoh): MW 100

Thutmose IV (king of Egypt): and

Great Sphinx, MP 57

Tiahuanaco: MW 79, *82,* 83-85

Tiamat (goddess): AE *93,* CD 24, 55, WW 13; background of, AE 92; and Marduk, WW 15. *See also* Mother Goddess

Tiberius (emperor of Rome): CC 34, MW 104

Tiber River: MY *37,* 70

Tibet: Buddhism in, EM 41, PV 120, *126-137;* death beliefs in, PV 58, 136; gods of, PV *126, 135;* lamas in, EM *31, 82-83;* masks in, EM *79;* monks in, EM *80-82, 102-103,* MA 18; oracles in, EM *51;* priests in, TN *42;* reincarnation beliefs in, PV 120; spirit trap in, MA 19. *See also* Book of the Dead

Tibetan Buddhism: PV 120, *126-137;* death beliefs of, PV 127, 135, 136; growth of, EM 133, 134; and Padmasambhava, EM

133; practitioners, CD 80; and reincarnation, PV 108, 120, 127; religious art in, PV *129, 133;* and Chogyam Trungpa Rinpoche, EM 133. *See also* Buddists and Buddhism; Shambhala; Tantric Buddhism

Tibetan healing: PH 62, 63. *See also* Eastern healing

Tibetans: as fortunetellers, TS 95

Tidworth: MW 19

Tiepolo, Giovanni Battista: paintings by, MB 95, MP 18

Tigers: ML *10-11, 105;* Chinese, SI 67; as sacred animals, EE *113,* 114, 115. *See also* Animals

Tiger Swami: EM 118

Tighe, Hamilton: PE *29*

Tighe, Virginia: MY *102,* PV *116, 117;* and previous incarnation as Bridey Murphy, PV 114-118

Tigris River: CD 55

Tihus: MA *46-47. See also* Dolls

TAROT. Ancestors of modern playing cards, tarot cards like the High Priestess and High Priest at left were suppressed by the Church for their supposed pagan symbolism. They are held to have special powers, used in divining the future.

Tilea, Virgil: CC 136
Tiles: marble, Egyptian, MQ *102*
Tilhaire, Pierre la: TN 86
Tillighast, Wallace E.: flying machine of, UP 25
Timaeus (Plato): MP 15, SE 46
Time: *See* TS *index*
Time clock: TS *110*
Time cylinders: TS *76-77*
Time dilation: TS 56, 57, 88-91
Time slips: TS 112-114, 126-128
Time-space anomalies: and UFOs, TS 134
Time travel: and Albert Einstein, TS 120; impossibility of, AE 119-120; and relativity theory, TS 71, 73; and rotating black holes, TS *72-73, 77*; and Michael Swords, AE 118-119, 120; and time cylinders, TS *76-77,* and Frank Tipler, TS 77; and wormholes, TS *74-75*
Time warp flight: and Bermuda Triangle, MP *44-45*
Time-zone system: TS *map* 110
Tincl, Father: and poltergeists, MM *37-38*
Tingley, Katherine (a.k.a. Purple Mother): EM *88-89*. *See also* UV *index*
Tintagel Castle: ML 49-51
Tipler, Frank: TS 77
Tippu Sahib: DD *40*
Tirio Indians: and transformations, TN 34
Tishman, John: PS 126
Tissa (feral child): TN *66-67*
Tisserand, Robert B.: PH 112
Titan: and *Titanic,* resemblance to, PP 28, *chart* 30
Titanic (ocean liner): CC 152, DD *132-133,* 139, MA 101, MY *29,* PP *30-31;* disaster premonitions of, PP 27-32; and *Titan,* resemblance to, PP 28, *chart* 30
Titans (gods): CD 24, EE 22, ML 25, TN 34
Tithonus: SI 26
Titian: VP 67
Titicaca, Lake: MW 79, TS 6, 12-*13;* and Incas, TS 13
Titmus, Bob: MC 119
Tituba: as witch, WW 74, 76
Titus (Roman emperor): CC 34

Titus, Nellie: DD 140-141
Tiv people: and time, TS 100
Tlacaxipeualiztli: MY 74
Tlaloc (god): MW 115
Tlalocan (heaven): TS 36
Tlatecme: MW 115-*116,* 117
Tlingit Indians: MA 74, MW 113, PH 9; culture of, TN 6; masks of, TN *16, 17;* and Raven, TN 49, *50-51;* reincarnation beliefs of, PV 108-109; shamans of, TN 16, 18, 19
TM: *See* Meditation; Transcendental meditation
Toads: SA *48, 51,* WW 12, *14,* 55, *60*
Tobacco: MB 116
Toboongkoos: EE 91
Toby, the Sapient Pig: PP 110
Tokyo (Japan): MW 34, 127
Toland, Reginald: and Exeter UFO sighting, UP 99, 102
Tolkien, J. R. R.: WW 122
Tolstoy, Count Nikolay: MQ *130;* at Hart Fell, MQ *134,* 135; on Merlin's Celtic associations, MQ 131, 136, 137; at Moat of Liddel, MQ *132-133*
Toltec: ML 115-116
Tombaugh, Clyde: CC 47
Tombazi, N. A.: MC 103
Tombstone (Arizona): MW 47, 50
Tombstone, Flamel's: SA *44*
Tomczyk, Stanislawa: MM *14;* hypnosis of, MM 17-18; levitation of, MM *14,* 17, 18; marriage of, MM 18-19
Tompkins, Peter: EE 108
Tondal (knight): AE *48*
Tondok Bombo: SE 39
Tonga: arch on, ML 97, *98;* giants on, ML 102
Tonna, Angel Maria: AE 61
Tontlewicz, Jimmy: and diving reflex, SI 101; hypothermia of, SI 101, *107*
Tonton Macoute: CD 86
Topazes: MA 101
Topilsky, Mikhail: MW 59-60
Topo (dog): AE 61
Top of the Tunnel (Osnato): AE *132-133*
Toraja people: EM 95
Tori-No-Ichi: MY *103*

Torno, Guy de: ghost of, HN 137
Toronto Society for Psychical Research: and levitation of table, MM *25*
Torque, Irish: MQ *136*
Torres, Maria: EM 134-135
Torres, Osel Hito: EM *135;* background of, EM 134, *135*
Torres, Penny: *See* Rubin, Penny Torres
Torrey, Edwin Fuller: MB 73
Torricelli, Evangelista: VP 41
Torricelli Mountains: CD 61
Tortoises: SA *108;* as sacred animals, EE *113,* 114, 115. *See also* Animals
Torture: SA *56, 58;* and Aristotle, WW 82; and Aristophanes, WW 82; of Clara Geissler, WW 72; of Johannes Junius, WW 92, *93-94;* of Margaret, WW 72; prices of, WW *66,* 72; and Friedrich von Spee, WW 83; tools of, WW *82-87, 84, 85, 86-87;* of witches, WW 70-72, 74-75, 82, 84, 87
Toscraec (magician): MA 45
Totem poles: of the Haida, TN *6-7;* of the Tsimshian, TN *8*
Totems: bears, TN *8;* bullheads, TN *9;* and clans, TN 8, 30; defined, TN 6, 30; octopuses, TN *14;* ravens, TN *9;* wolves, TN *8*
Toth, Max: and pyramids, MP 67
Toth, Robert: PS 84
Touch: and psychic healing, PS *95-103;* sense of, MB 54
Tourette's syndrome: CD 90, MB 90
Tournefort, Joseph Pitton de: and botany, EE 102-103
Tournouër, André: MW 51-53
Tours, Moreau de: MB 87
Toušek, Milan: PS *13*
Tower of Babel: ML 34, UV *20-21*
Tower of London: MW 19, MY 59, PE *102-103,* VP 40
Town crier: EE *31*
Towns, Captain: PE 50-52
Townshend, Roger: MW 21
Toynbee, Arnold: SI 23, UV 139, WW 115
Tozzi, Joseph: MM 44-46
Traces: defined, AE 75; types of, AE 75, 76, *77-79. See also* UFOs

Tradition, Wiccan: defined, WW 107
Traditionals: defined, WW 107-108
Tragicall History of Doctor Faustus, The (Marlowe): CD 84
Train, bullet: TS *98-99*
Trance healing: PH 10-*11, 12-13. See also individual trance healers*
Trances: as anesthesia, MB 103-104; and Catherine of Siena, MB *95;* of Edgar Cayce, VP 22; of channelers, SS 7; characteristics of, MB 93, 99; of Mina Crandon, SS 109; of Andrew Jackson Davis, SS 27, VP 22; and daydreaming, MB 103; and drugs, MB 93; effects of, MB 94; and Greeks, MB 93; and Joseph L. Greenstein, MB 96; and Patricia Hearst, MB 98-99; and Hindus, MB 96, *97;* inducing of, MB 93, 94, 97; of J. Z. Knight, SS 141; and magnets, MB 93; and mass wedding, MB *99;* and meditation, MB 103; and monks, MB *96-97;* and Sun Myung Moon, MB 99; and mystics, MB 93; and Nicholas II, MB 98; and oracles, MB 93; of Leonora Piper, SS 83, 86; and Bhagwan Shree Rajneesh, MB 99; and Grigory Rasputin, MB 98; and relaxation, MB 96; of Jane Roberts, SS 134, 136; and sadhus, MB *97;* and snake-handling ceremony, MB *94;* and Alfred Tennyson, MB 93; and Nikola Tesla, MB 53; and visualization, MB 96; of *völva,* WW 29; and voodoo, MB *94-95;* and yoga, MB *96-97*
Trance-state consciousness: defined, MB 77
Transataumancy: defined, VP 35
Transcendentalism: defined, SE 61
Transcendentalists: UV 57, 77, 81-84
Transcendental Meditation (TM): MB 122, PH 73, SI 23; Herbert Benson's research on, MM 119; characteristics of, EM 121, MM 120; criticism of, MM 122; effects of, EM 122, 124; and electrode caps, EM *124;* and "field of Being," EM 122; and levita-

TRIAD. Groups of three often convey mystical import. In this triad from the Cabala, the old Jewish mystical system, a triangle denotes the eyes and forehead of God, while the letter within is one of three "mother" letters of the Hebrew alphabet.

tion, EM 121, 122, MM 117-118; and mantras, EM 122; and Silva Mind Control, MM 120; uses of, MM 119; and Maharishi Mahesh Yogi, EM 121, 122. *See also* Meditation

Transformation ritual: of werewolves, TN 95-*103, 96-97, 98-99, 100-101, 102-103*

Transformations: of Diana, WW 12, 23; of Freya, WW 28; of witches, WW 9, 30, *43. See also* TN *index*

Transits: SS 54

Transkei (South Africa): MW 133

Transliminal mind: defined, MB 90

Transmigration: EM 37, MB 126, SE 32, 46; defined, PV 99, 120, SE 45. *See also* Reincarnation

Transmutation: *See* Gold; Projection; SA *index*

Transplants: of hair, SI *93;* of hearts, SI *83;* rejection of, SI 82

Transsexualism: CD 63-65. *See also* Gender

Trans Time: and American Cryonics Society, SI 116; and Arthur Quaife, SI 116, *118,* 119; and Paul Segall, SI 119, 122, 123

Transylvania: vampires in, TN 111-112, *119*

Travers, John Christopher: PP 98-99

Treadmill: MB *132*

Treasure of Priam (jeweled cache): MQ *36*

Treaty Oak: EE *98-99*

Treaty of Laramie: MW 79

Tree, Herbert Beerbohm: MA *112*

Tree of Bliss: UV 6

Tree of knowledge: CD *27,* EE 95

Tree of life: AW *28-29,* CD *25,* SA *50;* in Eden, EE 95, SI 13

Tree of Light (Cohoon): UV *71*

Tree of the Soul: EE *96*

Trees: MY *115;* magic, SI 13. *See also* World trees; *specific trees;* EE *index*

Treffert, Darold: MB 62

Tremaine, Kit: SS *147*

Trent, Mr. and Mrs. Paul: and UFO sighting, UP 47-48, *138-139*

Trepanning: MB *74*

Tressler, Marty: PS 116-117

Tres Zapotes (Mexico): archaeological excavation at, MQ *96-97*

Trevellyan family crest: MW *86, 87*

Trevilian: MW 86, 87

Trevortsent (character in *Parzifal*): MQ 117

Trew, Steve: PS 26

Triads: AE *120*

Trial by water: *See* "Swimming"

Trial of George Jacobs, The (Matteson): WW *74-75*

Trials: of Elizabeth Báthory, TN 126; of Victor Bertrand, TN 126; of Pierre Burgot, TN 83; of Hans Grans, TN 130; of Fritz Haarmann, TN 127, 130; for heresy, WW 50; of Michel Verdun, TN 83; of werewolves, TN 82, 83, 86. *See also* Witch trials

Triamates: legends as basis for Cyclops myth, MQ 53

Triangle: MA *38*

Triangle wave: MW 93

Tria prima: defined, SA 64, 93; and Paracelsus, SA 64

Trick-or-treating: MY 97

Tricksters: TN 42, 49, *50-51, 54-55. See also* Transformations

Trigrams: VP *118, 120-121. See also* I Ching

Tringale, Steven: and ghosts, HN 104; and poltergeists, HN 104

Trinity, Christian: VP 106

Triple Blessing: MY 41

Triplicities: CC 122

Triskaidekaphobia: defined, VP 108. *See also* Numerologists; Numerology

Tristan: ML 49, MW 87

Triton (god): CC *46*

Trobriand Islanders: MA 128

Trois Frères Cave: painting in, TN 27

Trojan Horse: MP *18,* MQ 49

Troland, L. T.: and psychic research, PP 48

Trophonious oracle: EE 54

Troposphere: defined, EE 62; and weather, EE 62-63

Trotsky, Leon: MQ 83

Troxell, Charlie and Romer: PE 63, 64

Troy (ancient city): ruins of, discovery of, MP *18-19,* MQ *36-37,*
40, 49

Trudenhaus: WW *90;* floor plan of, WW *91;* and Johann Georg II, WW 91

True-Light Supra-Religious Organization: MW 130

True (magazine): and UFO investigations, UP 46

Truffaut, François: AE 120

Trulli: MA *115,* MW 119

Truman, Harry S: PH 55

Trumbull, John: painting by, AW *78*

Trumpet séances: MW 106

Trumps Major: *See* Major Arcana

Truro (Massachusetts): MW 45, 47, 49

Truzzi, Marcello: SS 131

Tryptophan: SI 80

Tsampa: MY *108-109*

Tsantsa: MW 119

Tschirtner, Oswald: art by, MB *66-67*

Tse bit'a'i: EE *42*

Tséghahodzání: EE *49*

T7001: PS 131. *See also* RNGs

Tsiam: MY 120

Tsimshian Indians: culture of, TN 6; shamans of, TN 10; totem poles of, TN *8*

Tsinghai (China): MW 93

Tsiolkovsky, Konstantin: VP 28

Tsubos: PH 55

Tsunamis: defined, EE 74

Tuareg: MA *8*

Tuberculosis: SA 116

Tug-of-war: MY 98

Tujunga Canyon: abductions by aliens in, AE 121

Tulayev (shaman): PH *8*

Tulku: defined, PV 120

Tulku, Sidkeong: EM *76*

Tulley, T. O.: PS 113

Tulli, Professor: and alien visitors in Egypt, UP 16

Tulpa: defined, MB 85, PE 98

Tumey, David: MB 126

Tummo: defined, EM 50

Tumuli: defined, ML 96

Tuna Club: MC 33

Tunguska explosion: UP 23-25, *24*

Tunis (Tunisia): MW 133

Tunnels: natural, on Sesola Island, Greece, MQ *58;* and near-
death experience, PV 57, 67, *68, 74, 77,* 80, 86; Vietcong, PS 77-78

Tupinamba: CD 64

Turgenev, Ivan: SS 39

Turing, Alan: MB 128

Turing test: MB 128

Turkey: Antioch Chalice, discovery of, MQ 106; Hissarlik site, finds at, MQ *36-37. See also* Noah's Ark *in* MQ *index*

Turks: defeat of, ML 63

Turner, Mrs.: and hauntings, HN 34, 35

Turner, Dorothy: MB 70

Turner, Rick: AW 10

Turquoise: MA 101

Turtles: TS *82-83;* painted, SI 107

Turturro, Angelo: SI 105

Turvey, V. N.: and *Titanic* disaster, premonition of, PP 29

Tuskegee Institute: EE 105

Tutankhamen (pharaoh): MY *26-27;* tomb of, CD *12,* MP *64,* MY 27

Tu'u ko Iho (king of Easter Island): ML 96

Twain, Mark: *See* Clemens, Samuel

Tweedie, George R.: lectures of, PE *28-29*

Twelfth Night: MY 123

Twelve: in dice, VP 111; in numerology, VP 108

Twilight Man: TS *31*

Twins: CD *30,* 109, MY *38;* identical, SI *84,* 88

Twitchell, Karl: MQ 41-42

Two: in dice, VP 111; in dominoes, VP 112, 113; in numerology, VP 100, 108, 109

Tyagi, Sobha Ram: alleged reincarnation of, PV 110

Tyi Wara: MY *32*

Tylor, Edward: SE 21

Typhon: and Zeus, WW 15

Tyr (god): MA 29

Tyromancy: defined, VP 35

Tyron, Thomas: EE 104

Tyrrell, G. N. M.: PE 31-32, 90-91, 95; and hauntings, HN 86, 87, 88

Tzolkin: defined, TS 34

Tzuchinoko: MW 59, *61-62*

AE Alien Encounters; AW Ancient Wisdom and Secret Sects; CC Cosmic Connections; CD Cosmic Duality; DD Dreams and Dreaming; EE Earth Energies; EM Eastern Mysteries; HN Hauntings; MA Magical Arts; MB The Mind and Beyond; MC Mysterious Creatures; ML Mysterious Lands and Peoples; MM Mind over Matter; MP Mystic Places; MQ Mystic Quests; MW The Mysterious World;

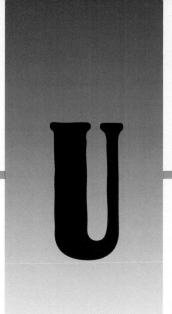

U

Uffington White Horse (England): MP 126, 127, *136*, MY 87

UFO abductions: *See* Abduction by aliens

UFO Attack (Robbins and Ostrow): AE *130-131*

UFO channelers: AE 124, 126

UFO Crash at Roswell (Schmitt and Randle): AE 81

UFO Experience, The (Hynek): UP 121

UFOs: MB *110-111*, MW *40-43*, *map 42-43*, 94, MY 18, 27, 34, 40, 56, 57, *58*, 66, 70, 71, 83, *86-87*, 92, 93, 97, 101, 102, 115, 124, 135, TS 136-*137*; aircraft mistaken for, UP 141; characteristics of, *82*, 86, 99, 102, 106, 114, *123*, *TS* 134-137; and Connie Cook, MB 90; and crop circles, EE 20; and electromagnetic energy theory, MC 122-123; and Charles Hoy Fort, TS 134; ground lights mistaken for, UP 51; and hallucinations, theory, MC 122-123; and ley theory, MP *108-109*; at megalithic monuments, MP 98; natural phenomena mistaken for, UP *18, 20, 21*; pseudo, UP 16, *42, 45, 89, 95, 97, 118, 130, 131*; sightings, MC 120-123, UP 121-122, 125; at Stonehenge, MP 99, 102; and time-space anomalies, TS 134; undersea civilization theory of, UP 131; in Upton Scudamore (England), EE 10. *See also* Abduction by aliens; Crash retrievals; Physical examinations; Traces; AE *index*

"UFO Show, The": AE *127-137*

Ujjain (India): SI 16

Ukobach (demon): MA 94, *98*

Ulf (berserker): transformations of, TN 36-37

Ullman, Montague: DD *146*; and archetypes, DD 79; and dreams, DD 76-77, 79, 119, 153, PP 66, 74; and precognitive dreams, DD 138-139; and telepathic dreams, DD 145-149; and vigilance theory, DD 145

Ulster Tape Recording Society: MW 24-25

Ultrasonography: PH 49

Uluru: MW 93, 95-96, *97*

Ulysses (Greek hero): voyage of, MQ *49-61*. *See also* Odysseus

Umbanda: PH *22-23*

Umberto I (king of Italy): TS *125*

Unarius Foundation: MY 93, UP 78-79

Uncertainty principle: SE 134, TS 66, 68

Uncle Tom's Cabin (Stowe): VP 78

Unconscious: DD 19, 73; and cerebellum, MB 41; defined, MB 39; and Sigmund Freud, MB 20, TN 31; infantile, DD 29; and Carl Jung, MB 20, TN 31; and lycanthropy, TN 31. *See also* Collective unconscious

Underground railroad: and ghosts, HN 111

Underhill, Leah Fox Fish: *See* Fish, Leah Fox

Undernutrition: *See* Diet; SI *index*

Ung Khan: ML 66

Unicorns: CD 14, *15*, EM *26*, MW *10-11*

Unidentified flying objects: *See* UFOs

Unification Church: MB 99

Unihipilis: MA 84, 85

Union of Soviet Socialist Republics: *See* Soviet Union

Uniped: EM *26*; defined, EM 27

Unitarians: CD 127

United Kingdom: MW *maps 18, 34-35*; crop circles in, AE 75; and psi-warfare experiments, PS *68-69*

United Society of Believers in Christ's Second Appearing: *See* Shakers

United States: AE *map 107*, MA 8, 9, 130, 134-135; biodynamic farming in, EE 130; seal of, MY *55*; and witches, WW 73-77, 98, 125-126

U.S. Air Force: and crash retrievals, AE 79, 81, 82-85; and UFOs, AE 78, 88, UP 38, 87, *88-97*; and UFO secrecy, UP 70. *See also* Project Blue Book; Project Grudge; Project Sign

U.S. Navy: PS 84-90

U.S. Nuclear Regulatory Commission: AE 57

United States Psychotronics Association (USPA): MM 80

Universal Doctor: *See* Albertus Magnus

Universal pool of consciousness: and dowsing, PP 138

University of Montpellier: SA 31, 33

University of North Carolina: EE 111

University of Ottawa: EE 111

University of Wyoming: DD 149

"Unknown, The" (television program): HN 128

Unknown Soldier of World War I: ghost of, HN 107

Unmasked Universe, The (Magritte): DD *16*

Unmoved Mover: SE 50

Unpreparedness: dreams of, DD *128-129*

Untouchables: EM 85

Uoke (god): ML 82

Upanishads: CD 24-25, 49, PV 99, SE 124; defined, EM 37

Up-Helly-Aa: MY *129*

Upper World: EM 63

Upton Scudamore (England): crop circles in, EE 10

Ur (ancient city): excavation of, MQ 64, *75*; seers in, VP 9

Urania (goddess): SA *27*

Uranium: PS 130

Urantia Foundation: AE 126

Uranus (god): CC *45*, CD 24, EE 22

Uranus (planet): AE *90-93*, CC 45, 139, 142, *151*, MY 119, 127

Urartu (ancient kingdom)· MQ 67, *map 67*

Urban II (pope): MQ 111

Urban IV (pope): SA 34

Urban VIII (pope): CC 104

Uribe, Melanie: PS 37, 38

Uriel: *See* Norman, Ruth

Uriel (archangel): CD *132*

Urinalysis: SA 66

Uromancy: defined, VP 35

Ur-plant: EE 105

Urquhart Castle: MC *64-65*, 66, 85, PS *88*

Ursa Major (constellation): MY 123

Ussher, James: MY 35, 96, 99

Uther Pendragon: ML 48

Utnapishtim (character in Gilgamesh epic): AE 97, ML 34, MQ 31-32

Utopia: defined, UV 17

Utopia (More): UV 16, *18-19*, 39-40, 42

Utskalar church (Iceland): SE 99

Uttarakuru: SI 13

Utzig, Harry: MW 76

Uvani (spirit guide): HN 116, 117-118, MY 22; and Eileen Garrett, PP 87

MY The Mystical Year; PE Phantom Encounters; PH Powers of Healing; PP Psychic Powers; PS The Psychics; PV Psychic Voyages; SA Secrets of the Alchemists; SE Search for the Soul; SI Search for Immortality; SS Spirit Summonings; TN Transformations; TS Time and Space; UP The UFO Phenomenon; UV Utopian Visions; VP Visions and Prophecies; WW Witches and Witchcraft

V

Vaccinations: MA 136

Vacuum fluctuations: TS 67

Vaidya: PH 63, *68*

Vajravarahi (goddess): EM 78

Valdivia (Chile): potters of, ML 116-117

Valentich, Frederick: AE 32

Valentine, Basil: SA 45; and Albert Riedel, SA 133-134

Valentine, C. S.: TN 60-62, *61*; and Sanichar, TN 60-61

Valentine, Saint: MY 133

Valentine cards: MY *133*

Valentinus, Basilius: EE 19-22

Valhalla: CD 124-126. *See also* Afterlife

Valhalla (British yacht): MC 32

Valiente, Doreen: WW 105-107, 126

Valkyries: WW 27

Vallee, Jacques: and abduction by aliens, AE 112-114; and deaths caused by aliens, AE 41, 42; and Ann Druffel, AE 123-124; and Carl Jung, AE 120; and parallel universe, AE 120, 121; and UFOs, AE 120-121, 123-124, UP 131-132

Valley of the Kings: MY 27

Valli, Eric: photograph by, EM *98-99*

Vämbery, Arminius: and Bram Stoker, TN 134

Vamp: Theda Bara as, TN *135*

Vampire, The (Summers): TN 122

Vampire bats: TN *128-129*; revenants compared with, TN 129. *See also* Bats

Vampire in Europe, The (Summers): TN 122

Vampire Night: MY 81

Vampire of Paris: *See* Bertrand, Victor

Vampire Research Center: TN 136

AE Alien Encounters; AW Ancient Wisdom and Secret Sects; CC Cosmic Connections; CD Cosmic Duality; DD Dreams and Dreaming; EE Earth Energies; EM Eastern Mysteries; HN Hauntings; MA Magical Arts; MB The Mind and Beyond; MC Mysterious Creatures; ML Mysterious Lands and Peoples; MM Mind over Matter; MP Mystic Places; MQ Mystic Quests; MW The Mysterious World;

VULTURE. *This ancient Egyptian bas-relief depicts the vulture goddess Mut. All vultures were believed to be female and to be impregnated by the wind, thus symbolizing both pristine motherhood and the means of rebirth for the dead.*

Vampires: AE *46,* MY *104-105,* SI *78-79;* victims of, AE *43, 46. See also* Lycanthropy; TN *index*

Vampire Studies Society: TN 136

Vampires Unearthed (Riccardo): TN 136

Vampyre, The (Polidori): MY 30, TN 132, 133

Van Buren, Martin: VP 75

Van Buuren, Clarence: PS 36-37, 39

Vance, Mary Lee: SI 73

Vancho, Eileen Jeanette: *See* Garrett, Eileen

Vancouver Island: MW 113

Vancouver Island monster: MC 38. *See also* Caddy; Sea serpents

Vandenberg, Hoyt S.: and Montgomery UFO sighting, UP 42

Vanderbilt, Cornelius: MY 40, PS 111

Van der Post, Laurens: DD 26

Van de Wetering, Janwillem: EM 95-97

Van Herwaarden (settler): MW 60-61

Vanir: characteristics of, WW 28

Vanishing Brief Case: MA 7

Van Steenburgh, Sally: DD 147

Van Tassel, George: SS 150; and Integratron, UP 78

Van Winkle, Rip: AE 114, SI 99

Varanasi (India): TS *92-93;* and Shiva, TS 93

Vardøgr: PE 100. *See also* Doubles

Varend (Sweden): MW 53, 55

Varieties of Religious Experience, The (James): MB 102

Varley, Cromwell F.: DD 150

Varney the Vampire: TN 133; illustrations from, TN *132, 133*

Vasectomies: and Eugen Steinach, SI 60, 62; of William Butler Yeats, SI 60, 62

Vases, Greek, depictions on: Aeson and Medea, MQ *35;* Ulysses and Sirens, MQ *59*

Vasiliev, Leonid L.: PS 78; death of, MM 26; psi research of, MM 23; and telepathy, PP *140-141*

Vasquez, Julio: and poltergeists, MM *49-51*

Vata: PH 65, 66, 67

Vaudreuil, Comte de: MY 68; and

retrocognition, HN *44,* 50

Vaughan, Alan: PS *14,* VP 25

Vaughan, Frances E.: PS 107

Vaughan, Joan: as witch, WW 61

Vecelli, Tiziano: *See* Titian

Veda: CD 24-25, EM 117, PH 63, TS 23; and Hinduism, EM 29; and sacrifices, EM 33; and soma, EM 33

Vedanta: CD 36

Vedanta Societies: and Hinduism, EM 117-118

Vedanta Society of Southern California: EM 117

Vegetalistas: MB *108-111*

Vegetarianism: PH 60

Vehicle Internal Systems Investigative Team (VISIT): AE 64

Velikovsky, Immanuel: ML 34

Vellutini, John: and vampires, TN 136

Venetsianov, Alexie: painting by, VP *128*

Vennum, Lurancy: SE 93-*95*

Venus (goddess): CC 40, MY 31, 88

Venus (planet): AE *90-93,* 114, CC 24, 25, 36, 40, 60-61, 117, MA *37,* MY 31, 88; background of, AE 92; symbol for, SA *24;* and time, TS *102*

Venus figurines: WW *16;* purposes of, WW 11-13

Venus line: VP 85. *See also* Palmistry; Palmists

Venus of Willendorf: EE 24, WW 16. *See also* Fertility symbols

Venus's-flytrap: EE 105-107, MC *134-135*

Veracruz (Mexico): MW 113, 115, 117

Verdun, Michel: and Pierre Burgot, TN 82, 83; crimes of, TN 83; as werewolf, TN 83

Vereticus (king of Wales): as werewolf, TN 78

Veridical apparitions: HN 30, 34, PE 89, 97

VERITAC: MM 70

Vernagallo, Ludovico: MW 36-37

Vernal equinox: *See* Equinoxes

Verne, Jules: CC 90, VP 27-28; airship stories of, UP 19; and Atlantis, MP 21; and hollow earth

theory, MP 146, 147

Verrall, Helen: SS 95; automatic writing of, SS 92, 97; and Frederic W. H. Myers, SS 94

Verrall, Margaret: SS 95; automatic writing of, SS 92, 97; and Frederic W. H. Myers, SS 94, 96

Verrill, A. E.: MC 24-25

Versailles: HN *40-41,* MW 34, MY 68, PE 122; and retrocognition, HN *42-49. See also* Hameau; Petit Trianon

Vertebrates: defined, SI 103

Vervain: WW 36

Vervet monkeys: CD 109

Vesakh: MY 41

Vesalius, Andreas: PH 20

Vespasian (Roman emperor): CC 34, PH 85

Vesta (goddess): EE 67, MY 18, 37, 52

Vestalia: MY 52

Vestal virgins: MY *18,* 37, 115

Vestricius, Spurinna: VP 35

Vesuvius, Mount: EE 67-68

Vevers: defined, MA *82;* and voodoo, MA 82, 83, *86*

Viatorum (Maier): AW 58

Vibhuti: defined, EM 24

Vibrograph: HN *122*

Vicitasara, Bhandana: MB 53

Vicki (split-brain subject): SE 120

Victor (feral child): TN *59;* and Jean-Marc Gaspard Itard, TN 59-60; and Richard Pillard, TN 68

Victoria (queen of England): AW 44, 45, CC 113, MA 101, PS 27, SS 22, 23

Victoria (ship): TS 84-85

Videodisk: AE 108, *109*

Videoplace: MB 130

Vienna (Austria): DD *64-65;* plans for morgue in, PE 92-93

Vietcong tunnels: PS 77-78

Vigilance theory: DD 145

Viking (spacecraft): AE 114

Vikings: MW 85, MY *129;* and America, discovery of, ML 17, 114, 117, 120-121, 122, 123; artifacts of, ML 124-131, 133-134, TN *36-37;* and sacrifices, TS 37

Vilcabamba (Ecuador): ML 73; characteristics of, SI 39-41; longevity in, SI 39, 41, 43

Vilenkin, Alexander: TS 67

Villa, Paul: and alleged UFO photographs, UP *89, 140*

Villas Boas, Antonio: and abduction by aliens, AE 21, 34, UP *84, 85,* 86

Villiers, George: PE *29*

Vimanas: ML 32-33

Vinalia: MY 100

Vinland: ML 124-126

Vinland Map: ML 130

Vinogradova, Alla: psychokinesis of, MM 27

Violet: sorcerer's, WW *34*

Violin: SA *128*

Vipassana: defined, EM 95; and Ron Ormond, EM 92-95

Viperfish (submarine): MC 76-77

Viper waters: SI 34. *See also* Snakes

Viracocha (god): ML 137, MW 82, 83, 113

Virgil: CD 99, MW 85, 90, SE 60, 72, *74-75, 78-85,* UV 23, 33

Virgin Mary: MW 85, 91, MY 36, 40, 84, 93, *117,* 128, 130, *132;* and angels, CD 122; appearances of, CD *119-122, 123;* and Bogomils, CD 32; and fertility, CD 59; and fig trees, EE 77; and Mother Goddess, CD 58, 59; veneration of, EE 76

Virgin of Guadalupe: CD *119*

Virgins of the Sun: ML 73

Virgo (zodiac sign): CC 24, 85, 139, MY 70-*71*

Virtual Programming Languages, Inc.: MB 130

Virtual reality: MB 129-137

Virtual transitions: defined, TS 118-120

Virtues: CD *131*

Vischer, Carl: PH 120

Visconti-Sforzas, Tarot of: VP *125*

Vise: WW *83;* leg, WW *92*

Vishnu (god): AE *44,* CC 26, CD 80, DD *28,* EM 124, ML 70, MY 30, *36,* 52, 67, 72, *91,* PV *98-99,* SI *16,* TS 23, *24,* 25, VP 106; and Asvattha, EE 93; and banyans, EE 82

Vision quest: DD 30-31, MQ *6-17,* PH 11

Visions: EE 105; and William

MY The Mystical Year; PE Phantom Encounters; PH Powers of Healing; PP Psychic Powers; PS The Psychics; PV Psychic Voyages; SA Secrets of the Alchemists; SE Search for the Soul; SI Search for Immortality; SS Spirit Summonings; TN Transformations; TS Time and Space; UP The UFO Phenomenon; UV Utopian Visions; VP Visions and Prophecies; WW Witches and Witchcraft

Blake, MB 102; and John Dee, SA 59; of Elisha, PS 73; of Ezekiel, AE 111-112, 123, MW 40, UP 12-14, 15; and Nicholas Flamel, SA 46; and Francis of Assisi, CD 116; hallucinations as, MB 71; and Rebecca Jackson, UV 68; and John, UV 23, 24-25; of Karl Ernst Krafft, PS 63; and Ann Lee, UV 56, 63, 64, 69, 71; and Ramon Llull, SA 33; and Albertus Magnus, SA 33; of Leonora Piper, SS 82; of Shawn Robbins, PS 127-128; and Shakers, UV 71; and shamans, MA 66; and Sitting Bull, MA 78, 80; and Rudolf Steiner, UV 109, 111-112; and Emanuel Swedenborg, SS 152, UV 34; and Teresa of Ávila, CD 117; and Katherine Tingley, UV 88; and Zoroaster, CD 26

VISIT: AE 64

Visual agnosia: defined, MB 50

Visualization: PH 116-117, 138-139, PS 46; and athletes, MB 125, MM 126, 132-133; and cancer, MB 96, 125, MM 136-137; creative, MM 126; defined, MB 123; and Shakti Gawain, MB 123; and Ben Hogan, MB 125; by Billie Jean King, MM 126; by Evel Knievel, MM 124, 126; in kung fu, MM 128-129; and pain treatment, MM 134-135; and Graham Potentializer, MB 48; purposes of, MB 96, 125; and stress, MM 130-131; and trances, MB 96; uses of, MM 126, 127-137

Visual-spatial skills: CD 65-66

Vitalism: SE 118; defined, MB 19

Vitamin C: SI 75

Vitamin E: SI 75

Vivarium, and Betty Andreasson: AE 30, 36

Vivation: PH 128-129

Vivekenanda, Swami (a.k.a. Narendranath Datta): EM 114-118, 116, 135-136

Vivienne (witch): MC 37

Vlad II (prince of Walachia): TN 104

Vlad III (prince of Walachia): See Dracula

AE Alien Encounters; **AW** Ancient Wisdom and Secret Sects; **CC** Cosmic Connections; **CD** Cosmic Duality; **DD** Dreams and Dreaming; **EE** Earth Energies; **EM** Eastern Mysteries; **HN** Hauntings; **MA** Magical Arts; **MB** The Mind and Beyond; **MC** Mysterious Creatures; **ML** Mysterious Lands and Peoples; **MM** Mind over Matter; **MP** Mystic Places; **MQ** Mystic Quests; **MW** The Mysterious World;

VAMPIRE. In books, plays, and works like the engraving below, the vampire has been a popular horror figure since the 1800s. But the creature symbolizes an older, almost universal fear that the dead will seek to regain life by drinking human blood.

Vlad Tepes: *See* Dracula
Vlad the Impaler: *See* Dracula
Vocabularium (Paracelsus): AW 53
Vogel, Marcel: AE 104
Voice of Silence, The (Blavatsky): AW 137
Volcanoes: DD *134*, EE 67-69
Volckman, William: SS 55
Vollrath, Hugo: CC 130, *134*
Voltaire: AW 64, 80, 90, MA 113-114, MW 34, PE 113, SA 100-101
Völva: characteristics of, WW 28-29; defined, WW 28; trances of, WW 29
Von Däniken, Erich: AE 99-101; and ancient-astronaut theory, UP *13*, ML 32, 97; and Ezekiel's wheel, UP 14; and Great Pyramid, MP 113; and Kiribati Islands, ML 97; and Maya, ML 32; and Nazca lines of Peru, MP 113-116; and nuclear holocaust, ML 33
Vonnegut, Kurt: CC 87
Von Werlhof, Jay: and geoglyphics of North America, MP 121
Voodoo: CD 86, *91*, MB *94-95*, MW 113, 133, MY 61, PH 23, *24-25, 26;* talisman of, MW *113. See also* High magic; Low magic; MA *index*
Voodoo chemist: MA *89*
Voodoo death: defined, MA 11
Vorilhon, Claude: AE *124-125*
Voronezh (former Soviet Union): MW 43
Voronoff, Serge: and gland grafting, SI *61, 62*
Vortices: EE 65, MW 79, 83
Vortigern (king of Britain): Merlin with, MQ *130-131*
Votive mask: EE *94*
Vox Stellarum (Moore): CC 112
Voyager (space probes): MY 70
Voyager 1 (spacecraft): AE 108
Voyager 2 (spacecraft): AE 108, TS 58, 69
Vrykolkas: See Vampires
Vulcan (god): CC 40, EE 67
Vulva: CD *67. See also* Womb envy
Vyas, Anand Shankar: CC *137*

133

MY The Mystical Year; PE Phantom Encounters; PH Powers of Healing; PP Psychic Powers; PS The Psychics; PV Psychic Voyages; SA Secrets of the Alchemists; SE Search for the Soul; SI Search for Immortality; SS Spirit Summonings; TN Transformations; TS Time and Space; UP The UFO Phenomenon; UV Utopian Visions; VP Visions and Prophecies; WW Witches and Witchcraft

WHEEL. *Like this 13th-century Thai example, wheels have meaning beyond that of mere circles. Because they rotate, they symbolize dynamic subjects: the sun in its daily passage, for instance, or the cycle of life, death, and rebirth.*

W, Mr.: as werewolf, TN 91

Wachter, Helen: AE 83

Waddell, L. A.: MC 100

Waddell, Leila: AW 117, *118*

Wadley, J. K.: PS 128-130

Wafts: *See* Doubles

Wagner, Cosima: DD *44*

Wagner, Richard: DD *44;* and hypnagogic state, DD 46, 117

Wahlgren, Erik: ML 129

Wainwright, John Ralph: alleged reincarnation of, PV *90-95. See also* Monica

Waite, Arthur Edward: AW 148, 152, 156, VP 127-129; Tarot cards by, VP 129, *142-143, 146-149*

Wakes Sunday: MY 85

Waldegrave, Henry: HN 68

Walden (Thoreau): UV 82

Waldensians: AW 28; and Inquisition, WW 58; and Satan, WW *59*

Waldo, Peter: WW 58

Wales: castle, MQ *112;* legends, MQ 109; poetry, Merlin portrayed in, MQ 133, 136, 137; witch hunts in, WW 80

Walford, Roy L.: SI *81, 108;* and biofeedback, SI 104, 109; and drugs, SI 109; and hypothermia, SI 103-105, 109; and immortality, SI 12, 46; and longevity, SI 46, 103-105, 109; and meditation, SI 109; and tetrahydrocannabinol, SI 104; and undernutrition, SI 46, 80-81, 103, 105, 109; and yogis, SI 104-105

Walker, Evan Harris: CD 118, TS 120

Walker, G. A.: PE 93

Walker, Jearl: fire-walking research of, MM 105-106

Walker, Kenneth: UV 98-101

Walking hypothermia: SI 102. *See*

AE Alien Encounters; AW Ancient Wisdom and Secret Sects; CC Cosmic Connections; CD Cosmic Duality; DD Dreams and Dreaming; EE Earth Energies; EM Eastern Mysteries; HN Hauntings; MA Magical Arts; MB The Mind and Beyond; MC Mysterious Creatures; ML Mysterious Lands and Peoples; MM Mind over Matter; MP Mystic Places; MQ Mystic Quests; MW The Mysterious World;

WITCH. *As an enduring symbol of men's fear of the power of women, the idea of witches perhaps sprang from lore of ancient goddesses who could create and destroy. Over time, they came to represent invulnerability and the power to cast spells.*

also Hypothermia *in* SI *index*

Walla, August: and outsider art, MB *65*

Wallace, Alfred Russel: MB 17, 21, ML 29, SE 118, *119*, SS 53-54; and materialism, MB 14; and mind, MB 14, 17, 21; and séances, MB 17; and spiritualism, MB 17; and theory of evolution, MB 13, 14, MP 26

Wallace, Henry A.: MQ 18, *20;* religious views, MQ 18-19; and Nikolay Konstantinovich Roerich, MQ 19-20, 22

Wallace, Wilbur: MC 119

Wallenberg, Raoul: CD 128

Wallenstein, Albrecht von: CC 98

Wallerstein, Susan: CC 7

Wall Street and Witchcraft (Gunther): PS 111, 113, 116-118

Walnut brain: defined, TN 91

Walpole, Dorothy: MW 21, *23*

Walpole, Horace: AW 64, SA 100; and poltergeists, HN 63; and séances, HN 64

Walpurga, Saint: MY 32

Walpurgis Night: MY 32, *33*

Walters, Edward: and aliens, AE 66, 67-68, 70; and Mutual UFO Network, AE 70, 71; photographs by, AE 66, 68, *69*, 70, 71-72, 73-74; UFOs, AE 66-67, 68, 71, 72; videotape by, AE 68, 73

Walton, George: and poltergeists, HN 58

Walton, Travis: AE *23;* and aliens, AE 8-9, 23-24, UP 129, 141

Wambach, Helen: and past-life therapy, PV 112

Wanamaker, John: CC 83

Wandering ecstatic: PH 10-11

Wandjina: ML *38-39*

Wands: VP 130, *138-139. See also* Magic wands; Tarot; Tarot readers

Wang, Robert: Tarot cards by, VP *136-137*

Wang Pi: VP 117

Warcollier, René: and psychic research, PP 49

Ward, Michael: MC 103

Waring, Jane Lee: UV *78*

Warkworth Castle: MW *19*

Warner, William: *See* Hamon, Count Louis le Warner de

War of the Roses: PE 105

War of the Worlds (film): and alien visitors, UP 28, *30-31*

War of the Worlds, The (Wells): MY 97

Warren, Joseph: AW 74, 76, *78;* burial of, AW *79;* monument honoring, AW *79*

Warren, Mary: and witches, WW 76

Warrior-monks: PS 94

Warriors: CD *12*, 49, 55; Pictish, ML *50*

Warsaw (Poland): MW 53, PS *66-67*

Washington, Booker T.: EE 105

Washington, D.C.: HN *map* 105; design of, EE 33; and hauntings, HN *105-113;* and UFO sightings, UP 53, 55

Washington, George: AW 73, *82-83*, 105, 106, EE 100, PH 59, UV *53;* Masonic apron of, AW *81*

Washington Monument: AW *106-107*

Washoe (chimpanzee): MB 42

Wassailing: MY *126*

Wassilko-Serecki, Zo: MM 40-41

Wasson, R. G.: EE 102

Waste Land: in grail legends, MQ 110; *Parzifal,* MQ 112, 114, 117

Watchers: CD 132, 133. *See also* Angels

Watchmen: defined, TN 7

Water: background of, SI 131; in Baden-Baden (Germany), SI 131-*137;* cults of, SI 131; as dream symbol, DD *35;* and Greeks, SI 131; gushes of, SI *28, 29;* and Hunzakuts, SI *53;* and Japanese, SI 131; and Romans, SI 131; and stress, SI 136

Water bath: SA 24

Water Bearer: MY *127*

Water buffalo: MY 131

Water bulls: MC 61. *See also* Lake monsters

Water clocks: TS *107*, 109

Water hand: VP *54, 62. See also* Palmistry; Palmists

Water horses: MC 61. *See also* Lake monsters

Waterhouse, Agnes: WW 58

Water kelpies: MC 61. *See also* Lake monsters

Water lily: WW *33*

Waters of life: MQ 32-34, 39-40

Water-tiger: MW 47, 51-53

Water torture: WW 85

Water trial: *See* "Swimming"

Water witching: MA 135

Watkins, Alfred: EE *37;* and ley lines, EE 36, 38, MP 94, 98, TS 129

Watkins, Graham: PE 128; and out-of-body-experience research, PV 42

Watkins, Leslie: CD 90-91

Wat Po: MW 127, 128-129, PH *67*

Watseka Wonder: SE 93-95

Watson, John: and behaviorist psychology, PP 49

Watson, Lyall: EE 125

Watton Abbey: and ghosts, HN 90

Watts, Alan: CD 34, EM *137*

Waugh, Evelyn: CC 87

Wave function: TS 66

Weapons: of leopard-men, TN *46*

Weapon-salve therapy: SA 90-92

Wear-and-tear theory: SI 66

Wearing, Clive (encephalitis victim): SE 114

Weather: EE 62-64; myths about, EE 64; prediction of, VP 41

Webb, DeWitt: MC 24, *25*

Webb, John: and Stonehenge, MP 85, 86

Weber (student): and rituals, MA 61-62, 63

Weber, William: HN 100

Webster, Daniel: VP 75

Wedding cake: MY 50

Weeks, Leon: PE 136

Weeping Woman: MW 27

Wegener, Alfred: and continental drift, EE 58-59; and Pangaea, EE 58

Weiant, Clarence: dig led by, MQ *96-97*

Weighing: of witches, WW *70-71*

Weinberger, Caspar: MA 6

135

Weinberger, Daniel: MB 75
Weinberger, Julius: PH 104
Weindruch, Richard: SI 59
Weiner, Jack: AE 16, *18,* 21, 27; and abduction by aliens, AE 17-20, 24, 34
Weiner, Jim: AE *18,* 19, 28; and abduction by aliens, AE 16, 17-20
Wei Poyang: SI 34
Weishaupt, Adam: AW 101-104, MY *33*
Weiss, Cecilia: SS *102,* 104
Weiss, Ehrich: *See* Houdini, Harry

Weiss, Gloria: VP 96-97
Well dressing: MY *40*
Welles, Orson: CC 81, MY *97*
Wellness Community: PH *132, 133,* 134
Well of Ishmael: MY 91
Wells: in British Isles, EE 76; Chalice Well, Glastonbury, England, MQ *116,* 123-124; and Greeks, EE 76; in Ireland, EE *74;* and prediction of earthquakes, VP *43;* Well of Life, Alexander's search for, MQ 33-34
Wells, Charles: MM 65

Wells, Charlotte Fowler: as phrenologist, VP 76, 78
Wells, David: SS 38
Wells, George: HN 34, 35
Wells, H. G.: AE 103, MY *97,* VP 28
Wells, Samuel Robert: as phrenologist, VP 76, 78
Welschkornnarro: MY *45*
Welti, Albert: painting by, MY *33*
Wentworth, Thomas (earl of Strafford): PE 50, *51*
Wen Weng: VP 117
Wereide, Thorstein: PE 100
Werewolf Hotline: TN 72, 91
Werewolf of Ansbach: TN *84-85*
Werewolf of Caude: TN 86
Werewolves: *See* TN *index*
Wernicke, Carl: MB 45, 49
Wernicke's aphasia: MB 45, 49
Wesermann, H. M.: PE 95
Wesley family: and poltergeists, HN 60-61; Rev. Samuel, HN *61*
West, D. J.: MM 62
West, Mae: CC 84
West Africans: as fortunetellers, TS 95; and time, TS 100
Westcott, William Wynn: AW 146, 148, 150, 153, SA 126-127
Western healing: PH 9-10, 15-16, 20, 45, 46, 54, 55, 57, 58-60
West Indies: burial rites in, PE 53
Westminster Abbey: HN 90
Westover Air Force Base (Massachusetts): and Exeter UFO sighting, UP 104
West Wycombe Park: MW 119, 121
Wetherall, M. A.: MC *68-69*
Wewelsburg Castle: PS 64
Weyer, Johan: WW *81;* and witch hunts, WW 72, 81
Whales: MC *18, 19, 39, 41;* and Loch Ness monster sightings, MC 85; mask of, TN *15. See also* Sea People, Zeuglodon
Whale shark: MC *39*
Whaling season: MY 76
Wharton, Edith: MW 25-27, *28*
Wharton, Edward (Teddy): MW 28
Wharton, George: CC 102
Wheel: WW *82, 87*
Wheel, Ezekiel's (vision): AE 111-112, 123, MW 40, UP *12-14, 15*

Wheeler, Jim: and Levelland UFO sighting, UP 68
Wheeler, John A.: TS 66, 67; and black holes, TS 63; and parapsychology, PP 60-61
Wheel of Becoming: PV *126*
Wheel of Fortune: CD *35,* TS *20*
Wheel of the Year: WW *123*
Wheel of Time (a.k.a. Wheel of Fortune): CD *35,* TS *20*
Wheel of Time (Kalacakra; Buddhist teachings): MQ 25-26
When Rabbit Howls (Chase): MB 82, 83, 87
Whirling dervishes: MY *114-115. See also* Sufis
Whirling gift: UV *70*
Whirlpool: EE *72-73*
Whistling: MA 129
Whitby Abbey: PE *16-17*
White, Anna: UV 69
White, Anthony: and Delphi Associates, PS 113, 115, 116-117; and ESP, PS 113
White, Donald A.: and UFOs, TS 136-137
White, Edward: AE 62, 85
White, Helen: and aliens, AE 63, 65
White, J. Claude: photograph by, EM *30*
White, Kerr L.: PH 139
White, Ralph: UV 144
White dwarf: TS 64
White God: MW 82, 83
White Goddess, The (Graves): WW 102, 104
Whitehead, Alfred North: MB 20-22, SE 43
White House: and ghosts, HN *108-109,* PE 112
Whitehouse, Charles: PS 84-90
White Indians: ML 125
White Lady (ghost): HN 15
White magic: MW 113, MY 56; in Assyria, MA 17-19; and black magic, WW 23-25; defined, MA 15, 48. *See also* Magic
Whiteman, J. H. M.: SE 108
White Mountains: SI *72*
White on White (Malevich): UV *124*
Whites: and *kahuna ana'anas,* MA 85-86; and voodoo, MA 82
White Sands (New Mexico): and

UFO sighting, UP 47

White stage: SA 48, 50

Whitley, Jan: AE 121-123

Whitman, Walt: VP 80

Whitmonday: MY 43

Whitsunday: MY 36, 50-51

Whitsun King procession: MY 42-43

Whitted, J. B.: and Montgomery UFO sighting, UP 42

Whole body suspension: SI 116, 118. *See also* Cryonic suspension

Why I Am Not a Christian (Russell): SE 65

Whyte, Constance: Loch Ness monster research of, MC 72, 76, 83

Wicasa Wakan: MW 79

Wicca: MY 23, 32, 65; and magic, MA 113; and rituals, MA 64-65. *See also* Neopaganism; Witches; WW *index*

Wiccan rede: and *Handbook for Chaplains,* WW 113-114; and Wicca, WW 113-114

Wiccan tradition: WW 107

Wicker, Joseph: gift drawing by, UV 73

Widdershins: defined, WW 107

Wiesner, B. P.: MM 63

Wife of Bath: CC 66

Wigner, Eugene: SA 136

Wigs: SI 93

Wilbur, Cornelia: and Katherine Castle, MB 85; and Sybil Dorsett, MB 79-80

Wilcher, Steven: MB 62

Wilcox, Gary: AE 62-63

Wild celery: WW 37

Wild child of Aveyron: *See* Victor (feral child)

Wilde, Oscar: AW 111, 127, 151, CC 86, UV 17-18, VP 82

Wildenstein Castle: HN 32-33

Wild Hunt: WW 26-27, 28

Wildman Gathering: CD 60-61

Wild Men: MW 53, 56, 59; hands of, MC 112, 114; sightings of, MC 112-114. *See also* Hominoids *in* MC *index*

Wildowsky, Mrs. Donald: and Silva Mind Control, MM 119

Wilhelm, John: PS 82, 84

Wilhelm, Richard (*I Ching* translator): SA 131, TS 32, VP 119, 121, 122

Wilkes, Charles: paintings by, MP 144-145

Wilkes, John: MW 124

Wilkes-Barre, Pennsylvania: PS 14-15

Wilkie, Ian: PH 92

Wilkinson, Jemima (a.k.a. Public Universal Friend): UV 74, 75

Willett, Mrs. (Winifred Coombe-Tennant; medium): SE 97, 104-107

William (archbishop of Tyre): MQ 122

William (spirit): and Chapel of St. Edgar, PP 121

William of Malmesbury: MQ 123

William of Newburgh: TN 117

William of Orange (prince of Holland): SA 14

Williams, Mrs.: CC 112

Williams, Abigail: and witches, WW 73, 74, 75-76

Williams, Arland D., Jr.: CD 106-108, 128

Williams, Brian: Tarot cards by, VP 132-133

Williams, Charles: MW 67, SS 54

Williams, David: and astrology, PS 119; and John F. Kennedy, PS 121; and stock market, PS 119, 120-121

Williams, Geoffrey: MW 66-67

Williams, Harold and Ida: MQ 75

Williams, John H.: TS 128

Williams, Rick: MQ 52

Williams, Tennessee: EM 117

Williams, Walter: CD 64

Williams, Wayne: PS 44

Williams, William J.: painting by, AW 82

William the Conqueror (king of England): CC 55-56, PE 102

William the Monk: ML 61

Willington Mill House: HN 28; and hauntings, HN 29

Willis, Albert S.: MA 86

Will-o'-the-wisp: EE 70. *See also* Lightning

Willows: EE 96. *See also* Trees

Willow-tree experiment: and Robert Boyle, SA 95; and Jan Baptista van Helmont, SA 93

Wilshire, Donna: CD 51

Wilson, Colin: TS 133

Wilson, Edward O.: CD 109

Wilson, Ian: and reincarnation research, PV 105-106, 110-112, 118, 122

Wilson, Jesse: and alleged UFO photograph, UP 92

Wilson, Patricia (Luna): SI 119

Wilson, Robert Anton: SI 119

Wilson, Robert Kenneth: Loch Ness monster photograph by, MC 71, 74, 81, 83

Wilson, Sheryl: MB 92

Wilson, Woodrow: ghost of, HN 108-109

Wilson House: and ghosts, HN 108

Wilton Castle: MW 19, PE 8-9

Wiltse, Gilbert: MA 85-86

Wiltshire (England): MW 85

Wimmin's Religion: *See* Wicca

Winchester (England): design of, EE 33

Winchester, Sarah: house of, HN 120-121

Winchester, William Wirt: HN 121

Wind Cave: MW 79

137

Window Rock: EE *49*

Windows: SA *74, 75*

Window sites: UP *133-135*

Winds in *Odyssey:* MQ 55

Windsor, Eugene: CD 106, 107

Windsor Castle: MW 19, 23, *24*

Windsor Hotel: CC 133

Wine: SI *35*

Wing, Marty: and John Catchings, PS 53, 56; and Gail and Steven Lorke, PS 50, 53, 56; and Ronald Phillips, PS 56

Wing, Vincent: CC 104

Winnie Mae (airplane): TS 85

Winnipegosis, Lake: MW 47, 48

Winnipogo: MW 47, 48-49

Winston, Harry: MW 129

Winterbourne Stoke (England): crop circles in, EE *6-7*

Winter Harvest: PS 91-92

Winter solstice: *See* Solstice, winter

Winthrop, John: UV 58

Wirkus, Mietek: PH *98*

Wirt, William: AW 84

Wisconsin: superstitions in, MA 135

Wise women: *See* Psychics

Wish fulfillment: dreams as, DD 62, 63, 64, 68

Witchcraft: *See* Wicca

Witchcraft Acts of 1735: and Spiritualism, WW 103

Witchcraft Today (Gardner): WW 102-103, 108

Witch Cult in Western Europe, The (Murray): WW 100-102

Witch doctors: MW *137;* and jackal, TN 20-21, *22. See also* Sorcerers

Witches: AE 112-114, CD *59,* 83, MA 118, MW 135-136, MY 32, *33,* 52, 53, 56, 64, 65, 72, 96, 120, 125, PS *29;* and Francis Bacon, TN 38; and elder trees, EE 92; and ergot, EE 101; flying of, TN 38; and Martin Luther, TN 38; and mandrakes, EE 96; and the Navajo, TN 43; and olive trees, EE 79; salves of, TN 38; and stock market, PS 117; and Montague Summers, TN 122; transformations of, TN 38-41, *39,* 43; wound doubling of, TN 38, 41. *See also* Sorcerers; *Tempestarii;* Wicca; WW *index*

Witches Anti-Defamation League: WW 126

Witches' Sabbath, The (Goya): WW *56-57*

Witches' Thanksgiving: MY 88

Witch finders: CD *59,* MW 135

Witch hazel: WW *34*

Witch hunts: *See* WW *index*

Witch of Lime Street: *See* Crandon, Mina

Witch's bridle: WW 7

Witch's marks: WW 75; defined, WW 63; and Cotton Mather, WW 77

Witch stones: EE 57

Witch's tools: WW *120-121;* defined, WW 107

Witch trials: *See* WW *index*

Witcombe, Al: shipwreck sighting by, PP *124*

Withers, Frank: SS 134

Wittgenstein, Ludwig: SE 65-66

Wittig, Monique: WW 116-118; and Wicca, WW 116-118

Witzelsucht: defined, MB 39

Wizard of Oz (film): and feeling of displacement, UP *71*

W. J. (split-brain patient): MB 47

Woden-lithi (Norse king): ML 133-134

Wohl, Louis de: PS 68

Wolcott, Josiah: painting by, UV *82*

Woldman, Susan *(Starlady):* AE 131

Wolf charmers: and wolves, TN *90*

Wolf-child of Hesse: TN 57

Wolf-children: TN *56-57, 60-64. See also* Feral children

Wolfe, Peter: PH 135

Wolfen, The (Strieber): AE 24

Wolfhounds: TN 78

Wolf-land: *See* Ireland

Wolfram von Eschenbach: MQ 111-112, 114, 117; foundations of writings by, MQ 117-118, 124, 125, 127

Wolfsegg (fortress): HN *14-15;* and ghosts, HN 15

Wolsey, Thomas: VP 14

Wolves: *See* TN *index*

Woman in grey (ghost): HN 68

Woman in the Wilderness: MW 105, UV 60

Woman with Feather Hat and Colorful Skirt (Hauser): MB *68-69*

138

WHALE. *Depicted in the Persian work at left, the story of Jonah being swallowed by a "big fish" and spat out a changed man forever linked the whale with the idea of resurrection. Yet the whale can also signify evil, its mouth the gateway to hell.*

WEREWOLF. *Werewolves embody the idea that humans have a dual nature, changing at night from those God made "a little lower than the angels" to bloodthirsty beasts. In the drawing below, werewolves wait by a cemetery to feed on corpses.*

Womb envy: CD 61

Women: CD 56, 58; and agriculture, CD 49, 55; brain organization of, CD 65-66; and fertility, CD 49-50; as healers, CD 59; and Industrial Revolution, CD 59; and intuition, CD 66-68; and magic, MA 63; and psi powers, CD 68; status of, CD 56, 58, 59; as witches, CD 59

Women's rights: SS 31

Women's spirituality conference: and Arlington Street Church, WW 96-97

Wonders of the Invisible World, The (C. Mather): WW 76

Wood: knocking on, MA 116-118, 122; from Noah's Ark, possible, MQ 70, 71, 76, 77, 79, 81, 84, 86, 87, 88-89

Wood, Forrest Glen: MC 25

Wood, John: and Stonehenge, MP 90-91

Woodbridge Royal Air Force Base (England): MW 43, UP 132-141

Woodford, A. F. A.: AW 146, 150

Woodhull, Victoria Claflin: SS 30-31

Woodman, Jim: and Nazca lines of Peru, MP 116-119, 118-119

Woodman, William: AW 148

Woodruff, Joseph L.: MM 61

Woods near Oele (Mondrian): AW 159

Wooldridge, Anthony B.: Abominable Snowman photograph by, MC 122-123, 124

Wooley, Leonard: Ur excavation by, MQ 64, 75

Woolf, Virginia: CC 90

Woolley, Richard van der Riet: VP 27

Word deafness: defined, MB 49

Wordless Book: *See Mutus Liber*

Words: and talismans, MA 38, 39

Word salad: MB 73

Wordsworth, William: EE 104

Work: and Georgei Ivanovitch Gurdjieff, UV 102, 108

World Conference of Astro-Economics: PS 124

World Council of Churches: and Selena Fox, WW 126

World Health Organization: PH 49-50, 68

World's Folk Art Church: UV 49

World's Parliament of Religions: and Swami Vivekenanda, EM 114-115, 117, 135

World trees: EE 96, 97; characteristics of, EE 92. *See also* Asvattha; Trees; Yggdrasil

Worm, prehistoric: and Loch Ness monster sightings, MC 84-85

Wormholes: AE 116, TS 70, 74-75; defined, TS 70

Worrall, Ambrose: PH 94, 95

Worrall, Olga: PH 93, 94, 95, 103, 104; psychic aura of, PP 147

Worth, Patience (spirit): SS 85; and Pearl Curran, PP 42

Wotan (god): WW 27; rites honoring, WW 43

Wound doubling: TN 38, 41, 42, 75, 89

Wounded Knee (South Dakota): MW 111, 113

Wovoka (Paiute): MW 110

Wreath: MY 114

Wren, Christopher: AW 90; and poltergeists, HN 56

Wright, Mr.: PH 123-124

Wright, Frank Lloyd: UV 104; architecture by, UV 104; and Georgei Ivanovitch Gurdjieff, UV 109

Wright, Lucy: UV 68

Wright, Newell: and Levelland UFO sighting, UP 68

Wright, Olgivanna Hinzenberg: and Georgei Ivanovitch Gurdjieff, UV 104, 105

Wright-Patterson Air Force Base (Ohio): and Project Blue Book, UP 98

Writing, automatic: *See* Automatic Writing

Writing, slate: SS 126-127

Writing systems: of Andes, ML 24-25; of Celts, ML 132-135; of Maya, ML 19; of Mohenjo-Daro, ML 20-21

Wu (emperor of China): CC 27

Wudewasa: MW 53, 56

Wundt, Wilhelm: DD 59

Wurtsmith Air Force Base (Michigan): and UFO sighting, UP 129

Wyatt, Ronald: and Phantom Ark, MQ 91-92, 93, 94

Wyck, Thomas: painting by, SA 38-39

Wyckoff, Charles: Loch Ness monster research of, MC 78, 85, 87, 89

Wyckoff, Helen: MC 89

Wyman, Jeffries: MC 30

Wyndham, Charles: ghost of, HN 31

Wyndham-Quin, Windham Thomas: SS 41, 42

Wynne, Charles Bradstreet: MM 115, SS 41

Wynona (dreamer): DD 152

Wyoming: MW 79

139

MY The Mystical Year; PE Phantom Encounters; PH Powers of Healing; PP Psychic Powers; PS The Psychics; PV Psychic Voyages; SA Secrets of the Alchemists; SE Search for the Soul; SI Search for Immortality; SS Spirit Summonings; TN Transformations; TS Time and Space; UP The UFO Phenomenon; UV Utopian Visions; VP Visions and Prophecies; WW Witches and Witchcraft

XYZ

X, M. de: and hauntings, HN 92, 93

X, Mr.: *See* Monroe, Robert

Xa:ls (god): MW 76, 79

Xenoglossy: defined, PV 118-119; Ian Stevenson's research on, PV 119-122; of T. E., PV 119-122. *See also* Reincarnation

Xerxes: DD 40

X Higgs bosons: EM 142

Xhosa people: MW 133, 135-136

Xian: SI 34; defined, EM 52, SA 112

Xipe Totec (god): MY *74, 75*

Xiuhtecutli (god): TS 30

Xi Wang Mu (goddess): SI 36, *37;* and peach banquets, SI 36, *37*

X-ray pictures: PH *67, 75, 77,* 104

Xylograph: CC *103*

Xylomancy: defined, VP 35

Yahoo: MW 63

Yahweh (god): CD 29, WW 13-15; and Leviathan, WW 15

Yajur-Veda: ML 32

Yakima Indian Reservation (Washington): and UFO window site investigation, UP 133-134, *135*

Yama (god): CD 85, PV *126,* SI 13

Yamabushi: defined, CD 111

Yams: MY 78, 100

Yamuna River: SI 16

Yang: EM 52; characteristics of, TS 27, 32, *33;* defined, EE 36. *See also* Yin/yang

Yang-chai Ching (Anonymous): EE 115

Yang dwellings: defined, EE 113; and feng shui, EE 113, *114-117;* and qi, EE 114-*115, 116-117;* types of, EE 114

Yang Lu Chan: EM 143

Yano, Michihiko: sea serpent drawings by, MC *43*

Yanomami Indians: PH *18*

Yantra: CD *11*

Yara-ma-yha-who: MW 63

Yasoda: DD 24

Yater, Verna: SS *147*

Yayati (king): SI 13

Yearam (Armenian guide): MQ 75

Yeats, William Butler: AW 114, 127, 151, *154,* 156, MA 64, MY 53, SE 104, 105, 106, VP 127; and Allan Bennett, AW 154-155; and Annie Wood Besant, AW 150; and Celtic Revival, AW 128; and Aleister Crowley, AW 122, 154-155; and Hermetic Order of the Golden Dawn, SA 126, 128; and Samuel Liddell MacGregor Mathers, AW 148-150; and Eu-

gen Steinach, SI *60;* Theosophical beliefs of, PV 103; vasectomy of, SI 60, 62

Yeh-teh: See Abominable Snowmen

Yellow-belly: MW 72

Yellow Bird: MW 111

Yellow Emperor: PH 74

Yellow Room, The (Chagall): DD *10-11*

"Yellow Springs": MW *127,* 128

Yen Tsu: CC 28

Yeshe, Lama Thubten: EM *135;* and Torres family, EM 134-135

Yeterian, Dixie: PS 47-48

Yeti: EM 16, MW 44, 59. *See also* Abominable Snowman

Yezidje: UV 105

Yggdrasil: MY 121, TS *18;* characteristics of, EE 92-93. *See also* World trees

Yin: EM 52, MY 89; characteristics of, TS 27, 32, *33;* defined, EE 36

Yin dwellings: defined, EE 113

Ying qigong: EM *54-55*

Yin/yang: CD *8-9,* PH 46, *47,* 54, SA *105,* SI 42, VP 119, *120-121;* characteristics of, CD 9, 35, 49, SA 103, *106,* 112; as duality, CD 49; and gender, CD 49; and intuition, CD 66; purposes of, CD 35; and qi, SA 104. *See also I Ching*

Ymir (giant god): CD 24, MQ 78, TS 20

Ynis Witrin: ML 52-56

Yodeling: MY 125

Yoga: PH 68, 70-71, 72-74, PV 102, UV 136-137; and Richard Alpert, MB 117; background of, EM 37; and Bhagavad-Gita, EM 37; and Bramasuganandah, EM 89, 90; and breathing, EM 40; and Paul Brunton, EM 89-90; and Buddha, EM 40; characteristics of, EM 37; and Haridas, EM 40; and longevity, SI 23; and Milarepa, EM 50; and monks, MB 96-97; purposes of, EM 37; and trances, MB 96-97; and Upanishads, EM 37; and xian, SI 34. See also Bhakti yoga; Hatha-yoga; Jnana-yoga; Karma-yoga; Kriya-yoga; Raja-yoga; Tantric yoga

Yogananda, Paramahansa (a.k.a. Mukunda Lal Ghosh): EM 118, 119; and Agastya, SI 11; and Babaji, SI 8, 9; and Kebalananda, SI 8, 9; and Self-Realization Fellowship, EM 119, SI 8; and Sri Yukteswar, EM 118-119, SI 8, 9

Yogi, Maharishi Mahesh: EM 121-123, MB 123, SI 23; levitation of, MM 117-118; and Transcendental Meditation, EM 121, 122, MB 122

Yogis: CD 111; and enlightenment, SI 99; and hypothermia, SI 104-105; live burials of, SI 99, 102; self-mutilation of, MM 108, 109; and Roy L. Walford, SI 104-105

Yokes: stone, MQ 96-97

Yokut Indians: and time, TS 37

Yolana (psychic): PS 128

Yom Kippur: MY 89

Yongden, Aphur: EM 77; and Alexandra David-Néel, EM 77, 81, 83, 84; death of, EM 84

Yoni: defined, CD 11, EE 57

Yorkshire Ripper case: TN 130; and clairvoyance, PP 133-134, 134-137

Yoruba: MW 113

Yoshimura, Masatoshi: and executive ESP, PS 107-108; and super-conscious, PS 108, 109-110

Yoshitoshi, Tsukioka: print by, PE 76

Young, Brigham: UV 59; and James Buchanan, UV 58; and Mormons, UV 58

Young, Jimmy: MM 6

Young, J. W.: PS 128

Young, Patrick: MB 73

Young-Man-Afraid-of-Indians: MW 111

Youngren, Fred: drawings by, AE 64

Yowie: MW 63

Ys: MW 87

Y Tylwyth Teg, Church of: WW 112

Yu (emperor of China): ML 115

Yu, Zion: PH 54-57

Yucatán Peninsula: MW 79

Yuchi Indians: background of, ML 134-135; harvest celebration of, ML 116, 134-135

Yugas: UV 23

Yugoslavia: vampires in, TN 116-118, 119-120

Yuka: defined, MA 80

Yukteswar, Sri: EM 118-119, SI 8, 9

Yulan, Gong: MC 113

Yule: MY 121, WW 123

Yule log: MY 121, 136

Yuletide Lads: MY 118

Yungtun-Trogyal, Lama: and Milarepa, EM 49, 50

Z., Miss: out-of-body experiences of, PV 35-36

Zabolotsky (Russian lieutenant): MQ 84

Zacharias (prophet): and Muhammad, DD 50

Zadkiel's Almanack (Morrison): CC 113

Zamora, Lonnie: and Socorro UFO sighting, UP 73

Zana (Almas): MW 60; history of, MC 106, 110-112. See also Almas

Zancig, Agnes and Julius (mentalists): and thought-transference act, PP 108

Zanesville UFO (Sokolov): AE 129

Zanfretta, Fortunato: and abduction by aliens, AE 26; alien seen by, AE 25; hypnosis of, AE 26

Zao Jun (god): MY 126-127

Zapatistas (Orozco): DD 147, 151

Zar: defined, CD 86

Zarathustra: MY 82. See also Zoroaster

Zazen: EM 55, 106-107, 137-138

Zebras: CD 109; migration of, TS 82

Zeitgebers: TS 81

Zekkum: DD 55

Zen Buddhism: See EM index

Zen Buddhists: MB 104; and intentional communities, UV 137; and paradise myths, UV 6. See also Buddhists and Buddhism; Zen Buddhism in EM index

Zener, Karl: and telepathic testing, cards for, PP 51-52

Zener cards: use of, in telepathic tests, PP 51-52, 53, 61, 63

Zenner: and rituals, MA 62, 63

Zeno: TS 38-40

Zeppelin: mistaken for UFO, UP 25

Zero: TS 29; and Buddhists, TS 29

Zeta Reticuli star system: and Hill abduction story, UP 84

Zeuglodons: MC 30, 39, MW 49; defined, MC 44, 85; and Loch Ness monster sighting, MC 85; and sea serpent sightings, MC 44. See also Whales

Zeus (god): CC 22, 43, 46, CD 24, 48, 61, DD 29, 32, ML 25, MQ 60, MY 51, SA 71, SE 31, SI 26, TS 20, WW 13-15, 23; and Atlantis, destruction of, MP 12-13, 19; characteristics of, EE 74; and numbers, TS 45; and oaks, EE 80, 92; transformations of, TN 34, 35; and Typhon, WW 15. See also Jupiter; Odin

Zhang Gualao: SA 113

Zhongli Quan: SA 113

Ziggurats: AE 95, CC 8-9, 15, 27, MW 133, WW 13

Zimbabwe: MW 65, 133; possession in, MA 13-15; search for King Solomon's mines in, MQ 41

Zimbardo, Philip: CD 94

Zimmermann, Johann Jacob: UV 60

Zinsstag, Louise: and Eduard Meier, AE 101, 102

Zodiac: CC 11, 99, 114-115; defined, CC 21; signs of the, CC 14-15, 65, 68-69, CD 34, TS 104. See also Glastonbury zodiac; Sun signs; individual zodiac signs

Zodiac, Madame: PS 90

Zohar (Moses de Leon): AW 24

Zohar, Danah: and precognition, TS 116, 118

Zolik, Edwin: and reincarnation research, PV 124

Zombie powders: MA 88, 89

Zombies: CD 86; and bokors, MA 88, 89; and Wade Davis, MA 88, 89; and tetrodotoxin poisoning, MA 88; and voodoo, MA 83-84, 88-89

Zoomancy: defined, VP 35

Zopa, Lama: EM 134

Zorab, George: and hauntings, HN 34, 35

Zoroaster: CD 26, 28, MY 82, TS 22; and angels, CD 122; and demons, CD 122; and visions, CD 26

Zoroastrians and Zoroastrianism: AW 22, CD 26-28, MW 99, 102, MY 82, 117; cosmogonies of, TS 22; decline of, CD 29; and dualities, CD 26, 28; and evil, CD 80; and resurrection, SE 51

Zosimus of Panopolis: and alchemy, SA 24-25; and philosophers' stone, SA 25, 44; and prima materia, SA 24-25; and transmutation, SA 24

Z-rays: and Zbigniew Dunikowski, SA 119, 122

Zug, George R.: Loch Ness monster research of, MC 78, 80, 85; and sea serpents, MC 40

Zugun, Eleonora: and poltergeists, MM 39-41

Zuiyo Maru (Japanese trawler): sea serpent carcass netted by, MC 42, 43

Zulus: DD 26, MW 133, 135; and beliefs about doubles, PE 85

Zuni Indians: DD 26, EE 24; cosmogonies of, TS 20

Zurvan: CD 28-29

Zurvanists: CD 28

Zwinger, Jacob: MA 33

ACKNOWLEDGMENTS

The editors wish to thank the following for their valuable assistance in the preparation of this volume:

Brigitte Baumbusch, Florence; Horst Blanck, Istituto Archeologico Germanico, Rome; Luigi Bottura, Soprintendenza ai Beni Artistici e Storici, Mantua; Marina Geneletti, Accademia Carrara, Bergamo; Justus Göpel, Axel Schmidt, Archiv für Kunst und Geschichte, Berlin; Andreas Holzapfel, Bildarchiv Claus Hansmann, Munich; Luisa Ricciarini, Milan.

BIBLIOGRAPHY

Bakhtiar, Laleh, *Sufi*. London: Thames and Hudson, 1976.

Bauer, Wolfgang, Irmtraud Dümotz, and Sergius Golowin, *Lexikon der Symbole*. Wiesbaden: Fourier Verlag, 1992.

Biedermann, Hans, *Knaurs Lexikon der Symbole*. Munich: Droemer Knaur, 1989.

Binder, Pearl, *Magic Symbols of the World*. London: Hamlyn, 1972.

Campbell, Joseph, *Mythologies of the Great Hunt* (Vol. I, Part 2 of *Historical Atlas of World Mythology*). New York: Harper & Row, 1988.

Cavendish, Richard, ed., *Man, Myth & Magic* (index). New York: Marshall Cavendish, 1985.

Christie, Anthony, *Chinese Mythology*. New York: Peter Bedrick Books, 1985.

Cirlot, J. E., *A Dictionary of Symbols*. Transl. by Jack Sage. New York: Philosophical Library, 1962.

Dickey, Thomas, John Man, and Henry Wiencek, *The Kings of El Dorado*. Alexandria, Va.: Stonehenge Press, 1982.

Dreyfuss, Henry, *Symbol Sourcebook*. New York: McGraw-Hill, 1972.

Eliade, Mircea, *Symbolism, the Sacred, and the Arts*. New York: Crossroad, 1986.

Encyclopedia of Witchcraft & Demonology. London: Octopus Books, 1974.

Fabricius, Johannes, *Alchemy*. Wellingborough, Northamptonshire, England: The Aquarian Press, 1976.

Faris, James C., *The Nightway*. Albuquerque, N.Mex.: University of New Mexico Press, 1990.

Ferguson, George, *Signs & Symbols in Christian Art*. London: Oxford University Press, 1975.

Gadon, Elinor W., *The Once and Future Goddess: A Symbol for Our Time*. San Francisco: Harper & Row, 1989.

Gettings, Fred, *Visions of the Occult*. London: Century Hutchinson, 1987.

Grof, Stanislav, and Christina Grof, *Beyond Death*. London: Thames and Hudson, 1980.

Huxley, Francis, *The Eye*. London: Thames and Hudson, 1990.

Ions, Veronica, *Egyptian Mythology*. New York: Peter Bedrick Books, 1968.

Jung, Carl G., *Man and His Symbols*. New York: Doubleday, 1983.

Kenton, Warren, *Astrology: The Celestial Mirror*. New York: Avon, 1974.

King, Francis, *Magic: The Western Tradition*. London: Thames and Hudson, 1975.

Lamy, Lucie, *Egyptian Mysteries*. Transl. by Deborah Lawlor. New York: Crossroad, 1981.

Leach, Maria, and Jerome Fried, eds., *Funk & Wagnalls Standard Dictionary of Folklore, Mythology and Legend*. San Francisco: Harper & Row, 1984.

Lurker, Manfred, *The Gods and Symbols of Ancient Egypt*. London: Thames and Hudson, 1984.

Mailly Nesle, Solange de, *Astrology*. New York: Inner Traditions International, 1981.

Pennick, Nigel, *The Ancient Science of Geomancy*. London: Thames and Hudson, 1979.

Piggott, Juliet, *Japanese Mythology*. New York: Peter Bedrick Books, 1983.

Rachleff, Owen S., *The Occult in Art*. London: Cromwell Editions, 1990.

Von Franz, Maria-Louise, *Time*. London: Thames and Hudson, 1978.

Walker, Barbara G., *The Woman's Dictionary of Symbols and Sacred Objects*. San Francisco: Harper & Row, 1988.

Wills, Geoffrey, *Jade of the East*. New York: John Weatherhill, 1972.

PICTURE CREDITS

Time-Life Books is a division of Time Life Inc.,
a wholly owned subsidiary of
THE TIME INC. BOOK COMPANY

TIME-LIFE BOOKS

PRESIDENT: Mary N. Davis

MANAGING EDITOR: Thomas H. Flaherty
Director of Editorial Resources: Elise D. Ritter-Clough
Executive Art Director: Ellen Robling
Director of Photography and Research: John Conrad Weiser
Editorial Board: Dale M. Brown, Janet Cave, Roberta
Conlan, Laura Foreman, Jim Hicks, Blaine Marshall, Rita
Thievon Mullin, Henry Woodhead
Assistant Director of Editorial Resources/Training Manager:
Norma E. Shaw

PUBLISHER: Robert H. Smith

Associate Publisher: Sandra Lafe Smith
Editorial Director: Russell B. Adams, Jr.
Marketing Director: Anne C. Everhart
Director of Production Services: Robert N. Carr
Production Manager: Prudence G. Harris
Supervisor of Quality Control: James King

Editorial Operations
Production: Celia Beattie
Library: Louise D. Forstall
Computer Composition: Deborah G. Tait (Manager),
Monika D. Thayer, Janet Barnes Syring, Lillian Daniels
Interactive Media Specialist: Patti H. Cass

Library of Congress Cataloging in Publication Data
Master index and illustrated symbols / by the editors of
Time-Life Books.
  p. cm.
  ISBN 0-8094-6509-4 (library)
  ISBN 0-8094-6508-6 (trade)
  1. Symbolism—Indexes.   2. Mysteries of the
unknown—Indexes.
  I. Time-Life Books.
  BF1623.S9M97 1992
  302.2'22—dc20   92-26586
                                              CIP

MYSTERIES OF THE UNKNOWN

SERIES EDITOR: Jim Hicks
Series Administrator: Judith W. Shanks
Senior Art Director: Thomas S. Huestis
Picture Editor: Paula York-Soderlund

Editorial Staff for *Master Index and Illustrated Symbols:*
Text Editor: Paul Mathless
Associate Editors/Research: Gwen C. Mullen,
Trudy W. Pearson
Assistant Art Director: Lorraine D. Rivard
Writers: Charles J. Hagner, Sarah D. Ince
Copy Coordinator: Donna Carey
Picture Coordinator: Greg S. Johnson
Editorial Assistant: Julia Kendrick

Editorial Intern: T. Nieta Wigginton

Special Contributors: Juli Duncan, Elizabeth Graham,
Anthony K. Pordes, Naomi Thiers (index)

Correspondents: Elisabeth Kraemer-Singh (Bonn), Christine
Hinze (London), Christina Lieberman (New York), Maria
Vincenza Aloisi (Paris), Ann Natanson (Rome).
Valuable assistance was also provided by Aristotle Sarri-
costas (Athens); Angelika Lemmer (Bonn); Gay Kavanagh
(Brussels); Nihal Tamaraz (Cairo); Bing Wong (Hong
Kong); Sarah Moule (London); Trini Bandrés (Madrid);
Andrea Dabrowski, Laura Lopez (Mexico City); Elizabeth
Brown, Katheryn White (New York); Ann Wise, Leonora
Dodsworth (Rome); Traudl Lessing (Vienna).

Other Publications:

THE AMERICAN INDIANS
THE ART OF WOODWORKING
LOST CIVILIZATIONS
ECHOES OF GLORY
THE NEW FACE OF WAR
HOW THINGS WORK
WINGS OF WAR
CREATIVE EVERYDAY COOKING
COLLECTOR'S LIBRARY OF THE UNKNOWN
CLASSICS OF WORLD WAR II
TIME-LIFE LIBRARY OF CURIOUS AND UNUSUAL FACTS
AMERICAN COUNTRY
VOYAGE THROUGH THE UNIVERSE
THE THIRD REICH
THE TIME-LIFE GARDENER'S GUIDE
TIME FRAME
FIX IT YOURSELF
FITNESS, HEALTH & NUTRITION
SUCCESSFUL PARENTING
HEALTHY HOME COOKING
UNDERSTANDING COMPUTERS
LIBRARY OF NATIONS
THE ENCHANTED WORLD
THE KODAK LIBRARY OF CREATIVE PHOTOGRAPHY
GREAT MEALS IN MINUTES
THE CIVIL WAR
PLANET EARTH
COLLECTOR'S LIBRARY OF THE CIVIL WAR
THE EPIC OF FLIGHT
THE GOOD COOK
WORLD WAR II
HOME REPAIR AND IMPROVEMENT
THE OLD WEST

*For information on and a full description of any of the Time-
Life Books series listed above, please call 1-800-621-7026 or
write:*
Reader Information
Time-Life Customer Service
P.O. Box C-32068
Richmond, Virginia 23261-2068

This volume is one of a series that examines the history
and nature of seemingly paranormal phenomena. Other
books in the series include:

Mystic Places	*Witches and Witchcraft*
Psychic Powers	*Time and Space*
The UFO Phenomenon	*Magical Arts*
Psychic Voyages	*Utopian Visions*
Phantom Encounters	*Secrets of the Alchemists*
Visions and Prophecies	*Eastern Mysteries*
Mysterious Creatures	*Earth Energies*
Mind over Matter	*Cosmic Duality*
Cosmic Connections	*Mysterious Lands and Peoples*
Spirit Summonings	*The Mind and Beyond*
Ancient Wisdom and Secret Sects	*Mystic Quests*
Hauntings	*Search for Immortality*
Powers of Healing	*The Mystical Year*
Search for the Soul	*The Psychics*
Transformations	*Alien Encounters*
Dreams and Dreaming	*The Mysterious World*